We felt like

We felt like grasshoppers

The story of Africa Inland Mission

Dick Anderson

Crossway Books
Nottingham

ISBN 1–85684–106–5 Paperback
ISBN 1–85684–107–3 Hardback

Unless otherwise stated, Scripture quotations in this publication are
from the Holy Bible, New International Version. Copyright ©
1973, 1978, 1984 International Bible Society. Published in Great
Britain by Hodder & Stoughton Ltd.

Typeset by Avocet Type, Launton, Bicester.
Printed in Great Britain for Crossway Books, Norton Street,
Nottingham NG7 3HR, by Cox & Wyman Ltd, Reading,
Berkshire.

Contents

Photographs, illustrations and maps

Maps

Foreword

The challenge of Africa is in many ways as great as it ever was. Almost daily we read about another crisis in that huge continent with its hundreds of Peoples Groups. What God has done in Africa, and continues to do, is not generally in our newspapers and that is one of the reasons that books like this one are so important.

The story of AIM is one that every Christian should know about. If we are to live for Christ where we are at, or across the seas, we must know something of this kind of love for Christ, sacrifice and perseverance.

As I listened to Dick Anderson speak in a meeting, I knew I was hearing from a man who knew God and the reality of God's grace and power. You will sense some of that as you read this book that he has prayed and worked so hard to give us.

How we rejoice over the growth of the church in so many places, yet we realize there is still so much to do. The need for missionaries, both national and international is still great. There are also many ways that we can all help and serve the work in Africa.

This book is about people – people who knew God, but also who were just as human as anyone else. The grace they appropriated in the midst of the problems and struggles is a powerful testimony to the power of Christ in their lives. As you read these powerful pages, you will realize that the reality of the people in Hebrews 11 is still flowing in the hearts and lives of people on the frontlines of evangelism in the world today. This is not just a book about missionaries, but a book about African believers and the African church. It is hard to realize how much they have suffered for Christ and his Kingdom.

My prayer is that this book will cause more people to become missions mobilizers on behalf of this giant continent of thousands of needs and opportunities. Most of us have Africans in our midst, and it is my heartcry that we will be an example to them of love and biblical faith. Reading a book like this must always lead to fervent prayer and practical action.

George Verwer

About the author

Dr. Richard (Dick) J. D. Anderson was born of British parents on the Island of Mauritius in 1928. He grew up in England and received his M.B. and B.S. from St. Bartholomew's Medical College, London University. He worked initially in England before serving two years with the British Army in Egypt as a medical officer. He then served a one-year assignment at the King George VI Hospital in Nairobi, Kenya, followed by one year of studies at London Bible College.

He joined Africa Inland Mission in 1956 and very soon became involved in medical safaris among the desert tribes of Kenya's Northern Frontier District. In 1958 he married fellow missionary Joan Boyd, who had been serving as teacher and translator with AIM since 1953. Together they were to serve among the Turkana people of Northern Kenya until 1975 when Dr. Anderson was appointed AIM's Associate Secretary for Outreach. While in this position, he and Joan were to test the waters themselves by becoming among the first in AIM to serve in the Comoro Islands (1975 – 76). Dr. Anderson directed the Mission to other potential countries of service and eventually doubled the number of countries where AIM served. In 1978 he was elected International General Secretary of AIM – a position he held until 1990. At present he holds the official title of IGS Emeritus, visiting various countries from which AIM recruits its missionaries and to which missionaries are assigned.

Although Dr. Anderson has published numerous articles, *We Felt Like Grasshoppers* is his first book. The Andersons have three children – Mary, Helen and Donald – and are presently living in Edinburgh, Scotland.

Preface

In 1937 a successful pioneer called Mabel Easton looked back over fifteen years in Africa. She saw them as 'years of difficulty, of many mistakes, of soul-searching revelation of one's own weakness'. Every missionary knows what she meant.

But this is a story of power. God honoured the faith of frail people. He used them to launch a movement which has swept millions into his kingdom.

I have chosen a few saints to represent thousands. When one couple read my piece about them they responded, 'We are astonished that we have such a place in the story. We are concerned that our fellow-missionaries are not shelved.' Others said something similar. They need not feel embarrassed for they were not selected on merit, but more because they tell the story of this mission – its principles, puzzles, methods and even mistakes. Many worthies do not appear for the book is not a roll of honour. If I have included one training hospital, I have glossed over others. If one or two people speak about theological training, they represent many. When God multiplied churches in one district, the same story could be told of regions elsewhere.

The Africa Inland Mission is an international organization. I have learnt that Americans organize a program while their British colleagues organise a programme. I have labored (sorry, laboured) to minimize (minimise) your irritation as you read. If I have failed here and there, please exercise your cross-cultural understanding – for the book describes a century of learning such sensitivity.

Family members have read every word. My son-in-law, Eric Robertson, and daughter, Helen Freeman, improved style, prevented repetition and ruthlessly eliminated needless lists of names. Eric's margin notes taught me a new phrase, 'too authorial'. This and Helen's comment, 'Yuk!' sent my finger scurrying for the 'Delete' key. Then my wife, Joan, offered advice and picked up typing errors. To each I owe a debt of gratitude.

Many others have helped – enduring long interviews, typing tapes, lending books, digging out information and allowing access to archives. Colin Molyneux drew the sketches and Darwin Dunham, the portraits. To all I say a sincere thank you and especially for those who prayed for the author on many occasions when Mabel Easton's words seemed relevant to this work.

Dick Anderson

Introduction

by Dr. Fred Beam, International Director, Africa Inland Mission

> Remark all these roughnesses, pimples, warts and everything as
> you see me; otherwise, I will never pay a farthing for it.
>
> Oliver Cromwell

With these words of caution, Oliver Cromwell commissioned the
artist Lely to paint his portrait.

The same spirit of realism and honesty seems to have directed
Dr. Dick Anderson in his portrait of Africa Inland Mission called
We felt like grasshoppers. Dr. Anderson claimed in his preface that
he has 'chosen a few saints to represent thousands' and thus 'tell
the story of this mission – its principles, puzzles, methods and
even mistakes'. But the book is more than just a history of the
first hundred years of AIM – it is the history of how a sovereign
God patiently works in moulding his children. Again quoting
Dr. Anderson:

> . . . missionaries often found themselves in the worst of conditions,
> when all sorts of stress threatened to rend relationships. That so
> few fell apart was a miracle of God's grace. That God could take
> up torn threads and weave them into a new and beautiful tapestry
> was a greater wonder, making us ask if he actually ordained the
> strains to show that this amazing power belonged to him alone.
> (pp. 57–8)

Thus, the book is a valuable addition to both missiology and
Christian devotional literature.

Dr. Anderson does not portray the mission as infallible in
either its history or its heroes; he paints the 'corporate warts'
of poor decisions as well as the weaknesses of men and women.
For example, he admits the mission made 'a series of errors' (p.
58) in its recruitment of the charismatic C. T. Studd – who
promptly resigned when the mission failed to comply with his
wishes. Dr. Anderson doesn't polish halos as part of his portrayals
of past or present, even though the original meaning of 'halo'
comes from the Greek word for a threshing floor on which oxen
made a circular path by going round and round. (The use of
halos in Christian art dates back to c. A.D. 400 and may be based

on the Scriptural accounts of Moses and Jesus having faces that 'shone as the sun'. In nearly a quarter century of missionary service and working with hundreds – if not thousands – of missionaries, I've never had to wear sunglasses while talking with any of them face to face.) Dr. Anderson's characters are a testimony of God's power made perfect in their weaknesses – and with their warts. He honestly tells of personality clashes among the saints, but gives them credit for piety and perseverance which God ultimately blessed.

> They might differ with each other – even squabble sometimes – and make many mistakes. But they thumbed through their Bibles, spent hours on their knees and pressed forward always with the saving Gospel on their lips. And God honoured their devotion. (p. 26)

This book will cost something more than a farthing, but it has painted missions and missionaries with their 'roughnesses, pimples, warts and everything' – without apology.

Chronology

1895   Africa Inland Mission (AIM), Pennsylvania Bible Institute, Central American Industrial Mission founded.

1895   The first AIM missionaries led by Peter Scott arrive in Mombasa, British East Africa.

1896   By first AGM, missionaries installed in Nzawi, Sakai, Kilungu, Kangundu. Peter Scott dies on 8 December.

1896–1901   The British build railway linking Mombasa with Lake Victoria.

1898   The last of the first sixteen AIM missionaries leaves Africa.

1901   Charles Hurlburt and family arrive in Kangundu, East Africa.

1903   Hurlburt moves AIM centre to Kijabe. John Stauffacher arrives.

1906   Josephine Hope commences school for missionaries' children at Kijabe.

1909   First AIM missionaries arrive in Nassa, German East Africa.

1912   Led by Stauffacher first missionaries settle in Kasengu, Belgian Congo.

1914–1918   The Great War.

1918   First missionaries to Mvara, Uganda, among four unreached tribes.

1920   League of Nations mandates German East Africa to Britain – a population of 5 million in 137 tribes.

1924   Paul Buyse crosses the Ubangi river into French Equatorial Africa (FEA) and suggests Zemio as the first AIM centre.

1939–1945   Second World War.

1942   First Ugandan ordinations – Revs John Dronyi and Silvanus Wani.

1949   CMS invites AIM to take over Opari and Torit in Sudan. Paul Buyse leads the first team.

1952–1955   State of Emergency in Kenya.

1956   Civil war breaks out in Sudan.

1960   Independence in Congo results in partial and temporary evacuation of AIM leaving an autonomous church in Congo of 32,000 members and 8,103 licensed and unordained pastors (see fn 146).

1962 Sudan Government enacts Missionary Society Act which restricts activities of missionaries. Expulsions commence.
AIM Kenya opens Scott Theological College.

1963 Africa Inland Church (AIC) Tanzania becomes responsible for the assignment of all missionaries.

1964 Simba rebellion in Zaire (Belgian Congo) results in AIM evacuation.

1971 AIM Kenya becomes a department of AIC.
American Council of AIM appoints first missionaries to Newark, USA.

1972 AIM's International Council meets for the first time.
Temporary cessation of war in Sudan permits AIC pastors to reestablish work to East of Nile. AIM and other missions set up ACROSS to work West of Nile.

1973 AIM abandons legal identity in Zaire and functions under CECA as one organization.

1975 AIM – AIR commences.
First missionaries to the Comoro Islands.

1977 A team establishes ceramics training in Seychelles.
Ugandan bishops elect Wani as Archbishop to replace Luwum, murdered by President Amin.

1978 Following their expulsion from Comoro Islands, a missionary couple moves to Reunion.

1979 Four missionaries enter Madagascar, working with the Bible Society.

1981 AIM and AEF establish a joint team of missionaries in Namibia, which numbers 36 by 1993.

1984 AIC Kenya holds a big prayer meeting to launch their new missionary college.

1985 Two AIM men enter war-torn Mozambique.

1986 AIM missionaries arrive in Lesotho.
CECA has 87,469 communicant members, 459 pastors of which 226 are ordained, 2,561 evangelists and 96 expatriate missionaries.

1986 Chad Evangelical Church welcomes an AIM team.

1992 While Sudan expels remaining missionaries, churches in other countries urge AIM to send more.

1995 AIC Kenya and AIM worldwide celebrate 100 years of ministry.

1

A dream dies

Peter Cameron Scott

Feet shuffled on grey stones, wandering between immense pillars which swept up to be lost in graceful arches. A fitful London sun occasionally set fire to brilliant reds and blues in lofty windows. To many carefree visitors, gazing at memorial plaques and effigies of the distinguished dead, Westminster Abbey that day was little more than a national museum. But a pale young man called Peter Scott, weakened from the onslaught of West African parasites, came with awe to this house of God. Still shaky on his legs, he turned into the centre aisle. Suddenly his eyes caught the name 'David Livingstone' cut in a slab on the floor. Under it he deciphered the words 'Other sheep I have which are not of this fold; them also I must bring'.[1] Oblivious of the crowds, he knelt on the floor and prayed for Africa, wondering again what God might require of him. Later he said that he 'seemed to see a line of mission stations passing through East Africa and on and on – into the mysteries of the Sahara Desert'. He asked himself, 'How can this be, without money, with no guaranteed church backing, with but few and uncertain supporters?' Another voice calmed him, 'If the venture be of God, it shall and must prevail'.[2]

Peter Scott had begun life in 1867, the child of Scottish parents who tried to teach their six children to love God. When Peter was six, two raw unordained Americans preached to a crowd of 3,000 in the City Hall, a few minutes' walk from the Scotts' home in Oswald Street. A teacher described how his dislike of the accent and informality evaporated as soon as he heard Sankey sing 'I am so glad that Jesus loves me'. Moody's preaching brought tears to his eyes.[3] Throughout that year the Bible suddenly became alive to thousands of Scottish people as they discovered the astounding fact that God loves sinners, for they had believed he loved only saints.

The Scott family owned little of this world's goods and life became more difficult when sickness struck Peter's sister Annie. After her death they decided to emigrate to Philadelphia. They joined a good Presbyterian church, where Peter's fine voice earned him a solo part in the choir and even brought a chance to sing on the stage. But his parents reacted swiftly, 'No son of ours shall use for a worldly purpose what God has given for His glory alone'. As he grew into young manhood, his conscience became a more formidable opponent than his parents and cornered him one day as he climbed the steps of the Philadelphia Opera House to respond to an advertisement for chorus singers. A small voice seemed to pierce his innermost being: 'Are you going to glorify God by going in there?' He heard it twice more and realized that God was speaking to him. He responded, 'No Lord, I shall never go into such a place again'.[4] Soon after this experience he yielded himself wholeheartedly to God.

In 1889 A.B. Simpson, the remarkable founder of the International Missionary Alliance, accepted Peter Scott into his training college in New York. The following year Simpson ordained him as an Alliance missionary just a day before Scott departed for Banana, at the mouth of West Africa's river Congo. His brother John joined him a few months later but recurring fever marred the joys of fellowship. Worse was to come; his brother died, leaving Peter to construct a coffin and dig a grave. He felt totally alone. As he bowed his head beside John's grave the iron entered his soul. He resolved to give himself completely to the task of taking the gospel to Africa's people. He never mastered the language nor, apparently, led a West African to faith in Christ. Two years after his arrival, he became so ill that he had to be carried to Banana unconscious and thence to England.

Peter's strength returned slowly in London. After his visit to the Abbey he had plenty of time to ponder the vision which he believed God had revealed. 'His plan for the new mission included nothing less than a work that would finally reach the very heart of the great unevangelized section known as the Soudan.' His experience on the west coast convinced him that the east offered the best approach. He saw 'much unoccupied territory' within two hundred miles of the Indian Ocean and could understand those who concluded that the priority lay there. But, comparing the coastal belt with the great untouched interior, he concluded, 'We will leave this field to our brethren (the Church Missionary Society, the German Lutheran Mission and the English Methodist Society) and press forward towards the interior.'[5]

Scott read all he could about Africa. He became aware of Arab traders up the Nile into Africa's heartlands in search of slaves and converts. The new line of Christian outposts might halt that advance. Fifty years before, Johann Krapf of the Church Missionary Society also wondered how to stop that trade in slaves and wrote, 'I used to calculate how many missionaries and how much money would be required to connect eastern and western Africa by a chain of missionary stations'.[6]

Studying the rudimentary maps, Scott noticed a mountain range sweeping through east and central Africa in a north-westerly direction towards Lake Chad along the line of his vision. The mountains attracted him for disease took a heavy toll of missionaries' lives in the low-lying areas. By living in the hills they might escape the fatal fevers. He hoped that Africans, more resistant to malaria, could be trained as evangelists and sent to the people on the plains.

Physically fit again and strengthened by God's marching orders, he sailed for Philadelphia to plan the new thrust. His infectious zeal lit up his family, who wanted to get involved. He met an interested group of missionary enthusiasts, including Arthur Pierson and Charles Hurlburt, who not only shared his dream but enlarged it. In

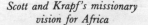

Scott and Krapf's missionary vision for Africa

1895 they established three organizations: Africa Inland Mission, Pennsylvania Bible Institute and Central American Industrial Mission. Although he surveyed part of Nicaragua in the spring of that year, Scott decided to devote himself wholly to the African venture while the Institute became the home base for the supporting Philadelphia Missionary Council and a school for training lay missionaries.

With a party of six recruits, Scott set off from New York on 17 August 1895 in the SS *Admiral*. They paused in England long enough to pick up another Scot, McLellan Wilson, and then continued their journey to Zanzibar, East Africa's most important port and the main centre of British influence. Scott and Krieger journeyed ahead to Mombasa and the rest of the group followed after a few days. Approaching Mombasa they marvelled at 'the deep green of the massed mango trees, the lighter green of the banana groves, the delicate tracery of the date palms and, high over all, waving fronds of the coconut'.[7] In gardens along the waterfront rioting colours welcomed them – creamy white jasmine, purple jacaranda, crimson bougainvillea and blue wisteria.

Threading their way through the narrow streets they were jostled by Arabs in white robes, Swahilis wearing red fezzes, Indian women clad in brilliant saris, poor tribesmen wearing next to nothing and jet black slaves. They crossed a narrow strip of water to Frere Town, the training centre which had first served released slaves. An Anglican missionary, Rev. H.K. Burns, welcomed the foreigners.

Safari and sacrifice

Scott had planned to travel inland immediately with the whole party, but he wrote 'the Consul General forbad our so doing as the country has been very much disturbed of late by the uprising of a rebel named Mbarak, an Arab chief'.[8]

The only European company in town, Smith Mackenzie, offered to arrange transport for any travellers to the mysterious interior. Before dawn on November 11th the firm's drums summoned porters and travellers. The task of gathering 250 men together and linking them to their loads took the whole day. Peter Scott had to leave the three ladies of the party behind in Frere Town. His sister Margaret described her sadness at remaining.

The whole town was in a state of excitement. The loads and porters were scattered here and there, and the boys were flying from place to place. I had quite a nice dinner ready for them but everyone had lost his appetite and they did not do justice to it at all. As they walked down the path to the beach in the darkness and I stood alone at the place where they had been, I felt quite broken-hearted for Oh! I longed to be with them.[9]

If the ladies had expected a quiet period of uninterrupted Swahili study, they were mistaken, for a few nights later they woke to the sound of gunfire. Mbarak was attacking Frere Town. Their hosts advised them to cross to Mombasa Island. 'Hurrying through the darkness, meeting armed men at every turn and unable to distinguish friend from foe, they reached a boat and were taken across in safety'.

Oblivious of the ladies' troubles, the five men were suddenly adjusting to blistered feet and aching limbs, to cruel insects that bit day and night, to perplexing contacts with strange people and to terrifying brushes with wild animals. Hotchkiss wrote of the night marches through the waterless Tara Desert,

> While daylight lasted there was the usual chaffing among the porters, as the long black line, like some gigantic worm, crawled slowly through the gathering dusk . . . there was no sound, save an occasional grunt as a weary porter shifted a load from head to shoulder or from shoulder to head . . . one after another would drop his load and, lying down beside it, fall asleep . . . we brought up the rear and our job was to rouse the slumbering porters, help them lift their loads and urge them on. It meant death to stay there . . . from thirst or from prowling beasts, for we were now in a region infested by lions.[10]

Malaria struck them hard when they were in sight of their goal, Nzawi Peak. For a week they lay on the rain-soaked ground, alternately shivering and burning, 'but one by one we recovered, wobbled about for a while with shaking limbs and giddy heads, and then turned our faces toward the hills'.[11] They had been walking for two months.

Scott stayed long enough at Nzawi to see the four men settled in a temporary grass home and then set his fever-ridden frame to tramp back to Mombasa. Travelling light he made it in nine days, arriving in time to pick up a rifle and take part in the final rout of Mbarak.

He found Miss Reckling, one of the party, in difficulties. The fierce attack on Frere Town probably unnerved her. After helping her onto a homeward-bound ship, he returned to Nzawi with the other two. Back in Mombasa again in July, Scott welcomed a second party of missionaries which included his parents and another sister, Ina. He now set out to spread his team.

The Wakamba, conditioned to regard every stranger as an enemy, did not embrace the newcomers with open arms. They reacted sometimes as friends, often as foes. At Sakai chiefs and armed warriors menaced them. Even with no knowledge of the language the missionaries understood the message – move on! The atmosphere was ugly. Scott responded with courage and humour: 'I began giving them an exhibition of juggling, tumbling, balancing sticks and axes and knives in various ways, and I soon had them all howling with laugher . . . the handspring evoked much praise'. Tension relaxed as the Wakamba responded by walking crab fashion bent over backwards. He added (perhaps allowing his usual cloak of humility to slip), 'I was glad to be able to do all they did, and more too'.

But he had not yet won their hearts. Although they rewarded his display of friendliness with gifts of milk, eggs, bananas and a chicken, they came back a few days later, heavily armed, to insist that the missionaries depart. He wrote 'I promptly told them that since they treated the white man so shamefully, "I now command every one of them to clear out" '. His display of authority impressed them. They departed and 'at about 2 p.m.

Peter Scott, DD

returned with a fine ram and an apology, requesting me to stay and promising anything I might desire'.[12]

Peter Scott set himself to befriend both Europeans and Africans. His diplomacy led Sub-Commissioner Ainsworth to offer a fine site and a useful building at Kangundo. The powerful chief, who had recently rebelled against British rule, welcomed him to the new mission station with the gift of a bull and a milking cow. Kangundo, in fertile hill country and free from malaria, subsequently became the mission's first ongoing centre.

By the first annual meeting of

AIM in October, he had installed missionaries in four locations: Nzawi, Sakai, Kilungu and Kangundo. He reported that he had walked 2,600 miles in the year. Opportunities abounded among the 500,000 Wakamba. 'In humble dependence upon our God we have moved steadily forward, no doubt in our blindness making many mistakes for we are still human, like most other people, but we ascribe all praise to Him for anything that has been done which can bring glory to His Name and honour to His cause.' None of the team had escaped fever, dysentery or 'dropsy and a serious affection of the heart and brain', but: 'we have been troubled so little that the attacks are scarcely worth taking notice of'.

The attacks could not be ignored for long. He planned to accompany the fever-ridden McLellan Wilson back to Scotland and then proceed to America. But first he needed to make a final visit to Kangundo and on to Kikuyu to prospect for a new centre among that huge tribe. The burden of the lost multitudes weighed heavily.

On November 27th he watched old men sacrifice a goat. They prayed: 'O God, send us food and rain, but let famine and sickness go far away. Preserve our cattle and our corn and give us a plentiful harvest . . . O God we love Thee and You love our people'. Peter commented in his diary: 'They have hazy ideas of God but, O how far from the truth! . . . Can we whose souls are lighted with wisdom from on high, can we to men benighted the lamp of life deny? Here am I, use me in life or in death'.[13] They were his last written words.

On December 3rd malaria forced him into bed. He began passing the dreaded 'black water'. Next day, confused by fever, he asked his mother if she was ready to go with him and said 'I am only waiting for you'. 'Let us go then', he mumbled. Mrs Scott humoured him, 'Where to, Peter?' 'To the eternal city', he gasped and then, raising his arm, he continued with his last breath 'I want the arm of the Lord of Hosts around me'.

Willis Hotchkiss

Willis Hotchkiss at Sakai was shocked to hear of the death of his 'beloved leader' late in the afternoon. He stumbled through the darkness for 23 miles and arrived at Nzawe in time to find the brethren hammering a simple casket together. Numbed by grief, the team of missionaries buried their pathfinder. Could they hear the death knell beginning to toll for the whole venture too?

Leadership featured as an important issue from the start. The members of the Philadelphia Council said that it was not for them; they described themselves as 'a prayer council and the home representatives of the mission, without forming any organic part of it, nor exercising any control over it'. They believed that 'the men and women on the field should know more about how to meet emergencies and how to plan to overcome obstacles than those at home.'[14] Before embarking, the first group of missionaries elected their officers: Peter Scott was to be Superintendent; Fredrick Krieger, his Assistant; Willis Hotchkiss was Secretary and Margaret Scott, Treasurer.

Now that the Superintendent lay in his grave, long informative letters from the missionaries – well salted with scripture – replaced Scott's reports. The mission magazine, called *Hearing and Doing*, mentioned no leader. Krieger, who should have taken over, was in such turmoil himself that at the end of 1897 he resigned, 'unwilling to continue on the doctrinal basis adopted at the founding of the mission'. At a time when the mission urgently needed encouragement and direction, it lacked any leadership.

'We like our own ways better'

Who could guide them into effective ministry? In the midst of spiritual darkness the missionaries longed to shed light, but the need to survive forced them to spend most of their daylight hours cultivating and building. Hard work and recurring fever (picked up in the coastal plains before they could reach the safety of the highlands) sapped their energy, leaving little strength for the arduous task of language analysis and learning. Scott had deliberately chosen people for their zeal and godliness rather than their schooling and skills; so they could boast few linguistic talents.

Hotchkiss encountered other difficulties. Before the missionaries arrived the Africans 'had looked upon the white man as a trader bent on making the most out of them'. They saw the missionaries exchanging beads, brass wire and colourful cloth for food and assumed they were traders too. As the missionaries spoke so little of the language misunderstandings inevitably arose. Sometimes trade ceased and the strangers went short of food. Occasionally tensions led to frightening confrontations. A hungry crowd, armed with swords, bows and arrows, threatened Hotchkiss and demanded food. He desperately pulled out a revolver and loaded it before they took fright and backed away.

Weeks of this sort of brinkmanship ended when a rhinoceros ran wild over the local gardens. The anxious villagers appealed to Willis and as he chased after the rhino in the company of thousands of men, women and children, he prayed for success, 'for my real target was a place in the hearts of these hitherto suspicious, hostile people. Why should God not help a man fire a rifle as well as preach a sermon?'[15] His second shot crashed into a vital spot. The Wakamba showered gifts of food on him and relationships looked up for a time.

Foul ulcers infected many of the local people. Missionaries impressed them by their patience as they washed away the pus and bound up the wounds day by day until they healed. But the Wakamba had no intention of accepting any change. They said the new customs were 'good for the white man but we like our own ways better'. Lester Severn wrote unhappily, 'With a few exceptions they are very indifferent to our presence'.[16]

The missionary team began to fall apart. Peter Scott's parents left first. The kindly Government official, Ainsworth, offered John Scott a job in a healthy climate and he accepted. John Ainsworth's motives may have been mixed for soon he married their daughter, Ina. Meanwhile the team sent Margaret Scott home to confer with the Philadelphia Council and to represent the mission at home. After a few months of impassioned deputation, she too resigned and the magazine notes somewhat ambiguously, 'Her parents need her in Machakos. She will return as the wife of Mr. Wilson who also resigns'.

Fever

Fever also ravaged the remaining members of the team: Jacob Toole died followed by Tom Allen. Soon Mrs. Allen and Minnie Lindbergh fell ill and Willis struggled with them to the new railway terminus, Kinani, and on to Mombasa where he helped the ladies board a ship. As they drew away from the quay, he painfully recalled disembarking with fifteen others two and a half years before; all so full of hope. Now, he only remained. Another distress added to his acute loneliness.

He was penniless and in debt. The Coast Agent had been setting funds he received for Willis against a mission debt. The Hotchkiss account stood in the red. Quite apart from the obvious material difficulties, this was a serious matter of spiritual principle. Scott and others had stated at the start that the mission would never appeal for funds (except to God in prayer). Every applicant must accept that 'where God leads, there God feeds.

He must be very sure of the former; then he can quietly trust for the latter'.[17] Such confidence in God prohibited debt.

Joining AIM Willis had gladly embraced this position. He now felt let down, not by God but by the mission. In fact money, forwarded by the Philadelphia Council, had gone to the Scott family who assumed it was theirs. But many months would pass before Willis heard the explanation. Meanwhile he wrestled with a bitter sense of betrayal.

Aware of his problem, Minnie had emptied her purse into his hands before she sailed, enabling him to board the train to Tsavo. The journey, which had taken two months on his first trip, lasted sixteen hours.

He returned to Kangundo to be greeted by devastating drought. Dysentery confined him to bed for long periods. At one time, in a haze of weakness, he looked on helpless while his servant sold his enamel dishes and made off with the proceeds.

Month after weary month passed without a cent coming from Philadelphia. Between bouts of fever Willis searched hard for food. Throughout two months he survived on beans and sour milk. The chiefs ordered that anyone bringing food to the white man would be killed. But God rewarded his faith in a remarkable way. Watching a woman return from her field in the evening, he was surprised to see a cassava root drop from a basket on her back. A day or two later another dropped at the same spot. He began to watch for her coming and observed her toss her head back as she drew level to his door, jerking a root out of her basket.

For seven months Hotchkiss soldiered on alone. Everywhere the unrelenting famine claimed lives. He just managed to survive from the game he shot. Confidence in God deepened. He befriended a young man, Kikuvi, impressing the lad more by his faithful ways than his faltering words. Kikuvi became a Christian and the right-hand man to a succession of missionaries.

Misunderstanding

As a result of his harsh experience, Willis determined that future mission staff should be largely self-supporting. He managed to sell a small crop of wheat and buy flour to make his first loaf in many months. At last, on 8 December 1898, he welcomed visitors from the USA – the new Director, Charles Hurlburt, and a missionary, William Bangert. The lonely man first caught sight of them on Mombasa railway station and described his gaze. 'Six months of longing were centered in that look and I must confess I haven't got over looking yet'.[18]

Initial encouragement turned into keen disappointment. Charles Hurlburt interpreted the financial policy even more strictly than Scott and disagreed with the veteran's new ideas of self-support. History draws a veil over their arguments but the two months together could not have been happy for either of them. Willis became more disenchanted with AIM.

After Hurlburt's departure famine, smallpox, cattle disease and tribal warfare continued to ravage the people. For many months Hotchkiss and Bangert endured 'the pitiful pleading of dying humanity from morning till night'. Often the crowds around the little mud hut became menacing in their demands for the little rice or other food the men possessed and they could only restrain them by brandishing their guns. He wrote home, 'Tell me what is the use of preaching the Gospel to people who are gripped with the awful pain of hunger? How can they grasp it? They want bread, and a fearful account will be laid to the charge of a self-satisfied church unless the pitiful cry . . . is heard.'[19] Later Ainsworth reckoned that half of the Wakamba perished at that time; Bangert estimated three-quarters.

In the midst of the carnage Willis resigned from AIM. No one had proved that God provides for his believing servants in answer to their prayers more than him. But disagreement on this issue led this godly pioneer out of AIM – the last of the first sixteen. Three had died (Scott, Toole, Allen); five were invalided home (Mrs Allen, Minnie Lindbergh, Jeannie Edwards, Severn and John Codd); four resigned (Hotchkiss, Krieger, Wilson and Margaret Scott); Miss Reckling returned home and Mr. Scott joined the government at Machakos with his wife and other daughter.

He learnt many lessons. In old age he wrote,

> As I look back over these forty years, the thing that stands out more clearly than anything else is the astonishing patience of the natives in the face of my abysmal ignorance. I was like a baby in toyland, smashing things in joyous abandon. Everything was topsy-turvy, but I was barging straight ahead, serenely unconscious of the absurd figure I cut in the eyes of those whom I had come to teach. I was glad at things that ought to have made me sad, and I was chagrined at things that ought to have delighted me. The only satisfaction is that one did learn after a while.[20]

He put his hard-won knowledge to good account when he returned to Kenya five years later as leader of the new Friends Africa Mission.

AIM was left with just William Bangert. He had shared the work with Willis for only four months but it was long enough to pick up something of the veteran's endurance. He bridged the gap for a further three months until reinforcements for AIM arrived in October 1899.

In a little over a year from his arrival Bangert returned home to recover from malaria. By then a new century had been born. And with its birth, AIM came to life again.

2
A seed germinates

In the midst of the apparently dying embers of AIM first Hotchkiss and then Bangert maintained their solitary glow. Who could have foreseen that such a dim glimmer would eventually set fire to millions? By calling Charles Hurlburt to take control and then bringing outstanding men and women to work alongside him, the Lord fanned the glow into a blaze in British East Africa (today's Kenya) and scattered some of its burning coals into German East Africa (now Tanzania) and Belgian Congo (Zaire), where they ignited new fires which continue to burn today.

The fire blazed with light and warmth, but it also consumed. In October 1907 a fledgling British AIM committee interviewed a new candidate. They recorded; 'Miss Soltau told briefly how God had led her' and then spoke of 'her parents' willingness to give her up'. She was not being melodramatic. When you said goodbye to a missionary son or daughter bound for Africa, you knew you may never meet again. Missionaries saw death not only as a hazard but also a privilege. Sweating out their fevers and doubling up with stomach cramps, they found solace in a Lord who knew all about suffering. If the final call came, colleagues sorrowed deeply but after the funeral rededicated themselves joyfully to searching for a harvest which must surely follow such costly sacrifice.

A rugged faith sustained these pioneers. God could take them to heaven or leave them to serve on earth as he chose. In illness, he could heal or give grace to persevere. Early they asked, can they trust him to provide all their material needs in Africa without appealing at all to friends at home? Their personal answer to this was almost always a resounding 'yes'. But the corollary was less easy to answer: could a rapidly expanding organization function in the same way?

They might differ with each other – even squabble sometimes – and make many mistakes. But they thumbed through their Bibles, spent hours on their knees and pressed forward always with the saving Gospel on their lips. And God honoured their devotion.

Charles and Alta Hurlburt

Deep snow blanketed the small Ohio town of Oberlin. At the end of their resources a teenaged lad and his recently widowed mother knelt to ask for fuel. Mrs Hurlburt's quiet confidence impressed Charles; she knew God would answer. When they opened their front door next morning they found a large pile of wood stacked against the wall. A kindly farmer had realized their need and set out to help them. Bad weather delayed him until well after dark, so he quietly dumped his load in the snow to avoid rousing them from their beds. Mrs Hurlburt was grateful but not surprised: her son was amazed and convinced.[21] From then on he never seems to have doubted that God lives and always responds to simple faith.

God, unerring in his faithfulness

For a lad of fifteen it was a vital step. In 1875 Charles almost totally supported his mother and the two younger children. During his growth to manhood God never failed the family. Charles married, set up a plumbing business, dabbled in dentistry and joined the Young Men's Christian Association. Soon he took up an appointment as full-time evangelist and then YMCA State Secretary. Even in his early twenties he felt restless with a sense that God was preparing him for a greater work.

For ten years he quietly asked God for further direction. Disappointed by the secular trend of the YMCA, he resigned to undertake door-to-door evangelism. Ignorance among Christians appalled him and led him to set up the Pennsylvania Bible Institute in 1895. He gathered like-minded men to pray for the school and called them the Philadelphia Missionary Council in recognition that their brief extended far beyond the college building. As he prayed for many missionary enterprises, he reached out to them, but he seemed to hear God telling him not to get too involved. Peter Scott came to share his vision and Hurlburt listened enthralled. As the group prayed together, he heard God say, 'This is the work that I have for thee to do'.[22]

Unsure at first how to respond, he found enough to occupy him in the infant Bible school. God continued to train him through the harsh reality of finance.

Charles Hurlburt, DD

The college commenced its third year with a debt of $120. Charles reluctantly refused to accept suitable students because they could not afford the fees. He led the staff and students to 'earnest prayer as to whether God would not have the school put wholly on the faith basis. This was finally done and the result was greatly increased blessing in every department of the work.'[23] This 'faith basis' meant they would ask no one but God for money. PBI ceased charging student fees; instructors gave their time without expecting a salary and all learnt to pray about every financial need. Occasionally they wondered how they would afford coal or butter but they never lacked. Miraculously to them, they paid every bill and closed the year free of debt.

As President of the Missionary Council when the news of Scott's death broke, Hurlburt felt the time had come to tell them, 'God has laid the African work on my heart'. After consulting the missionaries the Council asked him to become Director of AIM. But by the time this process was completed Hotchkiss was the only remaining member and the mission was in debt. Was God telling the council to close down or perhaps to ask another mission to take over the infant work? In the midst of the discussion Dr A.T. Pierson, a council member, said, 'Gentlemen, the hallmark of God on any work is death. God has given us that hallmark. Now is the time to go forward.'[24]

Hurlburt's first step to Africa was to free himself from the College by appointing a Superintendent. He watched with horror as the new man appealed to the Christian public for funds and was not surprised when the Institute sank again into debt. The Council insisted on its 'faith basis' and debts vanished. Charles, probably too gracious to say 'I could have told you so', determined that a renewed AIM would stick 'to a faith position in matters of finance'. He had no quarrel with other societies which followed a different method but for him God had made his will clear. Had he not said 'If I were hungry I would not tell you'? (Psalm 50:12) Had he not promised to 'meet all your needs according to his glorious riches in Christ Jesus'? (Philippians 4:19) Later he met old Hudson Taylor, the saintly founder of the China Inland Mission, who told him, 'Depend upon it, God's work, done in God's way will never lack supplies'. But the 'faith basis' meant much more than material provision. It expressed the mission's confidence that 'God is true to His promises and unerring in His faithfulness'.

Hurlburt expected missionaries to apply to God alone for their funds. He also trusted donors to ask the Lord to guide them in their giving and he valued such prayer: 'The AIM would rather receive the prayerful, free-will offering of a dime than a prayerless, solicited gift of a dollar'.[25] The guiding principle for the mission's approach to their constituency became, 'As to the work, full information; as to funds, no solicitation'.[26]

Although some, like Willis Hotchkiss questioned if Scripture was as clear as Charles believed, many warmed to a principle which laid such strong emphasis on faith and prayer and, at the same time, spared them the embarrassment of asking people for money. John Stauffacher spoke for them when he later wrote, 'How can it be possible that for a period of nearly thirty years a large number of individual workers . . . should unite on the one principle of absolute dependence on God and not one, as far as we are aware, fail at any time to have all his needs supplied?'

The Hurlburts amazed their friends by announcing in 1901 that they planned to take their five children, aged four to twelve years, to East Africa despite the terrifying scale of missionary mortality. They accompanied four new missionaries. Speaking of the need for equipment, passage money and houses in Africa, Charles wrote, 'God heard our cry and without any appeal save to Him, opened the way for us to go'. Even more remarkable,

Home from the garden, CM

God protected this family throughout their childhood years. All
five became missionaries, setting a precedent which many AIM
families later followed.

The Hurlburts found Kangundo, forty miles from the new
railway, too remote for the headquarters. In 1903 they moved
to Kijabe, alongside the new lines as they plunged dramatically
into the Rift Valley. Here the developing organization had access
to post and telegraph. He continually scanned the horizons of
God's purpose, always keeping the Lake Chad goal firmly in
focus.

Leading on his knees

Believing prayer formed Hurlburt's backbone. He rose early each
morning to meet God. One of the few rules he made for
missionaries was that they meet daily to pray together. He would
be the first to realize that such discipline could become sterile
and his letters to missionaries are filled with scriptural pleas that
they pray without ceasing. Having prayed over a matter, he felt
able to act decisively. But if a decision involved fellow
missionaries he recognized that the Lord spoke to them also as
they asked for guidance.

'In no other mission is there larger individual liberty', he wrote
to the mission family,

No officer of the Mission has any authority to force his personal ideas upon his fellow workers. Particularly is large freedom given to each head of a station who may shape the character of the work on his station, but all other workers are also free to choose as far as possible the station where they can work with greater liberty, and if not happy, may be changed to another point.[27]

He firmly based his leadership on and in the Bible. Not everyone agreed with his decisions but few doubted his godliness.

Hurlburt succeeded because he led not only on his knees but also on his feet. He pleaded for the salvation of those around him, planned to send people to them and plunged into action himself on their behalf. He exemplified his principle for missionaries, 'That direct soul winning shall be the first consideration, in everything'.[28] After visiting much of the Kamba tribal area he reckoned that 'two more stations than those we occupy now will enable us to evangelize all the Wakamba'. Following an extensive trip through the neighbouring Kikuyu area he purchased ten locations where he hoped to place missionaries but gladly gave them to the better-placed Church Missionary Society. He then opened others on the Kikuyu ridges closer at hand.

On a ship travelling to Africa in 1908 he met Bishop Tucker of the Church Missionary Society who talked about his mission's twenty years in German East Africa. The Anglican leader asked, 'Would AIM take this venture over so that CMS could concentrate on Uganda?' They crossed Lake Victoria together to visit Nassa and, after prayerful consultation with colleagues, Charles sent missionaries there the following year. Many recognized that, 'Hurlburt was diplomatic and adroit, both with chiefs and administrators, and it was due to him that the first "foot in the door" was often achieved in any sphere in the first two decades of the century'.[29]

His diplomatic skills reached higher than local chiefs and colonial officials. He had targeted North East Congo for many years but pessimists assured Hurlburt that the Belgian King Albert would never approve missionaries entering from the east. While recruiting in the USA a summons to the White House surprised him. President Teddy Roosevelt wanted his advice about an upcoming hunting trip to Africa. Quick to recognize an opportunity, Hurlburt invited him to lay the foundation stone for Rift Valley Academy, the new school for missionaries' children at Kijabe. On his visit Roosevelt admired the tough dedication of Hurlburt's team and likened them to the pioneers who opened up the American west. Before he left for his next stop, Brussels, he asked if he could help. 'When you get to Belgium,' Hurlburt replied, 'please put in a word for us to the King.' Permission granted, the mission trail-blazers moved into Congo.

Like his predecessor, Peter Scott, Charles abhorred competition. He summarized his attitude in a letter to CMS, 'It is our firm conviction that to trench upon territory occupied by others, whilst countless millions are unevangelized, would greatly limit God's blessing on our work'.[30] Many new missionary groups had followed the new railway into inland Kenya and leaders began asking if their converts could all join one church. Several meetings led to the Kikuyu Conference in 1913. AIM provided twenty of the sixty delegates and Hurlburt was asked to take the Chair. He gave a series of studies from 1 Corinthians chapter one. A new missionary wrote, 'Mr Hurlburt led the delegates into a true spirit of unity, conditioned upon absolute humility and surrender to the will of God.'[31]

Discussion ranged widely and resulted in proposals for federation leading to church union. The first clause of their agreement stated,

> the basis of federation shall consist in the loyal acceptance of the Holy Scriptures as the supreme rule of Faith and Practice . . . and in particular of our belief in the authority of the Holy Scripture as the Word of God; in the deity of Jesus Christ, and in the atoning death of our Lord as the ground of our forgiveness.

Five missions signed 'with a view to the ultimate union of the native churches'.[32] Bishop Peel led a joyful communion service before all the missionaries departed in the belief that the young African churches could be spared the divisive denominationalism of their western brothers.

Far off in his high-Anglican cathedral of Zanzibar another bishop, Frank Weston, was shocked when he heard the outcome of the conference. How could Anglicans agree to such an irregular form of churchmanship? How indeed could two Anglican bishops share communion with nonconformists? He wrote to ask the Archbishop of Canterbury to summon the offending bishops to trial for 'propagating heresy and promoting schism'. When the conference reconvened Weston presented proposals for a united church based on a high-Anglican view of episcopal authority and of the sacraments. While willing to go a long way down the Anglican road in the cause of church unity,

Hurlburt felt that 'no basis which placed the church above the Word of God, no ritual which would take the place of personal communion and no ecclesiastical control which limited personal liberty in vital things . . . was possible'.[33] All that could be salvaged was an alliance of missionary societies which provided a forum for cooperation while leaving each to develop churches along its own lines. One of their early accomplishments, the Alliance High School, educated a generation of church leaders and politicians.

Who's in charge?

By 1917 Charles Hurlburt was a sick man. He had to cancel a visit to England because doctors recognized 'emotional stress' and ordered long periods of rest. Parasites ravaged his health and travel sapped his strength. With his eye still on Lake Chad, Hurlburt decided that Kijabe was too peripheral for his headquarters and moved to Aba in Congo in 1919. Two deaths hurt him deeply. His daughter Alta and daughter-in-law Elizabeth, fellow missionaries in Aba, died within two years of each other. Several missionaries were disgruntled so that in 1920 he wrote that 'very few' did not complain to him about something or other. More ominous still, he was falling out with the American Home Council, the successor to the Philadelphia Missionary Council. A note of bitterness crept into his letters.

In 1912 the mission decided that its Home Councils in USA and Great Britain would supervise the work in Africa through the General Director.[34] Such was their confidence in Hurlburt that this change still left him in charge with the councils looking to him for advice. Ten years later the American council had second thoughts.

The council disliked his insistence on centralizing all moneys on Hurlburt's office in Aba. The Great War left the mission short of money. In particular the British missionaries felt the financial pinch and Charles used American money to make up the shortfall in their allowances. While most missionaries accepted this, the powerful council in New York objected. Moreover they decided that a public statement of their financial obligations did not contradict the 'faith basis'. Accordingly the mission magazine began publishing specific needs in 1922. It provoked an immediate response from Charles, 'failure in our work and grievous dishonour must follow'[35] such compromise. The answer to financial stringency, he insisted, was always 'genuine importunate prayer'. His friends in London, anxious to quench the fires of controversy, wrote to him, 'We have no reason to believe that the spirit of the faith principle has been changed. Giving full information does not necessarily connote definite solicitation of funds'.[36] But Charles saw it as precisely that. The British attempt only fuelled the disagreement and made him feel that all were apostasizing.

One source stated that 'Mr Hurlburt's attitude toward the AIM drastically changed after an operation for a brain tumour'.[37] Unwell in California, he felt hurt because the council ignored his suggestions and starved him of information. At the annual meeting in New York on 31 July 1925, fourteen council members and eighteen missionaries noted that 'Rev C.E. Hurlburt is forced to resign'.[38] They also reaffirmed their allegiance to the faith principle. The council appointed a five man 'Committee of Direction' to supervise the work in Africa while awaiting the appointment of a new General Director. Whether or not Charles thought he had resigned is doubtful. He sought to drum up support among missionaries for several months. In November 1926 he made a final, impassioned appeal for overall leadership, insisting on 'the need and necessity that a competent General Director be appointed and be given full confidence and power'.[39] Then he seemed to accept the inevitable parting.

Would he have handled the situation differently had he been fit and free of strain? Should the council have made allowances for his years of pressure? Had the advancing years and sickness made him dictatorial? Surely, in a relaxed atmosphere, his diplomatic skills could have found a way through the storm for the controversy was more over personal conviction than biblical principle.

His health improved dramatically as soon as he left AIM. He became Superintendent of the Bible Institute of Los Angeles and then founded a new society, the Unevangelized Africa Mission, to serve unreached tribes in Congo and French Equatorial Africa. He was still in harness in his seventy-seventh year when he suddenly collapsed. His doctors said his kidneys were 'shot all to pieces' probably as a result of recurring blackwater fever. He died a week later on 27 January 1936. His widow, Alta, returned to Africa where she died at the home of her daughter, Mrs Bell, in Oicha.

Charles Hurlburt defined AIM's doctrine, chiselled out its constitution, fostered two Home Councils in America and another in Britain as well as launching the work in Australia, recruited most of the 200 missionaries in place when he left, and directed the whole work with vision, care, wisdom and authority. His gracious shadow falls on every development in AIM's first three decades. Without him the mission would have been stillborn. The multitude of churches in east and central Africa who trace their origins back to AIM probably owe more to this man than to any other.

Kikuvi

A gulf of misunderstanding separated the early missionaries from the Wakamba. In the struggle for survival they had little time for language study and mostly they lacked the higher education which could assist them in this discipline. They wrote movingly about the horrors of the pagan darkness around them but were ill-equipped to understand the Kamba way of life. Even finding their way around a totally foreign country presented enormous hazards. They desperately needed a Mkamba to interpret for them, to mediate, to counsel and to act as their guide.

Scott's plan depended on African evangelists as much as on foreign missionaries. On his arrival in Kamba country, he saw the jostling villages and 'it became clear to him that the evangelisation of that area must be done by the Africans themselves and he longed for the day when such workers would be found among the Wakamba'.[40]

Hotchkiss befriended an intelligent young man called Kikuvi. On his lonely safari back from Mombasa in May 1898 he called at his friend's village. Kikuvi warned him that the Swahili porters, left by Willis to guard his property, had stolen it all and taken it to Chief Mwanamuke. Kikuvi led the way to the Chief's village, finding him 'just drunk enough to be thoroughly truculent'.[41] The Chief strongly resented the accusations and, picking up an axe, made for Kikuvi. They managed to disarm him, to find all the goods and return them to Kangundo. Kikuvi agreed to stay with Willis as a headman and immediately used his influence to persuade some local people to work for the mission instead of the coastal Swahili.

He was often eyes and ears to Hotchkiss. Hunting for food for the hungry people, Kikuvi suddenly stopped, pointed to a clump of bushes and told Willis that he could see a rhino. It looked like an immobile boulder to the missionary, 'but Kikuvi's eyes were better than mine and he whispered; "That's his shoulder Bwana" and I hastily fired. The great brute burst from the bush and came straight for us snorting with rage.' They jumped aside and he swept past at arm's length, falling dead seventy yards further on.[42]

With the departure of Hotchkiss, Kikuvi became companion to Bangert. The new missionary writes about one of their walks; 'Kikuvi pointed to a few bones and a scalp beside the path and said, "There's Kavulia; he died of hunger." ' They came across corpses beside every track; 'The drawn, agonized look on every face plainly speaks of the horrors of death by starvation.'[43] To Bangert the corpses formed part of a vast tragedy; Kikuvi knew them as friends and neighbours.

When Bangert left, Kikuvi stayed on with Hurlburt, who described a safari 'with the ever faithful Kikuvi as headman . . . Later in the second day, the path having faded out entirely, we struck for the camping place seen first by Kikuvi's practiced eye when none of the rest knew the way.' He led them to a cave where they could camp over Sunday. 'In the afternoon Kikuvi showed me the scene of some of the earlier raids, saying; "Before I heard the Words of God I was very bad and used to raid the Maasai and steal their cattle and kill their men; now I do not like such work. It is very bad." In the evening we gave a little talk and Kikuvi explained most earnestly that he had learned very slowly the words and ways of God. Then he asked God to give power to walk in His path and to reach God's village.'[44]

A few months later Hurlburt and Lee Downing led a series of meetings in the little 'Door of Hope Chapel' at Kangundo. Kikuvi gave a remarkable talk which led the two missionaries, after much prayer, to ask for definite decisions next evening. Hurlburt writes; 'About twenty came to the front and knelt on the earth floor, some of them with what appeared to be sincere prayers of repentance.'

A month before Hurlburt moved the headquarters to Kijabe Kikuvi was baptized at Kangundo. Out of his several wives, Hurlburt noted, 'all but one has come to a public acceptance of Jesus as Saviour.'[45] Later, missionaries insisted that a man must put away all wives except his first but Hurlburt at this stage avoided such a traumatic resolution of the polygamy problem. Before baptizing four people in 1910, Hurlburt asked them six questions including, 'Do you agree not to marry more than one wife?'[46]

Kikuvi must have disappointed Hurlburt for he married fourteen times. Like many others, material ambition may have motivated him initially as much as any spiritual desire. Certainly he became a wealthy (and sometimes wayward) chief. Charles never lost faith in him. 'Hurlburt's love, acceptance and friendship won him over and he eventually died in the Lord.'[47] His son-in-law, Bishop Wellington Mulwa, recounted the old man's calling his family to tell them, 'Tomorrow I will die.' He blessed them and instructed them in the details of his burial. Next day he quietly passed away.

William and Myrtle Knapp

The smell of death hung over Thembigwa River when the Knapps arrived early in 1899. The famine that halved the Wakamba struck the Kikuyu too and was just subsiding when a new epidemic of smallpox broke out. Thirsty sufferers crawled to the streams, where they perished in their hundreds and clogged the flow. The new missionaries flung themselves into the care of the starving and the dying.

The Knapps seem to have taken the appalling conditions in their stride and decided to penetrate further into the tribe. Their chance came when four enterprising Kikuyu arrived to ask for 'their own European' to live among them. The white man's gun may have impressed them with its potential for protection from the marauding Maasai and they stood in awe of God who gave him such powerful technology.[48]

Like most missionaries Knapp did own a gun but he seldom used it even to kill animals. He relied on love to win the Kikuyu and prayer to hinder the raiders. (In fact starvation, smallpox and cattle disease had so impoverished the Maasai that they had little strength to raid their neighbours.) In August 1902 William Knapp moved to the new plot at Kambui, where he lodged in a Kikuyu home while building his own. Although his diary complains of the cold and a strong smell of goats, he would not allow such minor discomforts to deter him. Myrtle's personality differed greatly from her husband's. While he was quiet, unexcitable and stolid, she was lively, talkative and hospitable. Resolution and dedication characterized both.

William as evangelist and advisor never gave orders or ranted. Myrtle, as faithful a hostess as any Kikuyu, welcomed all to her table – old men clad in skins, warriors painted red and earnest young Christians. Their assurance about the way to God impressed thoughtful Kikuyu, some of whom saw their own religious system failing in the face of disease and famine. The sponsorship of the four progressive elders, who had invited them to Kambui, gave the missionaries a standing in the community which encouraged people to listen to their message.

A large crowd witnessed the first baptisms in the river when the strong, visual symbolism of dying to an old way of life and rising to a new impressed many. William, convinced of a radical influence of the Holy Spirit in the converts, welcomed them at once into church life. 'As soon as the first converts were baptised, they shared in ordering the life of the community with him on a basis of complete equality, and, as their numbers increased, the entire control passed quickly into their hands.'[49] Never imposing his view, he only gave advice when asked. Whether or not his counsel prevailed, he always implemented the decision without hesitation.

In contrast to her phlegmatic husband, Myrtle freely shared her ideas. She could stimulate Africans to imaginative thinking without creating the suspicion of dominating them. The couple lived so simply that they encouraged their converts to develop initiative, self-reliance and community spirit. They had no desire to own property and rapidly passed the little they possessed into the hands of the emerging church.

Initially the Knapps had reached East Africa as members of the small, New England based, Gospel Missionary Society (a child of the Moody awakening). Hurlburt's genius for establishing good relations drew them into the family of AIM along with other GMS folk and held them until 1915 when *Hearing and Doing* announced that 'The Gospel Missionary Society, which has had a friendly alliance with our work for years, will now work independently.'[50] As usual in that era, discretion prevented the magazine from giving the reason but the 1912 Constitution would have made it inevitable. It stated that the Home Councils would direct the mission's work and hold the mission's properties. In contrast, Knapp and his colleagues not only insisted that leadership be Africa based but went much further, placing it firmly in the hands of Africans themselves.

The Knapps possessed the greatest of missionary skills – the ability to develop leaders. They nurtured a succession of pastors and church leaders. Early they baptized Waruhiu Kungu, who later became Senior Chief. They gave Harry Thuku a home with them for four years before he became Kenya's first major politician.

They served the Kikuyu for forty years. Soon after their deaths the church leaders invited the Presbyterian Church to take over their congregations. One of the conditions of merger insisted that

'Traditional customs of the Gospel Mission Church continue in the united Church until superseded by other customs by common agreement. Adult baptism by immersion and infant baptism by affusion to be acceptable practice throughout the Church.'[51] Hurlburt, with his passion for unity based on truth, would have approved.

Under British, German and Belgian rule

While Leopold reigned over Belgium, prospects for Protestant missions in his African possessions seemed remote. If missionaries must come at all he preferred Roman Catholics. Colonial enthusiasts in Germany formed the Berlin Evangelical Missionary Society for East Africa. They 'wished to harness the Christian mission to the national chariot and therefore regarded a German colony as an exclusive reserve for the German churches.'[52]

Sir Bartle Frere, the British Governor of Bombay who exercised jurisdiction over British interests in Zanzibar and East Africa, naturally looked to the Anglicans to care for released slaves. Even so the first CMS missionaries in East Africa came from Germany and the British officials seemed much more ready to receive missionaries of other nationalities than some other Europeans.

Most of the early AIM missionaries came from the United States. Under their leader Charles Hurlburt they managed to relate well to each of the colonial powers they met. Indeed, the pioneers often found a warm welcome from officials. As in the case of Congo, God undoubtedly prepared the way in answer to prayer. Also, remoteness made a European glad to meet any other white people and to assist them in their struggle against disease and a multitude of other problems which all foreigners shared.

Thrusting out from Kenya, AIM moved first into German and then Belgian territory.

John and Florence Stauffacher

When John Stauffacher arrived in the newly opened headquarters of AIM in Kijabe, British East Africa, he was assigned by the team, including the Hurlburts and Knapps, to work among the warrior cattle people called Maasai. Charles Hurlburt, always quick to encourage a new missionary, introduced him to their homes and urged him to learn their language. The colonial Government, wanting to settle European farmers onto the Maasai grazing lands, moved the tribesmen north to Rumuruti and John followed them. He longed for Florence, his fiancée, to join him, but she delayed. John now wrote full of assurance; 'Do you suppose I ought to believe that the doubt comes from the Lord? Don't be afraid . . . Let us go on planning as though your coming to Africa is definitely settled.'

She laid aside her fears and came. On 7 May 1906 she addressed her diary; 'Good night Florence Minch for the last time.'[53] John, full of malaria next day, could not walk to the church. Charles Hurlburt drove him to the mud and wattle church in an ox-cart and then carried him pick-a-back to a seat at the front. Florence's first duty as a wife was to nurse him at Kijabe for several weeks before they could move to Rumuruti.

Like Scott, John had cut short his college education in order to fulfil his call as soon as possible. But he read avidly, worked hard at the language and used his knowledge of Greek in translating the Maasai New Testament. Wherever he lived he sought a trysting place where he met God daily – a log in the Kijabe forest, a tree house at Rumuruti – and from such communion he could preach confidently and plan with assurance.

Under Hurlburt's tutelage John and Florence did more than any to realize the Coast to Chad vision. Hurlburt and John, assisted by a prominent young Maasai called Mulungit, thrust northwards into the thirsty plains of the Samburu and Rendille people. John investigated the tribes to the west around Lake Baringo. John and Charles were together again to accompany Bishop Tucker to Nassa in German East Africa. After saying farewell to the bishop they continued south with a Kamba Christian on a gruelling safari for two months. Dysentery dogged

Charles and malaria immobilized their companion until he had to be carried in a chair.[54] Tempers frayed.

One evening John sat by their camp fire frying chicken. The smell so sickened Charles that he struggled out of his tent, picked up the pan, flung its contents into the bushes and returned to his bed. Though sick and weary, neither could sleep. Towards midnight John heard a creak from Charles' camp bed and then a quiet shuffle of feet on the earth floor of the tent. He sensed the side of his mosquito net being raised and a hand sliding in to grasp his own. By the glow of the dying fire John could make out the bent form of his friend kneeling beside him, his shoulders shaking with great sobs. Tears streamed down John's cheeks as he reached to grip the penitent hand. Without a word Charles tucked the net in place and climbed back into his bed.

Another door swung open

John met Bishop Tucker again two years later at his home in Kampala, Uganda. He and another missionary, James Gribble, wanted to find a way to the millions of people in North East Congo. Tucker, aware of unrest between the tribes, advised against the venture. Joking about their five porters, the bishop told them they needed 200 and a military escort as well. Three weeks later they arrived at the River Semliki which formed the border. Suddenly all the tales the five porters had heard of violence and cannibalism in Congo took on new meaning. The party camped on the Uganda side for three days to pluck up courage but the five fled, leaving John and James to cross alone in a canoe.

A sullen group met them but, seeing they were armed with nothing more ominous than walking sticks, let them pass. With mounting anxiety they climbed past some houses, whose occupants turned out to scowl. Fear seemed justified when two men wearing tattered uniforms pointed rifles at them and demanded to know who they were. 'Come with us,' they commanded, 'Our white man is waiting for you.'[55] They led them to a tense meeting with an Irishman, a self-appointed local ruler. He traded in ivory and wondered if his visitors represented government. When he saw their helplessness and realized they intended him no harm, he welcomed them, told his African wife to feed them and then offered to carry them in his canoes to Mahagi Port where they could meet the Belgian official. In his pocket John carried King Albert's letter of authorization which President Roosevelt had negotiated. The official said yes to AIM's entry to Congo and another door swung open.

Hurlburt, unwell in the USA, appointed Stauffacher 'Extension Director' but told him to stay at Rumuruti until he could return to Kenya with fresh people for the new thrust. John built a comfortable stone house in which Florence gave birth to her first boy, Raymond. She did not find it easy to look forward to another pioneering venture but, once she had accepted it, she was eager to start. The months of waiting extended to two years. When Raymond's little brother appeared Florence may have seen God's hand in the delay but John became impatient and irritable. Why wait when he and his wife were ready to go? He knew of others who were willing to join them. Should he resign and commence a new work of his own? He found relief in preparing a paper for the January 1912 missionary conference.

John spoke to his colleagues on the subject, 'Side-Tracked for 2000 years'. He said 'The Church is absolutely without excuse in failing to obey the command to preach the Gospel to every living creature.' Africa's tribes were ready to listen. Missions had been diverted from the main task of proclamation. 'Many times more effort and money were spent in trying to reform, educate and civilize than would have been necessary to evangelize the whole world.' His passion mounted as he declared that 'the church . . . has ever been led aside from her real work to do that which in itself is good and true, but of secondary importance.' Referring often to the task of civilizing and education he urged, 'All we can hope for is to train those who shall do it while we speed on from tribe to tribe until the whole world has been reached.'[56]

John Stauffacher, DD

By April Charles Hurlburt's health had improved sufficiently for him to return. Immediately eleven missionaries, with the Stauffacher babies, set off to Mahagi Port in Congo. Despite the aid of Belgian officials they grappled with immense difficulties. Storms blasted their flimsy tents and tore apart huts hastily constructed of grass and poles. Mosquitoes hummed around them as soon as the sun set and then virulent malaria laid them low. Thieves, encouraged by their weakness, robbed them mercilessly so that one morning a lady rose to discover that she possessed nothing in the world save her night attire and a blanket. After two false starts they chose a base, Kasengu, high on a hill where, in the midst of their struggle to survive and to advance further, they gathered frequently to pray and to listen to God's Word. 'Without this,' John wrote; 'I feel certain that the continued annoyances and the prolonged strain would have caused us to go to pieces.'[57]

'I thought my heart would burst with joy'

By the time news of the Great War filtered through to Kasengu John's health was shattered both physically and emotionally.[58] Even so he found leaving difficult. He wrote, 'I think that was one of the hardest goodbyes I have experienced in Africa.' He knew the pioneer's bond with a population that he had introduced to the Gospel. Although he found some satisfaction in building a small home in Wisconsin, he never again felt comfortable in the United States. After a year there, 'he was restless and often moody and dissatisfied and couldn't settle himself to anything.'[59] His health forbad their return until 1918 when compassionate mission leaders, feeling that they should live closer to the Kijabe medical facilities and the missionary school, asked them to return to their first love, the Maasai.

Once again foreign settlers cast covetous eyes on the Maasai grazing grounds and the British Government ordered the frustrated nomads south. John and Florence followed them, to build yet another home – at Siyapei, where they met two old friends, the evangelist Taki and their colleague Mulungit. Together they threw themselves into the task of establishing a Maasai church.

Although veterans, God kept them in his school of suffering. Taki had never swerved from the faith since he first gave himself to the Lord as a young soldier at Rumuruti. Now the Stauffachers valued him as preacher, translator and brother in the Lord. After a morning of teaching he went to gather firewood, taking his rifle to scare off marauding monkeys. Leaning it against a tree, he bent to lift a fallen branch. A twig touched the trigger and the bullet entered his heart. At his funeral it seemed to John that they were burying 'the only hope of the Maasai work. We missionaries seemed to count as nothing compared to Taki and his influence.'

Mulungit brought them more pain and mystery. They had done so much for him but he turned away, and, in turning, took most of the Church with him (see p. 52 f.). The District Commissioner, disturbed by mounting Maasai hostility, advised all the missionaries to leave but they stayed and John gave himself to Bible translation, for by now he was fluent in the vernacular. When the rebels set up their own church, John humbly joined them in worship. Meanwhile Florence seized every teaching opportunity she could find.

A bright-eyed lad, John Mpaayei, looked forward to her visits to the Government Secondary School; 'Even when it was raining Mrs Stauffacher would arrive in her old Ford. The boys would hear it coming and flock to the classroom. One thing that gripped me was the way in which she pictured Jesus to us. To her He was real, one she knew and loved and one who cared . . . a personal friend.'[60] In the sixties Mpaayei, by then a Cambridge University graduate and respected Kenyan Christian leader, translated the Bible into his own language. When he first discovered Stauffacher's work, it thrilled him with its beauty. He said, 'I thought my heart would burst with joy as I read Psalms, Isaiah and other portions. The language expresses the deep heart feelings of the Maasai people.'[61]

The Stauffachers persevered through the disappointment of seeing the church dwindle to almost nothing in 1930. Ten years later people trickled back and some other small congregations sprang up. Raymond later wrote, 'Most of the effort they gave to win the Maasai seemed to be in vain'.[62] Four decades had to pass before the abundant Maasai harvest appeared. Who can say how much of that fruit grew from seeds faithfully sown by John and Florence? With new missionaries accepting the responsibility, John and Florence moved to a quieter life close to their sons in Congo, where he could still preach effectively in the Kingwana language. Eager as ever to serve, she ran a little rest home for missionaries at the foot of the beautiful 'Mountains of the Moon'.

We can imagine the praise in the hearts of these two faithful pioneers as they attended a missionary conference soon after their return to Congo. The tiny missionary team that had battled against fearful odds at Kasengu, had now multiplied to ninety-five. They discussed a 'simple form of church organization, welding together some 49,000 throughout the AIM Congo Field who have come out of darkness into marvellous light as a result of twenty-five years of prayer and toil and travail of soul.'

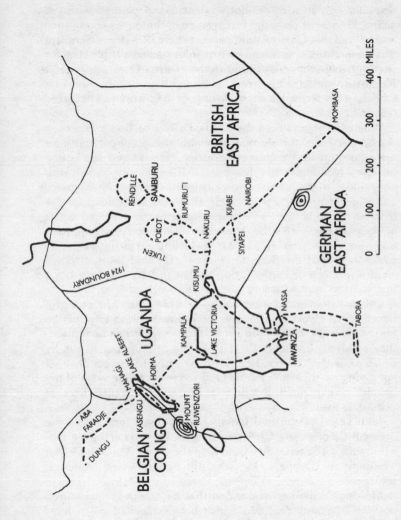

The Stauffachers' journeys in East Africa

Mulungit

When John Stauffacher first befriended Mulungit and Taki each was clad only in a single cloth garment and painted with red ochre. He saw at once the intelligence of these two young men and prayed that Christ would capture their allegiance. Sergeant Taki responded immediately when John started a Bible class for twenty tribal soldiers attached to the District Commissioner at Rumuruti and steadily grew in his faith to become the first Christian leader in his tribe. Mulungit had a more checkered career.

When Hurlburt asked the Maasai Chief to find a language teacher for John, the old man probably saw an opportunity for material gain and enhanced prestige. He offered his young relative, Mulungit. For his part, Mulungit responded with enthusiasm to the missionary's eagerness to learn the language and to get to know his people. He allayed Maasai suspicions so that John soon became a welcome visitor to the scattered kraals on the plains below Kijabe. Mulungit soaked up everything John told him in his faltering Maasai. Learning English quickly, he could soon read the Bible for himself. He told John, 'I don't want any sheep or cattle. I don't want to be a big man but I just want to stay with you and do the work of Jesus.'[63]

Others however did want him to be a big man. The powerful Chief, tribal elders and his own peers pressed him to return to his people and take his position of leadership. When he refused, they resorted to witchcraft. Too young a Christian to simply brush aside this danger, he eventually came to say goodbye. 'I am giving up the white man's God to return to the ways of my people,' he explained. But he soon rejoined the Stauffachers, as helpful as ever.

John heard of spiritual blessing following a time of intense persecution of young Christian men in Uganda. Hoping that fellowship with such men would help the young Maasai, he sent Mulungit to Kampala. He was still uneasy when Mulungit returned.

Mulungit's mother demanded that he accept the honoured position of young chieftain which his people had given him. Fearing lest she lose her son, she tried to keep him in the heart of his own culture. Her fears seemed well-founded when Mulungit turned down the appointment and talked about a trip to John's home country instead. He started collecting cattle to pay his passage. When the time came for John and Florence to visit America, Mulungit still had not collected enough. They decided to travel in the uncomfortable third class rather than second as they had planned so they could provide the balance for Mulungit's fare.

A man of two worlds

Mulungit and baby Raymond formed a sensational addition to the Stauffacher deputation team as they travelled widely in the United States. But he wanted to be more than a sensation. He longed to feed his alert mind. When the family returned to Kenya, he remained to study at a Negro school in Virginia. The Black Americans welcomed him and he always valued the Stauffacher and Minch homes which were open to him throughout the long years of study. But outside his trusted network 'he saw and experienced things which made him very bitter and distrustful of white people.'[64] The shock of racial inequality cut deep wounds which never healed.

In 1914 Mulungit at last journeyed back to Africa and sought out his old friends. John and Florence, approaching the end of their arduous years at Kasengu, invited Mulungit to join them for their final six months. When they left, he went home but did not feel so comfortable now among his own people. Were they upset because he had refused their offer of a chieftainship? Or had his American experience separated him from their ways? Nor was he at ease with the new missionaries and for four years we hear little of his activities. After the war John and Florence returned to Siyapei and he settled again to a life centred on the mission and church, inheriting Taki's leadership mantle when he tragically died in 1923. The mantle became increasingly uncomfortable throughout the twenties.

Taki had travelled widely as a soldier fighting the white man's war and Mulungit had been hurt as he studied in the white man's country. While never losing their gratitude to their own missionaries, they knew that white men could err and began to question some of their sweeping assumptions. Unfortunately Taki died before the storm broke for he might have steadied the more volatile Mulungit. As it was Mulungit had to face the full blast without mature, African counsel.

Confrontation arose around female circumcision. The Kikuyu and the Maasai initiated girls into womanhood through a long process of training which culminated in the excision of the clitoris and a variable amount of surrounding tissue. The brutal operation shocked missionaries. Haemorrhage, infection and scarring resulted in a significant number of deaths and much suffering in those who survived. They also observed that the long period of indoctrination led to spiritual decline. Most Africans (including many perplexed church members) were convinced that the very existence of the tribe depended on maintaining this tradition, hallowed through the centuries. Without it women would be unable to bear children, land would be stolen, herds would disappear and supernatural protection would be withdrawn.

AIM forbade the practice under threat of excommunication, insisting that all Christians vow to have nothing to do with it. Despite this ruling, the Stauffachers encouraged open discussion with Maasai tribal elders and Mulungit acted as mediator. Neither John nor Mulungit were sure of their ground. For a time Mulungit thought he could accomplish more by standing with the Maasai and occasionally speaking against the practice than by openly opposing it. But John eventually perceived that Mulungit was 'leading the opposition in spite of having enjoyed exceptional mission privileges for years'. On the first Sunday of 1930 they rang the Sunday School bell and no one appeared. Later in the morning the church bell brought no worshippers. After a few weeks of impasse the church elders met with John and insisted on leading 'their own church'. Mulungit attended the meeting but 'had little to say. He only looked miserable.'[65]

Ruth Shaffer, another missionary at Siyapei, said that Mulungit, in 1924, stood alone against some men who came to carry schoolgirls away for the rite. But she added sadly, 'In later years he was foremost in having his daughters circumcised for he feared the threat of having his cattle hamstrung'[66] – by bitter tribesmen who would regard him as a traitor if he deserted tribal lore in such a fundamental confrontation.

Throughout the controversy John's heart went out strongly towards the Maasai. While sharing the mission's revulsion against circumcision, he questioned the correctness of disciplinary expulsion of church members who countenanced it. He advocated another answer: 'I doubt if we should have done much harm if we had agreed that, since female circumcision must go, we would be patient and work and pray against it until the natives themselves had cast an overwhelming vote against it.'[67] Writing about this terribly painful experience, John said that the anti-circumcision vow was 'a huge mistake' which played 'terrific havoc with our work'. As a result the work was 'a complete wreck'.[68]

One casualty was Mulungit. He found no help in the separated church and drifted away from his Lord and his Christian friends. But Christians at Kijabe remembered him. Seven years later, when the African church leaders organized a large conference at Kijabe, they invited him. God's Word moved him. He asked permission to testify. 'Here are some charms I bought from the witch doctor,' he said; 'In my heart are hidden many of the things the preachers of yesterday mentioned. Evil thoughts, adulteries, theft, lying, covetousness, drunkenness, wickedness – they are all there. Today . . . I bring these evil things from this dark heart and ask the Saviour to forgive me.'[69]

Emil and Marie Sywulka

Bishop Tucker's request that AIM replace the Church Missionary Society (CMS) at Nassa in German East Africa came after twenty years of sacrificial Anglican service. As in British East Africa, Uganda and later in Belgian Congo, bitter birth pangs produced a lively child, destined to grow into a large, Christ-centred community of churches.

Before leaving England in 1876, at the head of a party of eight CMS pioneers, Alexander Mackay warned supporters that 'within six months they will probably hear that some one of us is dead'. In fact five succumbed during the first year and, at the end of the second, only Mackay survived. In words which Scott and his colleagues would echo twenty years later he continued; 'When the news comes, do not be cast down, but send someone immediately to take the vacant place'.[70]

Mackay led his party from Zanzibar, through German East Africa and then across Lake Victoria to the Baganda people. Arabs convinced the anti-Christian King Mwanga to expel him and he withdrew to the south shore of the lake, pitching his tent at Nassa in 1888. For twenty years the godly Anglicans preached and prayed while the little graveyard grew. A local Sukuma man recalled fire consuming a missionary's simple home, 'He sat on a box near the ruins of his home, weeping.'[71]

When malaria carried Mackay away two years later, Alfred Tucker took his place. With Baganda people pouring into Christ's kingdom, Tucker needed to concentrate his few CMS folk there. He was delighted when AIM accepted Nassa. Charles Hurlburt needed leaders with experience and vision to enter Nassa's maelstrom of malaria. He asked Emil and Marie Sywulka.

Emil Sywulka arrived in America at the age of four. His catholic parents brought him from Austria to the hazards of a new farm in northern Wisconsin. In the scramble to survive, he got work when he could as an errand boy. Walking along the railroad one day he talked to God in a simple, childlike way, repeating the Lord's prayer. Somehow he heard an answer, so real that towards the end of his life he said, 'The Lord spoke to me about Africa . . . From that time to this it was always my desire to be a missionary. Today that desire is a burning fire.'[72]

The errand boy's glimmer of faith caught fire a few years later when he met Christ in a more realistic way and yielded to the Master's claim upon his life. Soon after the start of the new century he left his school-teaching and enrolled at Moody Bible Institute. Then, in 1906, he achieved his childhood goal by arriving at Kijabe. After a short stay, the group asked him to start work high up on the misty ridges of Kikuyu country.

A year after his arrival Emil married a missionary nurse, Marie Schneider, and took her to his mountain home. She entered a life of change and movement. Someone said that Emil had 'Periscopic Vision'. When he was preaching on one ridge he was always peering over the summit wondering about the needs of the people living on the other side. In 1909 he received a summons to a new tribe way beyond the range of his powerful periscope – the Sukuma.

Although Emil and Marie had heard Charles Hurlburt's request for prayer that God would guide him in his response to the bishop's request, they could hardly have been prepared for the suggestion that they and their baby boy provide the answer.

Prayer among the graves

At Nassa the Sywulkas inherited a congregation of several hundred. On the first Sunday the people restlessly chattered, unsettling Mr Wright of the CMS until he realized they had heard rumour of a new baby in their midst. Borrowing Paul Sywulka from his mother's arms, he paraded round the church so that everyone could catch a first glimpse of a white one-year-old. Then they quieted.

The amazing Emil attempted to preach his first sermon in the Sukuma language on his fourth Sunday at Nassa. Soon he realized that many 'were living in sin although some could pray like bishops'.[73] The majority attended because Chief Shimba compelled them. When Emil asked the Chief to withdraw his command, all but a tiny handful departed. Emil and Marie felt

Emil and Marie Sywulka, DD

they had ruined the CMS work. They carried their bitter disappointment up the little Nassa Hill to share it with their Lord in hours of prayer and fasting.

Miss Jacobson joined them and they wondered why she had come for she seemed to lack any talents. But she too knew how to pray and this became her initial ministry. She loved the solitude and the inspiration of the cemetery, hallowed by nine Anglican graves, and often spent half a day praying there. Unbelieving Sukuma thought she went there to commune with the departed. Unwise perhaps in her choice of place, God honoured her cries and hungry souls began to enquire how they might find him. The church filled again. Decades later, senior pastors and African missionaries reckoned their spiritual birth back to those prayer vigils.

Blackwater fever, meningitis, typhoid and dysentery attacked reinforcements as they arrived. Miss Jacobson's fiancé, Mr Wall, typical of many setting out, said, 'I feel I am to go to Africa, if only to glorify Him there by my death.' Three weeks after he arrived in Africa he died. Marie, her baby and another missionary contracted meningitis while Emil was away: they survived.

The Sywulkas lived simply off their own cattle and chickens, local rice and fish from the lake. A visitor, running her hand over the smooth wall covering of dried cow manure asked, 'Is this paper imported or local?' Emil (with his periscope aloft) travelled widely on foot and bicycle usually eating and sleeping in African homes. He revised the translation of John's Gospel, printing it on a small hand press in 1913. The family departed late that year leaving a rich legacy of Sukuma Christians for the lean war years when the AIM team was reduced to only three – Mr and Mrs (Doctor) Maynard and Miss Bowyer at Kola Ndoto.

Whenever missionary numbers drop, those who remain clarify their priorities. Like Emil and Marie, the Maynards' prime concern was to develop African Christians. They called him 'Nangi' (meaning 'Teacher') because he spent his time expounding God's Word. His wife too was a trainer. As she laid the foundations of a strong health care programme, she determined to build it around African staff. 'We are here,' she said; 'not so much to do the work, as to get it done.'[74]

Emil and Marie could not return for ten years (the periscope had focused on Portuguese East Africa – present day Mozambique – for a while). Following the defeat of Germany in 1918, the League of Nations entrusted German East Africa to British care and changed the name to Tanganyika. Although no one consulted the people of the land about the change, the League expected Britain to govern it for the benefit of the Tanganyikans.

The Sywulkas' concern for a strong church, standing firmly on African feet, focused on the evangelists whom they called together for a week of training in every month. They taught the Bible, sang with them into the night and, long before the theorists talked about environmental concerns, they expected each evangelist to plant ten trees.

In old age, like the Stauffachers, they hosted a rest home for fellow workers. Missionaries called it 'Emmaus' – 'Em' for Emil, 'Ma' for their respected missionary mother and 'Us' for the guests.

Emil died in 1944 but his work lived on. Seventeen years later his elderly widow received the Kisukuma Bible. 'My, my,' she exclaimed, 'To think that after all these years I can hold the Kisukuma Bible in my hands.' Tears trickled down her cheeks as she fondled the cover of the thick black book. At eighty-seven she was celebrating the culmination of a dream for which she and Emil began to pray and work sixty years before.[75]

4
Straining the nets

Missionaries wove multiple webs of relationships with strands going off in many directions, all of them interdependent and each essential for the tough resilience of the whole. They worked hard to unite their own families and threw out cords of fellowships to other missionaries and African Christians, all the time drawing new threads of wandering souls. They tied themselves to leaders and to followers, to their organization in Africa and back at home, to other societies and to government officials.

Since the network functioned by effective communication, they studied the ways in which others spoke and thought, disciplining themselves to master languages and to understand cultures.

Most important of all, they communicated often with their Lord. By much conversation with God and diligent listening to all he said, the missionaries anchored their relationship webs firmly to the source of all love and humility, without which all else would collapse.

Under the best of circumstances none found it easy to maintain harmony and missionaries often found themselves in the worst of conditions, when all sorts of stress threatened to rend relationships. That so few fell apart was a miracle of God's grace.

That God could take up torn threads and weave them into a new and beautiful tapestry was a greater wonder, making us ask if he actually ordained the strains to show that this amazing power belonged to him alone.

Charles and Priscilla Studd

'Who will travel to cannibal tribes with me?' Charles Studd, a missionary veteran with long experience in China and India, was graphically describing his recent trip far up the River Nile in Sudan to an enthralled audience of Cambridge University students. He had amassed details of many central African peoples, some of whom still treated enemies with great barbarity. They all needed the Saviour to whom Studd was committed with every fibre of his being.

Hurlburt, also in England in 1912, shared with less sensationalism but equal sincerity, his burden for the same tribes. His Nile safari had convinced Studd that he needed to approach the Belgian Congo from the East. Hurlburt asked; 'Why not join us?' As a result Studd, in his early fifties, and four young men applied to AIM.

AIM already had some fine British missionaries. Hurlburt thought that, if he could establish a Home Council, the trickle might become a steady flow which would further strengthen the fellowship across the Atlantic. He asked several supporters to gather for a meeting on January 30th. They all knew that, twenty-five years previously, Studd had given up fame as Britain's number one cricketer in order to work with the China Inland Mission (CIM). His past commitment and present zeal led Hurlburt to appoint him immediately to the Council and, as soon as the Council accepted all five applications, to give him the title of 'Field Director, Congo' – two errors Hurlburt would soon regret.

The cavalry leader

Directors of CIM knew about Studd's inability to accept advice. Hudson Taylor once wrote of him, 'He is too independent.'[76] When the Church Missionary Society set aside two senior missionaries to show Studd around South Sudan with a view to reaching the 'cannibal tribes' from the north, he decided that he could not work with the Anglicans. Apparently Hurlburt did not seek the advice of either of these missions.

Council minutes are strangely silent about Mrs Studd. Priscilla

Studd submitted no application. In fact she opposed her husband's plan to leave her yet again, while she was suffering from a serious heart complaint and he was ill with asthma. Had she foreseen that this separation would be for two years and the next for eleven, she would have wept even more.

A few days after the new party left for Africa, Martin Sutton, C.T.'s son-in-law, wrote to Hurlburt on his behalf. He asked that the mission constitution (to which Studd had signed his name on the application form) be altered to ensure that the 'British Section' of AIM appoint all its own officers, handle all its own money and spend it only on British missionaries.[77]

The council minutes report 'a prolonged and friendly discussion' when three of Studd's friends argued his case. The friends admitted the root of the problem, that 'he would work more satisfactorily on his own and free of control'. The record continued, 'The acceptance of these alterations would practically mean the establishing of a new mission.' The council decided against the changes. Immediately Studd's friends produced a letter of resignation left with them in case his request was rejected. He had been a member of AIM for seven weeks.

The council explained to its handful of missionaries and supporters, 'These changes have all been made in the utmost good fellowship and with the unanimous conviction that they are occasioned in the best interest of the work.'[78]

Without knowledge of the heartaches he had caused in London, Studd wrote from Suez, 'The more I pray and the more I think, the more I am determined to have Jesus the Captain of this expedition and no other.' Then he expressed a desire to use the West African approach to his new mission area but for a reason that his Captain might not approve, 'I feel sure henceforth our route to the work will be up the River Congo . . . That will aid our independence from America more than ever.'[79]

For the time being he was still very dependent upon 'America' because he and his one remaining colleague, Alfred Buxton, could only enter the Belgian Congo as members of AIM.[80] The tiny team at Kasengu welcomed the party, gratified that it included new missionaries for AIM – J. Batstone and G.F.B. Morris – and glad to help Studd and Buxton establish their ministry. Still anxious to avoid the need to lean on AIM, Studd and Buxton moved south to await their baggage but malaria struck the old man and nearly carried him off. When they eventually reached Dungu, the goal towards which their thoughts and prayers had been directed for months, they found AIM already installed, despite a gentlemen's agreement (according to Studd) to leave Dungu to him. The old soldier fumed. Alfred sought to mollify his future father-in-law, persuading him to move on to the more strategic centre of Niangara where they exulted in enormous opportunities.

Studd was becoming more irritable. Of the new missionaries sent out through the devoted ministry of Priscilla at home, many remained only a short time with his 'Heart of Africa Mission' (later changed as a result of Priscilla's work to 'Worldwide Evangelization Crusade'). Relationships were not improved when some of Studd's people transferred to AIM. Hurlburt tried to resolve the misunderstandings but as late as 1919 he wrote to the British Council, 'Mr Studd replied refusing to have anything to do with me as a sinner'.[81]

In Britain Priscilla, with her heart almost broken by her husband's indifference, found solace in her Lord. She developed great gifts of administration, public speaking and diplomacy. As a result the AIM Council, six years after the original rift, had 'every hope of complete reconciliation between AIM and HAM.'[82]

Instead of restoring fellowship with others, 'the irascible old gentleman' drove his own team away. The Buxtons left to join the Bible Churchman's Missionary Society. In the last year of Studd's life, all the members of his home council except his son-in-law, Norman Grubb, left to form the Unevangelized Fields Mission taking some of the missionaries with them. Grubb, combining Studd's faith and zeal with his own humility, rebuilt WEC.

Alfred Buxton said, 'CT (Studd) was essentially a cavalry leader and in that capacity he led splendid charges. A cavalry leader cannot have all the gifts of an administrator or he would simply not have the qualities necessary to lead a charge.'[83] His charge launched a new movement which came to embrace thousands of missionaries and hundreds of thousands of African Christians.

Besides acquiring new members through Studd's Cambridge ministry, AIM registered other gains. Studd and his fellow applicants provided the impetus towards setting up a new home council. Controversy, handled constantly with an eye to the Lord's honour, developed maturity early in the life of that council and helped it refine the process of selecting new members. In

addition the mission developed an unshakable commitment to
the principle of international fellowship.

Studd's challenge to the Cambridge students was no idle
rhetoric. One of his life principles was, 'If Jesus Christ died for
me, there is no sacrifice too great for me to make for Him.' That
would certainly include the possibility of death at the hands of
cannibals.

Frank and Edith Gardner

Several strands, torn from C.T.'s net, joined AIM – among
them Frank and Edith Gardner.

A young shop assistant with a reputation for honesty and a
passion for reading, was enjoying her work with the young people
at Chipping Norton Baptist Church when a friend handed her
a note from Frank Gardner, home after five years in Nyasaland.
Somewhat awkwardly he enquired, could they develop a
friendship? She reacted first, 'I am twenty one and want to be
free for a time.' But she spread it before the Lord and a voice
seemed to say, 'This is my choice for you'.[84]

Edith filled in forms and visited the committee of Frank's
society, the Zambezi Industrial Mission. Their verdict: 'they
preferred Miss Seaton to wait two years – twenty one was too
young.' Her Dad thought she should wait four years. So in
March 1910 she stood forlornly on a Southampton quay and
watched Frank waving from the rail of his ship. Frank's brother,
Alfred, followed him a few months later.

Wedding in Nyasaland

Her own departure in September 1911 was traumatic too. Her
father broke down in tears at her farewell meeting. But Edith's
irrepressible interest in life rescued her from gloomy self pity.
When they reached the Zambezi, rough weather prevented the
ship from docking. She was packed into a basket with two
others, swung out over the side into a launch bobbing up and
down in the waves far below and carried to the safety of the
SS *Milliped*.

The tranquil travel up the heart of the huge Zambezi, watching
hippos and crocodiles by day and listening to croaking frogs on
the clear nights, prepared her for more turbulence ahead. A train
whisked her from the port to Blantyre. A rickshaw bounced her
over the bumpy roads until the tracks became too irregular. Then
teams of men carried her in a hammock, roofed by canvas to

protect her from the fierce sun, until she saw a solitary cyclist approaching and recognized Frank. Two days later they were married. The crowd of missionaries and African Christians rejoiced in their first white wedding but the girl around whom all the celebration revolved was tired and homesick. She wrote, 'It was then, most of all, I felt desperately lonely. They were all strangers and Frank whom I had not seen for nearly two years seemed one too.'

Her spirits bounced back as she wrote about the sweet perfume of lovely cream lilies, many varieties of orchids, the vivid red leaves of trees in Spring and the flashing brilliance of birds. After the wedding a woman told a missionary that 'Mr Gardner gave all his wealth to his wife at the wedding'. 'Whatever do you mean?' asked the puzzled lady. 'Why, he put it into her mouth'. The African had never seen adults kiss before.

Edith came to Nyasaland to be more than a wife. She longed to share her Lord's love with the local people and determined immediately to break the Chinyanja language barrier by the double discipline of four hours study each morning and frequent conversations. Soon she was visiting people in their homes, treating the sick, teaching in the local school and visiting schools throughout the district in her travelling hammock. She loved her studious husband and her new home with its watered garden and mountain views but 'longed for a friendly talk with some white woman . . .'

Soon she was pregnant. Ladies from other stations wrote advising her to stop her six days a week language study (it would injure the child's brain!) and move to the capital, Blantyre, to await her delivery in secure surroundings. But how then would she pass her language exams? And without Chinyanja how would she communicate with the women and girls? She asked two fellow missionaries – a nurse and a bachelor who had attended a couple of courses at Livingstone Hospital – to assist her. Birth was slow and possibly more dangerous than she realized as her untrained obstetrician needed to apply forceps. But he succeeded in bringing baby Edith into the home and her loneliness disappeared.

Due for home leave, Edith asked to stay another year so that she could bear her second baby in Africa. Mission leaders said no and sentenced her to an uncomfortable journey to England. The travel, the crowded home of her in-laws and the bitterly cold winter, provoked a premature labour. Little Grace appeared and lived for half an hour. The following month, March 1916, a second bereavement struck. The Zambezi Mission wrote to say that the war-time financial squeeze would prevent their return to the people they loved.

Misunderstandings in Congo

Before leaving Africa Frank had read about C.T. Studd's new work and once said to Edith, 'If God closed the door for me in Nyasaland I would try to go to Congo'. The Heart of Africa Mission accepted them, along with brother Alf, and arranged a farewell meeting in London's large Central Hall in July 1916, assured that the name of Studd would draw the crowds.

As the Southampton train pulled out of Paddington on an early summer morning to the triumphant hymns of supporters, Edith had a choking lump in her throat. She was leaving her precious three-year-old daughter with caring friends. She wrote sadly, 'She will forget us, a heart-breaking thought, but the best for her, and He will carry us through a day at a time.'

Warned that 'C.T. is erratic', Frank asked him about the policy of the mission. Studd replied, 'You will be free to be guided by the Holy Spirit. The policy will be drawn up after a conference on the field.' So they were surprised when they reached Leopoldville on the River Congo to receive the mission rules: missionaries were to speak the lingua franca and to use interpreters for the tribal tongues; they should complete the whole work in Congo in ten years and then move to another country; immediately an African professed faith he would be accepted into the church.

As they meandered for week after week upstream, first in steamers and then in canoes, Frank and Edith shared their reservations with the great visionary, C.T. They had no problem in learning the two simplified trade languages, but they coveted the tribal vernacular too. Their Nyasa experience had convinced them of two principles: if you want to get close to people, you must speak their heart language; and if you accept every profession of faith at face value, you'll inherit big problems.

Eventually the party of four men and Edith left the rivers and took to the paths. Malaria weakened Frank so that he too had to be carried in a chair supported by poles. Unable to communicate with the Africans at any depth, Edith again longed for another white woman – 'Oh to see someone with a skirt on.' Her Bible comforted her. She read *Martin Chuzzlewit* as she

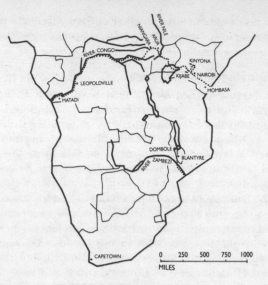

The Gardners' travels in Africa

swung in her hammock through the dim, unreal world of the Ituri Forest, with trees meeting overhead at great height. Drums flashed news of their progress along the narrow track from village to village so that people awaited them in hopes of selling fruit, potatoes, eggs and, occasionally, a chicken. The hot, humid air oppressed her; 'If only I could have my hair off – considered most worldly! Ah me.'

In January 1917 they reached their destination, Niangara, a Belgian administrative centre beside another huge river. 'It was good to think of getting on with a definite work of our own and getting to know the people.'

The young church served the Mangbetu and Zande tribes, who lived on opposite sides of the river. The people found it hard to sit together in their tiny, mud-walled church and complained to the Gardners, 'Did not their grandfathers eat our grandfathers?' Edith usually got her servant to canoe her across the river early in the morning so that she could cycle around the Zande villages for a few hours chatting to the women in the trade language, Bangala, while Frank worked on a brick house to replace their leaking home.

Fred Morris of AIM cycled over from Dungu, four days' journey to the east, and brought some language notes to help them. He preached in Pazande at both services and they noted,

'What a difference in the interest of the congregation listening to someone preach in their own language. We were more convinced than ever that we must learn it.'

C.T. disapproved. When Frank reminded him of his promise that 'he would be given freedom to be guided by the Holy Spirit', Charles replied; 'The Holy Spirit never guided a man to be disobedient to his superior officer'.

Malaria struck Frank, laying him low with the dreaded black water. Edith, heavy with her third pregnancy, nursed him night and day under the supervision of an Italian doctor who had treated thirteen cases of the fever and lost eleven. Frank survived a battle of several weeks and Edith gave birth to Beryl after a nightmare labour in the hands of the Italian who 'could not stand a headache himself, but did not believe in anesthetics for childbirth'.

Studd told them that 'unless we agree with his policy we are not needed'. By this time their friends included the AIM team at Dungu. Without pressing them, these colleagues suggested they join AIM. Two years after their return to Africa they set out for an eleven-day hike to their new location with Beryl, aged two months, securely anchored between her mother's legs in a swinging hammock.

They arrived in time for the missionaries' conference and revelled once more in Christian fellowship, particularly in Charles Hurlburt's messages on 'growing in the grace and the knowledge of our Lord Jesus Christ'. The missionaries discussed a new opportunity.

Sick pioneers in Uganda

During the previous months, illness delayed an AIM party at Vura Camp on the Ugandan side of the border. Only recently the British and Belgian Governments had agreed to transfer an area the size of Wales on the West side of the Nile from the Congo to Uganda. The whole district was in the grip of famine and the British administrator asked the missionaries to distribute food. They discovered that the border, like so many in colonial Africa, cut through tribes without any consideration of the wishes of the local people. AIM was working in three tribes in Congo, while people of the same tribes in Uganda were starved both of food and of God's Word. After helping to relieve the famine emergency, the mission sought an opening to preach. To avoid confusing Ugandans, the Government decreed that only two brands of Christianity be permitted in Uganda – Roman

Catholic and Anglican. Hurlburt easily agreed with his friends in the Church Missionary Society to plant Anglican churches. The AIM folk, meeting in their conference, saw nothing incongruous in asking their newest Baptists, the Gardners, to plant Anglican churches.

Edith made her home at Vura while Frank and Alf cycled ten miles every morning to work on a thatched house for them at the new centre, Arua, and then pedalled back in the evening. In a hurry to settle before the wet season, they moved into their new home before Frank had fixed doors and windows or given the mud walls time to dry. She wrote, 'The thatch soon became very poor and the rain streamed in. We had bowls all over the place and an umbrella over the mosquito net!' One bed was a strange affair, consisting of four poles dug into the soil and laced across with cow hide. The one in the better state of health used it, the other slept on the camp bed, in a drier position.

The house sat on a slight rise so that on a clear day they could see the Nile forty miles to the east. The Lugbara men wore no clothes and the women dressed with 'a bob of grass back and front'. None knew about working for a wage so much of the labour fell to the two brothers. They managed with neither nails nor paper. Every day Frank sent the workers to Edith for their pay. He scraped the number of cents owing onto their dusty arms. 'This was a marvel. How did I know by looking at marks on an arm? They began to get wise and when not working would scratch all kinds of marking onto their arms and come up to me, holding out their scribbles, expecting me to pay them!'

On Sundays they invited people to worship in their tent and were surprised to find five languages spoken by the small congregation. Their limited knowledge of Swahili helped a little but again they realized the need to speak the local Lugbara.

Malaria sapped their strength and twice Frank's life hung in the balance with blackwater fever. When all four lay ill at the same time, a Roman Catholic priest, unwell himself, responded to Edith's urgent plea for help, riding ten miles on his mule to treat Frank. Spanish flu and famine swept through the district, claiming many lives and further weakening the little missionary family. A colleague, John Buyse, and two ladies came from Aru on the Congo side of the border to care for them and to ensure that the vital work at Arua progressed. By February 1919 they sadly realized they must pass their dream of establishing a church to others. John urged them to return to England.

A steamer took them across Lake Albert. Travelling by canoe, a lorry, another ship, a train and finally a dog-cart, they came to Kijabe where 'the glorious panorama, the scent of the wild olive and the other trees made us feel we were in another world.'

Mountain fruit in Kenya

They felt better in the high altitude and asked AIM to assign them in Kenya. After so much lonely pioneering they revelled in the privilege of having a house to themselves in the midst of a loving, missionary community and a growing African church. As well as a beautiful church building, Kijabe ran its printing press, carpenter's shop, hospital, girls' home and school for missionaries' children. Frank was delighted to get hold of a good Kikuyu grammar and soon could preach in the villages with an evangelist.

The mission sent them to Kinyona. For three days they hiked over countryside 'like corrugated paper, just a mass of deep ravines, with the hill sides covered with brambles and bracken'. They climbed through clinging mists until they saw a white, wooden house atop a distant ridge – their next home.

Edith gave birth to Rex who became a firm favourite of the Kikuyu. He and Beryl chattered away to them with an ease which made their parents envious. Three quiet years passed, untroubled by the desperate struggle with sickness which had dogged their steps before. They watched a group of churches develop across the Kikuyu ridges and found great satisfaction in their friendships with the local people. When the time came to leave, their servant, Watari, begged them to take him to England. He asked Edith with tears running down his cheeks, 'How will you be able to look after the children and the Bwana and run a house too? I won't eat much and will need very little money for clothes.' But God planned a greater role for Watari – as one of the church's effective evangelists.

Back in an English spring the family reunited. Beryl and Rex met their eleven-year-old sister for the first time and their pioneer parents enfolded her with their love. Young Edith went on to become a mature woman of God despite the seven years of separation.

They asked AIM to send them back but the mission said no; Frank's three close encounters with death from blackwater fever were three too many. So they moved north, first to the Railway Mission in Carlisle, and then, to settle at last – for a quarter of a century – in a Scottish manse, where they spun a new web of relationships to the glory of the Master they loved.

Mary Mozley

Like Edith Gardner, Mary Mozley walked closely with God and enjoyed human companionship. She too realized that she could only weave weak webs without the local languages. As a young nurse she had asked God 'to put into my heart a passion for his glory that would send me in his will to the uttermost parts of the earth'.[85] In an agony of uncertainty about her call she cried, 'Lord if it be Thou bid me come . . . And He said, "Come".'

The two daughters of an English country parson arrived in Mombasa in January 1915 in time to glimpse the Stauffachers heading in the opposite direction with John's health broken. The name of the Belgian Congo was still ringing in their ears a couple of days later when they reached Kijabe and found Hurlburt's instruction to make their way to Dungu (see Map 4). They caught their breath for a few days at Kasengu before undertaking the first of many long treks on foot, first northwards for 100 sun-scorched miles along the Ugandan border then for a further 200 miles to the west. They packed all they had into fifty-pound loads for the men and then wondered if they would see their baggage again. They watched the porters tumble into the rivers and some mornings awoke to discover they had debunked in the night. Walking built up their muscles while the sun bronzed their faces. They needed thick skins too as the narrow path wound through villages and the people turned out to stare at the strange women in their unusual clothes. Once in a while the rigours of safari gave way to luxury. In Aru a kindly Belgian official gave them a leg of mutton, eggs, butter and cream cheese and they stayed for twelve days.

Their joy in reaching Dungu on the last day of May was spoiled by Mary's first brush with malaria confining her to bed for three weeks. She spent the time reading her Bible and talking to her Lord – 'He showed me how little I have glorified him. There is such a pressure of work here as I never felt at home . . . Do pray that I may be always kept abiding in the quietness of his presence, filled with the Holy Ghost.'

From her first arrival in Congo she plunged into Pazande study. During any pause on their journey, she and Catherine searched for Zande people in the villages, attempted hymns with them and faltering messages depending on the quick wits of their hearers to correct their hopeless pronunciation. Other pressures built up. Trained as a nurse, she tried to respond to the mass of physical suffering all around. Then there was the literacy challenge for how could Christians develop if they could not read? And always she yearned 'to preach the Gospel where Christ was not known' (Romans 15:20).

Alfred Buxton passed through and told her that the thirteen wives of a Chief Beka, two days' journey away, were anxious to hear the words of God. So she and her sister spent ten weeks in their home. Their hearts went out to these 'very intelligent' women, yet they could not be easily won. She wrote home from Beka's village, 'Every inch we have to fight. Pray we may be baptized with the Holy Ghost and with fire.' God must have understood for he drew several to his Son.

At the end of 1915 Charles Hurlburt called the dozen north Congo missionaries together for conference. A Mr Flinn reported that he had walked for forty days to the border of French Congo before encountering another Protestant missionary and Charles reminded them that between Dungu and Lake Chad lay '1000 miles of territory, absolutely unevangelized'. But he was concerned too for the tribes they had already bypassed. He asked the Mozley sisters to move into the Logo tribal area and tackle a new language. Three years later he asked Mary to move to her third assignment and yet another language. Once again she packed all she possessed – bed, clothes, blankets, table, deck chairs, medicines, basins, jugs, slates, tins, corn grinder, food, bicycle – into nineteen porter-sized loads and set off for the new centre, Aba. It was 'the third language in less than four years, and not one of them spoken with any real degree of fluency.'

Language and love

Language fascinated her, not only as a means of speaking to people but of understanding them too. A Logo man, Barangi, came to teach them after they had just slain a goat for their lunch. 'Now Barangi,' she asked, 'where do you think words?' He pointed to a spot at the lower end of his breast bone and gave her the word she had previously understood to mean 'heart'.

She produced a saucepan containing offal from the goat and enquired, 'With which of these do people think words?' He pointed to the liver and gave her the same word again. 'Yes,' he said; 'it stops and then the words stop in the liver and then people die.' Fortified by this find, she tried out a 'hard liver' as a translation for 'hard hearted' but her informant looked mystified. She described the condition. 'Oh,' he exclaimed, 'the Logo says "You have no ears" because you refuse to allow any words you hear to change your thoughts.'

The further she progressed, the more she realized that 'We are perfectly helpless apart from a good native teacher.' African patience with missionaries stumbling to speak their language always amazed her.

Approaching the end of her translation of Mark's Gospel into Logo, she wrote, 'Endless and unexpected difficulties arise, words mean not quite the same as ours, they often give wrong meaning if literally translated. Logo is a language of much idiom and picturesque expression but it is not easy to know what has an idiom to express its meaning and what may be literal.'

Despite her gruelling work schedule, she always made time for a visitor who wanted to discuss a problem: a small girl unable to wash the grime out of her only petticoat, a sick missionary several days' walk away, a young woman seeking to leave her evil ways and follow Jesus.

A faithful 'stand-by' called Wanji attempted to cook Mary's food and clean her room. 'Expert in nothing, yet willing in everything,' he was wise enough to keep his eyes and ears open in her home and recognize the Lord who meant so much to her. On 7 August 1920 Bwana Hurlburt baptized the first Logo at Aba and Wanji was in the group. When someone asked him what the ceremony meant, he replied; 'It is like a soldier putting his uniform on. A person may be a soldier but it is when he puts his uniform on the people recognize him.'

Blackwater fever prevented Mary attending the service. In the next two years it carried off her dear friends Alta and Elizabeth Hurlburt and she felt the loss deeply. Elizabeth asked Mary to care for her two daughters under the age of three and Mary gladly consented. But not for long. Her turn came on 4 December 1923, when the grim slayer of missionaries took her at the age of thirty-six to meet the Lord for whom she had always longed.

Mary wrote many letters. All of them throb with desire for Christ. She asked prayer that she might be kept 'abiding in the quietness of his presence, filled with the Holy Ghost'. As she contemplated the fate of sinners, 'It makes me long to live so near to God that through me He may reach those He is longing after with such tender love'. She revelled in the writings of Amy Carmichael and Madame Guyon. When Hurlburt moved the mission headquarters to Aba, she 'could not help thinking how privileged we are, stationed where Mr H is. He gave a lovely message yesterday in Romans 8 verse 29, "conformed to the image of His Son" ' and she outlined his talk in her letter and her own longing for that conformity.

Catherine once peeped into her room after dark and saw her in bed under a mosquito net, bending over her Bible. With her book of prayer open, she ran through name after name in her wide network of relationships, bringing the needs of each to God. Next morning the light was on again at 4 a.m.

Not long afterwards her Lord again said, 'Come'.

Moro Sheeba

Others besides the missionary pioneers faced enormous hazards. The first converts too had to contend with the very powers of Hell. Their courage, often totally alone in a hostile village, led many onlookers to acknowledge the superior might of their God.

Although the African Christians learnt to depend on God alone, the role of the missionaries was crucial. They would trek for days through the villages proclaiming Christ and demonstrating his love. Their homes, enjoying the protection of the powerful colonial government, provided havens where converts could grow for a time unmenaced, and their clinics offered health care unencumbered by spirit veneration. Later mission stations, with their foreign sub-culture, would tend to separate missionaries, and even African Christians, from the real world where God wanted the salt of the kingdom to season society.

In 1912 a ten-year-old girl called Moro lived with her Alur parents and only surviving brother close to big Lake Albert. By looking towards the setting sun, she could have made out Kasengu Hill where the first missionaries were constructing their simple homes.

Moro's mother experienced deep trouble. Ten babies died, including twins, always branded as 'devils'. Caring friends and her dutiful husband convinced her that she had upset the great god Jok and his army of lesser spirits. They helped her greet each tragedy with sacrifices of goats, chickens and grain and eventually persuaded her to offer herself as the possession of two evil spirits.[86] Not even this surrender halted the relentless cycle of maternal sickness and infant death. Seeing her mother's devotion, Moro began to wonder; 'Why do her gods not reward her?'

When Moro developed into an attractive teenager, a missionary visited their village and invited people to accept a new God. Moro's father listened politely but commented in the privacy of his home; 'We cannot afford to placate any more gods.'

A drought paralyzed the gardens around which the whole of life revolved. Strangely, the gardens at Ara Mission flourished. The missionaries also distributed food to the hungry villagers on the dry plain. Moro was puzzled. Her father had always given the firstfruits of his garden to Jok, but now the great spirit was ignoring their plight. Did the God of the newcomers care more than Jok? Could he even be more powerful? She began to listen to the white women as they spoke about God's Son. Seeing her interest, one of them invited her to stay at Ara.

Jok or Jesus

At first she found life strange at Ara. She dressed differently; although she still hung a fresh bunch of leaves back and front from a cord around her waist every morning, she now wore a cotton dress as well. The ladies asked her to work in their kitchen and learn new ways of cooking. And she learnt to read in the little mud and thatch schoolroom, where her quick mind, like a sponge, soaked up all she heard – especially in the daily Bible class.

When the Bible told her that Jok was a liar, Moro was not surprised. The news of God's love gladdened her even more. Her mind, soaked from infancy in a costly religion of vain sacrifice, warmed to the tale of the very powerful sacrifice of Jesus which God himself had provided for her and for her people. She 'turned her liver to Jesus' and received his forgiveness. The salt of the gospel flavoured her whole life. Slight and young though she was, she knew that the Spirit of Jesus inside her was more than a match for all the powers of Jok and his host of demons.

Jok mounted his counter-attack with great cunning. One Sunday afternoon Moro was walking from her home to Ara when some men jumped out of the long grass beside the path to grab her. 'You belong to us,' they claimed; 'Your parents say you are to go with us.' In a sense they were right. Years before, her parents had agreed to a marriage proposal from a man called Pilipili and the two families had negotiated a costly bride price. Moro disliked Pilipili from the start but no one consulted her. A Christian now, she determined that she would only marry a believer. She wriggled free from her attackers and darted into the thick grass like a flash.

Pilipili had paid the costly bride price in animals. Now he

demanded his wife. Having failed to snatch her by force, he turned to the village court. Tribal elders were amazed at the courage of this slip of a girl as she explained how her new faith forbad her to marry an unbeliever. The Chief, anxious to maintain his good relationship with the mission, and to uphold justice at the same time, told Pilipili; 'If you want to have her, you must become a Christian too.' So Pilipili moved to Ara, where he submitted to the external changes required of a new Christian but failed to experience Moro's inward transformation.

The missionaries gave Pilipili a job at Ara while his young wife's faith blossomed through the Christians' fellowship and teaching. Missionaries, quick to recognize leadership potential, trained her in the villages as an evangelist. Before long Moro was travelling on her own, with the help of a younger girl, and leading many of her people to faith in Christ. Through the loving care of Christians, her half-brother recovered from smallpox and abandoned the worship of Jok to serve the God who had healed him.

Moro's first baby died at birth. In her grief she found solace in her Heavenly Father so different from the agonies her mother had endured. In 1924 little Daniel appeared and within a couple of years she was pregnant again. Moro wanted to stay always at Ara, but Pilipili's life there was artificial and he longed for his own village, Awasi. Moro helped him build his house and dig his garden but had to stay at Ara until harvest. As soon as she had gathered it in, her baby Matayo arrived.

Traditional belief dictated that infants be kept at home, secure from the menace of evil spirits. When Matayo was only three days old Moro tied him to her back, descended Ara Hill, forded a river (where the powerful spirit Andranga dwelt), passed some big rocks (the home of another spirit), skirted the forest (where numerous demons inhabited the trees) and endured the horrified cries of the women she met, 'You are killing your child', 'Your milk will dry up'. The cordial welcome of the ladies of Awasi soon turned to dismay, and then to abuse, when they saw how Moro rejected any practice related to the spirits.

Once settled in Awasi, Pilipili abandoned all appearance of Christian faith. He only wanted wealth and respect which came with having a big garden. Their son Matayo became ill. The Chief demanded that Moro offer a sacrifice. Village pressures increased the closer he came to death. Moro decided to carry the lad to the mission doctor at distant Rethy. Amazingly the child was still alive when they reached hospital and she told the staff that God's glory was involved in this sickness. Slowly Matayo recovered.

The experience strengthened her for the next great test when Pilipili's leg swelled. Again Moro rejected all the pressures to placate the gods and decided to return to Rethy, telling her neighbours, 'The doctor there is a servant of the true God who has power to heal.' All Awasi turned out in amazement when Pilipili walked home and told them; 'If it had not been for the faith of my wife, you would have sacrificed for me and I would have died. The true God spared my life.' Pilipili too gave his liver to the Lord.

Under a hail of hostility Moro opened a small school which grew until the mission sent a teacher, releasing her for more evangelism. Slowly a church developed in Awasi.

One Sunday, when Pilipili could have been in church, he rowed out on the big lake with three friends to check fish traps. A squall struck their two frail canoes overturning one of them. Pilipili's partner could not swim so Pilipili volunteered to remain with the upturned dugout while they paddled ashore with his friend and then returned for him. As they ran onto the beach, they raised the alarm. Men rushed for their canoes while women wept. But no one knew where to look for the lost man and darkness closed in. The news spread fast and soon Awasi filled with anxious friends and wailing women. Who had ever been lost on the lake and survived through the night?

Moro sat quietly at home with her Bible open and prayed through the dark hours, 'My Father show your power to these people by restoring Pilipili to us so that they may know that you are the true God.' People scolded her, 'What sort of wife refuses to mourn for her dead husband?'

Out on the lake, waves buffeted the weary man clinging to the rough undersurface of his canoe. Again and again he wrestled to right it. Suddenly, in the middle of the night, it rolled over and he clambered in. Water kept splashing over the sides until he faced the new danger of sinking with his boat. Through the long hours of night and the hot morning he baled out the water with his cupped hands. At noon next day, when tempted to abandon the search, a man in a large canoe noticed a speck on the horizon. It was Pilipili. For the second time Pilipili staggered back into Awasi when everyone thought he was dead.

Derision turned to praise. People marvelled at the woman who quietly prayed for her husband when others panicked. Moro led many to Christ. Jesus wove them into webs called, 'Women

Messengers of Jesus Christ' and they asked her to be their president even though she was still only in her mid thirties.

Soon after the birth of a baby girl, Moro became sick. She may have known that her time was short for she called the infant, 'Will of the Lord'. At Rethy the doctor diagnosed tuberculosis. Slowly her sun set, the more radiant the closer it came to the horizon.

5
Cultures clash

When tribal Africans first met missionaries, they thought them very strange. Physical appearance, dress, language and smell immediately set them apart. As an uneasy acquaintance developed they noticed that their visitors built rectangular houses, ate different foods and carried powerful weapons. Getting to know them more they discovered huge differences in attitudes to such vital areas of life as sickness, harvests, family and the spirits.

More damaging to relationships, each assumed his own way of life better than any other. The newcomers seldom questioned the rightness of sharing, not only the Christian religion, but also the assumed benefits of their western civilization. For sure, missionaries differed from the officials over many issues but, 'where the missionary found the African customs wicked, the government administrator found them a barrier to progress; and in breaking down their solidarity the administrator saw the missionary as his ally'.[87]

A historian may have been too sweeping when he wrote, 'most missionaries considered African culture, religion and customs to be of the devil and to be discarded as soon as possible'.[88] In 1897 Tom Allen, one of the mission's second batch of pioneers, said, 'There is no home life among the Wakamba. The system of polygamy prevents any idea of home life. Thus the children are deprived of a mother's training and grow up in the presence of immorality and drunkenness, terribly common among such tribes'.[89] But his colleague, Margaret Scott, sounded a note of caution. After suggesting that 'Christendom' would do well to copy the Kamba law relating to murder she continued, 'There are also laws relating to family life, but I am not enough acquainted with them to make a definite statement'.[90] She wanted to learn.

Learning from the Africans was the only way forward. Miraculously some became Christians and were then able to help missionaries understand their language and culture better. While depending heavily upon these converts in many ways, the missionaries often felt unable to trust their judgment in ethical issues. In such matters they relied on the Scriptures and on personal observation. So missionaries quickly condemned polygamy and circumcision without considering the impact of their decisions either on unbelievers or on the young church. John Gration concluded, 'It would appear that the missionaries precipitated and aggravated the crisis by demanding too much too soon'.[91] Could they have prevented the crisis by focusing more on patient biblical instruction and less on traumatic church discipline? Should they have looked to the Holy Spirit, even in the early days of the church, to lead godly Africans to make the decisions on these delicate cultural issues? In practice they felt they must wait fifty years before ordaining the first Kikuyu minister.

This hesitancy to rely upon African opinion led to the educational controversy. In an age when false teaching was eroding the western churches and, moreover, when Jesus Christ could return at any moment, nothing was more important to the missionaries than to spread the gospel. They must resist any sidetrack. Their commendable zeal often made them insensitive to what the local Christians thought about this vital issue and hindered serious consultation. When at last the mission capitulated, seeds of distrust had been sown which bore bitter fruit for many years.

By this time many relied on Africans. 'Speak not one word against Nandi customs,' said Stuart Bryson, 'The Holy Spirit will do the correcting'.[92] Another, Linnell Davis, asked Africans why they adopted a certain approach to traditional behaviour. They told him that they studied the Scriptures and came to their own conclusions.[93]

In the confrontation with Mau Mau the African Church proved her maturity. By God's grace she was ready for the battle and fought it out faithfully. Despite terrible suffering the Church triumphed and became stronger still.

A scholar wrote, 'If the early missionaries had not been spiritual giants they would not have got away with what they did, but they were holy men, of immense courage and personality. Their goodness was transparent, and their intolerance, though completely baffling to non-Christians, was nevertheless forgiven.'[94]

Lee and Blanche Downing

Lucile Downing sat enthralled as her father preached. AIM's Kenya Director spoke equally well to Africans, to missionaries or, as now, to their supporting church in Ohio. After the meeting she felt resentment when one of his boyhood friends wrung his hand and said, 'Who'd ever have thought that rabbit-eared Downing would amount to so much!'[95]

He had more than big ears to contend with. His abiding memory of his mother was of her supporting him as he fought for breath. Asthma and hayfever racked his thin frame throughout his life (but never troubled him in Africa). His parents, devout Irish Presbyterians, died before his tenth birthday, leaving him to a succession of foster homes.

A wide intellect made up for a weak body so that, in 1896, when he was thirty, Charles Hurlburt appointed Lee Downing lecturer in New Testament Greek at Pennsylvania Bible Institute. From the start the older man trusted Lee Downing for he also invited him to be a College Trustee and Treasurer to the Philadelphia Missionary Council.

One of his students called Blanche Hunter, weary perhaps with Greek verbs, mused about her teacher, 'If I cooked for you, I'd fatten you up'. As her year progressed she looked into his intense, dark blue eyes to see a man who loved his Lord with his whole being. They married in Dayton, Ohio, in October 1899 in a ceremony without flowers for fear of triggering his allergy. But she never achieved her goal of adding flesh to his skinny frame.

Two years later they arrived at Kangundo with the Hurlburt family to take part in the renaissance of the mission. Blanche gave birth to Lucile in a two-roomed house roofed by overhanging grass, wide enough to prevent the rain from washing away the mud walls. The family graduated to a house at Kijabe, possessing iron and glass windows, in time for the births of the two boys, Herbert and Ken. Four-year-old Herbert heard his baby brother's first cry in the next room and sang, 'The fight is on O Christian soldiers'. Nevertheless the brothers grew up to be good friends and both distinguished themselves in mission leadership.

Blanche loved the Kikuyu women even though she never mastered their difficult language. She grieved over the inferior position their society assigned them and sought to help them. In long sewing classes they would laugh at her claim to the love of her husband for they measured a husband's affection by the number of goats and chickens he paid to possess her. 'How then was it possible for a white man to love the wife for whom he had paid nothing?' On her side Mrs Downing could not understand how a woman could share her husband with one or more other wives.

Like Blanche, Lee was a perfectionist. Even his few hairs (his daughter said 'a dozen or so') had to be carefully cut and combed. He hated to appear in public without a clean white shirt, tie and freshly pressed suit. He could not stand shoddy work in others and was even more demanding of himself. He would wrap, tie and address a package as if it was a work of art. He knew Greek and Latin well, along with a smattering of Hebrew, and quickly mastered Kikamba and Kikuyu. He could recite large sections of the New Testament from memory. In his photographs he looks austere but his children found him full of affection – a love, however, that knew the value of an occasional stinging slap when a child erred.

Africans too were amazed at the strength in his scrawny limbs and nicknamed him, 'Arms of Iron'. He was more renowned for his spiritual power. A young missionary visitor heard him scraping the living room fire together two hours before sunrise so that he could settle down with his Bible. Immersion in God's Word enabled him to feed people, both Africans and missionaries, by his godly conversation. Mabel Easton reported on the 'great, outstanding blessing' of his daily Bible message to the Congo Missionary Conference in 1927 – the fruit of 'a life enriched by years of loving absorption in the Book of books'.[96] At times of special perplexity he would disappear to his prayer hut in the forest.

African church planters

Problems perplexed him throughout twenty-one years as Field Director for Kenya. Pressures increased still more during a further six difficult years as Deputy General Director when Hurlburt's leadership was crumbling. While Downing was in charge, missionaries laid the foundation for enormous church growth. Yet for much of the time the mission seemed confused in vital policies and, more damaging in the long run, insensitive in its relationships with the Church which it was nurturing. Without doubt God honoured Lee Downing's priority of prayer and his insistence that the Bible mould both his own life and the lives of all believers. He had the joy of leading a team which, despite many human weaknesses, shared these same basic commitments.

When he arrived in 1901 AIM's three missionaries occupied only one centre, Kangundo. Twenty-five years later he reported fifty missionaries serving in fifteen locations in Kenya with 144 'native helpers'. In 1926 missionaries baptized 299 Kenyans bringing the total church membership to 1,804. With his concern for details he listed an additional 1,698 as 'inquirers' – presumably believers under instruction who had not yet satisfied the leaders that their faith was genuine enough to warrant baptism. Over the next eight years the number of church members doubled and missionaries opened three more centres. But the mission could not match this church growth with trained leaders. Despite the fact that two Bible schools opened their doors

Rural church, CM

during that period (at Machakos and Kijabe) for the purpose of training church workers, the number of evangelists was the same and still no Kikuyu had been ordained.

The 'native helper', later known as outschool teacher or evangelist, was the key to church growth. A missionary started to preach in a locality and a few would respond. Often one or two of these early converts grew rapidly in commitment and understanding so the missionary concentrated on teaching them to read and write. He used them as valuable bridges into a foreign culture.

Before long these dependable people began to teach too. The next step in developing the work was to send them to open 'outschools' where they gathered a few children for instruction in Bible and literacy during the week and a wider congregation for worship on Sundays. They taught the embryonic church by rote – simple hymns, a few Bible verses in the local language and an early catechism. They could travel freely to the villages with a rolled blanket over the shoulder. In the evening they chatted about God's words while their food cooked and then stretched out on a hospitable mud floor. In contrast the foreigner on safari moved with his train of porters and slept in his remote tent. Wisely the missionaries recognized the greater effectiveness of their young converts and concentrated on encouraging and training these raw messengers at the weekends and during holidays.

Are schools important?

Soon after its formation, the Philadelphia Missionary Council minuted, 'In view of the many untouched millions, we feel called to do a thorough evangelistic work, rather than to build up strong educational centres'.[97]

Margaret Scott had opened the first school in 1896. Others welcomed the orphans from the great plagues and famines. Peter Scott wrote in 1896, 'Our school work has not been large but has been carried on faithfully since March'.[98] Missionaries, recognizing that youngsters must learn to read and write in order to understand the Bible, urged parents to send their children and often bribed the youngsters with food, clothes or even money. But 'African parents, elders and headmen opposed the establishment of schools because missions required Africans to cast out the old traditions with the result they became detribalized.'[99] Lee Downing tried hard to influence the leaders. In 1910 his secretary, Hulda Stumpf, told Charles Hurlburt, 'Mr

Downing is in Nairobi since Tuesday attending a meeting of the Governor with certain chiefs in regard to sending their sons to the different missions to be educated'.[100]

Despite the inspector who criticized the teaching at Machakos school as 'having little educational value, being parrot-like',[101] the government valued the early mission schools. More important, this simple programme produced a slow but steady flow of converts.

Lee watched African attitudes change. By 1924 he was writing, 'Fully ninety-five per cent of our church members have passed thru' our schools. Genuine interest in the gospel has led to thirst for knowledge of reading which will at least enable them to read the Scriptures.'[102] That thirst led to a major confrontation between AIM and the young church.

At the start most AIM missionaries desired simply 'to open a school where the only textbook is the Word of God and the sole object in teaching the people to read and write is that they may have access to it'.[103] Other missions in Kenya arranged for their brighter pupils to go further. They reaped the benefit of educated leaders at a much earlier stage than AIM as well as producing a growing, Protestant, educated elite in Kenya. AIM believers, their appetite for learning whetted in the simple village schools, found themselves left behind and began to agitate. Some missionaries saw that 'we have not only lost the confidence of Government but of large sections of the native people also'.[104]

The government, short of money after the war of 1914 to 1918, looked to the missions to educate the masses. Officers grumbled about AIM's poor educational standards and reluctance to expand beyond the elementary phase. Realizing that missions lacked cash, the Director of Education offered generous subsidies, which other missions used gladly. In 1922 the American council of AIM ruled against accepting such financial aid.

Dedicated missionaries argued. One said, 'Education, like a vampire, is sucking the blood of all missionary power'.[105] Another wrote, 'We are believers in education in so far as it will enable Christians to read the Word of God, and (we believe) that further education is the responsibility of Government'.[106] Some objected on the grounds of cost and, when government proffered grants, feared that official interference might hinder spiritual ministry. In any case the mission would have to apply for such financial assistance and that would contravene the 'faith basis' of asking no one but God for money.

Money was short everywhere. As the number of African

teachers swelled, the source of overseas money, augmented from the missionaries' meagre salaries, proved increasingly inadequate. For a few years AIM vainly appealed to the African workers 'to live like missionaries on a faith basis'.[107] Without adequate salaries, even the best were tempted to join a different mission able (through accepting Government grants) to pay them a standard wage.

An exasperated Government announced its Kenya Education Ordinance in 1924 which demanded the closure of all unlicensed schools. They would only issue licences to those schools which met Government standards for buildings, equipment and trained teachers. Faced with the closure of their schools thirty-nine missionaries wrote to Hurlburt in America, 'the majority of missionaries in Kenya now feel the mission should receive grants'. Lee urged the American Council to 'appreciate the seriousness of the situation . . . and that if immediate remedial steps were not taken it could spell disaster to the work of the AIM in Kenya'.[108]

The Council reluctantly agreed. Glad to have the issue resolved, Lee Downing applied for a grant. But his joy did not last. The Director of Education told him that he had already allocated all available funds and AIM must wait. The Council probably took this as divine overruling for they reversed their decision.

By 1928 the whole argument was in full swing again and through the thirties and the Second World War the debate continued uneasily inside the mission. One missionary summed up the dilemma, 'Now that the Mission has succeeded in attracting a large number of followers . . . it proved incapable of deciding the extent of its obligation to meeting the educational needs of the converts'.[109] Downing's alert secretary commented, 'Education is like a red tablecloth to a turkey gobbler'.[110]

African Christians felt frustrated. Some had gone outside

Lee Downing, DD

AIM circles to become better educated than many missionaries. Why, they asked, when they were paying taxes, would their church not accept educational grants? Were missionaries deliberately trying to hold them back? At Githumu, one of the mission's most fruitful centres, the outschools withdrew from AIM control to form an independent denomination. Kamba, Kikuyu and Luo Christians railed against their mission. Some saw that, after working for fifty years, the mission broke one leg of their child by failing to provide education.[111] More ugly, Christians at Machakos reviled the missionaries for lack of interest in Africans' welfare and demanded that they leave.

By 1938 Lee Downing acknowledged, 'Only recently have I come to realize how far we are behind other missions in teacher training. The pupils in our schools failed to pass the examination, set by the Government, which hundreds in other missions pass, since they have better native teachers.'[112] Only ten per cent of AIM's 280 teachers possessed a recognized qualification and a typical Government Inspector of Schools said, 'The schools are thoroughly bad.'[113] Their closure by the authorities seemed possible. At a stroke the mission stood to lose 10,000 boys and girls from the most fruitful environment for conversion and spiritual growth.

Downing's successor, Harmon Nixon, could see no end to the debate and mournfully declared, 'We are between the anvil and the hammer for both the Government and natives are trying us to the breaking point.'[114]

By 1945 most missionaries realized that they could not hold out against the almost universal demand from their converts. The Home Council, bowing at last before the insistent cry from Africa, turned round yet again and decided, 'We will maintain schools at least to Government standards. We will seek qualified educationalists to carry out teacher training and act as trustee of education grants funded by Government taxation.' They applied this radically new policy to Congo and Tanganyika as well as to Kenya.

The decision had come too late to halt the defection of multitudes of Africans. Although many departed over the cultural confrontations, the mission's failure to understand their depth of resentment over educational mismanagement resulted in a haemorrhage of Christians and adherents which was almost fatal. Lee Downing, unsure where he stood at first, had seen it coming for three decades. Sadly he died of cancer a year before the Council's change of heart. Miraculously neither the Church nor the mission bled to death – probably because a man with rabbit ears prayed regularly in his forest hut.

Virginia Blakeslee

In a grey Kijabe dawn an anxious voice summoned Virginia Blakeslee, 'Wanja, your Wanja is sick'. Calling her Kikuyu nurse, she followed a guide until she found her friend Wanja lying among bushes where frightened relatives had dropped her, with her upturned face unconscious of the cold drizzle. She had been in labour for three days, trying to deliver through a dense band of circumcision scars. Her baby was already dead. Before Virginia could snip through the barrier, Wanja breathed her last. A multitude of similar experiences convinced Virginia that she must oppose circumcision and help free the girls and women from the bondage which forced such suffering upon them.

Dr Blakeslee had arrived at Kijabe ten years after Lee Downing and, while still practising medicine at the time of Wanja's death, had become one of the most committed educationalists in his team.

Pioneer blood flowed in her veins. Her grandfather founded a village in Pennsylvania and served its people as judge, postmaster and principal trader. In gratitude they called it 'Blakeslee'. Virginia practised her profession of osteopathy in her home state until she met Charles Hurlburt at a Bible conference. She could find many answers to his searching question, 'Is there any reason why you cannot go?' Her Lord swept her reservations aside and she sailed for Kenya.

En route to her first assignment at Matara, a Kikuyu man in tattered red blanket offered to help her cross a river. With great care he guided her from rock to rock 'as carefully as if I were a piece of rare old china and as gallantly as though I had been a queen'. Forty years later Virginia said, 'That day love for the Kikuyu was born in my heart'.

Love grew as she discovered the depth of her dependence upon the first Christians at her new home. They wandered with her through the villages, helping to unravel the complexities of Kikuyu language and customs. After a few weeks in Matara she was asked to preach. Her first sentence was broken and hesitating and then a verb failed her. A young pupil teacher, Johana, rolled his eyes heavenwards in a desperate effort to find her lost word. Suddenly he blurted it out. She stumbled on, looking to him to interpret while the tiny congregation politely hid their smiles.

One day she heard the student teacher tell his own story. He said,

> I was a small boy herding my father's sheep and goats. The first white man I ever saw came to our village. The women and children, very frightened, cried, 'Kill a sheep and sacrifice it or we die. We looked upon a face like the face of God; it is white.'
>
> He was Bwana Sywulka who first opened Matara. He called us together to tell us about the love of the Son of God. His words were to me like the taste of honey. After a few days he left our ridge to camp on another. I left my father's herd with another herdboy while I went to the ridge where the tent was pitched to hear more. My father gave me a beating and forbade me to listen to the white man.

The lad ran away from his father's cattle to hear more of the Son of God but the old man followed to plead with him to return home. When entreaty failed, he beat him and finally disinherited him. Johana felt he must remain and learn to read the words which 'burnt like a fire' in his heart so that he might 'go over all the ridges of Kikuyuland to explain to the herdboys the good affair of salvation'.[115] As soon as he could read a little, he helped teach other errant boys who contrived to escape from their herds for a period.

White ways

Keige ran away from home too, fleeing a fate she dreaded. She had discovered her father's plan to betroth her to old Njoroge who already had several wives. As Njoroge had by now handed over a quantity of goats and beer, Keige knew that she could be carried off to his home any day. Should she not escape to Matara and learn the path of the God she heard the mission lads speak about in the market? When she reached Matara, the other girls insisted on removing her dirt-engrained skins, scrubbing the oil and clay off her body and dressing her in a cotton garment. Her parents implored Keige for hours to return home and her father was furious but her only response was to thrust into her mother's hand a bundle of her ornaments wrapped in her goatskins. The old man growled, 'These will be thrown on a grave. To us you are dead.'

The new missionary, committed to loving the Kikuyu, was perplexed. She saw these young folk obeying the command, 'Come out from them, be separate, touch no unclean thing' and described this exit as 'leaving the ways of the Kikuyu'. The young

Christians were convinced that 'to wear a Kikuyu outfit while professing to live the Christian life was hypocrisy' because they would always link their attractive ornaments with heathen practices. But the radical change to foreign dress, environment and life style troubled her. She wished she could have taught them 'a Christian way of life which was distinctly African, rather than try to fit them to the cumbersome, complicated and, in many ways, mistaken customs of the white man's Christianity'.

Johana and Keige found a way to placate their parents. Johana asked Keige's father for her hand in marriage and presented him with an adequate dowry. They had a western style 'white' wedding and set up a home in which Christ was Head of their family and, wherever they lived in the troubled years to come, their home always shone like a beacon for righteousness.

Matara church grew and new congregations multiplied across the ridges. Eventually the Matara missionaries appointed church elders and left the station in their hands. Virginia moved several times, working as school teacher or doctor as the need demanded, but always eager to teach God's Word. In 1927 she arrived at Kijabe convinced that Kikuyu women would only find release from their cruel bondages through the ministry of trained Christians of their own Tribe. She established a new training school for girls and soon had 170 on the books.

While the Kingdom of God advanced in the twenties, opposition to the white man's rule found country-wide expression. In 1922 Harry Thuku addressed a crowd on their grievances about land and about forced female labour. Police arrested him and several thousand Africans sat outside the police lines where he was held. After waiting for twenty-four hours a restive group led by women moved in on the guard. In a nervous moment someone fired and this signalled a volley into the crowd. Twenty-one died.[116] The colonial Government had baptized the infant African protest movement in the most powerful element of all – blood.

Circumcision

The stream of political protest widened. One evening a group of Christian men, whom Virginia had nurtured in their faith many years before, brought disturbing news from the villages. Many who had called themselves Christians were insisting that, if their land was not returned, they would drive the white man out. The visitors added, 'The leaders want all the Kikuyu to take a strong hand against the mission churches in the affair of the circumcision of girls'.

When Virginia moved to Kijabe she was delighted to catch up with her old friends, Johana and Keige. While missionaries still controlled the church, they leant heavily upon Johana for the pastoral ministry. If, at this stage, they could have entrusted the delicate confrontation between Christian faith and Kikuyu culture to mature African Christians, they might have been able to avert the approaching tragedy. Johana, like many others, watched the infection spreading but was powerless to advise his white friends.

Jomo Kenyatta was emerging as a dominant politician (although from 1929 to 1946 he lived in England). He wrote that circumcision 'has enormous educational, social, moral and religious implications'.[117] By selecting this emotive issue, emerging African leaders aroused Kenyans to decide who would determine their future way of life – themselves or the white man.

AIM, like the other missions, had long taught against this dangerous practice and regarded it as evil. Many precious teenagers disappeared from mission schools for training in tribal lore for several months before the physical operation. A cloak of secrecy surrounded the ritual and hindered most foreigners from making a careful investigation. One answer for the boys was to keep them at the mission for training and then circumcise them in hospital. Mission doctors could not permit the mutilating operation on the girls.

In 1921 the missionaries discussed female circumcision at their annual conference. They decided to 'condemn and forbid' it. Not only would 'all transgressors be subject to church discipline,' but also any who ridiculed an uncircumcised person.[118] Every church elder and every teacher must sign a repudiation. Many Christians rebelled, masses deserting the churches. When Lee Downing discovered that the elders at a village church refused to accept the official ruling, he immediately dismissed them. His secretary, Miss Stumpf, wrote that on a day after Mr Downing left Kijabe, 'several daughters of our very best Christian elders were circumcised'. The missionary response to widespread defection was to excommunicate the offender 'for ever unless he was willing to confess his wrong and swear allegiance to the white man and his rulings'.[119]

Church attendance throughout Kikuyu plummeted to a tenth of the former level. Independent schools and churches, led mostly by mission educated people, welcomed those who wished to escape white domination, offering them a path which claimed to be both Christian and Kikuyu. Discontent spread among

Virginia's girls at Kijabe until, at the end of one term, all but one proudly walked out.

Virginia's fellow teacher, Hulda Stumpf, felt uneasy about the mission's rigid line. Privately she questioned if it was right 'to thrust upon African Christians rules of conduct that have not grown out of their own convictions'. They needed to be taught why one custom should be avoided, another utilized and a third purified; 'but the teaching will have to be done in LOVE and not by legislation'.[120]

On the evening of New Year's Day, 1930, Virginia mounted her mule and rode across a

Virginia Blakeslee, DD

narrow gorge that separated Miss Stumpf's home from Kijabe mission. The two friends enjoyed a meal together with good chat and some prayer.

The next morning Pastor Johana interrupted her breakfast. Distressed, he blurted out, 'Miss Stumpf was killed last night!' Hurrying to her friend's little brick cottage, she found a totally different scene from the previous evening's peace. Rocks and shattered glass littered the bedroom floor. On the bed lay Hulda's body, brutally battered and partly covered by a mattress. Large black and blue patches on her neck showed where cruel hands had finally squeezed out her life. A rumour (which Dr Blakeslee denied) spread that she had been circumcised.[121]

As if an angry abscess had burst, Hulda's murder marked a turning point. The Government ruled that no girl could be forcibly circumcised against her will and unrest quietened. AIM backed away from the signed pledge, reserving it only for teachers. Independent churches and schools continued and went on to provide many members for the politically active Kikuyu Central Association. Slowly people trickled back into churches in the AIM heartland while Kikuyus working in the large white-settled farms turned to Christ in large numbers.

Mau Mau

Sixteen years after Hulda's murder, Virginia moved to her old home, Githumu. Many friends greeted her but without the spontaneous goodwill she had always known before. The circumcision controversy still rankled, undermining the old relationship of trust. A costly theft from her home and the murder of an outstanding Christian shocked her. An African sister told her, 'Some Kikuyu say you pretend to be friends of the people, but in truth you are Government spies and live among us to learn all about our affairs'.

Despite these warnings she was unprepared for a letter signed by leading teachers and elders of the district. These fellow workers who had shared many burdens with her over the years wrote, 'You missionaries have done a good work during pioneer days. We are grateful, but now we ask you to leave Githumu District'. The missionaries, still unable to appreciate the gravity of the rejection, took no action. The African leaders met again and laid down a list of prohibitions: no one may attend the mission hospital; none may join the missionaries in their meetings for women; if a missionary ventures into a classroom all pupils must walk out; people may not sell food to missionaries. All the schools and churches joined the independence movement. A small group of faithfuls worshipped with the missionaries on Sundays; the majority formed a separate congregation.

Following an attack on several mission buildings one night, the District Commissioner posted six police guards on the station. Order returned and, even though the district schools remained independent, Githumu Primary and Secondary Schools filled beyond their capacity in 1949. The lull lasted for three years and then a horrendous storm broke.

A society called Mau Mau appeared, dedicated to deliver the Kikuyu from the white man. They would reclaim all occupied land, drive out foreigners, destroy Christianity, restore ancient customs and encourage modern education. Quickly the movement gained control of the independent schools and used them as centres for propagating their message. People were rounded up and taken to a place of sacrifice where they had to swallow blood and meat while a vow was repeated over them committing them to secrecy, obedience, theft from Europeans and murder.

Some Christians acquiesced. Others refused. Many, who had been forced to take the oath, courageously renounced it. Throughout Kikuyuland Christians were under fire again as in

1929, but this time church attendance increased, proud hearts were humbled before God, people trusted in the blood of Christ over against the bloody sacrifice of the evil oath. In the midst of battle, Christians spoke of revival.

Faithfulness cost many lives. The Githumu evangelist, Onesimus, refused to take the oath. After communion one Sunday, he took his son to a local shop for a snack. A gang leaped on them, pounding their bodies with clubs and demanded, 'Who are you to refuse the words of the Kikuyu?' 'I go to live with the Lord', came the quiet reply. They carved his body into several pieces and buried them.

Johana too remained faithful. He and Keige survived to minister to Mau Mau detained by the government in a large camp. Before Virginia left in 1953, he travelled up to Kijabe to spend a morning with his mentor. She enquired about his work and he replied, 'Every morning we evangelists move among the prisoners and talk to them. At first they bit us with words . . . Finally some began to listen . . . Ten of these have confessed their sins and been truly saved.'

With the disappointment and horror of Mau Mau still churning in her mind, she wrote to Johana from her American home, 'Men are saying, "You have labored in vain. You have wasted your lives. Christianity has failed in Kikuyuland." You and I know better. The Lord did not send us to change the whole Kikuyu tribe. He sent us to give them the light and trust him for the results.' Soon she heard that Johana's ten disciples in the camp had multiplied into hundreds. In prisons across the country and out on the Kikuyu ridges, the Spirit of God moved to bring new life out of the carnage and ruin.

Ken and Hazel Phillips

As Ken Phillips lay in his hospital bed, paralyzed but at peace, he could not have guessed that God had chosen him to minister to the Mau Mau.

As manager of AIM schools among the Tuken people of western Kenya he suspended an unsatisfactory teacher. Tribal leaders resented his action, claiming that the white missionary still insisted on holding back the black. The local government official, probably aware of the old educational controversy between the mission and its adherents, asked him to leave.

Within a few days Ken's two-year-old daughter, Pearl, collapsed with poliomyelitis. A week later Ken too was driven seventy miles to the hospital powerless from the neck downwards and in great pain. He felt concern for his wife, Hazel, expecting their fourth child, as she set about packing up their home in the midst of antagonism. Despite the turmoil, both knew that God was quietly working to a plan. 'Be of good cheer', he quoted the Lord's words to Hazel, 'It is I; be not afraid.'

Ken and Pearl survived with much of their muscle power restored, but needed two years' convalescence. Then, in 1954, the mission surprised them – would they evangelize the Mau Mau?

Division among the Kikuyu

The Kikuyu rebellion had reached a climax while Ken was grappling with polio. Convinced that Europeans robbed them of their land and suppressed their culture, they determined to drive out the aliens.

Before the first British soldiers arrived in Kikuyu country, famine and disease forced many Kikuyu off their land. The newcomers settled on the deserted tracts. As conditions improved and the birth rate escalated, families moved back to their old gardens only to find them occupied by the 'Red Strangers'. With mounting hostility, they demanded, 'Give us back our land.'

They forced the government to acknowledge the justice of their claims. The settlers too insisted that government had approved their applications for the new farms. With cultural blindness they later regretted, the officials arranged compensation. But how can a cold business deal rectify the loss of land where revered ancestral spirits are known to reside in its hills, streams and trees? Resentment simmered.

Piling insult onto injury, the government appointed new tribal chiefs to recruit labour, including women and children, to work on the stolen land. In addition chiefs enforced the colonial laws, raised hated taxes and conscripted soldiers to fight in foreign wars.

On the whole the races kept apart. Woe betide the new missionary who wandered into a white restaurant with her African friend! An Anglican missionary, Rev Bewes, wrote at that time, 'The European attitude of calm aloofness and patronizing superiority stirs the flow of anger more than political injustice.'[122] Educated Africans visited other countries, where they were often treated as equals, only to return to an inferior position and life style in their own country.

New schools, independent of the missions and with scarcely any Government supervision, fostered hatred and a sense of injustice. In the British army Kikuyu soldiers had seen the bubble of white prominence burst. At the same time they learnt modern fighting skills which would serve them well in the wild forests and the city ghettos.

To the non-discerning all whites were part of the same anti-Kikuyu conspiracy. They blamed missionaries for attacking their sacred institutions of circumcision and polygamy. They saw the mission occupying land at Kijabe known to belong to a Kikuyu family. Although missionaries opposed government on such issues as child labour and the enforced moves of the Maasai, they mostly cooperated, even to the extent of deciding petty legal cases on behalf of officials. Bewes was right to affirm that 'it is never desirable that the Gospel of Christ should be regarded as something foreign, too closely associated with an alien rule, nor that missionaries should appear as Government agents, still less as Government policemen.'[123]

But many Kikuyu Christians saw this clash differently. Mau Mau oaths repelled them. The second oath for example stated, 'I have become one of the company of killers. If I fail to do so, may this oath kill me.' The initiate had to swear to 'always carry a rope for hanging people' and to 'help drive out the Europeans from Kenya'.[124] As he advanced through seven grades, oaths increased in horror and the accompanying rites became more foul. The choice between darkness and light was clear. Controversy about circumcision and education had emptied the churches; this issue filled them.

Mau Mau hated such loyal Christians and found them softer targets than the white farmers with their powerful weapons and police force. They visited the home of a recently converted teacher and persuaded his wife and brother to take the oath, but he repeatedly refused. 'Every man has to choose which world he wants,' he told them, 'you have chosen this world, but I have chosen the world of Jesus and His Kingdom. Kill me if you like, but I shall go to be with him.' They shot him through the mouth and with the blood flowed words, 'Lord, forgive them, for they do not know what they are doing.'

Ken and Hazel Phillips were part of God's answer to that dying prayer.

Christ in the cages

Government rounded up and detained thousands of Kikuyu in camps across Kenya. They confined 23,000 in two huge settlements at Mackinnon Road and Manyani. At 'Mac Road' Ken met the prisoners in huge iron hangars divided into six cages, each holding 250 men. Every time he entered a cage, the guard would snap a padlock onto the gate behind him leaving him alone with a mass of sworn murderers. He sensed, 'Something right from the start seemed to break down every barrier, and I never once found myself in an ugly situation, nor yet had any fear.' That 'something' was his ability to empathize as a sinner who needed God's grace just as much as them.

Sometimes he spoke to 1,000 at once. 'I speak to them using Swahili for half an hour or more' about 'sin, the All-sufficient Saviour, cleansing in his precious blood and a holy life. You could hear a pin drop all through the service, hardly a soul stirring. We close in a word of prayer, and they seem reluctant to disperse.'

The Camp Commandant allowed him to use the public address system that carried his message to every person in Mac Road. As his preaching continued month after month in the hangars and over the tannoy people asked for literature. Everywhere in the camp men read the Kikuyu Bible and began to respond.

> In one of the compounds twelve men asked me to meet with them, saying that they were ready to follow Jesus utterly – all they wanted was Jesus . . . One prayed, 'As a fish is in the sea and cannot be hurt by the sun's heat, so I want to be so deep in Thee that I shall be unaffected by the fierceness of temptation.'

The Commandant wanted to rehabilitate these men although some cynical guards distrusted professions of conversion. But Ken knew that converts had to live in the cages among hardened Mau Mau who threatened to take their lives, if not there, then back in the villages later. As believers multiplied, Ken arranged for more intimate meetings for fellowship, always aware of spies trying to infiltrate the Christian groups.

God had already prepared some for Ken's message. A teacher, educated in a mission school, slipped a New Testament into his pocket when he fled his home to join the gangs in the forest. He then taught people to murder. The Mau Mau rewarded his zeal and ability by promoting him to the rank of Lieutenant General. When he stopped to read the only book he had with him, he trembled at the prospect of God's judgment. He found another soldier who shared his predicament. They feared execution by the Government if they gave themselves up but, by refusing to

Ken and Hazel Phillips, DD

kill, they risked severe discipline from their fellow 'freedom fighters'. After two years in the forest he surrendered and came to Manyani.

Listening to Ken preach about Saul of Tarsus, the General recognized his own fierce enmity towards God. That night his conscience told him again and again that he was lost. He asked God to forgive him for Jesus' sake and found peace. As he reached this point in telling Ken his story, he broke down and cried out, 'How can I undo the great harm I have done? There are men in all these compounds whom I have taught to be murderers.' He mentioned one who, like himself, had risen high in the hierarchy. 'You need not worry about that man now,' Ken replied, 'he was saved four months ago.'

Another educated man worked as a clerk on two European farms before his arrest. At Manyani he responded to Christ's offer of forgiveness. In fluent English he said to Ken, 'I have been detained for twenty months but it seems like one day to me because I have Jesus. And if I am here for twenty more years it is all right. There is barbed wire all around me, but there is no barbed wire above me.'

The Governor declared a State of Emergency on 20 October 1952. His successor claimed the defeat of Mau Mau in February 1955. In a military sense he was right. But the struggle convinced the politicians (apart from the white settlers) that independence must come soon. The anti-white movement cost ninety-five European lives compared with 13,423 Africans, many of them Christians. They did not give their lives in vain for the churches, already growing before the Emergency, boomed after it.

While some who professed faith in the Lord failed to persevere, Ken met many others afterwards who had joined these congregations. Typical was a Nairobi taxi driver who waved frantically as he drew alongside Ken's car in a busy street. Their vehicles slowed to a crawl and they compared notes through their windows. With a smile he reminded Ken of his conversion in Mac Road. 'Are you still loving the Lord?' Ken enquired as the traffic behind impatiently hooted. The smile broadened, 'Ndiyo, sana, sana' (Yes, very, very much).

6

Progress and peril in Uganda

Albert and Florence Vollor

In 1923, Frank and Edith Gardner, who had so nearly died in Uganda (see pp. 66–7), were completing their service at Kinyona, a few miles north of Kijabe. They heard that a new couple had passed through on their way to Arua.

The seventeen workers at Kijabe welcomed the Vollors and showed them around the high school for white children and the industrial centre which trained Christians in carpentry, building, blacksmithing, metal work, quarrying and agriculture. Bert wrote home about the surprising rainfall – three to four inches in their first few days – and fires in every home, 'And all this within sixty miles of the Equator'. Missionaries told them, 'we must wear helmets until one hour before sunset because the penetrating rays of the sun are said to be just as powerful in pouring rain as in the clear. Sun-glasses likewise must protect the eyes from the invisible sun.'[125]

Florence, at the age of thirty-three, was so tiny that when Hurlburt first met her he asked, 'My dear, is your mother anywhere about?'[126] Reared in London's poverty-stricken dockland, she left school at twelve to care for nine younger brothers and sisters. Albert joined a Christian boys club and became part of a missionary prayer group called 'The Praying Out Band'. They could already count three of their number as missionaries. They prayed for Albert as tuberculosis threatened his life. They rejoiced later when a godly parson sent him to Cambridge University.

From Albert's letters, Sunday worship at Kijabe sounds a bit regimented. A bell at 9 a.m. summoned the congregation of about 200 to the church. They waited outside for a second bell at 9.25 which allowed them five minutes to get in and take their seats. Men sat on one side and women on the other; Christians at the back and heathen in front. Discipline went to the wind, however, when the service finished and the women swarmed around their small son, Ronnie.

The missionary community buzzed with news of African unrest and Government reactions. Although Bert only stayed three weeks in Kijabe he developed some strong opinions. 'Natives are ill-treated and virtually forced to work as slaves and magistrates will not do justice. No wonder the mission is not popular . . . I hate to couple the name of English with, not only flagrant acts of injustice and brutality, but with the general trend of official Government.'

In Kampala they were guests of the bishop who secured them invitations to a reception for the new Governor in 'the native parliament'. The representative of the King of England sat beside the King of Baganda to receive the homage of the chiefs and to exchange speeches. The Governor's task was easier in Uganda than in Kenya for he did not have to wrestle with the demands of a growing white settler community.

They stayed in the comfort of the capital long enough for Bert to pass an ordination examination. By now the bishop led a large and lively Anglican diocese, refined in the crucible of suffering. He headed a procession into the broad, brick-built cathedral. Bright cassocks fluttered in the breeze, choirs sang, dignitaries settled in their seats and hundreds worshipped. The bishop, flanked by five ministers (including one Ugandan) laid hands on Bert, commissioning him to the work of the Church of Uganda.

When they reached Mvara, on the edge of Arua, they found that the church was still a struggling infant. Four years after the Gardners' costly pioneering, missionaries had baptized the first flock of twenty-six believers and now, a year later, Albert Vollor arrived as their shepherd and teacher.

West of the Nile

The Vollors moved into a large, brick-built house standing on a hill with a magnificent view, sharing it with Florrie's monkey, lizards, crickets, spiders, etc.

While they wrestled with the Lugbara language, they did all they could to persuade children that the white people would not eat them if they came to school. Florrie's clinic on her back doorstep and Bert's exuberance disarmed suspicion and the school steadily filled. By the end of 1923 two of the Christian men had opened new centres and several hundred people poured into Mvara for the Christmas service. Afterwards Bert organized games – races, a marathon and a pillow-fight between contestants balancing on a pole above a water-filled pit. In an archery contest, 'We threw a ball into the air and one boy pierced it with each of his three shots.'

They did not find the language easy and Florrie never became fluent. Once she asked a boy to fetch a tape measure which she had left beside a precious two-foot-high water filter. Two lads returned staggering under the weight of the filter. Bert did better and later on managed to produce the first New Testament in Lugbara. But even he was far from perfect and the Lugbara enjoyed imitating his mistakes.

How they found time to concentrate on study is hard to understand. Florence sought to bring women to Christ and, having made the vital link, strove to strengthen their faith.

Albert and Florence Vollor, DD

Despite her total lack of formal training she became an excellent school teacher. Shy and retiring, she hated speaking to a western group she did not know, but never shrank from her Bible class in Uganda. Africans saw beyond the rather stiff, colonial formality to her loving heart. They responded with affection and respect. Bert described himself as 'farmer, butter maker, baker, cobbler [his father's trade], schoolmaster, metal worker, doctor, poultry farmer, gardener, parson, bricklayer, plasterer, ink maker, miller, clock mender and solderer.'

A year after the Vollors arrived, one of the young evangelists was invited to preach in a village and immediately people crowded around to hear. Soon he gathered 100 believers for daily teaching. The surrounding villages heard and asked him to preach to them. As the converts learnt God's truth, they wanted to read it for themselves, so Bert sent the early believers from Mvara as teachers and evangelists. When the next Christmas party came round, over 1,000 crowded in.

Training shepherds

Bert appointed such raw workers out of necessity. Although quick to appreciate good aspects of their culture, he learnt from the early Christians that many traditions were evil and about these he complained, 'It is difficult to get them to make a clean break with their old pernicious habits and customs.' He determined to give the young leaders all the teaching he could so that they might stand firm in their faith and, in turn, develop many other Christians. When a man started a little group under a tree he usually became the evangelist. As soon as possible Vollor called him and his wife to Mvara for a year of Bible training. He expected all the evangelists to attend conferences every six months. Later he called them back for a second year of training and eventually a third. Churches multiplied rapidly and eventually required several evangelists' schools.

Together the Vollors stressed the importance of schools. Tied initially to Mvara school during term-time, they moved around the district extensively during vacations to encourage teachers and evangelists. At first they travelled with porters on foot, then by bicycles over the rough tracks. Occasionally, Fred Morris (another member of the dockland Praying Out Band), would squeeze the family into his motorbike and sidecar to launch them into their first day of a two-week safari. When babies Eva and Bertha arrived, the sidecar became too small and the little ones swung in hammocks suspended from two pairs of sturdy Lugbara shoulders. Arriving at a school, they gathered everyone for a Bible lesson. Then, while Florence listened to the teacher and examined his curriculum, Bert checked classroom equipment and dropped stones down the latrines to ensure they were not too full.

More and more Florence moved out of her own classroom into teacher training and school supervision. Unlike the missionary team in Kenya at that time, they saw Christ-centred education as part of their message and usually kept a few steps ahead of the government. As soon as possible they established teacher training and a secondary school at Mvara. When they retired, they left thirteen secondary schools.

In line with his great desire to help Christians grow, Bert imported a small printing press and, with an understandable hint of pride, sent a sample booklet of twenty-five Lugbara choruses to his family in England in mid 1925. A year later he was turning out 10,000 primers for another language group in West Nile that had responded to the Gospel, the Alur, and colleagues in Congo were asking him to print for them too. He stuck with his principle of training Africans even in the face of so much frustration that he once came home from the print shop to cry out in a letter, 'The inability and the slackness and the irresponsibility of the native is always trying.' But six months later he is telling the folk at home that he has appointed a man called Sila to take charge of the press and he adds with a sense of satisfaction, 'I have long been on the look out for someone with a little initiative and gumption that I could trust.'

This ability to select and develop trustworthy people characterized Bert. He trained two clerks to relieve him of much of the administration of the schools in the early years. The Vollors instilled dignity; 'They did not just give us things but made us rely upon ourselves,' said the Africans, 'We learnt not to look to the missionaries for everything.' Before the Vollors reached their twentieth year in Africa, the Lugbara had 120 churches and two trained supervisors who visited each congregation every two or three months and then came to report to their own leader, Bert. He was a good accountant and introduced simple book-keeping into all the churches, insisting that it always be in the hands of a layman so that the pastor or evangelist avoid the temptation of borrowing.

When local training resources were exhausted he searched for opportunities elsewhere and sent suitable people away. In 1942, only twenty-four years after the work started in West Nile, two men from the Kakwa tribe returned from theological college to be ordained. John Dronyi became a key figure in translating the Kakwa Bible. The other, Silvanus Wani, was consecrated bishop in 1964. Bert sent a succession of able men to a year's course in an Anglican college in North London.

Keys of the Kingdom

They were fortunate to arrive in the quinine era so he was able to answer an anxious query from home, 'Life is not a constant battle against illness. The freedom, the sunshine and brightness and the fresh cheering winds, and the general geniality of the climate give quite a different outlook on such things as illness. What little there is goes in a couple of days.'

If humour is good medicine, the Vollor home had plenty to keep it healthy and Bert loved to tease Florrie. Their daughter-in-law Olive noticed that Bert and Florrie were accustomed to being in charge and he would occasionally bark at people but the people appreciated their work. When some criticized, they responded in deep humility. Olive came across her seventy-year-old mother-in-law on her knees scrubbing the church floor with a group of African women.

After the Vollors left Uganda severe tests fell upon the church (see pp. 106ff.). Idi Amin murdered Archbishop Luwum and the bishops asked Silvanus Wani to take his place as their leader. When they all gathered in the great cathedral to celebrate Wani's appointment, he insisted on going through the ceremony with his feet bare in order to identify with Uganda's poor who were suffering deeply at that time. 'In heaven there will be no archbishops,' he would say later, 'just those who have washed their clothes in the blood of the Lamb.'[127]

The Vollors finally retired to England in 1966 but found it hard to settle. Three years later the elderly saint tumbled downstairs, fatally fracturing his skull. When the news broke in Mvara hundreds of Christians crowded into the large church which Bert had built. Rev Benoni, one of his early disciples, walked up the aisle carrying a big key and said, 'God gave the keys of heaven and hell for the whole world to Peter, but He gave the keys for West Nile to Bwana Vollor.'[128]

Seton and Peggy Maclure

During their first night at Mvara in 1942, Peggy Maclure roused her husband with an urgent summons, 'Seton, I'm being bitten.' When Seton put a cautious hand out from the protection of his mosquito net and touched the floor, pinching ants swarmed up and started consuming his flesh too. A night or two later the ceiling fell down. They found the culprits in the morning – white ants. The hungry hoard had also eaten the curtains.[129]

On Seton's first morning, Albert Vollor took him to the primary school to supervise some building. 'The best way to learn the Lugbara language is to get working with the people,' he told the young English curate, 'Get up on those rafters and show the workmen how to set the tiles in perfect line. They don't know any English but you speak in Lugbara and see what you can do.' Seton, who had never handled a tile in his life, did his best but thought he would be more at home teaching the Bible.

He was in for another surprise. Three weeks after his arrival Bert introduced him to the evangelists' school and told him to start teaching, using the Lugbara language. His first lesson was on Solomon's judgment between the two mothers who both claimed the same baby which, he wrote, 'was quite an easy story to demonstrate, so I didn't have to speak much to make the point clear.'

Toil of translation

Language fascinated him and he soon became fluent. Another missionary, Laura Belle Barr, and Seton were asked to revise the New Testament but they soon found that they needed a totally new translation. This fairly small project grew into a fifteen-year assignment to translate the whole Bible into Lugbara. The church appointed a committee to work with them. Laura Belle and Seton wrote the initial drafts but then Africans did most of the work, checking every word and phrase in long sessions together. They arranged these committees in different churches so that in the evenings, after a communal meal, they could sit around the fire to chat over the day's work with the local Christians and introduce them to scriptures they had not heard before. Stories, familiar to the missionaries from childhood, were striking their brothers for the first time. 'Stop, we can't go on,' exclaimed Noah Yii from Adja in Congo, 'This is such a wonderful verse. I have never heard it before and I want to copy it in my notebook so I can preach on it on Sunday.'

The translators needed a whole morning to wrestle with Paul's idea about shedding the earthly tent of his present body in order to get his new resurrection body (2 Corinthians 5:4). Lacking a word for tent in their language, Seton suggested a Swahili word, *hema*. They did not like it because Amin's soldiers used it.

Someone had a flash of inspiration, 'What about a snake sloughing off the old skin to reveal the shining, new skin in all its beauty?'

The Africans rejected many expressions which the missionaries had thought were straightforward. They would not permit 'pride goeth before destruction' (Proverbs 16:18, AV), because in Lugbara you must state where pride goes. A long discussion came up with, 'If you are proud, you will be destroyed'. Similarly it made no sense to tell them, 'they are dead which sought the young child's life' (Matthew 2:20, AV), for they were actually seeking his death not his life.

Upon completing the initial translation they had to read through it searching for any concept which appeared in more than one place to make sure that the translation was the same. With a sigh of relief they posted it to the Bible Society. The consultant linguists came up with many queries. After digesting these, they produced a new draft and the Society prepared proofs again.

Expectation mounted as the date for delivery of the Lugbara Bibles drew close. Before dawn on the great day, Peggy's cook hammered at their door to make his claim. A later consignment arrived during the chaotic weeks after President Amin fled the country and in time for people to carry away when they crossed the border into Zaire (former Congo) as refugees. One of the first they unpacked had a piece of shrapnel lodged in the pages.

Next Seton learnt the Alur language and plunged into more translation. As he became more and more familiar with the hazards and techniques of this task the Bible Society requested his assistance with other languages. He chaired the committees which worked through the Acholi and Lango translations in northern Uganda, Madi and Kakwa in West Nile, and Bari in Sudan. In all he shared in the production of five complete Bibles and three New Testaments.

Revival and revolt

But the Bible alone does not produce mature churches. When they first arrived, the 150 churches in West Nile impressed them. Then a prominent Christian committed adultery, another took a second wife and someone else became a notorious drunkard and they began to be cynical: surely the whole work was bad and they were wasting their time. James, in his New Testament letter, rescued them from this sort of depression with his plea, 'Let patience have her perfect work' (James 1:4, AV) and they were able to see the wonder of God's grace in planting a church at all, however weak, and in steadily leading it on. They shared the Vollors' determination to focus on teaching Christians the Bible and, in particular, training people for ordination.

As the exciting days of rapid expansion passed, a dreary formalism crept into the church to displace the Holy Spirit's vibrant leadership. In southern Uganda the Spirit swept many people into an experience of forgiveness unknown before. Suddenly the Lord Jesus became a real person and they wanted to maintain a moment by moment relationship with him which they described as 'walking in the light'. Living in this way required open confession of all sin, particularly evil attitudes towards fellow believers. As the movement gained momentum, the 'Revival Brethren' developed a style of meeting which stressed confession and the repeated singing of a chorus in the Baganda language, 'Tukutendereza Yesu', from the English,

> Glory, glory, Hallelujah;
> Glory, glory to the Lamb.
> Oh! The cleansing blood has reached me.
> Glory, glory to the lamb.

The Brethren met in enormous conventions to hear preaching which emphasized the theme of 'bending the stiff neck' of pride and being washed in the precious blood of the Saviour. Testimony was usually more important than accurate exposition and the testimony must be right up to date. Leaders would quickly discern and correct any hypocrisy.

One of the first to be touched by the movement in West Nile was young Silvanus Wani.[130] He met with a few others in church early each morning to pray that God would fill his church with the Holy Spirit. An African doctor in Arua hospital testified to a revival type of experience but felt slighted by the leaders and developed a following of his own. They soon became known as 'The Trumpeters' because they shouted denunciations at missionaries and church leaders through home-made megaphones, telling them they 'must be saved'. They accused the other Brethren of coldness and demonstrated their own zeal by leaping up and down in noisy meetings after the regular church services. Many, who had heard of the movement in the south said, 'If that is revival, we want nothing of it.'

Silvanus and his group prayed on and steadily the Trumpeters dropped away. Almost all the pastors and several missionaries found their lives deepened in some degree through the revival.

Seton and Peggy Maclure, DD

The church leaders wisely adopted the 'Tukutendereza Yesu' chorus into their repertoire and welcomed the Trumpeters into their fellowship. Thus God gave the West Nile churches three vital ingredients for mature growth – a Bible they could read, godly teachers they could understand and a living experience of their Lord. He now added a fourth – suffering.

When the Ugandan Army commander, Idi Amin, overthrew President Milton Obote in 1971, the Maclures felt relieved. Obote had threatened to withdraw missionaries' residence permits and they thought that the new leader, although nominally a Muslim, would allow more freedom. How wrong they were! No one knew who the secret police would next drag away to prison or brutal murder. The bishops paid for their courageous rebuke of the President with the bullet-pierced body of their leader, Luwum.

For eight years the economy sank. To pay his army Amin invaded Tanzania, inviting the soldiers to help themselves to all the loot they could carry. Seton and Peggy watched with sinking hearts as proud conquerors returned with lorries piled high with corrugated iron stripped from Tanzanian roofs. Retribution followed swiftly. The Tanzanian army, bolstered by Ugandan refugees who had fled to their southern neighbours for military training, swept into Kampala and on towards Arua where Amin was expected to make his last stand. On Easter Monday he fled in a small aircraft. His drunken soldiers pillaged and murdered as they tried to force the whole community to cross into Zaire.

Shells fell on Arua and Mvara during the days and bullets whistled past at night. The bishop and his staff, including Seton and Peggy, wondered if they too should leave. Some were following the Scripture Union system of daily Bible reading and came to Jeremiah chapter 42.[131] 'If you stay in this land, I will build you and not tear you down; I will plant you and not uproot you . . . Do not be afraid . . . for I am with you and will save you . . . I will show you compassion.' So the church leaders remained.

The Maclures could hear the tanks rumbling along the main road and realized the Tanzanians were close. Their hearts beat faster. They saw soldiers advancing across the field spread out in a line. Seton said to himself, 'We're in for a sticky time.' An officer came to their open door and reached out a friendly hand. Seton grasped it with relief. The men had been eating mangoes and, as each shook hands in turn with Seton, he left a smear of sticky juice. They searched the home for Amin's men and took a radio. Seton saved his watch by taping it inside an uninteresting-looking theological tome. As he washed the oily mess from his hands, Seton gratefully murmured, 'Not too sticky after all.'

The Ugandan soldiers were less friendly, being Acholi people who had suffered greatly under Amin. Because Amin had lived close to Arua, the Acholi assumed the people in West Nile were his supporters. They came repeatedly intent on looting. One night pillaging soldiers dragged the Maclures and their guest, Gail, an Australian missionary, out of bed and pushed them outside to what they assumed would be a firing line. Their house was ransacked but eventually they were permitted to return unharmed.

Another evening they heard a knock on the door. As he rose from their supper Seton muttered, 'Not another soldier at this time!' The uniformed man greeted them, 'Praise the Lord, I'm your brother in Christ.' He gave them a small tin of Nescafé he had bought at the soldiers' shop.

Worse came the next year. Wrongly thinking that the people would rise to support a rebellion, Amin's people invaded from Zaire but the National Army easily pushed them back. Then the army falsely accused the Lugbara and Kakwa of collusion and battered them with reprisals. They destroyed Arua town.

Laura Belle Barr was at her desk in her home alongside the Bible school when gunfire to the south signalled the advance of army reinforcements. Soldiers arrested her, rounded up staff, students, some primary school teachers and their older pupils and marched them off towards the school with their hands above their heads. Flames crackled and consumed teachers' villages. 'When I was almost there,' she wrote, 'a Tanzanian officer stopped me, looked at the Bible in my hand, talked to me and turned me back along with the other women and small children.'[132] They set the Alur people to one side and made the eighteen Lugbaras lie down. Soldiers lined up with their guns ready. They decided to release two ordained ministers, one of whom pleaded for the others to be spared and then dropped to his knees in prayer. The prostrate Christians sang the song of the Ugandan martyrs.

One young man, Manassi, turned his head to the lad lying beside him and asked, 'Joseph, can I be saved before I die, like the thief on the cross?' Joseph just had time to assure him that he must simply trust in Jesus. Then the bullets tore into their flesh. Joseph and Manassi survived but ten perished.

Who would dare show sympathy for the dead by burying them? A man with leprosy said, 'I'm just an old leper and it will not matter if they return to kill me for doing this.' And he dug a shallow grave for them.

Laura Belle stayed with a colleague. Soldiers, searching her empty house, claimed to find ammunition and set it alight. Laura Belle grieved over her Royal typewriter, blackened and twisted. 'At this desk and typewriter I prepared the whole Lugbara Bible manuscript between 1956 and 1963. A strange end to my thirty-six years of service in Africa . . . And why should those innocent Christians die thus, not as martyrs to the faith, but as victims of tribal hatred and revenge?'[133]

The army swarmed into Arua to pillage, burn and blow up what refused to catch fire. They set churches alight and murdered many, including Christians. Pastor Adroa ran out of his back door, with nothing but his Bible in his hand, at the same moment as soldiers burst in through the front. When he eventually met his congregation again they counted seventeen deaths.

Each morning, long before the soldiers were astir, over 150 people gathered in the large Mvara Church to pray. Throughout West Nile the churches filled. Where the buildings had disappeared they gathered under large trees. People, who had allowed their faith to slip, repented. Many trusted Christ for the first time. When people returned home and met long lost friends, they would embrace and exclaim, 'Praise the Lord, you're alive!'[134]

Ted and Muriel Williams

Chief Ajai's stomach hurt less once he started drinking the new medicine. So he walked the forty miles from his home alongside the Nile to talk to the sharp-faced doctor about another problem which he feared to share with medicine men. His fingers ran over a mass on his face, the size of an orange, and he noticed again the spongy feel of it and realized that it was getting larger, uglier and perhaps, for all he knew, threatening his life. He could feel around his muscular flank to several smaller swellings which also distressed him. The doctor explained, 'I'll stick a needle into the skin to deaden all pain and so that I can cut the lumps out.' Could he trust him? Idly he fondled the ivory rings around his arms – trophies from his hunting exploits – and asked himself why he found it easier to face an angry elephant than the surgeon's knife. Suddenly he came to a decision. 'Slaughter them,' he commanded the doctor.[135]

Ted had performed more difficult operations as an intern in London's Mildmay Mission Hospital but none as important. He was launching an ambitious health programme for West Nile's 300,000 people. He needed a notable success to establish confidence. It was not without risk. In 1941 no one knew about penicillin so infection was still the chief enemy of the surgeon. He operated in the same mud-walled hut in which he saw all his patients and dressed their many ulcers. In preparation, he and his wife Muriel (who had first caught Ted's eye above a surgical mask at Mildmay) moved out some of the furniture so that they could unfold their portable operating table and then strung up a square of cloth to protect their patient from hornets' mess which powdered the area beneath the grass roof. Muriel sterilized the instruments in a handy pressure cooker and Ted got to work. The Chief, with his contours corrected, sent a stream of patients to Mvara Hospital as it steadily enlarged over the next ten years.

Other cases were more hazardous, especially those who came late. Typical was a man with a groin swelling which suddenly became painful. His belly enlarged and he began to vomit. Anxious relatives called tribal elders who decided to test for poisoning by making many small cuts over the distended abdomen and pouring on oil. When the oil and blood mixed, froth bubbled up – a positive sign of poison. Four men carried him twenty miles in a bed. Ted recognized a strangulated hernia and, despite the poor prognosis, decided to operate. Fortunately he recovered, earning Mvara the reputation for power over poison.

Africans recognized spiritual forces at work behind all sickness and, early on, medical missionaries realized that they contended with more than microbes and masses. A real confrontation with evil powers demanded prayerful trust in their mighty God.

Christians were often severely tested. Penina, wife of Silvanus Wani, suffered from chronic dysentery and relatives administered the poison test. When she reacted positively, they insisted on taking her away from hospital to die in comfort at home. Silvanus stood firmly against them and their barrage of accusation: 'You don't care for her; you don't respect us, your relatives.' She recovered with Ted's treatment and the believers, while rejoicing in 'western medicine', chalked up another victory in the spiritual realm.

God did not immunize his servants from tragedy. Ted performed a hysterectomy on the wife of a seminary student but unexpected complications killed her a few days later. That evening, while Ted was sitting at home nursing a glum sense of failure, a wild dishevelled man wearing an ex-army greatcoat burst into the room and, pointing a spear at him, demanded to see what Ted had removed from his sister. Ted showed him the diseased organ, quietly explaining the nature of its tumour. He listened, turned on his heel and disappeared into the night. Twenty years later he walked into Ted's evening clinic and reminded Ted of that alarming night. He said, 'I intended to kill you, but God stopped me. Christ has now forgiven me for all my sins. Now will *you* forgive me?'

Even in death God gave victories to young Christians which impressed unbelieving relatives. A child died in the middle of the night and Ted tensed as he waited for the harrowing death wail but the father said, 'God has taken him' and both parents quietly bowed their heads as Ted prayed and read to them about Jesus returning with our loved ones who have 'fallen asleep in him'.

A fourteen-year-old boy called Owor told the doctor, 'I have rabies and am going to die.' Months before a mad dog had bitten him and now the scar itched and the sight of water threw him into a violent spasm. Owor continued, 'I am not afraid because

I am a Christian.' He gently comforted his distressed mother. Two weeks later he passed on.

Creative caring

After ten years in Mvara, they moved a few miles to a larger site where, in addition to 200 acres for the hospital, they managed to negotiate a further 1,000 acres for leprosy patients.[136] They came from the whole of the West Nile District to live in eighteen villages – one for each county. Ted experimented with the new drug, dapsone, and found the results exciting.

As the workload increased Ted and Muriel needed more help. His brother, Peter, joined the team and soon married another nurse, Elsie. Ted's father, a retired civil engineer offered his services just when they were developing the new hospital and leprosarium at Kuluva. So, despite a few warnings from some colleagues that the work was becoming too much a one-family affair, the elderly Mr and Mrs Williams added a precious dimension of practical skill and spiritual maturity. Missionary nurses came as well. All the time they emphasized the need to train Africans.

Eriamu was a typical trainee. He walked twenty miles to apply for a job as a carpenter and built a little round hut of mud, wattle and grass for his wife and two babes. He graduated onto the wards, became a nursing aide and was still on the staff forty-two years later. Daniel Biaka earned a few cents by carrying water to the doctor's house in Mvara. He and his wife moved with the team to Kuluva and both found work in the new hospital. Forty years later he was working as the hospital evangelist. Owing to the educational foresight of the Vollors, secondary school graduates went on to study nursing and some became doctors. Whenever they came home Kuluva gave them a warm welcome so that, after the Williams families left, much of the health care passed into the hands of Ugandans.

Life always brought a busy variety. Morning would find them walking around the wards and out-patients, working in the hospital office, often operating or visiting the leprosy villages. Afternoons were for more mundane tasks: puddling mud to make mortar, clambering onto roof timbers to nail on iron sheets or rebuilding the hospital generator. Evening might involve a Bible study, sometimes interrupted by an emergency operation. They shared their father's flair for innovation. Ted mastered the art of making false teeth and artificial eyes. He fitted his first plastic eye into a boy's empty socket. On the road home people stopped

Kuluva Hospital, Uganda, CM

him, tipped up his chin to have a good look and asked, 'Can he see with it?'

Ted struggled with himself. Shortage of money, which later on became an exciting challenge to faith, used to depress him in the early days. How could he build a hospital estimated to cost £3,000 on an income of £16 a month? Had he and Muriel made a mistake in joining a mission which did not appreciate the cost? When the move to Kuluva was imminent, the AIM British Council advised delay and Ted wrote a hasty letter to the godly Secretary, D.M. Miller, in which he sarcastically misquoted Nehemiah's statement, 'And the rulers knew not whither I went, or what I did.' He admitted, 'I was rather too aggressive and critical in pushing ahead with developments . . . trying the patience of fellow missionaries.' Matters became worse when the Maclures went home leaving him as the senior missionary. 'It was a very bad year when I made many bad mistakes and antagonized some of the recently arrived missionaries.' But he maintained his early morning hour of prayer and Bible study. Moreover revival was in the air for any questioning soul. He could write, 'Such things I am ashamed of now and pray that the Lord will forgive me.'

Ted and Muriel never doubted the need to relate health care to Christian witness. God called them to proclaim good news,

Ted and Muriel Williams, DD

especially to the poor, and they seized every opportunity to read the Bible to patients in private or to preach in public. They exulted in the evangelistic opportunity of caring for people in hospital and trained their staff to see that the Lord's compassion sought spiritual transformation as well as physical healing. They proclaimed Christ by the way they lived as much as by what they said. They insisted, 'Our witness is enhanced by the best possible medical service.' After Ted had performed a Caesarean section in the middle of the night, Muriel counted all the blood-stained gauze packs and missed one. Although Ted was certain he had not left it inside the patient reluctantly he opened her up again but found nothing. Finally they located it by lamplight at the bottom of a rubbish pit, where it had been thrown with the afterbirth, and Ted clambered down to retrieve it. Only then could they go to their beds.

Expulsion and progress

Amin, playing on the popular nationalistic sentiments, expelled all the Asian people. At this one stroke Uganda lost half its medical practitioners and every pharmacist. As relationships between Britain and Uganda worsened in the light of Amin's brutalities it became clear that the missionaries could be the next to leave. They organized a Board of Governors, chaired by the

113

bishop, to ensure that the service would continue. Missionaries exercised great care in all they said because Government informants quickly twisted anything into a seditious statement. Arua school went on strike. Tension mounted as the British refused to allow the President to attend the Queen's 25th anniversary celebrations in London.

Family reasons forced Peter and Elsie to leave after twenty-six years working alongside Ted and Muriel. Ted, the only doctor now, slipped on one of his ward rounds and felt his thigh snap. Archbishop Wani persuaded President Amin to rescind his order forbidding all flights into Arua so that the Flying Doctor plane could evacuate Ted. By this time he had trained the staff to diagnose and treat half of all the patients attending hospital and had laid in supplies sufficient for two years. Although he was eventually able to return, it was only for a short period.

In the troubles that engulfed Uganda after the Williams' left in May 1979, Kuluva hospital never closed. When the dust of war settled, the African governors insisted that it was a vital part of the church's ministry. They recruited Ugandan doctors and nurses, initiated a vigorous programme of modernization and invited AIM to send people to join the team in a real partnership under African direction.

7
Growth and crisis in Congo

Earl and Helena Dix

Earl stumbled into the mission through a misunderstanding. Soon after his arrival at Chicago's Moody Bible Institute he was shocked to hear that a bank back home in Nebraska had failed, swallowing all his slender savings. The College accountant kindly arranged for him to earn his fees by scrubbing floors. Night after night, as he carried his broom and bucket around the huge building, he passed a picture of an African homestead on an office wall. In an idle moment he nodded towards it and said to his colleague, 'Maybe some day I'll go to Africa and see a village like that.'

His fellow student, an accepted candidate for the AIM, quickly urged him to meet the AIM committee chairman in Chicago. By mistake the chairman thought Earl had applied to join AIM and he was interviewed as a missionary candidate. The chairman, realizing his mistake, thrust some forms across the desk to Earl and said; 'If you want to be a missionary you should fill out these papers.' An impulse prodded Earl; 'I felt so uneasy,' he wrote later; 'I had to fill out the form, even though I had no intention of going overseas.'

At the end of his first year in Chicago Earl clattered home in the train with his mind far from Africa. The young farmer was praying about a pretty teacher, Helena Sieler, who had already completed two years' study at Moody.

They started dating and the excitement of falling in love put AIM out of his mind until an official letter from the mission jolted him. AIM welcomed him as a new member. He reacted, 'I was stunned. My life was taking a direction I didn't want it to go.'[137] The mission office wrote again two weeks later to say that a New York business man had promised to provide all his financial needs; in fact, they added, 'he is anxious to have you on the field as soon as possible.'

What about Helena? Would she marry him with all that missionary commitment might involve? She anticipated the twin challenge by praying for God's direction over several weeks. When he asked the crucial question, she answered with an unequivocal yes. In three months he swung from uncertainty about marriage and indifference about mission to an assurance that 'God had unmistakably called us and we were going in obedient response to that call.' They knew so little about AIM and Africa that Earl confessed, 'Helena and I had to be the greenest missionaries who had ever gone.' On 26 October 1929 they walked up the gangway of the SS *Milwaukee* in New York as an engaged couple on their way to Congo.

They might have been ignorant at the start but they were eager to learn. Mission policy required a lengthy period of language study and orientation before an engaged couple, coming fresh to Africa, could marry. Earl felt privileged to share the home of the Congo Director, George van Dusen. George taught well and his pupil quickly grasped the principles under which AIM established churches.

Although the local congregation looked back on many years of growth, the missionary still played the leading role as teacher and pastor. Like his 200 colleagues in the mission, George determined to develop a pure church through faithful instruction supported by diligent discipline.

George conducted Earl and Helena's wedding on New Year's Day 1931 and, a few months later, accompanied them far west to an unreached section of the Azande people. They approached a huge symmetrical mound, visible fifteen miles across the plain, called Banda. Clambering through the forest which clothed Banda Hill, they saw houses and gardens everywhere and decided to make it their new home.

Friends, fears and fortitude

Nearly twenty years had passed since John Stauffacher and his party had first made contact with the Azande at Dungu but these

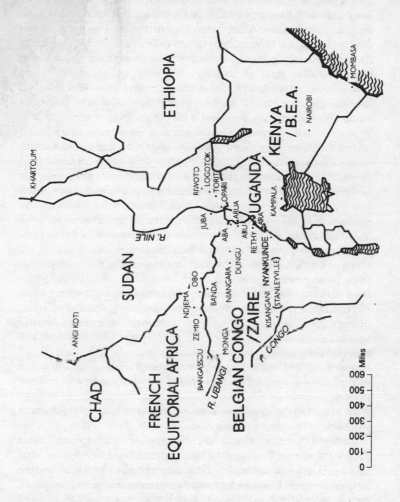

Central Africa

generous-hearted people still showed little interest in the Gospel. As Earl and Helena sat on low stools around the village fires in the evenings and struggled to pick up the difficult language, they began to understand the awesome fears which gripped the minds behind their smiling faces. If someone became sick, it must be the result of sorcery and the witch must be hunted until discovered and purged. Ancestors, reincarnated in a forest animal like the eland or the red boar, must be honoured. Bengi was a vine which crept along the ground, passing under all obstacles in its path. He had become a silent god who could get to the bottom of any problem you might encounter.

A more serious menace, Mangu, resided in a person's belly, appearing when the possessor was angry or jealous to burn a house down, to call elephants into a garden, or even to kill. Earl knew villagers who had arrested a suspected host, split open his belly and found a finger-sized recession alongside the small intestine where Mangu dwelt. Until indicted in this way the accused was unaware of any supernatural powers.

The Azande perceived all foreigners as cannibals. From time immemorial marauders from other tribes took captives and ate them. Then the Arabs came to chain slaves together and march the columns away – obviously to the same fate. Finally the white man arrived. Earl describes a typical reaction of a young man who pointed to the lush peaches on the label of a tin of fruit, 'That's what's in there, isn't it?' Earl had to agree. Pointing to the sleek man featured on a Quaker Oats carton, he announced, 'White man in there', and, before Earl could respond, he indicated the robust figure of a black woman on a sack of Aunt Jemima Pancake flour; 'Now look at this . . . Black person!'

In the early days Earl and Helena were careful in their message, 'We knew their beliefs were false, but we also discovered that they would not believe us if we told them.' And they were wary of hastily proclaiming judgment to a fear-ridden society. They started with a determined bid to befriend people in their homes. Long treks took them to distant villages, where they avoided formal meetings but simply sat with the people, listened and, eventually, reasoned with them about God's offer of forgiveness and a new heart, free from fear.

Slowly people responded. When a member of a secret society called Bili died, his family refused to bury him. They explained; 'For one who is not Bili to bury a Bili is enough to bring a curse that would cause his death.' Some new Christians volunteered and, when Earl asked why they were unafraid to bury a Bili, they told him; 'But you don't understand. We are Christians. If we should die, we will go to heaven and that will be much better than living here.'

Through divination a man near Banda reckoned that a Christian named Kuraboroyo was having an affair with his wife and determined to destroy him through black magic. Three times he tried, using more powerful spells each time, and they all failed. Totally defeated he told the chief; 'I've tried everything but God has protected Kuraboroyo. Nothing has an effect on him.'

Chief Mboli could not have been pleased to hear of such spiritual protection for he felt threatened by the power of Christ. As long as he gave due deference to a remote Belgian official, his position gave him a dictator's control over the land as well as everything that moved on it or grew out of it. So when Earl needed fifty workmen to assist in building a house and a road, he had to apply to this potentate. Mboli was too wise a politician to say no. To their surprise Earl gave his labourers a salary and two hours of school every day.

Chief Mboli subtly visited the Belgian, to tell him that the mission had become a haven for criminals. He asked permission to take action against them. Arriving at Banda in the middle of the night with a force of seventy-five 'soldiers', he arrested the men and demanded that they leave their new employer. His soldiers punished each of them with twelve strokes of a hippo-hide whip.

Next day Mboli angrily asked them again if they wished to continue working for the white man on the hill, 'Do you believe his God is greater than me, Mboli?' Twenty-five men survived a daily beating on their naked buttocks for eight days, emerging with hideously infected lacerations to continue their work and their studies, and eventually to become the core leaders of the Zande churches.

Mboli knew that Earl would soon go home to America. He boasted about the coming revenge against his rebels once the protection of the white man was withdrawn. Meanwhile the missionaries prayed for the infant church and held out a hand of friendship to their opponent. Sickness struck him. In fear of evil spirits he fled at night to Banda, where, in a whisper which later reverberated throughout his realm, he said to his son; 'I am safe here. They can't touch me here on the hill.' He died a few days later.

Mboli's son, Solo, established a friendship with Earl and

Helena which endured through his thirty-year reign. His own son and grandson maintained the tradition. Earl wrote; 'All of them have come to us for advice and counsel, much as a son would come to his father.'

Skill and stamina

Understandably the Azande respected Earl and Helena as their spiritual parents. With his fluency in the language and understanding of their ways, they told Earl that he was a Zande himself. His talent as an evangelist resulted in a network of schools and churches. He travelled widely, shepherding raw believers and encouraging new leaders. His greatest sorrow was the spiritual bondage of the Azande and his greatest joy was their deliverance. He also grieved over sickness, poverty, hunger and ignorance. He spent his fifty-four years in Africa pitting his alert mind and immense skills against these ills. He built the first AIM secondary school in Zaire, drilled wells in South Sudan, erected a power line for the important health care programme at Nyankunde and fostered a trade in a local root with valuable medicinal properties.

Helena shared his safari ministry despite having five children, travelling in a chair borne by four men. When the motor era arrived, she often needed to drive across two logs forming a bridge over a swirling river. Unable to see the wooden trunks beneath, she fixed her eyes on her husband ahead as he pointed the way.

Earl's homecall came in 1985 and Helena's the following year. Tributes poured in. One missionary said, 'Earl perfected the art of getting things done through people.' Several commented on the lifelong romance between the couple and remembered that, as an old man, Earl often spoke about their wedding and said, 'We've been on our honeymoon ever since.'

Carl and Marie Becker

Few succeeded so well in 'getting things done through people' as Carl and Marie Becker. As a twenty-two-year-old clerk in a Pennsylvanian iron foundry with only a few dollars to his name, Carl had no idea of the consequences as he rashly knelt beside his bed and prayed, 'Lord, if you help me to become a doctor, I will give you everything.'[138]

God answered Carl Becker by strengthening his small body so that he was able to work in a soda fountain from 6 p.m. until midnight while keeping abreast with a full university programme. Soon after President Wilson brought America into the war in 1917, Carl enlisted in a medical reserve corps. The government allowed him to continue his studies at their expense, providing free accommodation and issuing him with a uniform.

Carl still wore his army shoes when he finished his studies three years after the armistice. As he approached the graduation ceremony he thought his mother and sister would feel ashamed if he appeared in his old army shoes and shabby clothes. He told a friend, 'I just sat down and asked God about it.' Five cheques arrived in the mail and he received his degree wearing a new suit, new shirt, new tie and new shoes. Prayer for provision of his material needs became a principle which stuck.

Early in his student days he wrote about a schoolteacher with dark brown hair, 'I was attracted to Marie . . . perhaps because of her evident interest in knowing and doing God's will', but he felt he had to warn her about his promise to God, 'I don't know if it means I'll go to China or Africa as a missionary or what. But he has first claim to my life.'

Marie waited through his long years of study and into his early months of practice in Boyertown. They married in September 1922 and, by the time little Mary arrived a year later, the reputation of the young doctor had spread widely. Ever since his father's death eighteen years previously the Becker family had tasted poverty; now, at last, he could relieve his mother's financial distress.

A letter from AIM made him uneasy for a few days. Hurlburt, whom Carl knew from his student days, wrote to friends of the Mission to tell them of the sudden death in Aba of his daughter-in-law, Dr Elizabeth Hurlburt. Who would replace her? Carl replied that his responsibility to his mother prevented his going.

The practice boomed. Becker hired a physician, two nurses and a secretary. He installed an X-ray machine and a laboratory. Boyertown citizens talked of building him a hospital. Hurlburt got in touch again. Once more he turned from the challenge, but not without a niggle of conscience for now he could provide for his mother for the rest of her life.

That niggle kept troubling him, especially as he met with God day by day. 'Marie,' he said one morning, 'I think God wants us to be missionaries, but I don't know exactly what to do about it.' She suggested contacting Hurlburt, who urged them to get to Africa as soon as possible. They sold the practice and home and placed all the money in trust for his mother's use. With a wife and two children to support he turned his back on an annual income of $10,000 for an uncertain monthly allowance of sixty. Their perplexity increased when they heard too late of Charles Hurlburt's resignation from AIM. Instead of being members of AIM as they had thought, they had joined Hurlburt's fledgling Unevangelized Africa Mission.

'Any person is precious'

Charles' eldest son, Paul, led ten missionaries to Belgian Congo the year before the Beckers arrived. To accommodate the new family, Paul added two rooms to his own house, so small that, when they had squeezed their four camp cots into the bedroom, the only way to get into bed was by clambering over the foot. Mud walls were still wet. In answer to Marie's question about her kitchen, Paul told her it was behind the house. She whispered to her husband, 'I looked and all I saw were three large stones.' 'That's your kitchen Marie,' Carl replied.

Marie was not the only one to acquire new talents. In Boyertown Carl always referred patients requiring major operations to the trained surgeons. When a frightened Congolese woman showed him her painful hernia, he knew that her life depended on his own untried skill with the scalpel. Marie scrubbed the Hurlburts' kitchen table and swept the manure-plastered floor. They held hands to pray. Marie administered her first anaesthetic. Saucer-eyed relatives, crowding the doorway, watched Carl incise the skin and perform the delicate repair. Despite Marie remonstrating with her in the pouring rain the patient ran home that night. He must have sewn her up well for she made a good recovery.

Carl was puzzled by the anomaly of two missions working side by side to accomplish the same goals. He wrote, 'Added to the difficulties of living was my own unhappiness at finding ourselves in a splinter group.' He urged Paul to seek reconciliation with AIM but without success. Two years after their arrival in Congo the Beckers transferred to their original mission, AIM. But fellowship was not severed. For the rest of his life Carl was ready to serve the UAM clinic when they needed his help.

For the next few years Carl and Marie worked in the two AIM hospitals, Rethy and Aba. From each of these they supervised a network of small clinics. So Carl quickly got to know the whole area served by the mission. Impressed by the immense medical needs, he realized that they could only be met by training Africans.

The local people often called the tribal dentist to deal with rotting teeth. Using a chisel he tapped the tooth on each side until it was loose enough for him to pick out with his fingers. Carl found that he could teach his illiterate African assistants to become adept in the use of dental forceps. A simple training programme brought relief to thousands of sufferers.

The principle of multiplying his effectiveness through developing the skills of others served him well when he was asked to open a hospital at Oicha, in the dark, steamy forest, 200 miles south of Rethy. Patients of all races soon converged on the clearing. The hospital grew so that by 1941, 1,989 major operations had taken place. The 102 leprosy patients rocketed to 3,315 in a dozen years[139] making Oicha the largest leprosarium in Africa.

The Beckers and their small group of missionary colleagues could only cope with the crowds by delegating the straightforward diagnosis, treatment and care to trusted Africans. By this time the developing school system provided him with staff who could just read. He tried to make time each day to instruct them. 'As a teacher Dr Becker was a strange amalgam of infinite patience, inveterate optimism and nearly impossible standards.'[140] Over and over he insisted that 'any person is precious in the sight of the Lord.' Students must learn that God valued an alien tribesman, an insignificant pygmy or a filthy pauper enough to send his Son to die for them. At the same time he would not allow a brand of medicine in Oicha which he would be ashamed to practise in Philadelphia.

A visiting mission leader was surprised to see a nurse from his own area. 'He had a bad reputation – insolent, surly and you couldn't trust him out of your sight,' he told Becker. 'Maybe so,' the doctor murmured, 'but he's one of our most trusted staff members now.' The leader called him over to ask him how he changed. The African hesitated and then answered, 'Many missionaries preached Jesus Christ to me, but in the Munganga (Doctor) I saw him.'

This hard-working doctor who began each day at 5 a.m. with an hour of personal prayer and Bible study, seemed austere to some. But his colleagues recognized his quick sense of humour. A patient, coming round from anaesthesia, demanded a fee for allowing the doctor to remove his tumour. Reaching for his scalpel Becker replied, 'Very well, I'll put it back.'

Although he acknowledged that others could preach better than himself, he set an example by sharing the news of Christ as he moved around the wards during the week and visited the villages on Sunday. Nothing thrilled him more than to hear of people turning to Christ after listening to a staff member or a chaplain. To some who felt that AIM should not expend precious resources on health care he pointed out that it was 'an essential outworking of love'. He could certainly see how his ministry broke up the soil for the gospel seed. But he watched God accomplish more: hundreds of needy people from far away heard the message every day and experienced the healing touch of God; believers in the wards, the staff houses and the leprosy settlements grew in their faith and some were already mature in leadership roles in both church and hospital.

Could AIM depend upon the leaders' maturity? In the mid fifties Congo was seething with change and increasingly radical expectations. Some were demanding better education, higher wages, more leadership, even self-rule in the state and in the churches. As the mission leaders met, Dr Becker counselled, 'I think it would be a good idea to set a time limit on the number of years we should give ourselves to get out of Congo and leave a strong established national church to carry on.' Few agreed.

Becker himself could not be sure. He watched the Oicha Church grow until, by 1958, 1,350 baptized members worshipped in the simple building. Masses more crowded into

Oicha Church, Zaire, CM

thirty smaller district churches to listen to several gifted evangelists and teachers. But he remembered many fallen believers, overcome usually by immorality or theft. When he heard Christians criticize wrong attitudes in certain missionaries, he wondered if the complaints arose from carnal jealousy or from godly concern.

Pastor Zefania prayed in the Oicha church, 'Lord we're standing at the door of independence and we don't know what is on the other side.' Less stable people looked forward to an era of free education in the schools, free treatment in the hospitals and free money in the banks. Many failed to dig their gardens believing that the government would distribute free food.

On New Year's Day 1960 Carl read, 'Do not be afraid. Stand firm and you will see the deliverance the Lord will bring you today.' He made it his verse for the year.[141] Excitement mounted as the great day, June 30th, approached. The doctor quietly arranged for Africans to take over the Management Committee of Oicha Hospital.

Missionaries go: Africans grow

Following the advice of the British Government AIM decided to cross over into Uganda until the danger of possible violence passed. But many, including the Oicha team, were reluctant. Yonama, the senior African on the staff, rounded up some newly-appointed government officials to persuade the team that they could safely remain. Seven months later another scare forced Carl to hand over to Yonama and head for Uganda. Although a number of vehicles got across the border, Becker's was halted and he agreed to return, recognizing that God wanted him to remain.

Once the dust of these two evacuations settled everyone acknowledged that old patterns must change. 'Mission and Church came together in a new way, though awkwardly at first for both,' Carl wrote. They held joint sessions on all matters of common interest, such as the assignment of missionaries, and a new spirit of brotherhood developed. Africans balked at some of the responsibilities thrust upon them; they complained, 'Mnatupa sisi (You are throwing us away)'. Years later they 'thanked us for having forced them into positions of authority and value.'[142]

In the medical work more and more patients came as the government health care facilities collapsed. Scarce supplies taught the workers to pray for such practical needs as penicillin and cotton wool. Dr Becker heaped responsibilities on Yonama's shoulders and found him increasingly capable. The Africans on the committee handled finances, personnel and sensitive problems with patients. Meanwhile storm clouds gathered once again.

Disillusioned with the national leaders of Zaire (formerly Congo), young people gathered in rebel bands, proudly calling themselves 'Simba – The Lions'. Communists skilfully organized them into an effective fighting force which depended on witchcraft and terror. Carl Becker listened with horror to tales of rape and murder wherever they went. At last he thought it was time to leave. To the question, could the church stand on its own feet he replied, 'For the past four years we've been living on borrowed time here. If the church isn't ready now, it never will be.'

The Simba tide swept closer. This time Yonama pleaded with government officials to let the Oicha missionaries depart. He knew that their presence would only add to the dangers for the African Christians. He and Benjamina, who had already been trained in some surgical procedures, took over for a time until Yonama too had to flee for his life.

Apart from one couple, Charles and Muriel Davis, trapped in distant Stanleyville, all the AIM folk crossed Zaire's eastern border. While most continued into Kenya, the Beckers located Yonama and many of their old staff in south Uganda. They started work at Kagando in a collection of abandoned huts which once housed leprosy sufferers.

When the Beckers returned to Oicha, they found Benjamina and his colleagues running the hospital. Benjamina complained of a smaller patient load, 'Only about 500 to 600 a day now'. More important to Carl was the state of the church. How had it held up to torture and persecution? Zefania beamed, 'Many of our members were lukewarm but the Simba growled so loud that they became afraid and got on fire for God again.'[143]

Carl and Marie decided against settling again in Oicha. Yonama clearly could run a hospital and Benjamina had saved a person from a strangulated hernia. Carl was sure these successes could be multiplied many times to provide a wide service for suffering people in Zaire. He recalled talks before the evacuation with doctors and leaders from several societies about pooling resources in a large training hospital which would provide a stream of well-qualified health care workers for the five million people of north-east Zaire. They would refer difficult cases to the well equipped Centre. Now was the time to realize the dream.

The group met again and selected the Brethren centre of Nyankunde. The Missionary Aviation Fellowship based a small Cessna aircraft there and supervised a strip. Earl Dix found the source of a water supply and later laid on electricity. Helen Roseveare of the Worldwide Evangelization Crusade took the lead in the training school and the group asked Carl to be the first Director. In his seventies now, he travelled widely to get the project launched.

Carl Becker, DD

No one was surprised when a heart paroxysm forced him to leave his car and lie at the roadside for two hours while Marie sat anxiously beside him. He survived to continue his heavy schedule. Told by one of his nurses that he ought to be in bed, he replied, 'If this is to be my last day on earth, I certainly don't want to spend it in bed.'

The pace was telling on Marie too. For years arthritis forced her to wear a leg brace and now her spine was complaining. At the age of eighty-one they decided that their continued stay in Africa could cause problems to their fellow missionaries. As their light aircraft lifted off from Nyankunde on 5 May 1976 they looked down for the last time on a medical centre staffed by seven highly qualified doctors, six dedicated nurses from overseas, a training school for nurses and midwives and an efficient pharmacy. In their minds' eye they could see masses of Zairois people gathering at eight hospitals and sixty rural dispensaries, all linked by radio and plane to Nyankunde. With joy in their hearts they knew that five church/mission groups were working together to ensure that all these people would receive good health care as well as the message of God's grace. They rejoiced to hear of the appointment of African Medical Directors for both Nyankunde and Oicha soon after they left.

Vera Thiessen was one of many missionary nurses whose awe for Dr Becker turned to loving respect. She would often call him to cases at night and then find difficulty in getting back to sleep, concerned lest the night nurse fail to care for the patient. Even if she had to tap on the doctor's bedroom window three times in a night, she would always find him asleep. 'How can you do that?' she asked. 'Vera,' he replied, 'If I have done my very best before God, then why should I lie awake?' They flew to Pennsylvania knowing that God had enabled them to do their best and now they could confidently leave the outcome to him.

David and Joyce Richardson

David and Joyce Richardson knew Carl Becker from their childhood. When they completed their education in the early fifties and returned to Congo as missionaries, their respect for the hard-working doctor grew. But they valued him most as their Field Director at independence when the whole AIM team looked to him to resolve the issue of evacuation. The missionaries talked regularly on the radio net. David and Joyce would switch on, apprehensive of approaching danger and listen to his quiet voice as he summed up the situation throughout the mission's area; 'You would leave the radio feeling calm; that all would be well for the Lord was with us.'[144]

David and Joyce shared Becker's burden for developing African leadership skills. David, in particular, used his London Bible College training in theology to train pastors and evangelists for the maturing church and the brother and sister both exercised a wide ministry of Bible teaching.

The youngest church planter

Joyce was the elder and began her church planting ministry on the day of her birth in 1926. Her parents had struggled for two disappointing years to persuade the Kakwa to abandon their little grass spirit huts and turn to Christ. The Kakwa regarded them and their message as irrelevant . . . until they heard the electrifying news of the birth of a white baby. Soon the whole community seemed to be gathering round the thatched home and little Joyce could get no time to sleep. 'Come to the house of God on Sunday,' decreed her father, 'and you will be allowed to see her after the service.'[145]

At sunrise on Joyce's first Sunday in Adi, hundreds of people converged on the mud chapel along the winding paths. For several Sundays crowds swarmed to Adi, some from twenty miles away; they listened in church and then peered at Joyce. When the novelty of the baby wore off the crowds continued to throng in, drawn by a message which spoke to their deep needs.

Joyce and her younger brother David grew up and returned to the Congo as missionaries. David learnt to preach to Africans in the rough and tumble of church life in Aru. The Aru church, increasingly confident in a world of changing expectations, appreciated their missionary founders but resented their continuing control.

Feelings came to a head when the Belgian Government instituted a minimum wage for all workers. On the whole missionary incomes were low (although immeasurably higher than African wages) and missionaries often financed much of the work they developed. They assumed that pastors, evangelists, teachers and household servants would likewise be content with a lower salary than their contemporaries. In any case, the 'faith policy' prevented them promising a fixed wage.

The Africans ignored the enigma of the faith policy and focused on lifestyle. They reasoned (as others have argued since), 'How could there be such a great difference in the standards of living if the white man did not misappropriate the funds that were earmarked for African advancement?'

The Government agreed that, because the mission was not a profit-making organization, their workers could sign a statement waiving their right to the minimum wage. When this arrangement was explained to the Africans, suspicions mounted. Unfamiliar with the western concept of a signature guaranteeing a contract, they asked, 'Is it not the white man's ruse to deny our rights?'

A Belgian sat on the verandah of a mission house in Aru to talk to all the African workers. He asked the two pastors, 'Are you going to sign?' They answered, 'No.' 'Then you are dismissed.' Over a hundred district teachers lost their jobs. When David preached in church on a subsequent Sunday, cries of . . . 'We don't want a white man to teach us' shouted him down.

The Central Church Council sent a largely African delegation to mediate but Aru Christians refused to welcome them. Hostility displaced hospitality. Contrary to all their traditions they offered neither food nor fellowship. The central leaders decided that all the missionaries should leave Aru and wondered if the work would collapse.

But the disturbances were growing pains. Aru became the model church outstripping all others in their giving and progress. Thirty years later David preached to thousands at their

Adi Bible School, CM

convention and felt a throb of spiritual life. He visited their Bible school to talk to 100 students.

When he had to leave Aru, David moved to his old home, Adi, to a heavy teaching load in the Bible school. Joyce, enjoying her work among girls at another centre, Todro, did not feel as lonely as her brother.

Looking back David says, 'Single ladies have a difficult task but the missionary bachelor's life is harder. You have your own turmoils within and keep wondering if the Lord has someone for you.' At missionary conferences he knew that many were watching to see if he chatted to any young woman. Every conversation was noticed and normal friendships became impossible, isolating him more than ever. Well-meaning friends would tell him he ought to get married. One twisted the knife in an already painful wound at the end of a conference. 'David, think of me. I'm going back to be welcomed by a wife and you're returning to an empty house and a cold bed. Don't you envy me?'

'You must leave at once'

Anti-white rhetoric spread as the country tottered towards independence in a haze of euphoria. Communist youth, recruiting heavily in the schools, fed their followers on propaganda. They accused a missionary of saying, 'The white man is the head; the black man is the tail and it will never be any different.' People marched around missionary homes and sometimes threw stones through windows.

Independence Day was set for 30 June, 1960. Adi church elders sent two men to guard each missionary's house during the night. A Belgian official stayed with him but trusted no African. He told David, 'I have a sub-machine-gun and a revolver. If anyone approaches the house, I'll fire.' David expected the red youth to march and prayed for rain to thwart their plans. God answered with a deluge, which only lifted in time for the church service.

The missionaries invited the Belgian to church to hear their old friend, Pastor Akudri, boldly thank God for all the colonizers had done. A week later troops in a camp 150 miles away rioted and started moving towards Adi causing mission leaders to order everyone to leave. David collected Joyce from Todro and they drove across the border into Uganda. In five weeks the situation settled enough for them to return, but only for a while.

Civil war engulfed Kivu Province to the south. In January David took in a new class of evangelists. On his radio he listened to the Baptist missionaries far to the south debate the dangers and finally decide to evacuate. The American Consul in Kampala broke into the network to urge all remaining missionaries to follow their example. A new voice broke in, 'This is "X-ray",' he said mysteriously, 'I have clear information that serious action against whites is planned in the next 48 hours. You must leave at once.' 'X-ray', David discovered years later, was an amateur radio buff who had intercepted a call from Moscow to the ousted President, Lumumba, advising him to start killing all white people.

They set out again to Aru and had completed all the formalities for crossing the border when drunken soldiers drove up in a lorry and announced, 'You don't move an inch forward or backward or we shoot.' They later allowed them to return to Adi. On their third attempt they managed to get into Uganda through another crossing point.

David returned to his students in a few weeks. When the Simba prowled in 1964, he and Joyce were in England with their sick parents. Joyce stayed to care for them leaving David to return to Africa alone in 1965 for a stint of ten years in the Scott Theological College at Machakos. Then, with Joyce released by the death of both parents, they represented the mission to the

British churches in a roving commission based on London, returning in 1981 to Adi for a final decade of African service together.

A confident denomination welcomed them. Thanks to the foresight of their parents, Carl Becker and many others, the Church achieved autonomy before national independence. The storm which followed swept away any remaining reliance on the parent mission. After the Simba menace died the church leaders invited missionaries back on condition that they would now work under African leadership. David and Joyce felt privileged.

They devoted themselves to training pastors in the Bible school and encouraging them later when they went out into their church assignments. David was asked to preach at huge conferences but they enjoyed more their visits to the villages when they could spend three days in prayer and Bible study. As understanding dawned, women prayed with tears, sometimes of repentance and often of gratitude. After a discussion of James' teaching about the tongue, an old man spoke to God, 'Lord, if we could not see it with our own eyes in the book here, we'd think people had been telling tales about us.'

David and Joyce longed that more would 'see it with their own eyes'. Instead of discussion, students wanted lectures: 'We've come here to be taught, not to give our own ideas.' David reckoned, 'Some have the idea that you open the flap, push in information and shut it down again.' Senior men resisted attempts to update the curriculum, 'The first missionaries did it like this and we should not change.'

In the midst of massive multiplication of churches they recognized danger signals. CECA[146] inherited the AIM system of committee leadership. Gifted preachers travelled slowly, sometimes for hundreds of miles, to attend meetings. They would be called away from a fruitful ministry of Bible teaching in the local church to attend weddings, funerals, school functions, etc. and the pressures of administration swallowed their days. If they opted out they would appear either proud or uncaring. David, on the other hand, equipped men for the pulpit by emphasizing time in personal prayer and study.

In most societies autocratic chiefs ruled. The new church communities often looked to their senior pastor to adopt a similar role. Local people became unwilling to take action without direction from the top – even for choice of Bible passages to study in a conference or a day of prayer. For a time respected elders squashed young visionaries graduating from Bible College, calling them 'children' and dismissing their initiatives as 'title seeking'. In the nineties massive growth in the congregations brought these younger preachers their opportunity.

But David and Joyce enjoyed this bumper harvest from afar for arthritis in Joyce's knees sentenced her to surgery in London. The babe whose birth first sparked the Adi church learnt to work hard on those knees throughout her life. Her brother, living with Joyce in Britain, reckoned that God's Spirit sets fire to the work of missionaries as they concentrate on Bible study and prayer 'as a personal, group and church priority'.

Yoane and Maria Akudri

A tall African, weeping without shame, caught the attention of gravediggers in a London cemetery. Surprise turned to embarrassment when his voice boomed out in a strange language and the Londoners realized he was praying. They stopped digging, took off their caps and bowed their heads. 'Oh Nzambe (God) . . . Oh Nzambe,' cried the elderly man from Zaire, 'You remember how this man taught me to pray – Mericee! Mericee!'[147]

Yoane Akudri's memory flashed back forty-five years when he was cook to the Richardsons' parents, Ken and Dorothy, in Adi. Hearing that Ken visited a little hut near his home every day and behaved strangely, Akudri hid behind an anthill to watch. He saw his dignified employer fall on his knees with a groan and call out to Nzambe. Sweat poured from the missionary as he lifted his arms in intercession. Akudri could not understand the English but repeatedly caught the name, Kakwa, and knew Ken was pleading with God for his tribe.

They first met in 1925 when Akudri worked for Ralph Davis, pioneer to the Kakwa. Ralph handed the embryonic work over to Ken and then left to commence a new ministry among the Azande, taking Akudri with him for six months. Akudri came home looking for more work and Ken asked about his experience of Christ.

Saved to serve

Akudri told him that, at a time of drought, a dreadful plague broke out, called 'the Walking Sickness' because it spread so rapidly from house to house. It walked into his family home to steal his two brothers, sister and parents. The disease struck

Akudri. The strapping young teenager came so close to death that relatives kept the last grave open, planning to drop him in when his time arrived. But he cheated the grim invader, convincing villagers that the spirits decreed some important leadership position for him, perhaps even the village chieftainship. As he grew into manhood his fine physique and stentorian voice qualified him for the post of Leader of the Dance.

Ralph and Ellen Davis fascinated Akudri. They offered to teach him to read and write and to tell him more from their book. Soon they convinced him that he needed to trust Nzambe's Son to save him from the power of evil spirits which terrorized the Kakwa world. When his cousin died, an uncle asked him to participate in the sacrifices ordered by the witch doctor and to lead the dancing. Akudri refused saying, 'All my life I have believed as you do but now I know Yesu Kristo and can no longer take part in these practices.' The witch doctor attacked him with a sharp knife but fell powerless in a frenzied convulsion. Akudri, with his faith fortified, asked to be baptized in the first group of four Kakwa believers. He selected a new Bible name for himself, Yoane (John).

He worked in the Richardson home and used all his spare time in visiting the surrounding villages to call people to turn from their evil ways to the Lord Jesus. Then Joyce was born and Ken needed help in preaching to the throng coming to church. Ken set out to develop Akudri's powerful voice and eager personality in the service of God. He often invited his disciple for a day of prayer far from the people.

Ken Richardson determined to establish a church rooted in the Kakwa people and to do this recognized the need for Kakwa leaders. A first step was to appoint elders to decide church issues – placement and pay for some evangelists, a policy for polygamy, church discipline for a Christian who beat his wife, a request for a new village church, etc. Although Ken was still in charge he deliberately left many of these puzzles to the elders. His part was to teach them the qualifications for leadership and then to pray much with them about the people they would choose. The process became more demanding as Ken steered them towards selecting a pastor. They had no suitable Bible school graduate but one man stood out. They recommended Akudri.

In 1935, after working in Adi for only twelve years, few other missionaries expected an ordination so soon. A committee of missionaries and Africans came to Adi to examine Akudri and his wife Maria. They already knew he could preach but now they saw the extent of his Bible knowledge and his close walk with God. The respect of the local community for both Yoane and Maria convinced the visitors. In a solemn ceremony they laid their hands on Yoane, appointing him the first Kakwa pastor.[148]

Regularly Pastor Yoane led a team to the local market to preach in short, pithy, Kakwa sentences. The powerful voice and dramatic presentation attracted many people to faith. A local priest disapproved. After listening on one market day he tackled the pastor, 'There is only one God, Yoane, whether we worship him as Catholics or

Yoane Akudri, DD

Protestants.' Yoane agreed but politely enquired about the new birth, direct confession to God and the saving value of the sacraments. When he discovered that he could not silence Yoane, the Catholic invited the local Belgian official to his home after mass.

'My dear son,' he said, confidentially offering him a cigar and then lighting his own. 'There is a pastor at Adi who is a serious trouble maker. He can sway an audience of 2000 people at the Chief's market . . . He makes all the people stop their buying and selling . . . With his loud voice he controls the people . . . He will certainly lead the whole tribe into an insurrection.'

The administrator arrested Yoane and decided to deport him to a distant province. Yoane thanked the official,

> There is a large church at Adi with over a thousand members . . . dozens of strong pastors will take my place . . . I want to go to a new territory to preach. The Gospel is for all the Congolese. It is even for you, Monsieur. You too must confess your sins to Christ and believe that Jesus is Lord and that only his death can cover your sins.

Yoane's words breached the Belgian's indifference and he concluded that he could not send away such 'a real man of God.'

Listening ears and weeping eyes

As the young leader of the dance in his village, Akudri needed to pierce his ears so that he could decorate them with rings. Infection followed the simple operation and persisted for years. Healing left large scars, like a pair of hanging golf balls. Four doctors removed the tissue on seven different occasions but the ugly pendants always returned. He learnt to smile when strangers stared at his thorn in the flesh.

His ears might be deformed but they were always attuned to human sorrow. The baby of a young missionary couple took sick. Despite the pastor's prayers the child died. Both parents wept uncontrollably. He put his arms around them and recited verse after verse, 'Suffer the little children to come to me. Forbid them not . . . Weep not for the child is not dead but asleep.'

He wept much for his own sons when they rejected the pathways of their parents but rejoiced for his daughter, Roda, who responded to a missionary challenge and went to work with her husband among the pygmies. Today she is a stalwart back in the Adi church.

In the late fifties, talk of revolt disturbed the pastor. He was aware of the brutalities of the Belgian regime but always taught the Bible attitude to the governing authorities. When necessary he would openly rebuke the officials; he stood against them when they insisted that everyone grow tobacco. But his resistance was always peaceful and, when independence finally arrived, he taught his flock to be grateful for the good things the Belgians had brought them.

Yoane's sons joined the rebel Simba who, often under the influence of drugs and witchcraft, committed the most appalling atrocities. White mercenaries came to Adi searching for rebels and accused him of protecting his sons. They tortured him and he would have died but for the intercession of a Christian interpreter with the mercenaries. He still bears the scars.

During the brief period of Simba power he suffered again. As they heard of many pastors being imprisoned and murdered, Christians advised their pastor to keep a low profile and warned, 'The Simbas will kill us if they see us carrying on the work of missionaries.' Akudri replied in the words of his Lord, ' "I must work the works of him that sent me while it is day" . . . We shall have our services. We shall preach to the Simbas. They need it more than our own people. The Lord is on our side; we will not fear what the Simbas can do to us.'[149]

Then it was the Simbas' turn to search Adi. They wanted money and guns. They rampaged through the missionaries' houses, in their fury and frustration smashing furniture, doors and windows. They triumphantly turned up a box of ammunition 'Show us the guns or you will die,' they demanded. His calm readiness to go to heaven unnerved them.

The Simbas ordered everyone to a market square four miles from Adi where their leaders made speeches. Soldiers shot several 'enemies of the people'. Yoane asked, 'May I speak please?' Clambering onto the platform, he turned to the crowd and told them 'the wages of sin is death, but the gift of God is eternal life through Jesus Christ our Lord'. He pointed to the bleeding corpses and said, 'We have been told that these died for their sin against Congo. But our sin is against God . . . and God's gift is eternal life.'[150] He pleaded with them, 'God loves you Simbas. He gave his only Son to die for your sins. If you believe you will have everlasting life.' Several poorly aimed shots whistled past him and he was ordered down.

By the age of seventy Yoane Akudri was preaching in Britain and America. His outgoing personality made friends for Africa wherever he went. He preached with a team in Kenya and then set out for Sudan. In northern Uganda machine gun bullets ripped into the side of the lorry and the driver braked to a stop. Amin's soldiers roughly hauled out the evangelists and led them to their barracks. They promised, 'Tomorrow you will die.'

Hunger, thirst and fear gnawed at the young men that night as they lay under their lorry, surrounded by soldiers. Yoane tried to comfort them with descriptions of Heaven but they thought more of wives and babies back at home. A twig broke. They all froze in fright. A woman's voice whispered timidly, 'Don't be afraid It is I, a Christian, I have come with food.'[151] Quietly they crept past their sleeping guards to where she stood with a large pot of steaming chicken, manioc and gravy.

Next day a senior officer shouted at them, 'You Christians! You are enemies of Allah and friends of the hateful Americans. You must die.' To their astonishment another woman came to their aid. She introduced herself as the wife of the bishop and demanded that the soldiers keep their prisoners alive until she could contact their superiors in Kampala. A few days later they were released.

The Adi church invited David and Joyce Richardson to their New Year conference in 1994. David preached to 2,000 on each of three days and to 5,000 at a service lasting six hours on

Sunday. They consoled Akudri on the loss of Maria the previous year after sixty-seven happy years together. Akudri's youngest son, who was once a great source of grief to his parents, gave David and Joyce a live duck and asked if he could tape each of David's messages. He told them that he was studying at the Bible school.[152]

Akudri's response was a loud 'Nzambe – Mericee'.

Charles and Muriel Davis

Akudri escaped the Simbas' bullets; others perished.

When, in the early days of August 1964 the rebel army advanced rapidly towards Congo's second city, Stanleyville, Government leaders trusted the huge river to hold them back. Well-armed soldiers guarded the only bridge, forty miles out of the city. If all else failed, a touch on a detonator would send the bridge hurtling into the current and halt the invaders.

The defenders expected an ill-clad army, fortified mostly by fanaticism. But their first sight of the Simbas struck terror into their hearts: four weird figures danced at the head of the advancing column; each wore a grass skirt decorated with feathers, leopard skins on their heads and a pair of goat horns testifying to their confidence in demonic powers. As they drew closer, drug-glazed eyes set in whitened faces stared at their enemies with unearthly intensity. The national army, first at the bridge and then in the city, flung aside their bazookas and fled in panic.

Forty miles north of Stanleyville, Charles and Muriel Davis continued to settle into their four-day-old home at Banjwadi Seminary. Despite three months' language study in the AIM heartland to the north-east, they still felt new and raw. As they wrestled with the challenge of helping four-year-old Stephen and little Beth, nearly two, to adjust, events in Stanleyville seemed remote. Only a short time before a senior colleague wrote, 'It is hard to imagine trouble in Congo when all we know is peace.'[153]

Three Simba soldiers shattered that peace. They arrived on a Saturday afternoon looking for Americans. 'Oh, I'm American . . . and my family,' said Charles guilelessly. The officer told them they would not need to take baggage as they would return in the evening.

A few hours later a surging mob in the city forced the car to halt. 'Daddy,' shrieked little Stephen, 'They're going to tip us over.' Just then a man sprawled over the front of the vehicle. Angry hands flung him to the ground. In a moment bullets riddled his body. 'Daddy. They've killed him!' the boy sobbed, 'Oh, they've killed that man!'[154] The lad's sobs angered the Simbas. Eight or more men thrust their guns, still smoking, through the windows. 'Dear God,' Davis choked, 'take us all together. Don't leave the children alone with them.' Suddenly the guns withdrew. The officer stamped on the accelerator calling back to his passengers, 'We'll go to the airport now.' When they arrived, the driver ordered them out of the car and hurriedly left them in the midst of another angry crowd. More guns prodded them into a low stinking toilet. As their eyes adjusted to the gloom, they found the room packed with people.

Forty minutes later the door opened and a soldier commanded them to come out. 'You go home,' he told Muriel and when Charles objected, he curtly insisted, 'You stay here.' Numb with worry, Charles scarcely noticed as soldiers forced him to undress and pelted him with mess from the toilet. One struck him with the flat of his bayonet. They returned his clothes after emptying the pockets and told him to sleep. As he settled on the filthy floor, fear gripped him.

Outside, Muriel carried Beth to a waiting car. Stephen cried, 'I want Daddy to come.' An angry Simba raised his stick and shouted, 'Be quiet.' He bundled them into the back seat and asked, 'Where do you live?' But her home was too far away and he said he would take her to the barracks. In horror Muriel searched her mind for a secure place in this strange city. She suddenly recalled a name heard in a casual conversation at Banjwadi. 'Take me and my children to LECO,' she demanded, 'the place where they sell books.'

Alone in the street outside the Christian bookshop, she remembered another name from that discussion – a missionary known as Kinso. Seeing a light above the shop, she pounded on the door and shouted in desperation, 'Kinso, Kinso, Kinso!' A voice answered, 'I'm coming.' An elderly Englishman opened the door and Muriel rushed upstairs to collapse into the outstretched arms of Ma Kinso, Mrs Jenkinson.

For weeks Stanleyville reeled under oppression. Mass trials, sometimes before thousands, resulted in mass murder. Maddened by the scent of blood and the fear of opposition, rebel leaders executed people almost daily in front of a monument to Lumumba, Congo's first Prime Minister, killed in a suspicious

Charles and Muriel Davis, DD

air crash. Kinso, listening from his apartment in the city centre, learnt to fear the silent executions for they took place with unspeakable cruelty. Better to die in a hail of machine-gun fire.

The rebel President visited Charles' prison and inexplicably ordered his release. Quickly he made his way to Kilometre Eight, a centre belonging to the Unevangelized Fields Mission, for a happy reunion with his family.

America showed increasing concern for the violations of human rights in Congo. Rumours spread of bombers on the way. At the same time the Congo Government enlisted the aid of an international force of mercenaries. Simbas became more nervous. Their President threatened, 'The Americans and Belgians we have in our claws will be massacred in case of bombing attacks.' As anti-American feeling escalated they rounded up all the US citizens they could find and placed them in Stanleyville hotels. Once again they arrested Charles. Anxiety for the family at Kilometre Eight churned through his mind and each morning he awoke to the question, 'Is this my last day on earth?'

A small notebook shows Charles' source of strength in those tense days:

November 1 'I sought the Lord and he heard me; and delivered me from all my fears.' (Psalm 34:4)

November 3   'Commit thy way unto the Lord; trust also in him
and he shall bring it to pass.' (Psalm 37:4, 5)
Bunyan: 'Stay in the middle of the path and the chained lions
can do you no harm.'
'Be not afraid of their faces, for I am with thee to deliver thee,
saith the Lord.' (Jeremiah 1:6)
November 7   'My times are in thy hand: deliver me from the
hand of mine enemies, and from them that persecute me . . .
Be of good courage, and he shall strengthen your heart.' (Psalm
31:15, 24)[155]

Suffering galvanizes the Church

On November 24th low-flying aircraft jerked Charles out of his
sleep. A Simba ran through the halls screaming, 'Everybody
outside! At once, outside!'[156] As they ran into the street Paul
Carlson, a missionary doctor who had already been badly
mistreated, suggested to Charles, 'Maybe they're planning to
use us as a human shield to slow up the Belgians.'

Gunfire from the airport direction came closer. Soldiers argued
about killing all 250 prisoners but held their fire in indecision.
Two of them shrieked in terror, 'The paras are coming!' A
machine gun crackled in the next street and bullets ripped off
the corner of a building ahead.

Panic took over. A rebel sent a bullet into the waiting crowd.
Restraint snapped. A score of Simbas opened up on the helpless
captives. Worst was a rebel machine gun at the side of the road.
'Wait,' shouted one of the missionaries, Al Larson. From his
position on the ground Charles could see people running, falling
and lying still. A burst of fire cut a Belgian child in half. The
rebel gun came to the end of its belt of ammunition. 'Now run
while they reload,' Al cried, and Charles ran towards a house.
He reached a chin-height wall at the same moment as Paul
Carlson. The doctor signalled him to scramble over first. Charles
sprang for the top and slithered over.

Paul, weakened by malaria, beatings and long imprisonment,
managed to pull himself up by his hands and plant his elbows
on the wall. He swung a foot up and reached down to grasp
Charles' steadying hand on the far side. One more effort and
he would be over. A Simba ran up behind him, aimed his sten
gun and fired. The first shot smashed into Paul's head. Charles
felt the hand slip from his as Paul slumped to the ground.[157]

In turmoil, he dashed into the building. Looking for
somewhere to hide, he flung open a low door and squeezed inside

a windowless store. His hand touched another trembling body and, as his eyes adjusted to the darkness, he made out several others. Minutes passed like hours. Voices approached outside the door and muscles tensed in the hide-out. Then they heard the words – English! The paras had come.

Al and Charles thought immediately of the extreme danger to the families at Kilometre Eight. They raced to the airport where Al persuaded three tough, bearded, Cuban mercenaries to drive him to the centre. As Director of the Unevangelized Fields Mission he insisted on Charles catching the first plane to Leopoldville. They would need all the space in the jeeps for the families. The mercenaries shot at anything that moved beside the road as they sped to Kilometre Eight.

They arrived too late. Simbas had got there first and left grim evidence of their brief visit. Outside the house Al paused sorrowfully beside the body of his long-standing friend, Hector McMillan, murdered only a short time before by panicking rebels. They had no time to bury him nor space on the vehicles to take his body with them.

Al found Ione McMillan and her six sons in the house. His own wife, Jean, and Muriel Davis had taken refuge in the jungle with their little ones. Quickly he rounded them up and helped them climb onto the jeeps. Simbas fired at them on the way back to the city but the Cubans replied with volley after volley until they delivered their passengers safely to the airport.

For fourteen more years Charles and Muriel served Zaire (Congo) until the American Council appointed them to represent AIM in universities at home.

Thirty years after that fateful November day, Charles reflected, 'Suffering is normal: if the Master had to learn obedience through suffering, how can we avoid it. Suffering purifies the Church. AIM, with its history of suffering down through the years has galvanized a church which glorifies the Lord.'[158]

8
Spread across Kenya

Scott's team brought God's Word to the Wakamba. Charles Hurlburt extended the work among these responsive people but saw also the importance of the populous Kikuyu ridges and established his first headquarters on the railway skirting their southern rim, from which pioneers planted Kikuyu churches. At Kijabe he met the Maasai and immediately planned to evangelize them, in the process running across the Tuken, Njemps, Rendille and Samburu. He noted these tribes for future penetration.

As Hurlburt thrust into Tanganyika, Congo and Uganda, he could not rest realizing that, behind the line of advance, many Kenyan peoples knew nothing of the good news of the Lord Jesus.

An American, Miss Boldt, heard God's call to Kenya while working among Zulus in South Africa. Moving north, she met farmers, Mr and Mrs McLellan Wilson (who had first arrived with Scott ten years previously). They pointed her to the Luo of western Kenya. She established The Independent Nilotic Mission close to Lake Victoria in 1906 and called her friends, Mr and Mrs Innis, to join her. They gladly surrendered their autonomy to become part of AIM and the nucleus of a team for the Luo.

Four missionaries came to the village of Aldai in 1919 to

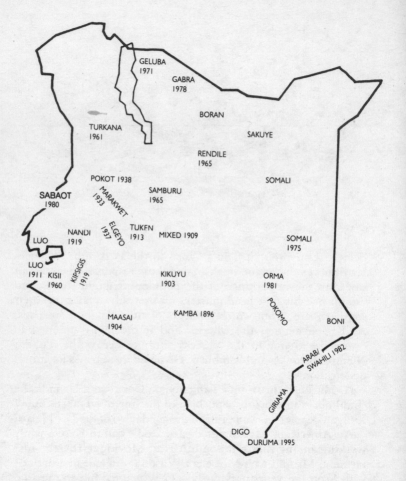

Note:
Dates refer to the year in which missionaries
took up residence. AIM missionaries visited
those places without dates.

AIM ministry to Kenyan tribes

establish churches among the Nandi, warring neighbours of the Luo, while others preached to the Tuken, Kipsigis, Marakwet, Elgeyo and Tiriki (map 5). Churches grew rapidly after the trials of Mau Mau and even faster once Kenya achieved independence in 1963. As Europeans put their farms up for sale, many Kenyan Christians moved out of their old tribal reservations to seize the opportunities. Settling on new farms, they usually planted churches as soon as they sowed their first seeds.

Half a million nomads wandering across the inhospitable northern half of Kenya called AIM and AIC pioneers into the Pokot and Turkana areas first and then eastwards to the Rendille, Samburu, Gabbra and Somali peoples. To make the circle complete, Kamba entrepreneurs settled along the coast where they too spread the Gospel in their new situations, among the Swahili and Mijikenda (meaning literally 'Nine Villages' but actually the name for nine tribes).

Often the pioneers – black and white – in these daunting ventures felt their frailty. Weakened by disease, satanic opposition, inadequate preparation, and ethnic prejudice, they leant heavily on God's power, trusting him to work despite their deficiencies. Through him, they rescued sinners, nurtured churches, translated the Scriptures and built up leaders.

Stuart and Elise Bryson

On a dusty farm, far to the west of Australia's Blue Mountains, the Bryson family seemed happy in their busy life. But, when they invited a travelling preacher to stay, Mrs Bryson felt empty and plied him with questions. He returned to Sydney and sent her a New Testament.

Stuart, who had been glad to see the back of the evangelist, was astonished when his wife told him after a sleepless night reading John's Gospel, 'I'm born again.'[159] Blind resentment welled up in him at this inexplicable change that had invaded their lives. Each night Elise prayed with the children; she talked to the married couple who helped on the farm and she tried to lead Stuart to Christ. His anger built up but, confronted by her changed life and quiet consistency, gave way to confusion and eventually to a conviction that he was a sinner. One day while harvesting he cried out to God for forgiveness. 'Suddenly,' he later testified, 'I realized that it did not depend on what I could do or be, but that Jesus Christ had already borne upon the cross the punishment for my sins. I was free and forgiven. I had

145

nothing to do but accept the work of Christ for me; and as I did so the burden of my sin was lifted.'

Word of this dramatic change spread throughout the small farming community. An old shepherd and a dirt-covered drunk whom they took into their home were among those who turned to Christ as a result of their witness.

Two ambitions increasingly mastered these two farmers – to know their Lord better from his Word and to share him with others. Different Christian leaders brought each of these desires into focus. The Principal of the Sydney Missionary and Bible College met Stuart and convinced him of the need for a period of uninterrupted Bible study to equip them for effective service. Charles Hurlburt visited Australia to set up an Australian Committee of AIM. Soon Stuart and his wife were reading about the young mission and asking God if he wanted them in Africa. So, early in 1918, they sold their farm and moved into the Sydney College with their faces firmly set towards Africa.

Kikuyu, Luo and Nandi

Their arrival at Kijabe coincided with a meeting of the Field Council under Hurlburt's leadership. Two missionaries, recently invalided home, had left the carpentry shop, saw-mill and printing press without leadership. Immediately the leaders realized that God had sent Stuart to step into the gap. Even Stuart did not see at the time how valuable the experience in printing would be to him later. He determined to be more than a technician, setting his heart on speaking to people about his Lord. First he must submit to the severe discipline of learning Kiswahili and Kikuyu. As he gained a few phrases he would boldly try them out only to discover that his hearers often misunderstood.

Despite these frustrations they both persisted until, just as they were beginning to feel free in these two languages, the Council told them of an urgent need to continue the work of Mr and Mrs Innis in the Luo tribal area. They agreed to the transfer even though it meant tackling another language.

Their new home, Nyakach, sat 1,500 feet above Lake Victoria. In the rainy season three rivers gathered water from the surrounding mountains and poured it across thirty miles of plain into the lake. The soil was so fertile that thousands of Luo put up with the recurring floods and peppered the plain with their villages.

Mr and Mrs Innis had set a typical pattern. Patiently hiking,

Western Kenya

often through clinging mud and across swollen streams, they fostered thirty-two little centres. In each they placed a young Christian who taught school all week and led worship on Sundays. The experience of planting and nurturing these simple churches for another two years further prepared the Brysons for their own strategic ministry which still lay in the future.

In 1923 they returned to Australia, concerned to educate their children, aged 14, 11 and 9. Stuart's passion for the Bible led him to travel throughout the country speaking on behalf of the Bible Society. But Africa had captured their hearts. After four years at home, a friend offered to care for the boys if Stuart and his wife decided to go back. They felt God nudging them. But the family, never separated before, did not realize how much the parting would hurt. The lads were camping when departure time came. Mother Bryson described one of the most agonizing experiences of her life: 'In the morning we went to the camp to say goodbye, thinking they would not notice so much there. We boarded our bus and they ran alongside for some distance.' Sorrowfully the boys rose before dawn next day to watch the ship slip down Sydney Harbour and out to sea.

The Brysons began work on another totally new language – Nandi. The Nandi are neighbours to the Luo so, at the start, they could sometimes find people to interpret for them as they

Quiet in the village

spoke Luo. But they knew that no language speaks to a person's heart so much as the language of the home. Soon they were stringing Nandi sentences together. They collected words on scraps of paper which they kept in bundles inside a large biscuit tin.

Missionaries first settled among the Nandi in 1919. By the time the Brysons arrived a church and school were thriving at Kapsabet. They set out to develop this centre and to use it as a base for starting the 'outschools' that had helped the Luo so markedly. The key to success in each of these was the teacher-evangelist.

Reuben Seroney and his wife Leah were the first. The Brysons helped them settle at Surungai, thirty miles from Kapsabet. They immediately established a routine of preaching in the villages each morning and teaching children in the afternoon. One by one fine Christian men and women, mostly with very little education themselves, started churches and schools across the hills of Nandi country while the Brysons built up the Kapsabet church. Ten years after their arrival, church membership stood at about five hundred throughout the district.

Kenya's first complete Bible

Today the name of Bryson is honoured among the Nandi churches for their work on the Bible. Soon after their arrival at

Kapsabet Stuart asked the church elders to choose a translator to work with him. They selected an evangelist-teacher called Samuel Gimnyige and suggested that he translate with Stuart through the week, returning to serve his church at weekends; Maria could stay at home with the children and care for their large garden on her own. Would they be ready to accept such hardship for the years it would take to complete the Bible? He responded; 'My wife and I are willing to make any sacrifice in order that our people may have the Bible in their own language.'

Samuel lacked any formal education to equip him for this exacting task. Elise set out to teach him English as they would base their work on the 1611 King James version of the Bible for Stuart's training as a farmer had not included the biblical languages of Greek and Hebrew. Aware of his own inadequacy Stuart wrote; 'I know how much of my own work was spoilt or delayed through ignorance of phonetics.' The study of three African languages before learning Nandi had given a useful background. They may have felt like amateurs but the little team shared a deep commitment. Stuart said; 'From 1929 onwards the translation of the Bible into Nandi became the dominating purpose for us.'

They puzzled over many words and concepts like salvation, forgiveness, the cross. The Lord's hair, 'as white as snow', held them up. One morning, as they sat down to work, Samuel said; 'I received a telegram in the night,' (his way of saying that he had been praying and God had shown him an answer to some difficulty). 'Have you noticed how the sun shines on the morning mist as it lies low in the valleys? Can we write, "as the sun shines on the white mist in the valley and makes it sparkle, so our Lord's hair was dazzling white"?'

In September 1931, the Brysons took the manuscript of the New Testament to Australia, returning after eighteen months with seven cases of the volumes. Samuel received it with awe. This book, which had transformed his own life, was now available to all his people. It whetted his appetite to press on to complete the whole Bible.

In 1934 Samuel became the first ordained Nandi Pastor. Later, as the Africa Inland Church spread widely across Kenya, he was appointed Vice President of the denomination.

By 1938, with the Old Testament's drafts corrected and the whole New Testament revised the Brysons were free to return to Sydney where they entered a totally new role in their own country. He became General Secretary of AIM's Australian work and inspired many others to serve in Africa. Their African service reached its climax six months later when the Nandi Bible arrived in Kapsabet and then multiplied as thousands read it.

A drunkard, called Arap Kibor, in the neighbouring Marakwet tribe got hold of a copy. He had been a cruel husband and father and lived alone in a small hut far from any Christian or school. He read slowly, mostly at night by the dim light of a primitive oil lamp – about Cain and Abel, Abraham, Isaac and Joseph – and wept about his own uncleanness. After finishing Genesis, he turned to Matthew, where he found the Saviour living, loving, caring, healing and teaching. He came to Calvary. 'As I knelt there, reading of His death,' he later told a friend, 'I realized He had died for my sins. God opened my understanding and filled me with peace.'

Tom and Ruth Collins

Tom's toes puzzled the missionary elders. Under the chairmanship of Stuart Bryson, they met as the Field Council of the 'Eldoret Area' to consider the mission challenge of the mountains and desert plains of North West Kenya. The cut and bleeding toes of their newest missionary figured on the agenda.

These men had asked their British constituency to pray that God would send pioneers into the spartan, desert conditions of East Pokot and Tom Collins was the unlikely answer. Scorning hardship and heat he walked from home to home learning the languages (first Swahili and then Pokot), adjusting to a fascinating culture and sharing his Saviour with new friends. The Pokot taught him to cobble up cheap sandals from discarded tyres. In these he could average fifteen miles a day, wandering around the scattered dwellings.

Back at the newly opened centre of Kapsowar the mission doctor noticed his grazed toes and warned him of infection. Tom's response was a courteous thanks but 'I can trust the Lord to keep me from harm'. To the doctor's suggestion that he buy a pair of boots, he replied that he needed his money to finance the walking trips and could not spare it for such a luxury.

The Council shared the doctor's concern for Tom's feet. They not only insisted that he wear boots but also used precious mission funds to buy him a pair. He wore them at the mission centres but left them behind when he went on safari.[160]

Tom had been born in Johannesburg in 1910. Before his first birthday the pupils of both eyes misted over with cataracts. For some reason South African surgeons were reluctant to operate and his parents took him first to Germany and then to England. Although surgery cleared his vision he was always helpless without thick spectacles.

When his father went to Iraq with the army, he sent Tom to school in England until the war ended and the family linked up again in South Africa. But not for long. Rheumatic fever ravaged his heart valves and sent the little lad to bed gasping for breath. Doctors told his father that he could not survive at Johannesburg's height of 5,500 feet so he arranged for Tom to live with his grandmother in London. The journey almost killed him and he spent the next six months in bed.

By the age of eleven Tom was battling against poor vision, a serious heart disorder, the loneliness of boarding school and the emotional trauma of separation from his parents. Seven years later his headmaster reported that 'his health is above the average. He has a pleasant disposition, first-rate common sense and tact . . . signs of leadership, and marked energy and enterprise.' He had become a crack shot with a rifle (in the absence of lenses in his eyes!) but the Army, less impressed by his physique, would not take him and he settled for Peterhouse College, Cambridge.

In 1931 two AIM veterans, Reg and Zan Reynolds, from Githumu in Kenya travelling home to South Africa on the *Caernarvon Castle* entertained their fellow passengers with films of Africa. Tom, on vacation from university, was interested and helped with the equipment. On the last night of the voyage Reg searched for Tom and found him in the library. Walking up and down the deck they talked about the Lord. For Tom, 'It was the first time anyone had asked me about my relationship to Christ, and the first time I confessed Him as my Saviour.' Confession of Christ meant immediate obedience. By the next day, when he walked off the *Caernarvon Castle* Tom knew that he was to work among the East Pokot people of Kenya about whom Reg had been speaking.

During his last year in Cambridge Tom applied to the AIM and was astonished when they did not immediately accept him. They asked, 'What about in depth study at a Bible school?' and recommended the Missionary Training Colony, run by Captain Godfrey Buxton (which grew and eventually moved into the Buxton family home in Hertfordshire becoming All Nations Christian College). In 1933 the Colony was housed in ex-army huts and the ex-army Principal deliberately kept living conditions simple so that he might equip the students for pioneer ministry among unreached people.

Tom's feet were itchy. Studying hard, enjoying evangelism, relishing the tough challenges of the Colony, he chafed at the enforced delay. God had called and he was sure he was ready even though the mission and Colony leaders both advised further preparation. While some wrote about his 'staying power . . . patience . . . perseverance . . . uncomplaining spirit,' one probably summed up what all felt, 'At times he could be as stubborn as the mule he later rode.' By New Year he reckoned he knew enough of the Bible to help the Pokot and decided to sail without the mission's approval.

Reg Reynolds wrote from Kenya counselling delay. His parents cautioned against going off 'into the blue' with neither financial backing nor logistic base which, said his father, 'are just as much the gift from the Almighty as anything else and I don't see your point in rejecting them.' But Tom's mind was made up. As for needs, God would provide; as for a base, he was wary. 'Mission stations' develop a routine and a way of life inimical to the itinerant role among the Pokot to which God had called him. He wanted 'to get right in amongst them, and live with them as much as possible.'

Chip of the desert

Although Tom had not heeded his advice, Reg invited him to Kapsowar. The ministry at Kapsowar was still in its infancy. When Tom arrived in 1934 the little hospital was only four months old. Tom fitted well into the atmosphere of faith and expectancy which a new work encourages. He was a man of contrasts – a mix of thoughtful submission and tough self-sufficiency. He told Reg that he wished to work under his direction and so his host set him to learn Swahili throughout his first six months.

High on the next mountain ridge to the east an Australian couple, the Dalziels, had started preaching to the Tuken people in 1926. They asked Tom to help and he agreed provided that he be free to travel in Pokot country whenever he wished. He immediately discovered that the rough roads and high hills defeated his motor bike so he sold it and bought a mule. The mule disliked the steep ascents as much as the machine, but it possessed a will of its own. After three somersaults over its head, Tom forced it into submission but he soon decided it made more trouble than it was worth and sold it too. For several years he relied on his own feet. He paid two Pokot lads to walk with him, carrying the very few bits and pieces he needed on safari.

He developed a programme of a month's safari in the hot Pokot plains followed by a month either at Kapsowar or at Kabartonjo in the Tuken hills. By the end of his first year he could speak Swahili with fair fluency and make himself understood in Pokot. At last Britain's cautious Council officially accepted him into the AIM family.

Over a five-year period Tom visited every Pokot home on at least three occasions. He would never pass a Pokot without pausing to greet that person for a chat about the Lord Jesus. As he approached the low, grass-covered huts of a Pokot home he would await the father's welcome and then sit on a stone. After discussing the rain (or the lack of it), the latest cattle raid by the neighbouring Turkana tribe, and a local wedding perhaps, he would go on, 'I have good news for you from God,' and launch into a simple description of man's need, answered by God sending his own Son to die for us.

As the sun plunged behind the western ranges boys, away since dawn with the family flocks, drove in their animals. Whistling and threatening, they cajoled them into their thorn-fenced enclosures. The women and girls took over, deftly squeezing udders until, if the rains had been good, the old man handed Tom a wooden mug full of foaming milk. Hunger helped him ignore the fact that vessels for water and milk are cleaned either with a smoking stick (possibly sterile) or human urine (probably not). In times of drought, which came only too often, Tom would settle down for the night with his stomach empty. At the end of the month, when he climbed up into the cool forests again, his colleagues saw a shadow of the man who had left them – a dry chip of the stony Pokot desert.

Rheumatic fever still troubled him. If he was on safari when it struck, he lay for a week chewing aspirins and then slowly got moving again. Malaria sometimes laid him low. Once he was so weakened that he had to shelter in the shade of a large rock, far from water. As his temperature mounted, so also did his thirst. Remembering Elijah he prayed for rain and God sent it, sufficient to fill a hollow in his sheltering rock. He carried medicines to help the many sick people he met but, if he ran out when he needed to treat himself, he calmly asked the Lord for healing and waited. Tom became indifferent, almost contemptuous, to personal hardship. Each fresh difficulty was a challenge to faith and ingenuity.

He continued to question the standard policy of a central mission station, observing that it clogged the feet of many missionaries. Tom wrote of the Enemy's intention 'to make the Lord's messenger directly disobey orders – "Go ye therefore" . . . A person can stop on a station for months on end, working hard of course, being little less than a degraded schoolmaster seeing that rather unwilling workmen carry out the petty orders of the day.' His senior, Reg, tactfully spoke of the need 'for a central camp . . . where there is permanent water . . . to which we could periodically send mail and provisions.'

Long treks failed to produce the believers for whom Tom longed. Reluctantly he agreed to establish a small school and a simple home for himself on a dusty river bank called Kinyang, where the Pokot knew they could always find water if they dug deep enough. By no means would he erect a church. He reckoned, 'When a few have truly believed, they will want a church, will ask for it and build it. Then, and not till then, perhaps we might step in and help – just a little – but mostly it must be theirs, in initiative and defrayment of expense.'

Two Pokot evangelists and a Kikuyu missionary from Kijabe called Laban were the first to settle at Kinyang. The government forbade Tom to stay there without a white companion. Before that person could appear, war broke out.

Tom and Ruth Collins, DD

In 1939 when war erupted Tom enlisted but five years later, following recurrent bouts of malaria and rheumatic fever, he was medically discharged from the army.

During the war he had met and married Ruth Barnett who was in charge of the hospital at Kijabe and the daughter of AIM missionaries Albert and Elma Barnett. Following Tom's medical discharge they visited their home countries to speak on behalf of the mission. Tom was reticent to say much of his own work, always reluctant to attract credit to himself. He refused to paint romantic pictures of a work he knew to be hard and tedious, reaching an unresponsive, nomadic people. Nevertheless he created an impression of dogged determination to serve his Master whatever the cost and people responded in various ways.

In America, friends handed him some keys and invited him to the front door where he was surprised to see a jeep with the powerful gear ratios needed for the hazards of Pokot. In an Irish gathering, a young doctor heard God's call to AIM and, a few years later, set off for Kapsowar. Most important of all, wherever they went, the Lord stirred people to pray for the tribes of northern Kenya.

Beautiful feet

For a time they were asked to replace Ken and Hazel Phillips in charge of the Tuken work. Tom may have thought this hard because he disliked mission stations as they always usurped the priority of itinerant evangelism. In any event he submitted to the mission leadership. He found an ideal situation for taking Ruth and baby Malcolm on long thrusts into Pokot, as well as serving the rapidly developing Tuken churches. For Ruth it was God's gracious way of introducing her gradually to the harsh and lonely life of the pioneer.

A busy mountain situation was bad for an ailing heart. Doctors ordered the Collins' to the coast so that Tom could rest for a couple of months. In solemn conclave they then decreed 'several more months of complete rest at a low altitude and follow that by a very sedentary job at as low an altitude as possible'. One added to his report, 'I take a gloomy view of his future'. With a heart the size of a rugby football, what else could the doctors say?

The doctor's task is to preserve life but Tom and Ruth acknowledged a higher principle – we must do God's will even at the risk of shortening life. Tom had written, 'In the Army I am counted "C3", but that does not count for much for one who could raise Christ from the dead.' Mission leaders, rightly wary of presumption, recognized that they faced a vast evangelistic need and an evangelist who, with his wife, was sure of God's call and had proved God's care. They consented to the Collins' return to Kinyang.

As well as continuing their patient work among the Pokot, they took long swings in their jeep northwards into the even more barren and drought-riven country of the sworn enemies of the Pokot, the Turkana. Tom began to learn the Turkana language and wondered if God wanted them to move into their desert.

One evening Tom and Ruth came across an escaped convict, Lukas, stirring a Pokot crowd to rebel against white rule. Tom quietly listened as Lukas outlined a plan to slaughter all the foreigners in a town 120 miles away. Tom drove his jeep several hours to alert the police. The Pokot, convinced that bullets of their enemies would turn to water, recklessly attacked with spears. People fell on both sides until the police withdrew and the Pokot lost heart. In the eerie night that followed local villagers heard the cries of the wounded as the sharp teeth of hyenas finished the work begun by spears.[161]

Tom and Ruth were fighting a battle with different weapons. The most powerful was God's own Word. For thirty years Tom studied Pokot. Early he translated some simple hymns and verses, but he set his sights on the complete New Testament. For this he had two allies in Mr and Mrs Totty serving the West Pokot, close to Kitale. They worked separately and then met together with a committee to revise their manuscripts. Not long before his death, they completed the task.

Tom and Ruth moved their base to Liter, at the foot of the mountain range which supports Kapsowar. Here at last the people, a mixture of Marakwet and Pokot, responded to his preaching and asked for a church. It was opened with great joy in June 1964. Within three months Tom went home to his Lord whom he had served so faithfully.

To the end he felt his ministry had been a failure. Many years after his death older Pokot men still remember the visits of the Collins' to their homes. Possibly these hardened nomads needed to hear the simple message several times over the years before it fitted their own rugged culture. Certainly missionaries are now reaping where Tom and Ruth patiently sowed and small churches are springing up at last. Perhaps just as significant are those whom Tom and Ruth have challenged to follow their steps into the northern nomad tribes.

As a new missionary to the Turkana in 1956, I looked to Tom as my mentor. His thick cataract spectacles magnified his eyes in contrast to the thin, disease-riven body. An austere personality had mellowed over the years into a dependable, resilient person always ready to help. His iron will drove his slender frame too hard. I sometimes looked at his feet while he prayed before climbing into bed at night. The soles were thick, calloused and fissured. Large oval scars on the shins testified to old ulcers. The skin was blue, its veins twisted, gnarled and heavy with the blood which a weak heart could never quite handle. I used to ponder Paul's words, 'How beautiful . . . are the feet of those who bring good news' (Isaiah 52:7: Romans 10:18).

Peter and Roda Mualuko

African feet followed Tom's into the sandy wastes of the North. Their owner was to become the principal architect of the Turkana church, the main motivator of a new missionary thrust by the Kenyan Africa Inland Church.

God delivers

A boy in his teens lay in a dark hospital ward in Kenya, apparently unconscious. A fiery sore on his leg had sent his temperature rocketing and he now appeared comatose. In fact he was conscious – not of the ward, nor of his fellow patients, but of menacing figures crowding around him, the size of children, but with the proportions and intelligence of men. They threatened him and he called the name of a nurse from his own area, 'Matolo'.

A nearby patient asked, 'What do you want to tell Matolo?' Mualuko described the demons who were still lurking at the foot of his bed, listening, and said, 'They want to take me. I am going to die.'

'Are they greater than Jesus Christ?' enquired the friendly patient.

'Who is Jesus?'

'He is God's son, greater and more powerful than those you can see. He can help you if you will trust Him.' He prayed for him and Mualuko mumbled an Amen before lapsing back into stupor.

The demons threatened him again but Mualuko heard another voice, kind and gentle, immediately above his head, 'Don't mind their spears. They cannot harm you. Don't be afraid; just ignore them.'[162] He awoke to find his mother beside the bed. He had been unconscious for three days and they had given up all hope for him.

Back at home, healthy again, he quickly took up his old ways: a thief, drunkard and idol worshipper. He would pray both to the demons and to Jesus. Jesus amazed him with answers, but he quickly forgot his own promise.

He found work as a stone cutter with a group of Christians. Coming home one night with some stolen vegetables in his hands he was embarrassed to find one of the group waiting for him. He threw the vegetables into the bushes and hoped his friend had not seen them. Someone else had witnessed the crime. Mualuko continues his story,

> That night I did not sleep. I realized that I was facing God's judgement for my sin of disobedience, especially for rejecting Jesus . . . God had saved me from suffering and from physical death . . . I remembered how God met my needs and I had told him lies. I shed tears as I asked God to pardon me. I made a final decision to abandon my old life and all that was not pleasing to God.

Two months after his conversion Peter Mualuko returned home to discover that his wife, Roda, and mother had already started attending church. 'After some explanation, my wife and mother decided to accept Jesus Christ as their personal Saviour.'

The family had a problem. Roda became pregnant eight times, but only one live birth resulted. Neighbours laughed. They insisted, 'Unless you turn to the witch doctors you will have no more children.' Mualuko's time for the demons and their servants was over. They prayed to Jesus who had been so kind to them before and he gave them seven sons and two daughters.

God calls

Challenged in a sermon to ask God what spiritual gift he was to exercise, Mualuko heard that familiar, kindly voice answer, 'Prophet.' The Lord continued, 'I shall make you a soul cutter; from now on you will cut no more stones, but souls.'

When he asked, 'Where Lord?' the answer came from the apostle Paul, 'It has always been my ambition to preach the gospel where Christ was not known' (Romans 15:20).

First Peter had to spend three years in Machakos Bible School and then an apprenticeship as an evangelist. He visited a remote area among his own Wakamba people called Kalawa and felt a great sympathy 'for the lost souls that had been made captives of the devil'. He told his wife about the need and she agreed with him that God wanted them to work at Kalawa.

Over ten years God used Peter and Roda to plant eight churches. The AIC leaders then encouraged Peter to study for two further years in order to prepare for ordination. In 1958 Sid Langford (AIM's leader in Sudan and recently moved to be American Director) visited the Pastors' School and told of the need for someone to take the Gospel to the Taposa of Sudan.

In the next year the AIC established the 'Africa Inland Church Missionary Board (AICMB) and appealed for missionaries for the Turkana in Kenya and for Sudan. Mualuko applied for Sudan and another pastor offered for Turkana. Neither succeeded. Mualuko could not obtain a visa and the other man had family problems.

White families too experienced difficulty in getting to the Turkana. The colonial government forbad western women entrance into such a harsh wilderness. For this reason I had reluctantly assumed that God wanted me to remain a bachelor. Then I met Joan!

Happy in her teaching role and already fluent in Nandi, she felt settled among the hills of Kapsabet – as green as her own emerald Ireland. Some questioned whether she could adjust to semi-desert conditions. But God gave us assurance of his will and we married. As an early seal upon our union, the government lifted their ban for her benefit.

We travelled through the whole Turkana district, half the size of England, and met many of the 120,000 nomads. Hearing of Pastor Peter's interest in the Taposa, we got in touch with him to urge him to join us in Turkana. 'The Taposa live just across the border, and their language is almost identical,' we told him; 'Why not come here first? When the way opens, you can go on to Sudan.'

The Pastor consulted his wife. Her neighbours frightened her, 'The Turkana are cannibals,' they warned; 'and their climate so hot that the skin of people who wear clothes splits and their entrails escape.' The couple laid the matter before their Lord.

Again the missionary Paul provided the answer, 'A man of Macedonia [was] standing and begging him, "Come over to Macedonia and help us." And when he had seen the vision, immediately we sought to go, concluding that God had called us to preach the Gospel to them.' (Acts 16:9).

Kalawa had been hot, but nothing prepared Peter for the fiery

Turkana plains. Our jeep lurched and jolted, often achieving only a dozen miles in an hour. In two days we arrived at Lokitaung, a small town close to Ethiopia and Sudan, where the Kenya Police headquarters guard the borders. In a rocky, dry river-bed behind a couple of corrugated iron shops, Peter captured the attention of about a hundred Turkana with a gramophone record in their language. ('Is there a man inside that little box,' some asked incredulously; 'How does he know our language?') Then he preached about the spirit world, Jesus and the resurrection, and finished with an invitation to all who wished to believe to raise a hand. Everyone raised a hand, several lifted both.

For two years no rain fell on the Turkana. Normally they kept alive by moving their herds of cattle and camels, as well as their flocks of sheep and goats, to grazing wherever rain has fallen. Dependent on their animals for all their food, they possessed remarkable skills in conserving them and resilient stamina in survival themselves. If food was short they tied a strip of hide around their stomachs to ease the pangs of hunger and then waited for conditions to improve. But the vicious drought of 1959 and 1960 swallowed half the animals and the tribe teetered on the brink of starvation.

The government responded with an immense famine relief programme. Twenty thousand gathered in camps, the largest at Kalokol on the shore of Lake Rudolf (now Lake Turkana). This life-saving exercise was wide open to abuse and the British Commissioner, seeing the love of the pastor for the Turkana (in sharp contrast to most more 'civilized' people – black and white – who tended to despise them as 'primitive') asked him to settle at Kalokol and to assist in the programme. He told us, 'We are desperately short of honest men.' The AICMB agreed and sent Roda north to join her husband.

Pioneer missionary work is always hard. The drought broke with torrential rains which poured through the palm leaf roof of their simple home. Roda, pregnant again, became sick. With great difficulty Pastor Peter got her to hospital, 250 miles away, where three pints of blood saved her life. The harsh climate and the different culture added to their difficulties.

Despite her almost total lack of formal education, Roda was as sure of her missionary call as the Pastor. Within six months she was back at Kalokol, smiling through her typically filed Kamba teeth, as she suckled yet another answer to prayer.

The Lord was answering other prayers too. He was working

among the paupers of Kalokol. When food corrected the prevailing apathy of hunger, Peter found many Turkana intelligent, full of good humour and willing to ponder his message, but they could still be more irritating than any other people he had ever met! Love and patience, prayer and preaching brought people to Christ – indicated more by changed lives than raised hands and Mualuko taught them for months before taking them to the lakeside for baptism.

With the help of Kikuyu Christians on the famine relief team, Peter started a school. AICMB had sent him metal

Peter Mualuko, DD

sheets to solve the leaking roof problem in his home. He put them on the first classroom instead. As elsewhere in the history of the church, the school proved a powerful recruiter of Christians.

The Lord answered other prayers too. He sent a multinational missionary team of westerners and Kenyans to plant churches in other parts of Turkana and all looked to Peter Mualuko for leadership.

God enlarges vision

For sixteen years the Mualukos skilfully built the Turkana church. Then the AICMB needed Peter for a wider ministry. Twenty-six Kenyan missionaries were pioneering in unreached tribes and discovering, like their American and British colleagues, that they had much to learn for they too were foreigners. Of course they were less foreign than the westerners and probably made fewer cultural mistakes but Africans automatically expected that someone with a black skin would be like themselves in every way. AICMB asked Pastor Peter and Michael Donovan (a Briton) to give them encouragement, care and supervision. Increasingly the two leaders saw that the Bible school training given to all their missionaries was not sufficient. They began to pray about specific missionary training.

As well as helping the men and women in their remote

assignments, Peter and Michael visited the established churches and their big conferences to deepen understanding and foster support for the missionaries. For four years they crisscrossed Kenya, stirring Christians to get involved, and establishing African missionaries in their ministry. Although Peter recognized the importance of this work, his heart was elsewhere.

One of Peter's joys was to send a young missionary couple to the Taposa. The Zaire churches had sent missionaries to Sudan, but these two were the first Kenyans to venture outside their own country expecting to devote their lives to serving another people group. The Sudan AIC welcomed them and accommodated them in a rebuilt house in Kapoeta, where they set about learning the language and building relationships with the people.

But Sudan perplexed them. As well as reeling before strangely different ways of life (like many missionaries when they first arrive), they could not understand the attitudes of Sudanese church leaders. Westerners had learnt hard lessons in relating to the new leadership of the young African churches and the Kenyan missionaries faced the same difficulty. After struggling for a few months they returned home.

Peter Mualuko visited Kapoeta and met a warrior, Lotome, who said he wanted to believe. The pastor talked with him for a long time about his bondage to witchcraft. Reluctantly Peter had to leave his eager enquirer for his flight back to Nairobi. Looking down from the plane on the massed Taposa villages, he pondered his Lord's words, 'I have other sheep that are not of this flock. I must bring them also.' (John 10:16 – the verse that spoke to Peter Scott in Westminster Abbey, p. 17.) He thought of Lotome and many others who needed to meet Christ. When he got home he asked the AICMB leaders to release him for Sudan. He told them, 'The Lord is reminding me that the Taposa are waiting to hear the Gospel from my mouth. I regard my stay in Turkana as preparation for Sudan.'

Lotome was one of the first to greet Pastor Peter when he returned to Taposa in March 1982. He stripped fetishes off his wrists and neck saying, 'Now I want to follow Jesus.' It was a good beginning, but tests followed.

The supply flight came in but, although it brought food for others, none arrived for Peter. How would he survive in this remote place?

He visited another church centre, where dysentery struck him. Cholera was around and someone told him that people did not normally recover from his brand of infection. A Sudanese pastor called elders and prayed, 'Lord we have waited many years for you to bring this servant of yours. Now he is close to death. Please raise him up for ministry.' He recovered rapidly.

Peter spoke the Turkana language which the Taposa could understand without difficulty. The tribes hated each other and recently the Turkana had slaughtered some Taposa people close to the border. Fellow missionaries advised Pastor Peter to remain close to the mission centre where the team was well-known and accepted.

Rains failed and people became hungry. Witch doctors said that the ancestors demanded sacrifices. They could not satisfy the spirits with a donkey and offered an ox. No rain fell; the diviners blamed the Turkana-speaking stranger in their midst. Pastor Peter realized he was in danger.

Before dawn the Chief's raucous voice roused him, complaining bitterly that since the new teacher's arrival the spirits' anger had rested on the land. He wrote a farewell letter to Roda and went out to conduct his regular morning meeting, to which more and more people were coming. The Chief arrived accompanied by two spear-wielding warriors.

The Pastor greeted the visitors and asked them to sit, determined that they would hear the Gospel before slaying him. He preached, 'Repent of thieving, murder, witchcraft, adultery and turn to Jesus. Then you can ask God to send rain. You won't need to sacrifice any more oxen and donkeys.' He told the penitents to raise their hands and the Chief was the first to respond. Then they prayed for rain.

He heard the first drops in the middle of the night and wondered if this was the answer. A downpour followed and continued all next day, washing out the normal Sunday service. Late in the afternoon, when the deluge eased, a few gathered to worship, awed at God's response to repentance and believing prayer.

Peter's flame burned brightly for a time and many Taposa came to its warmth. Soon the tide of war swept in, forcing the missionary team to depart. The elderly soldier could have retired with honour but he heard of other sheep, in north-eastern Kenya, who needed someone to draw them into the flock of the Lord Jesus. Always driven on by obedience to his Saviour and the longing to bring people to meet him, Peter testified, 'The Lord has really done marvellous things using me, a poor and weak vessel, with little education. May the glory be to Him, who enabled me to persevere through hardship and temptation.'

Alan and Coleta Checkley

Stuart Bryson, well established now as the Australian Secretary of AIM, visited the Sydney College for Bible and Mission thirty years after his graduation there. Listening to him speak about Kenya, Alan Checkley thought he heard the Lord say to him, 'This is it.' The more he learnt about Kenya, the more certain he became of God's command to go there.

The Mau Mau emergency was at its height in 1952 when Alan arrived in Kenya but he saw little of troubled Kikuyu country. He travelled directly to Kapsowar, where a hospital, church and school jostled for space on a high ridge. If he rose early and looked south-east, he could sometimes see, 150 miles away, the sharp profile of Mount Kenya outlined by the rising sun. Three thousand feet below, a river wound northwards through increasingly thirsty land to Lake Turkana while, behind him, forest climbed through the morning mist towards a jagged peak at 11,000 feet.

Alan soon felt at home. He developed an aptitude for forming Nandi sentences, for building hospital wards and, most important of all in a missionary, for making friends. As he worked he got close to people. The mud and wattle church, alongside the hospital, housed a vigorous congregation led by elders who, despite their sparse education, were effective evangelists. Alan enjoyed his preaching safaris with these men and learnt from them. When Zekaria taught, he always chose his text from John chapter fifteen, encouraging his hearers to draw life from Jesus, the vine. Dropping in for a friendly cup at Elder Job's little tea shop, he would hear him introducing a customer to the living Lord Jesus. Isaya had the quick intelligence that made him the doctor's right hand in the hospital for nearly half a century. While they had the skills to bring their own people to Christ, they still depended on Alan and his missionary colleagues for regular Bible teaching.

Alan and Coleta met at Northside Church when she was still in her teens. They were engaged before Alan left Sydney but she still needed to complete her nursing and Bible training. So he had waited two years before he led her up the pressed-earth aisle of Kapsowar Church as his bride.

The Field Council assigned them to Kapsabet, Bryson's old home, where Alan supervised schools and Coleta nurtured their four boys and a girl. Christians, alive to the spreading spirit of progress and wanting to upgrade their mud-walled churches and schools to brick, valued Alan's building expertise. Increasing fluency in Nandi enabled him to teach in Kapsabet Bible School for more and more wanted to understand their Nandi Scriptures.

Alan's capacity for friendship embraced a rising band of leaders. He travelled widely with teachers at the weekend sharing the good news in villages and preaching in churches. Some of his companions later rose to high office. Ezekiel Birech invited Christian lads from Kapsabet Secondary School on Sunday evangelistic trips – including a boy called Daniel Arap Moi. Twenty years later the nation chose Ezekiel's disciple to follow Jomo Kenyatta as Kenya's second President and the AIC appointed Ezekiel as their second bishop. Another friend, Joel Malel, became Kenya's High Commissioner to Great Britain.

The churches did not grow without pain. Stuart and Elise had held powerful personalities together but, after their departure in 1938, their first teacher, Reuben, led a group out of the Africa Inland Church to become Anglicans. To AIM the issue was straightforward – the seceders wanted freedom to drink, dance, and smoke, which the missionaries had forbidden. But perhaps the problem went deeper. In the early days missionaries often laid down rules for their converts rather than allowing the Bible to convince the Christians themselves. Some of the Checkleys' friends resented such foreign imposition.

Alan and Coleta ran into the problem of the tithe. Missionaries employed many people for all sorts of work, but pay was small. They strongly taught Christians to give a tenth of their income to the church. If an employee forgot to pay this month, then he would pay double next. Rather than run into that inconvenience, Africans asked that their employers cut the tithe before handing over the salary. While some resented the interference in their pay, others regarded it as a test of spirituality. The Checkleys felt glad when giving became voluntary and more personal.

Pulled up by the roots

The political gale in Kenya gathered momentum and everybody sensed major changes approaching. Foreign farmers in the fertile 'White Highlands' realized that they would soon cease to have a white monopoly and might, indeed, have no place at all. The British Government bought many farms and then sold them cheaply to Africans.

Those with money to buy were often Christians who had been the first to seek education and to learn to farm well without squandering their profits on drink. Their pioneer mentality equipped them for new ventures. Having developed skills in caring for twenty to fifty acres, they quickly learnt to care for 400 to 3,000. They quoted the Psalm, 'The earth is the Lord's and everything in it', and then added, 'I'm his caretaker'. So many Nandi church members moved from the traditional tribal reserve into the adjoining farmlands that the rumour spread, 'If you want to own a farm there you have to be a Christian.' On the farms they found a resident labour force and immediately established churches for them.

Kapsabet Bible College continued to flourish. A previous graduate, Timothy Kendagor, took over as Principal, determined to meet the new needs. Nandi churches, denuded of many of their ablest men and women, looked for new leaders, while all the churches springing up like fertile shoots in the farms cried out for pastors. Some expected the old work to be crippled by the demands of the new but this did not happen. Both thrived.

Alan and Coleta watched with wonder as Christians pulled up ancient roots in obedience to their Lord and planted them elsewhere. With such exciting progress to keep them busy, they never expected God to tell them to do the same. In 1964, the Australian Council, acutely aware of the burgeoning challenge to AIM, needed to strengthen their recruiting base at home. They requested the Checkleys to take over the direction of the work in Australia.

Back in Sydney Alan found the new assignment difficult. Years later he confessed,

> I wrestled with it and never came to proper terms with it. I only wish now that I had looked at it as the Lord's will and done more in the early days of '65. I thought we would perhaps extend our furlough by one year, giving us two years in Australia; we ended up staying sixteen. In the absence of an obvious replacement, I did not feel I could demand another field assignment. Over forty years that's the way I've worked – if you're given something to do, you go and do it until it's time to do something else.[163]

Once settled there they gave it their best. The support built up – more prayer partners, an increase of missionary membership and a solid financial base – but, when the call to return to Africa eventually came, Alan found it easy to respond because his heart had never left. The International Council asked him to join its leadership team in Nairobi as Associate International Secretary responsible for administration.

Coleta found it harder to leave Australia. Their four sons were settling into their own homes and jobs while eleven-year-old Lynne was happy at school. Coleta loved the contact with the family and enjoyed her secretarial role in the office. But it was God's 'time to do something else' and they moved into a fruitful five-year ministry which introduced them to the AIM family all round the world.

Joan and I valued the help and friendship of Alan and Coleta. His decisiveness clarified issues although he occasionally upset people. Of one group he candidly admitted, 'They or I were not easy to work with.' Busy though he was, he always had time to respond to a need, whether of a missionary or an African. His old friends, the Nandi Christians, recognized his love for them and appreciated the mastery of their language which never left him.

9

Towards Africa's heart

Scott's vision, arrowing from Mombasa to Lake Chad, gripped Hurlburt with sacred intensity. He moved his headquarters from Kijabe to Aba in 1919 in order to be more centrally placed along the arrow's shaft (see p. 36). In missionary conferences he reminded his colleagues of the unknown peoples who lay along Scott's visionary line. Every month of 1917 the front of the mission magazine proclaimed the goal by a wedge drawn across East Africa with its point tilted north to rest on the shore of Lake Chad. Although lines on the map indicated that missionaries must yet traverse thousands of miles, the caption beneath boldly declared 'The Last Frontier'.

Ten years later Hurlburt no longer led AIM and, with his eclipse, the vision of striding across great swathes of the Continent for the sake of Christ and the lost became blurred. Missionaries saw the mass of human need immediately around them. They evangelized their district: they taught, healed and translated, always wishing they could do more.

By 1935 it seemed to some that 'the days of pioneering are drawing to a close as slowly but surely the untouched areas are being occupied by one society or another'.[164] The mission needed to consolidate: to build hospitals, start schools, open Bible training institutes. The enthusiast who pined after the past sacrificial days of evangelism might be dubbed old-fashioned, out of touch with the modern reality, perhaps a trifle rebellious. John Buyse rescued AIM from its loss of wider vision. Convinced of the need to strengthen the local churches, he never allowed them to deafen him to the cry of the remote unreached.

'The Last Frontier' probably applied to the international border between Belgian and French Africa. Buyse hiked across it, opening the way for others. Of course it was not the last frontier at all. As an elderly man, when many might feel they had done enough, he and his wife pressed across another border, into Sudan, opening a new and dramatic chapter in the fulfilment of Scott's dream.

John, Helena and Mabel Buyse

An elderly Dutch couple groaned inwardly as they prayed together. Mr and Mrs Buyse had experienced the trauma of letting go of their children as each grew into a young adult, but John still needed his home. An obstinate, unbelieving fifteen-year-old, he determined to sail on the windjammers that plied out of Rotterdam. How could their youngster survive? What had God done about their pre-birth covenant to give this child to his service?

Their prayers followed him around the world for several years until a letter came from Canada to share the glad news that Christ had captured his rebel will. Soon the letters told of an American Bible School; then of a girl called Helena, 'well educated and refined'[165] in contrast to his uncouth, sailor's toughness; next of a needy land called Congo and, at last in 1916, of their expected arrival in Holland on their way to missionary service in Africa, eighteen years after John had left home.

On the mountains overlooking Lake Albert, John and Helena pioneered a ministry to the Alur around Ara. He, with his thick skull, and she, much quicker to learn, were beginning to converse in the difficult language when she told him that she was pregnant. Despite his arguments, she insisted they could not spare the weeks necessary to reach Rethy Hospital for the delivery: 'I have prayed much concerning our baby,' she told him, 'We will remain here at Ara and trust God to help in the delivery.'

After five excruciating days in labour Helena gave birth to a lifeless little girl. John wrote that his wife felt well that day until

she suddenly took ill. She had a chill at night which caused a high fever. I had buried baby with my own hands that same day, but

I took it up again and placed it in the same bamboo coffin with my wife. Wish you could have seen them lying together, baby in wife's arms. They just looked as if they were enjoying a peaceful sleep . . . My dear little wife and baby girl are in glory . . . We were married thirteen months.[166]

British Uganda and French Equatorial Africa

The young widower moved to Aru where he heard of famine in adjoining Uganda. A hundred porters helped him carry food for the starving, but he recognized at once a deep spiritual emptiness. Later he slipped across the border to help the Gardners set up their home in Arua. When malaria drove them out, he took their place.

Any spiritual void challenged John. Five years after participating in the Uganda thrust, he set out on his bicycle for French Equatorial Africa. The rough tracks ruined his machine, forcing him to abandon it except for the front wheel with a precious milometer in its hub. He asked an African friend to push it all the way for he was travelling on uncharted paths and must know the distances in order to draw his maps.

He crossed the wide river on the Zaire border, sent word back that he recommended nearby Zemio as a new centre, built a small mud hut and settled down to await reinforcements. When they arrived, he was off again looking for new sites until he wandered into the Baptists' compound in Bangassou just before Christmas.

His hostess smiled when she saw the state of his safari clothes, patched with anything he could find – yellow into one trouser leg, lavender into the other and a piece of red striped rag holding the shirt together. She laughed outright at his 'evening dress' on Christmas Eve – a pair of tired pyjamas – and sat up late to make him a Christmas present of two pairs of shorts, shirts and handkerchiefs.

Others followed John to establish churches among the 40,000 Zande people of French Africa and John, with his pioneer task accomplished, returned to Congo.

He became engaged to a fellow-missionary, Mabel Easton, before leaving for furlough in 1928. On his return they were married by Lee Downing in Kijabe and commenced their united service at Kasengu among the Alur whom they both knew so well.

'Their characters were complementary. John was typically Dutch, with a strength of serious conviction. Mabel had a humorous way of tempering his sometimes outspoken opinions and smoothing over situations created by his bluntness of speech.'[167] One of his aversions was 'the home where the woman wears the overalls'. He declaimed against this weakness at a missionary conference. Next time all the missionaries met, Mabel amused them with a photo on the notice board of John in a well-patched pair of overalls. The caption read, 'Overalls over'auled'.

John found that 'village work is but one continued planting and watering, sowing and praying'.[168] But, as Africans like Moro Sheeba proved more effective as evangelists, his emphasis shifted: 'The greatest duty before the missionary is that of training teachers and evangelists . . . If he can train and send forth 25 Africans he will reproduce himself that many times.'[169]

Mabel shared his vision. At a course for fifty primary school teachers she wrote, 'There was always before us the vision of an "invisible audience", the scores of boys and girls in the little bush schools to whom they would be going back. It was like talking into a sort of human amplifier.'[170]

Most missionary households picked up one or more servants. They too could become human amplifiers. Some quickly learnt the skills of kitchen and garden, releasing the missionaries for a multitude of other tasks. They often traced the roots of spiritual life to this close relationship as they listened to the missionaries' message and, perhaps even more convincingly, observed their lives. A surprising number rose to leadership in the churches; one became the national President.

Proximity in the home led to strains and surprises as Mabel describes,

> One day our house boy Ukumu came with his month's wages in his hands. Something in me stiffened for a fray. We have a classic little protest here if wages are considered to be inadequate. We simply cast it scornfully on the table and depart with chin up, and a 'Too-proud-to-accept-such-a-pittance' air. I was all braced to deal with this impudence (not too gently, I fear), when Ukumu said shyly, 'This is for the Cup of God.' 'All of it?' I asked weakly. 'Yes,' he said, and put it into the Bwana's hands. I felt like a very small long-since-gone-out-of-circulation-one-centime-piece (which by the way has a hole in its midst). And yet something in me sang 'God moves in a mysterious way his wonders to perform.'[171]

While they marvelled at the great sweep of God's church planting programme, they never lost their sense of awe when confronted by his work in individual saints like Neema for example who is an almost toothless, wrinkled, old, Lugbara widow. She will never learn to read. She still wears a fig leaf and grass bustle. But Neema has given three children to the Lord's work. When we visited her village recently, we found Neema with half a dozen other women busy hoeing in 'God's Garden', the proceeds of which go into the Cup of God.

The Cup of God took an important place in a church which accepted the burden of paying its own workers. The Elders knew their responsibility for discipline too. At their local church council meetings,

> final decisions are made in the light of scripture precept. For example – a young teacher's helper had slapped one of his students in the interests of discipline and probably under provocation. 'What does the Word of God say?' demanded Noa, the presiding elder. 'What did Jesus say to Peter? He said "Feed my sheep," didn't He? Did He say, "Slap them?" ' And there the case rested.[172]

Nine years after their wedding, they visited America (for John's second time away from Africa in eighteen years). He studied dentistry in order to assist missionaries before giving another unbroken period of nine years to the Alur – this time at Goli in Uganda. A colleague, who appreciated John's skill, questioned his belief that fillings must be replaced every few years. He replied, 'Open your mouth wide and I will fill it.'[173]

South Sudan

Looking northwards they saw many mouths wide open with no one to provide the bread of life. After several years of prayer John and Mabel goaded AIM into sending a survey party into the south-eastern corner of Sudan in conjunction with the mission's old friends, the Church Missionary Society (CMS).

In their early days in Sudan, CMS hosted a visit by C.T. Studd but Studd decided against working with Anglicans. Now they told AIM that their work in two small centres could not possibly meet the needs of seventeen tribes, representing over 500,000 unreached people, scattered across 300 miles of rough mountain and plain, desert and swamp. To the north Islam held sway over millions more.

At the age of sixty-seven John drove his wife and another couple through Arua, where he had pioneered forty years previously. Soon after crossing the Sudan border, they manoeuvred their two vehicles onto a ferry consisting of a platform lashed astride two huge dugout canoes. Anxiously they watched muscular men pole the contraption across the Nile. With a mixture of relief and excitement they arrived at Opari a few hours later.

CMS had built their Opari rest house as an overnight stopping place for a visiting missionary. Now its three little rooms sheltered two couples and a baby. 'Black friends appeared from nowhere. There was no question of their welcome as they thanked the white people for coming and told them of the long, long hope now realized. It was heartwarming. It is not always thus in Africa.'

The AIM team grew and John set out to open new centres, Katire Ayom among the Acholi and Logotok for the Lotuka. The Sudanese welcome continued for the remaining eight years of their leadership. They returned to America where doctors detected a weakness in John's seventy-five-years-old heart. Forbidden to work any long in Africa they continued to battle for Sudan in prayer. They had passed on their vision for the three countries in which they served. Little did they realize the tragic blows that would pound their colleagues over the next half century.

Martha Hughell and Barbara Battye

Martha, a nurse from Idaho, gazed downwards from the airliner approaching the end of an overnight flight from London.[174] As she watched the Nile far below twisting like a green serpent through the Sudanese desert, she recalled the conviction God gave her while studying in Oregon University. He wanted her in Africa. She pondered too the years of preparation in hospital and Bible College which followed. The plane lost height and a mixture of excitement and apprehension gripped her. It touched down on a sandy runway. As she stepped through the door, a blast of heat took her breath away.

Old John Buyse met her and shepherded her through the airport formalities. They drove past smart colonial offices, through shabby suburbs which seemed to be peopled mostly by goats and naked children, over a bridge spanning the Nile and south for ninety miles to Opari.

John asked Martha to learn the Latuka language while waiting for a team to gather for a new centre. During her months at Opari, Martha met interesting people. Pastor Andrea Vuni told her that he was about as old as the century. Rev Davies of the CMS had helped him to find Christ and had baptized him at the age of twenty-three. CMS then trained him as evangelist, teacher and pastor, and eventually placed him in charge of all their work to the east of the Nile. In the end they graciously took their hands off their disciple, suggesting that he work in fellowship with AIM.

In August 1951 the medical team moved up to Logotok. The Latuka crowded around, enthralled by the unpacking process, and offered to help Martha settle in. At the end of the day she discovered that they had helped themselves too – to several small items.

The clinic, with bamboo walls and grass roof, acted as a magnet. Healthy warriors swaggered up complaining of 'too much spit'. Rather than dismiss them as a joke, the group decided to give each a few bitter tasting drops of quinine, which won sufficient confidence to persuade mothers to bring their genuinely sick children.

Martha was too good at the language to spend all her time in the clinic and soon began teaching, along with a new arrival, Barbara Battye. She discovered that she and Barbara possessed different personalities which God welded into a friendship destined to survive more than forty tumultuous years.

Barbara, a Home Economics graduate from New Jersey, reached Logotok on a Friday almost a year after the medics. Martha sat her under a tree on Monday morning to start learning Latuka vowels. As soon as she could string a few words together, Barbara taught the boys – falteringly at first causing much mirth. As people lost their fear of the newcomers, she started classes for girls and, later, for women. The two valued the health care and the mind-stretching three Rs, but they knew that only the power of Christ could transform lives.

By Barbara's first Christmas they wondered if they could detect the first sprouts of spiritual life. The Buyses drove up from Opari to celebrate two births – the Lord's and little Susan Reitsma's. Mabel described the congregation which included Barbara and Martha and a hundred Latukas, 'a little group of schoolboys in neat white shorts and shirts, . . . women in goatskin skirts and girls in more scant attire, . . . an unexpected number of stalwart warriors and recent workmen standing about with spears in their hands. Royalty was represented by Chief Lotura (a potent rainmaker), very resplendent and conspicuous among his unclad brethren.'[175]

Drawn by a desire to read, a young man asked for a job. Martha employed Lohima and admitted him to the classes. Teaching in the home and the school soon bore fruit and he asked the Lord Jesus for forgiveness. Christ responded by changing his life. He celebrated his transition into new life by changing his name to Tomaso. Wary lest his hopes be set more on a job than on Christ, the missionaries continued to teach him for a further two years before baptizing him. Later, seeing his love and zeal, Martha and her friends decided to send him to Adi Bible School in Congo as a potential pastor for the Logotok Church.

Besides teaching and nursing, love appeared in other ways. The people in each of AIM's four centres suffered in the recurring droughts. Earl Dix arrived with his well rig – 'two truck-loads of heavy clanking tubes, pistons, pumps and other mechanical paraphernalia'. Few who have never endured thirst can understand the relief when he struck a water table 200 feet underground. To the missionaries his ugly machinery became 'a symbol of power and of loving concern.'[176]

Although serious sickness occasionally struck the team and living conditions were far from easy, a spirit of optimism prevailed.

First friction

The first indication that the spread of God's kingdom in Sudan would be painful came early in 1955. Doug and Kim were in Zaire for the birth of their third child and Martha at home in America. On a hot February night in Logotok, Barbara woke to the cry, 'Come quickly . . . Fire!' Once out of doors her heart sank. Most of the hospital roof was ablaze. While she watched, the roof caved in, flinging sparks high into the sky. A brisk wind swept them onto the doctor's home and soon flames consumed all the Reitsmas possessed and equipment worth thousands of dollars.

The ashes smouldered for days and then local men, sifting through the debris for clues, found a baked print of a crooked foot. It matched the Reitsmas' servant who belonged to a clan, the Ebaree, recently at war with the Logotok people. Jealous because the local wounded received care in the hospital which they dared not seek, the Ebaree reasoned, 'If we destroy the hospital, the Americans will rebuild in our own village.'

Barbara soon became enmeshed in a more sinister conflict – between massive ethnic blocks rather than neighbouring clans. She knew that two different races populated the Sudan: Arabs in the north and indigenous Africans in the south. The north was desert, peopled by Muslim tribes; the south, fertile, and the home of traditional African religionists. Between them an immense swamp prohibited links by either rail or road; only the river steamers and aeroplanes travelled the thousand miles between the capital Khartoum and Juba. The slave trade a century before left such a legacy of northern contempt and southern resentment that the colonialists administered them almost as separate nations.

In mid 1955 Arab officers in the South Sudan Defence Force attempted to disarm the southern troops, who then mutinied, killing seventy-two Arabs. In the midst of the fracas, too close to Logotok for comfort, Barbara misread a radio message and decided to leave with the only other missionary there and her children. Night fell as they drove and, with darkness dangers increased. They tensed as they saw headlights approaching only to find they belonged to their new director, Sid Langford. Sid accompanied them to Congo where they rested for two months while the dust of rebellion settled.

Although reinforcements quelled the rebellion, they drove resistance underground where it festered – to burst out again and again in tragic confrontation.

New Year 1956 gave birth to independence for Sudan, centred in the Muslim north. AIM's fifteen missionaries in four centres thanked God that 'The Government is cooperative . . . we may expect to occupy other areas to the East.' Two African missionary couples from Congo joined the team and five young Sudanese Christians crossed the border in the opposite direction to study in Bible schools. Even so, the combined African and western missionary force seemed woefully inadequate for the many still unreached tribes. They wrote of the need for reinforcements so that they could break out of the 'beachhead' which they had established.

But the beachhead was coming under increasing pressure. Further violence forced the missionaries to leave the country again for a few weeks. Joy at getting into harness again was shortlived as the Government took over the mission schools just a week after they reopened and banned all village and market meetings. New laws forbade missionaries to speak of Christ to any non-Christian over eighteen. The Provincial Governor, jealous of the drawing power of compassionate health care, ordered the Reitsmas and Martha to leave.

In 1962 the 'Missionary Societies Act' prohibited witness to Muslims and confined missionaries' ministry to Christians and pagans in specified areas.[177] By the following year the

1. A North Kenyan warrior

2. A Rendille man in North Kenya

3. Soldier in Belgian Congo

4. Pilot Les Brown with hospital fee for a sick passenger

Photo: Ed Arensen

5. Martha Hughell

6. *Radio work*

7. *Friends*

8. *Jonathan Hildebrandt*

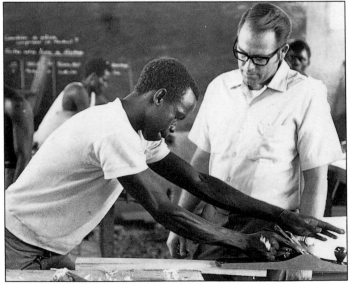

Photo: Ed Arensen

9. *Bill Stough*

10. Kattie
    Mackinnon

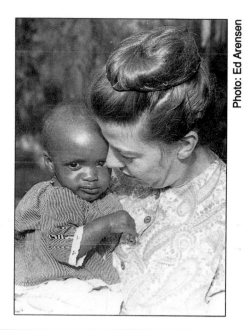

Photo: Ed Arensen

Photo: Ed Arensen

11. Barbara Battye

12.
Listening

Photo: Maurice Wheatley

13.   *Africa Inland Church, Kijabe*

Government had terminated the service of ten of our missionaries. A wave of unrest made travel hazardous and forced hundreds of Africans to flee south across the borders.

A sniper's bullet wounded a United Nations couple. A new AIM leader, Harold Amstutz, replaced Sid (who became American Director). Driving one day, he heard a rifle shot and ducked just in time to avoid another bullet which missed him by 'a millimetre and a second', dislodging some metal that struck him in the arm.

Government accused missionaries of supporting the rebels and then expelled the three hundred missionaries of all societies in the three southern provinces.

Reluctantly Barbara and another colleague left Pastor Tomaso Lohima to continue at Logotok with eleven church members while fighting escalated. The Muslim noose tightened around the south, threatening Christian leaders and murdering some. Two years after the evacuation of the missionaries, Tomaso escaped, travelling by night with his family to Kuluva hospital in Uganda. After rest and healing, he moved into a Sudanese refugee camp to continue his work as a shepherd.

Martha and Barbara worked at Becker's hospital, Kagando, for most of their seventeen years' exile. Martha pressed on to complete her translation of the Latuka New Testament in 1965.

In 1972 the President of Sudan, General Nimeiry, achieved a peace agreement with the 'Anyanya' army of the south. The civil war had displaced a million southerners, most of them across the southern borders into Kenya, Uganda, Zaire and Central African Republic; but many were never seen again.

Pastor Andrea Vuni survived the war. Two of his sons, Abednego and Nikolao, returned after using their refugee years to study theology in Kenya's Scott College. With Tomaso and other homecoming leaders they determined to see AIC rise again from the ashes. AIM first assisted them with transport and with money for rebuilding but they requested more than money; they wanted resources for a Bible school, health care, schools and a farm. They wrote to Barbara and Martha and asked them back.

The ladies arrived at the District headquarters, Torit, once a smart government centre, to find a shattered ghost of a town. The AIC director now occupied the AIM leader's home. But driving north little had changed. They splashed through a familiar marsh in low gear, frightening storks, hammerkops and a lazy heron. On the track to Logotok they paused sometimes to level step-like wash outs. Long grass waved above the

Landrover, often obliterating the path, and rammed seeds into the radiator so that no air could penetrate. A field of sorghum spread across the old road.

Hesitantly they walked over the old airstrip, hidden now by bushes, and suddenly the stark gable end of Dr Reitsma's brick house poked up above a sea of millet. Roof iron and timbers had long since been rifled but the bricks, cemented only with mud, still stood firm against the weather. A frustrated rebel had scrawled across the wall, 'Do people dominate us to be the servants. Why?? Think deeply.'

As they pondered whether this was a reaction against Arab oppression or missionary imperialism, excited people came running from the villages around to welcome them and help pitch their tents.

Others responded to the request of the church leaders until the AIM personnel tally reached a record of thirty-four. Sudanese pastors fostered little congregations. Other agencies came to help the war-torn country. Over the next few years a tide of development swept South Sudan: huge machines scraped smooth roads across the plains while others bored down to deep water tables; youngsters crowded into schools and newly trained community health workers set up clinics; agriculturalists demonstrated appropriate techniques and trained Sudanese counterparts.

Frustration and fruit

Changes in government soon threatened peace and progress. A new religious experience persuaded the President to commit himself more fully to Islam and to institute Muslim 'Sharia' law. Church leaders, upset by the barbarity of amputations for theft and the lack of legal rights for Christians, boldly protested. Southern warriors stirred.

Soon armed bands roamed the southern plains. They began to coalesce into the Sudan Peoples' Liberation Army (SPLA). Life in the city was safe but out in the bush anything could happen. Early in 1985, Lanny Arensen, AIM's team leader, brought the missionaries out to Kenya for two months. Five transferred to the north, where thousands of Chadian refugees were fleeing aggression in their own land.

Barbara and Martha returned with a depleted team but faced mounting violence. Lanny and his wife, Janis, visited Riwoto, where a church was growing. Travelling homewards, Lanny heard a gunshot on the left of his Landrover and realized at once that it had blown out a front tyre. Wrestling with the steering, he accelerated. A second shot caught Janis in the side. A mile down the road he stopped and was devastated by what he saw. Janis was writhing in agony from an ugly abdominal wound. Many hours later, still in great pain, she died on a plane flying to Nairobi.

Once again missionaries left the remoter homes. At one hurriedly abandoned centre, Keyala, rebels found the mission houses and stores heavily padlocked. Sniffing around four big drums they smelt petrol. They scattered the fuel everywhere and, with great glee, set it alight. Thatched roofs roared into flame and aluminium walls melted. Martha and her friends lost most of their personal possessions in the blaze. Other homes disintegrated more slowly before the onslaught of pilfering fingers and the invading 'bush'. The missionaries withdrew into the city of Juba.

Like green shoots thrusting through Keyala's black ashes at the first scent of rain, the Spirit brought life in the midst of suffering. Through the Latuka grapevine the ladies heard about baptisms at Logotok. In one of the dilapidated houses the Christians found a bath with piping to the roof tank intact. Although no water had run into the tank for several months, none had been drained out either. They filled the bath, immersed several people and refilled it with clean water. Forty-three new believers demonstrated their faith in the Lord Jesus amidst great joy.

When AIM returned to assist AIC in 1978, Martha learnt new concepts of health care, less dependent on costly hospitals, more on training local people to prevent and treat common ills. Convinced of the value of this approach, she followed it again when forced into Juba in 1985 where thousands of displaced folk placed overwhelming demands upon the few nurses. Also, with the tide of fighting advancing and receding all the time, she doubted the sense of spending precious time and money on costly buildings. Slowly Christ-centred care for the poor spread in the huge camps and people responded to his love in a measure unknown in the prosperous years of peace.

In the late seventies missionaries built a Bible school and Pastor Nikolao Vuni became Principal for a time. Although they had to abandon the precious new buildings when war surged through, the AIC continued the teaching programme in Juba. With churches beginning to multiply in Juba, Barbara became increasingly involved in this effort to prepare pastors.

She faced another unexpected challenge. Lanny departed to take up an outreach ministry ranging across many countries. In the tradition of AIM the missionaries (including the women) appointed other men to take the lead. At times they could not find a suitable man and then they turned to Barbara. To her own surprise, Barbara felt comfortable as a leader. The team supported her. Other women, especially the singles, shared their concerns in a way they could not with a man. Government officials welcomed her. She thought they figured, 'Oh well; here is a woman. She doesn't threaten us and doesn't really know what is going on. So let's help her.'

Over seven years tensions built up until the team left in 1992. The crew of a Russian jet welcomed them. As they rose from Juba, spiralling up to ten thousand feet to evade rebel missiles, Martha sadly thought, 'I've had enough of that shelling, fighting, insecurity and government suspicion. We have done what we could.' The future for the remaining Christians seemed grim; she wondered, could the church survive? In fact the church was on the threshold of her greatest expansion.

Douglas and Gill Reitsma

ACROSS

Gill Livsey, in England after six fruitful years of teaching in Kenya, heard an Australian doctor, Tony Atkins, appeal for teachers in Juba.[178] She discovered that Tony directed the African Committee for the Rehabilitation of South Sudan (ACROSS), a conglomerate of Christian societies (with AIM as one of four founder members) who wished to pool their resources to help South Sudan recover from its disastrous war.

When she arrived in Juba, Gill joined a growing team of doctors, nurses, well drillers, teachers, engineers, agriculturalists and administrators. ACROSS established a four-year agreement with the government but sought to cooperate as much as possible with the churches.

Like others, Gill wished that the churches controlled ACROSS. But they needed to find their own feet after their fiery ordeal and to tread cautiously with a new government, still Islamic, although much more friendly to the south than its predecessors. African pastors warmly welcomed ACROSS workers but advised, 'Please continue to deal directly with government about your projects.'

She experienced the teething troubles of a new group drawn

from up to twenty different organizations. Inevitably she missed the warm, family fellowship she had known in AIM. With the rather short-sighted emphasis on accomplishing projects, ACROSS made no provision for language learning and cultural orientation at the start.

Juba Girls' Secondary School tested Gill's fortitude. She analyzed the smells: urine dominated the entrance; further down the path frying onions prevailed; elsewhere Juba's universal stench of decaying vegetable matter hung over the school. The lack of discipline among the girls surprised her for African youngsters normally value education so highly that they almost revere their teachers.

She rejoiced when ACROSS asked her to join Juba 'Model' School with a go-ahead committee of intelligent Sudanese Christians who sought an example of quality education. The name confused westerners (one pilot thought it was a school for mannequins) but the Sudanese understood it and, in fact, one of the first African teachers set up a similar school when her husband was appointed a bishop.

The AIC sent a young pastor, John Moi, to start a church in Juba. Gill joined the tiny congregation trying to make sense out of the chaos they had experienced. They met in a dusty classroom but there was nothing dusty about the message nor about their desire to see churches multiply among the increasing numbers of displaced people drifting into the city.

Gill visited a clutch of three small churches of refugees from Zaire. When the tide of war had turned against the Simba, a group of them arrested a pastor and demanded at gunpoint that he accompany them 'to teach the words of God'.[179] Rev Alfonse faithfully stuck to his call. As the refugees fled across borders, he carefully taught them that even wild murderers could experience God's forgiveness. Unwanted in Central African Republic (the old French Equatorial Africa) and blamed for all the local crimes when they tried to settle in Juba, they wandered a few miles south of the city and planted gardens in fertile land along the Nile where they erected their grass-covered churches.

ACROSS depended upon an air link with Kenya. Missionary Aviation Fellowship and AIM's own AIM–AIR served the team. In February 1977 an AIM pilot, Hal Bowman, flew in with passengers and supplies. That night Gill was asleep in a school dormitory when gunfire jolted them all out of their dreams at 2 a.m. They scrambled under their beds. The more timorous crawled over to Gill, who comforted them with Scripture and prayer until the gale of shooting subsided with the dawn. They emerged cautiously to hear that the Sudan Air Force had failed in an attempt to overthrow the government. Evening brought bad news. Hal, taking advantage of a lull in the fighting, made a dash for the airport. Although stopped by a patrol and ordered to turn round, he went forward and was shot in the neck. He died at once – Another AIM martyr in Sudan.

In the turmoil surrounding the end of Idi Amin's reign in Uganda, many refugees fled into Sudan. The government and the United Nations High Commissioner for Refugees requested ACROSS to provide schools, health care and water supplies for the new camps. When a similar situation developed far to the north with 23,000 refugees from Chad, they again asked ACROSS to help.

Several workers settled the Chadians into a loosely organized city of low huts called Angi Koti. They served food, treated sickness, aborted a deadly outbreak of cholera, delivered pregnant mothers, nursed starving babies back to life and, in every service, trained Sudanese counterparts. Mutual respect blossomed into many friendships and a happy atmosphere pervaded the huge camp. They needed more workers and AIM asked Dr Doug Reitsma, now a widower at 65, to consider serving there. He got no closer than Juba.

The nightmare of any feeding programme is long-term dependency. An ACROSS director borrowed a visiting helicopter to search for unused land which the Chadians might farm. A camp official, frustrated by close supervision which prevented his selling famine food for his own profit, produced a battery of complaints against ACROSS: the director photographed military positions from the air; he used the helicopter at night to transport supplies for rebels; ACROSS fostered SPLA cells in Angi Koti; it passed radio messages to the British government; and, most damning of all, workers held secret Christian meetings designed to convert Muslims. The government, ignoring all denials and refusing to discuss the charges, expelled ACROSS from the north. Doug met the disappointed team as they returned to Juba and became their doctor.

Roaming SPLA bands made life dangerous in the southern rural areas. Three times they kidnapped ACROSS personnel. A nurse resolved the first crisis by preparing stew for the rebel guards and spicing it with phenobarbitone. While they dozed, the captives crept away and were picked up by an army patrol.

On another occasion, rebels inflamed by a visiting Marxist propagandist, arrested an AIM pilot and beat him viciously with a hippo-hide whip. They confined him and his passengers in a hut until the Sudanese army rescued them.

The third arrest caused even more anxiety. The rebels held four workers for six weeks in a situation of extreme discomfort. Eventually ACROSS located them and negotiated for their release. AIM–AIR (the flying service of AIM) flew the Nigerian director of ACROSS on a hazardous mission through gunfire to rescue them.

Romance among the ruins

At these times of crisis, the missionaries in Juba met each evening for special prayer. Doug noticed that Gill visited friends before the meetings and often arrived hungry. He invited her to share his rice and beans. Amused that he kept his tea warm by wrapping a towel around the pot, she made him that most English of articles, a tea cosy. His thanks were more profuse than she felt the act merited ('including physical contact' as she coyly tells it) and suddenly she became aware that he had fallen in love. Through a ham radio link into a British telephone, she told her delighted mother that Doug had proposed. When he shared the news with his family, they all said, 'Go for it Dad.'

No one could remember a white wedding in Juba. Church leaders made it into a big occasion with a reception continuing until well after dark. Children kept it alive for weeks with such specially composed songs as 'Oh Dr Doug come and meet Mrs Gill'.

The Liberation Army captured some important towns and advanced on Juba. War devastated the villages scattered across the southern plains, forcing their impoverished people to flee to the city. Juba's population of 30,000 swelled to 450,000, mostly living in simple dwellings around the outskirts. At times, when the rebel stranglehold on the city tightened for a while, aircraft offered the only food route. The Lutheran World Federation and Missionary Aviation Fellowship attempted to maintain supplies but came close to losing the battle. The death toll mounted with people falling to undernutrition, sickness, SPLA shells and government bombs.

The AIC pastor in Torit heard Sudan Air Force bombers overhead and ran to shelter in an old shell crater. As he was about to jump down, a cobra reared its head and he swerved to seek refuge elsewhere. A bomb whistled towards him and he ducked.

Looking for the point of impact, he found that crater and cobra had collected the full blast.

In the midst of danger, people turned to God and found strength. Hardly a family escaped bereavement but believers multiplied. The solitary AIC congregation which Gill joined ten years previously developed into fifteen churches in several different tribes. AIM had hoped to send evangelists to the seventeen tribes east of the Nile; instead God brought the people to the evangelists in Juba. A core of veteran pastors and missionaries supported youngsters graduating from the Bible School and together they cared for the churches.

1988, according to the London *Times*, 'was a year of tragedy which has displaced two million people, killed 250,000 from starvation, a year in which Sudan had its best harvest in ten years'.[180] SPLA seized crops, planted mines, raped, tortured and stole while the government 'deliberately denied food to its southern towns to depopulate the rebellious region'.[181] Despite their explanations, government leaders continued to pillory the relief agencies and Sudanese churches for assisting the naked and starving, claiming that they fed and clothed SPLA. Khartoum's *Sudan Times* was aghast at the Arabic press which 'unleashed a barrage of spurious allegations and outright abuse against the Red Cross in order to discredit them in the eyes of the public'[182] and at the 'Minister who stood up in the National Assembly last Wednesday and announced that the Islamic trend government intended to phase out all western-backed relief operations and replace them solely with Islamic and Arabic organizations'.

ACROSS was now ordered to abandon all their work in Sudan. Churches asked some of the workers to remain under their direction and Doug stayed to run AIC clinics while Gill taught in the Bible school.

In 1989 another quarter of a million starved because of war. But good news spread too. The Reitsmas wrote, 'Atanasio, Anton and Juma walk several miles – across the Nile – to hold Sunday School under a tree.' Funerals went on for three days and provided the evangelists with the opportunity 'to point the mourners to the hope they can have in Christ'.[183]

In the rest of Sudan, hundreds of thousands left home in search of food and security. Over a million settled around Khartoum where food was known to be available to those who would convert to Islam. Some became Muslims but thousands turned to the Lord.

ACROSS became the kind uncle with a long arm stretching

out from its Nairobi base to help Sudanese wherever they could with food, medicine, clothes, student bursaries, Bibles and other Christian literature. The spiritual harvest had never been so ripe. A Sudanese pastor wrote, 'Christians have nothing, but they are rebuilding the churches. The worse the war is getting, the more people are coming to the Lord. Since 1905, when the first mission station opened in our land, nothing has happened like what is going on now.'[184]

The siege of Juba intensified. Shrapnel pelted through the roofs of the two missionary homes. When rebels mounted a successful raid into the centre of the city, killing 200 army officers as they slept, government blamed collaborators. Soldiers retaliated with sudden dawn arrests, tortured their captives and executed many. Corpses floated down the Nile. Bulldozers and tanks flattened the homes of 100,000 settlers around the city, mercilessly crushing occupants who failed to leave in time. Some returned to search for food in their gardens and stepped on freshly laid mines.[185]

Doug fought an expulsion order for two weeks. On 3 September 1992, security police roared into their compound to force them out. Pastors and friends quickly gathered for a final hug and prayer. At the shell-pocked airport Doug was too dejected to resist when the customs official confiscated his radio (in spite of an export certificate) and opened their cameras to rip out films of their final gatherings with the Juba saints.

Over the next two years Doug and Gill watched the Sudan from their British home. By early 1994 they reckoned one-fifth of Sudan's 27 million people had been directly hit by the previous ten years of civil war: 1.5 million had died, 4 million were displaced within Sudan (about 2 million southerners as squatters in and around Khartoum), about half a million refugees existed in Kenya, Uganda, Zaire, CAR and Chad.[186] Outside Sudan, missions and aid agencies mounted relief and training programmes. But within, the Spirit of God used Sudanese 'human megaphones' to spread his word. The Reitsmas wrote, 'Various missions have reported finding huge congregations of believers in remote areas.' But, tempering optimism with caution, they added, 'Few of these have pastors or trained leaders.'[187]

10
The wind of change

In 1960 the British Prime Minister, Harold Macmillan, completed a lengthy safari across Africa. In Cape Town he addressed Parliament about emerging African nationalism. 'The most striking of all impressions that I have formed since I left London is the strength of this African national consciousness,' he told the South Africans; 'The wind of change is blowing through the continent.'

Of the countries where AIM worked, Sudan had already been independent since 1956. Over the next four years the cry of *Uhuru* (Freedom) shook off the colonial yoke in Uganda, Congo (Zaire), Tanganyika (which fused almost at once with Zanzibar to become Tanzania), Kenya and French Equatorial Africa (Central African Republic).

During the years following Macmillan's speech, the new African consciousness brought muscle into the churches. Under African leadership, church growth exploded. Masses responded (even if sometimes superficially) to a Gospel which was relevant to them. The Bible became a bestseller. Bible schools multiplied. Many observers concluded that the Holy Spirit, who like the gale blows where he chooses, not only rode high on this wind of change but was its Author.

Despite the mission's long-standing commitment to indigenous church principles, the new African attitude of 'we can do it ourselves' surprised the western leaders. Their correspondence reveals uncertainty, alarm, complacency and, at times, indignation.

Philip Henman, Chairman of the International Conference which the mission set up in 1955 to foster cooperation between all the mission councils, addressed the influential American Council on 14 December 1960, 'The situation that faces us in Africa is like the smog in Los Angeles, difficult to describe and, in some ways, indefinable.' He recalled Congo's recent tragic stumble into national autonomy and told the council, 'Our tendency for the moment seems to follow the same Belgian path of not having policies outlined that will prepare the way for the future.'[188]

He insisted that the mission base its new policies on the principle of taking second place, 'in other words that the Mission should become the handmaid of the Church . . . subject and obedient to their authority.' For this to happen, AIM needed 'to be integrated into the organizational setup of the African Church' and the missionaries must become members of that church. Henman recommended that the same Constitution govern church and mission. The Council agreed with Henman and asked for the International Conference to convene within a few months to discuss the new situation and to invite African leaders.

Looking back now, we can wonder why Mr Henman seemed a revolutionary. But mission leaders in Africa at that time disliked the appearance of a home council dictating policies for a field situation, feeling that none understood the African scene as well as themselves. One wrote, 'In the AIM we have a very close integration . . . African and European work together in the closest harmony, and full administration in the work is being handed over to the Church as it will take it.' Henman could not believe him and resigned.

If some African church leaders in the early sixties thought of their relationship with the mission as 'integration' and 'the closest harmony', the gathering storm of nationalism forced them to think again.

Congo led the way. Well before independence, the far-sighted Dr Becker urged the Africans into an autonomy they scarcely sought (p. 125) so that, when the storm struck repeatedly in the sixties, they grasped the helm and steered the church through troubled waters. In 1965 they warmly welcomed the missionaries back from their third evacuation into a new era, no longer as supervisors but as servants. Seven years later the Church in Zaire completely absorbed the mission. God had used the ugliest possible face of nationalism to fashion a strong fellowship.

The mission, guided by its councils, learnt little from the Congo/Zaire experience. Tanganyika's church and mission leaders struggled through years of contention before achieving a similar result. Kenya possessed AIM's largest band of missionaries (175 in 1961 which rose to 255 in the next ten years) as well as a strong strain of foreign settlers. These influences, combined with President Kenyatta's benign attitude of forgetting discords of the past, lulled the mission into believing that its identity would continue strong. With controversy threatening the future, the International Conference met in May 1962 and confidently assured the mission family 'that relations between the Church and mission are generally satisfactory in all our fields and we confirm our faith in the policies already adopted.'[189]

AIM groped through the ensuing smog with difficulty. Exasperation often marred fellowship and fed confrontation. The wind of change gusted for two decades before producing in each country an organization akin to Henman's vision.

Erik and Emily Barnett

Erik Barnett, more than anyone, steered the mission's largest team through the troubled sixties. His background had prepared him well.

When Erik's parents arrived in Kenya in 1908, their party of twenty-three doubled the mission membership. They took over the Maasai work from the Stauffachers. Two years later Mrs Barnett gave birth to twins, Arthur and Erik.

Entering the mission school at Kijabe, Arthur and Erik swelled the enrolment to eleven. Rift Valley Academy could only take them up through their first seven years so they continued schooling in America. Erik met Emily, the daughter of the Professor of Greek and Church History at Columbia Bible College. They married and sailed for Kenya in 1934 and went first to Litein among the Kipsigis people.

One church and three preaching points served the two vast Kipsigis districts for which AIM accepted responsibility. The Barnetts set out to increase these through the generally accepted strategy of preaching, teaching and multiplying schools. Today the AIM-related churches number six hundred.

When the Japanese attack on
the American fleet in Pearl
Harbor precipitated the USA
into war, Erik and Emily were
drawing to the end of their first
home leave. The war forced
them to remain until 1945 but
Erik benefited by joining the
staff of Wheaton Academy. Back
in Kenya again, Erik's reputation as an educationist led his
colleagues to appoint him
Education Secretary for the
whole mission. AIM's long
vacillation over the value of
schooling was over. Erik could
now plan beyond the meagre
four basic years of elementary
reading and writing.

Erik Barnett, DD

His enthusiasm paid off. In
some of the schools 70 per cent of the pupils became Christians.
The church was born in the classroom.

He was too late on the scene to prevent the tragic loss of many
of the original Kikuyu schools and churches, but he could help
the recovery. He remembered his parents visiting a Kikuyu
church in the 'White Highlands' (named because European
settlers developed farms in the lush hill country, with the
assistance of Kikuyu labourers). A rival group threatened the
worshippers with death. One by one the congregation withdrew,
leaving just the two missionaries and Pastor Samuel Wandudu
on their knees. The mob outside wanted to burn the building
down, but prayer prevailed. Years later Erik returned to the area
and, over a period, baptized more than a thousand new believers,
most of them from AIM schools. In 1949, the missionaries in
Kenya chose Erik as their Director.

Then the Mau Mau storm burst, threatening to empty the
AIM churches again, but Christians stood firm, strengthened
by a deeper knowledge of God's word through the improved
teaching in schools and churches. Many paid for their faithfulness
with their lives.

Hundreds came one day to witness the baptism of seventeen
young people. After a communion service an elder asked Erik,
'Did you see what was down there in the baptismal pool?' He

pointed to an ugly crucified dog which Erik had not noticed. 'Mau Mau have sent us a message to show how they will treat anyone we baptize today,' he said. Each of the youngsters read that threat but entered the water undeterred.

Uhuru

Cars crawled bumper to bumper along the road leading out of Nairobi towards Mombasa. Some spent four hours on the four-mile stretch from the city centre to a new stadium erected for the Independence celebrations on 12 December 1963.[190] To the rhythm of tribal dancers, newly appointed Kenyan Cabinet ministers took their places alongside seventy-six foreign ambassadors. Erik and Emily, in their reserved grandstand seats, watched the crowd gather with apprehension. How would the new chapter in Kenya's history unfold under the direction of Jomo Kenyatta, recently released from his seven-year prison sentence for managing Mau Mau?

After the initial speeches, the Duke of Edinburgh, representing his wife, the Queen, told the multitude that Great Britain formally relinquished government to independent Kenya. Lights dimmed. At the stroke of midnight a band played 'God Save the Queen' and the Union Jack dropped, marking the end of seventy years of colonial rule. Slowly a new flag mounted the pole – crossed spears over a shield on a background of red, black, green and white. Erik and Emily joined a bit awkwardly in the unfamiliar words of the Kenyan national anthem.

250,000 throats yelled, 'Uhuru' again and again as Kenyatta moved towards his microphone. He waved his fly switch and the crowd roared back. The master orator began, 'Let's forget about the past and build a new nation.' Cheers echoed around the stadium, 'Freedom . . . Uhuru . . .' The President ended with a rousing cry which was to characterize his fifteen-year reign, 'Harambee . . . Harambee (Let's pull together).' Erik sighed with relief.

Erik's emphasis on education fitted the new Kenya. He foresaw the boom in secondary education and persuaded the mission to recruit many graduate teachers. Kenya, he was convinced, needed Christians in her schools. Along with other mission leaders he petitioned Government for Bible teaching in all schools. President Kenyatta encouraged them, 'My Government recognizes the importance of the spiritual development of our children and I would like to give an assurance that this will continue in our schools.'[191]

Scott Theological College, CM

The Field Director wanted tertiary education as well. He sponsored a conference to consider leadership training for the churches. The speakers appreciated the six Bible Schools and two Pastors' Courses which provided strong leaders but they realized that these schools would not meet future needs on their own. In two days of prayer and discussion God gave them a vision to develop a central Theological College offering higher leadership training for the churches. Remembering the mission's founder, with his dream of African evangelists, they called the new venture 'Scott College'.

The mission magazine of July 1965 pictures the first six graduates of 'Scott' with their teachers. The accompanying article lists two diploma courses – for students successfully completing ten and twelve years of schooling respectively – and it mentions plans for a Bachelor of Divinity programme. Under Erik's leadership, AIM in Kenya had come a long way in the twenty years since their first grudging decision to give more than simple reading skills to young Christians.

One body or two?

In a commendable drive for a mature, self-governing church, AIM formed the Africa Inland Church in the early forties as a separate body, although its doctrine and organization drew heavily from AIM patterns. AIC control extended to evangelism and pastoral care. The mission retained responsibility for Bible schools, Literature, Radio, Medical Departments, and negotiated with the colonial government on behalf of both bodies. AIM saw two sister organizations working as partners, each respecting the other's autonomy.

In 1955 AIM internationalized. In the new setup each Field Council sent delegates to a Central Field Council (CFC), the 'co-ordinating authority' of AIM's ministry throughout Africa. A larger umbrella, the International Conference, covered the CFC as well as the Home Councils. The two bodies first met at Kijabe and appointed Erik Chairman of CFC.[192]

Erik and his colleagues puzzled over the question, 'Should missionaries become members of AIC?' Dedication to the principle of 'separate but equal', led the CFC to the surprising decree, 'that missionaries should not be considered as members of the local church . . . but as members of the Church Corporate, which is Christ's Body, they are enjoined to enter faithfully into the fellowship of the local church.'[193] Philip Henman, watching from afar, felt uneasy about this theological juggling.

At its next meeting CFC further emphasized the organizational difference between church and mission because, unlike the church, the mission 'is an intermediate agency, not a final goal in itself. The duration of its life does not depend on its inherent nature, but on the need for its services.'[194] Erik and his colleagues on CFC believed that God called missions to temporary ministry but churches to a permanent witness. A mission should establish the church and then move on. But Henman saw the stark contradiction of the two working side by side in parallel relationship without belonging to one body, the church.

In subsequent years AIM learnt from the two viewpoints. At the time a third was ignored – the Africans' – and, in the prevailing conviction of national identity, Kenyan opinion inevitably dictated the outcome.

When the Field Council met with AIC leaders, the missionaries came with policy guidelines already prepared. Harmony prevailed in initial discussions. On 26 March 1963 (nine months before Uhuru), five church leaders and five missionaries signed an agreement along the lines of the CFC directive. If misgivings flitted through the African minds, they did not surface until a year later when the Church's General Secretary urged a closer working relationship.[195]

On the national plane the Government demanded rapid

Kenyanization of its own departments as well as commerce and industry. While courteously welcoming the continuing input from westerners, Kenyatta insisted on African leadership. The media asked, 'When will the churches become independent of foreign control?' AIM could answer, 'the church is autonomous'. AIC had doubts: could their yoke to a foreign and autonomous mission compromise their own Uhuru?

At the same time, AIC leaders began to suspect the AIM theology of the local church; surely, they reasoned, all the members of the Body of Christ in a locality constitute the church, regardless of race. In a joint meeting of mission and church leaders they asked that AIM 'be joined in one organization with the AIC'.[196] They did not convince Erik and his Council to abandon the principle of dichotomy. The AIM leaders asked, 'How will the AIC handle such technical departments as Health Care, Printing and Radio?' Andrew Gichuha, President of AIC replied, 'You may still drive the car, but the car now belongs to us.'

The discussion dragged on, trying patience and testing fellowship. Early in 1969 the Church presented a demand for 'One name in the place of AIC/AIM . . . one leader . . . one constitution . . . one body of Trustees . . . one treasury . . . one central office . . . one set of rules for the work.' The missions responded, 'There must be two organizations, the Mission cannot be dissolved.'[197]

A Kenyan stated in amazement, 'When Uhuru came, many denominations tried to bring forward the Africans in the Church . . . But it appears that AIM is not going forward but backward . . . If we speak of bringing the Africans forward, then we are talking of something that AIM is not interested in.' At the same meeting another bluntly stated, 'Missionaries need to change to be more like the missionaries of long ago, and identify with the Church . . . Are we not one?'[198]

The American and Canadian Home Councils recognized an explosive situation fraught with danger and sent their two directors to listen and learn at first hand. While possessing no authority over the Field Council, their seniority gave them great respect in both mission and church. They found on the one hand that Erik was seeing a need to compromise and, on the other, that church leaders could understand some of the missionaries' fears and allay them. At a final joint meeting in June 1970, AIM agreed to the Church's demands with only a few reservations which AIC readily approved.

Thousands of Christians gathered on October 16 1971, in the presence of Kenya's Vice President, The Hon. Daniel Arap Moi, for a new Uhuru celebration. Ed Arensen, editor of the mission magazine, described it as 'The Day The Mission Died'.[199] Both mission and Church had new leaders. They read the Agreement, one in English and the other in Swahili, 'The AIC in Kenya shall govern itself and be responsible for all its activities. The AIM Kenya takes the position of a department in AIC.' AIC would direct all the church-related work and take responsibility for missionaries, properties, and money.

'Suddenly I realized our Mission was not dead,' wrote Arensen; 'It had simply allowed itself to be buried in the Church it had brought into being. Now through the Church the Mission could spring forth in renewed growth and service.'

Erik and Emily could not join the great celebration for family responsibilities took them home to USA. A great innovator in education and in many other spheres, Erik reluctantly recognized the necessity for the mission to relinquish all leadership in Kenya. Gration served with him for several years and says, 'He was a strong leader, had a great vision and could make things happen. We knew where the Kenya field in his mind should be going.'

The Barnetts demonstrated their willingness to work under Kenyan leaders by returning for a further ten years of Bible teaching. Eventually Emily's Alzheimer's disease sent them to the mission's retirement centre in Florida where Erik said, 'Even though both of us are hitting eighty-three, the Lord has given me strength to help my sweetheart for these four years. It's a tremendous privilege. She has looked after me for fifty-five years so I can certainly look after her.'

Yeremiyah Mahalu Kisula

A strong and godly African prodded AIM into the new era in Tanzania.

Had you heard a British judge sentencing young Mahalu to six months in jail, you would never have suspected that God's hand would rest so powerfully upon him. He was one of six guilty of breaking their contracts to work in the sisal plantations in Pangani on the coast. Although the law required sentencing, their foreman pleaded for their release and the exasperated colonial official ordered ten lashes for each.

After two more years of unrewarding work in the plantation,

Mahalu's conscience troubled him. He heard a voice, 'What are you doing here? When will you serve me?' Yeremiyah Mahalu Kisula recognized that voice and remembered his youth. As a careless sixteen-year-old beginning to dance, steal and lie, he had received an unexpected shock – his clever brother suddenly died. Mourning beside the grave, he asked himself, 'What can save me when my own day comes?' After much questioning he first heard that voice saying, 'Believe me.' Mahalu told himself, 'These are just my own thoughts' but the voice persisted until he determined to test its truth. Against his father's wishes he went to church. At last, in 1920 (aged seventeen now), he listened to an evangelist asking, 'Who wants to believe in Jesus?'

Mahalu wrote later, 'My heart trembled with fear but I did not believe on that day. No believers lived in my village. In fact, any convert would face the charge of contempt for tribal custom and would not obtain permission to marry.' For a week he counted the cost and, on the next Sunday, 'I believed Jesus Christ to be my Saviour totally. I left church full of joy.'[200]

His furious father threatened to kill him if he returned to church. He pondered the prohibition and decided to face the threat squarely. Next Sunday evening the old man asked, 'Where did you go today?' 'I went to church.' Father asked a second time, 'Where did you go?' Then he picked up a heavy stick and began to beat Mahalu about the head. Fortunately a visitor restrained him but his enmity continued until the youngster moved ten miles away to live alongside the church.

Five months later, the missionary at Kijima baptized Mahalu, who chose Yeremiyah as his new name. He chose aptly for, when he went home again, his family continued to criticize his faith and to blame him for sickness which struck his three sisters and himself. One died and he longed for the same release, especially when his parents begged him with tears to consult a diviner. But God healed him and he decided to go to school in Mwanza.

He must have learnt quickly for, after only a year there, the missionary admitted him to Kijima Bible School. Sent out at the age of twenty to assist an evangelist, he found a wife and persuaded his reluctant father to pay the bride-price in cattle. Three months in another assignment failed to suit him so he requested a transfer and was told, 'You can either stay or quit the work of evangelism.' He chose to quit.

Surely, he thought, his education would open the door to a lucrative job in the regional centre, seven days' walk away. But no one wanted his services. Finally he accepted a contract in a distant sisal estate, reached after a long train journey and a further fifteen-day hike. Backbreaking labour, from dawn to dusk, for a mere 24 shillings a month (20/- = £1 Sterling) forced him to break his contract and end up on the ground outside the Tanga Commissioner's office with a kiboko (a whip of hippohide) biting into his flesh.

Evangelist and leader

Challenged by the voice, Yeremiyah decided to go home. He knew the risks from evil men and wild animals along the way. 'Lord,' he promised; 'If you will care for me along the road and bring me safely home, I will serve you in any way you wish.' For six days he walked night and day, collapsing beside the path to sleep a few hours in the hunting grounds of lions, rhinos and buffalo. At last he reached the railway and a train brought him to Tabora where he set out again for a four-day walk to Emil Sywulka's mission station, Nyida. Here the prodigal found a warm welcome from the church and told them 'all the sins I knew I had committed against God'.[201]

He made his way home and immediately began to preach in fulfilment of his vow to God. Many trusted in the Saviour and a church began to grow. Soon the leaders of the work recognized his call and placed him on the official roll of evangelists. They sent him to a church ruined by two promising evangelists who had slipped into sin. With Yeremiyah's ministry for the next five years the church became strong again.

Missionaries sent him to a new work on Ukerewe Island, from which he travelled widely preaching as far as Musoma. Ten new churches sprang up through his sacrificial ministry. To Yeremiyah's surprise, the missionaries transferred many of his churches to the care of the newly arrived Mennonite Mission without consulting him. The pain of that presumption rankled for many years.

Although the missionaries sometimes acted insensitively, they never faltered in their commitment to find God's chosen leaders and to equip them for service. They sent Yeremiyah back to Kijima for two further years of study and then, in a solemn celebration on 8 January 1939, Emil Sywulka, assisted by two Tanzanian and two missionary pastors, laid hands upon his head to set him apart as a Minister of God's Word. One of his first official duties was to baptize his younger brother.

A year before Yeremiyah's ordination, the AIM Field Council took a momentous decision with implications beyond the imagination either of the mission or their church. On 22 January 1938 the council gave the church 'self rule but under the authority of the AIM'.[202] Although no Africans sat on the Council, Yeremiyah, as a student at Kijima Pastors' Course must have taken part in the buzz of discussion occasioned by this step towards indigenization.

African colleagues recognized gifts in this young pastor in addition to his great ability as an evangelist for they elected him Synod Secretary in 1938, Vice Chairman three years later and Chairman in 1943 at the age of forty. Meanwhile Pastor Yeremiyah busily planted and pastored churches in a succession of assignments, appointed no longer by missionaries but by the Tanzanian Synod of AIC.

In missionary thinking, 'self rule' included self-support. Previously they had supplemented the giving of the churches in order to ensure that pastors and teachers received their full salaries, tiny though these were, but now the churches must find all the money themselves. Although this unilateral decision struck the Africans as harsh at the time, Yeremiyah later used it to emphasize that 'they [the missionaries] simply came to the realization under God that we were ready and able to care for our own church. We were the very first church in all of Tanganyika to become autonomous.'[203]

Towards the end of the next year war broke out between Great Britain and Germany. Missionaries recalled that in the previous war most AIM people were forced to depart. Although Britain now controlled Tanganyika, many Germans still lived in the country and it could again become embroiled in fighting. They asked themselves, 'What will we do with our property if war makes us leave?' They discussed it with the church leaders and agreed that the Africans would inherit it. To the Tanzanians, 'self rule' suddenly assumed the larger dimension of a take-over.

No evacuation took place and the arrangement, always only provisional as far as the missionaries were concerned, faded. It niggled in some African minds as an unfulfilled half promise.

Political consciousness heightened in the late fifties. Denominational missions handed full responsibility to their daughter churches for the ongoing work, giving them homes, offices and often a foreign financial subsidy as well. As Independence approached, AIC looked for similar freedom from all AIM control. Although misunderstanding marred subsequent discussions, a fundamental bond of fellowship held the two organizations together.

AIC wanted to appoint a leader. 'Beware,' warned AIM, 'It is not fitting for the Church to have a Head like the Pope or Bishop, but all Christians are alike.'[204] The Synod expressed surprise, noting that missionaries always appointed a Director. On 4 and 5 February 1958, the leaders appointed Yeremiyah their first Director. Later, to the horror of some missionaries, they changed the title to Bishop.

'Born by the wrong mother'

With the newly independent Government of Tanganyika driving its 'Africanization' policy, the Church became more confident, demanding not only full freedom from mission control, but also the right to rule the missionaries. The leaders decided that new missionaries should fill out an application form and submit it to the Church for their approval. In addition no missionary would return to Tanganyika from overseas leave without the consent of the Synod.

AIM resisted. The mission felt obliged to stand by the principle of two parallel organizations promulgated by the Central Field Council. This stated that, in addition to the mission acknowledging the full autonomy of the Church, 'The Church in each Field recognizes the AIM as a fully autonomous body established for the purpose of fulfilling the Great Commission.'[205]

Bishop Yeremiyah asked, 'Why can you not become members of our local churches and unite with us?' The mission replied that membership of churches in America prevented their joining another church. The answer sounded hollow even to many missionaries and their leaders. Other reasons lay deeper. Some objected to the submission to African leadership which church membership implied. Many, while recognizing the Church's spiritual ability to lead the evangelistic and pastoral ministries, doubted that she had adequate skills to direct the technical departments. They wanted to keep these separate, under mission control. More fundamental and scarcely discussed at the time (except by a few men like Erik Barnett and his colleagues in the CFC), a basic difference exists between the work of a church and a missionary society.

AIM agreed to withdraw any control over 'Church Work' and AIC interpreted this as including all the ministry of the mission apart from personal financial matters and the education of missionaries' children. Subsequently the Field Council pointed out that 'Church Work' to them meant preaching, Bible teaching, and Bible Schools but not such departments as

Education, Medicine and Literature.

The bishop and his colleagues, propelled by the force of the successful struggle for political independence, insisted on total leadership of the work. The Field Council, despite pressure from CFC to uphold the dichotomy policy, began to compromise. In 1962 they agreed to pass on the Evangelism and Education Departments immediately, with the Medical and Literature to follow a year later – the delay allowing time to prepare African managers for these technical ministries. But they continued to reject the contentious application form.

Yeremiyah Mahalu Kisula, DD

Courteously grateful for the concessions, the Church Synod refused to give ground on the form. Several missionaries wished to return from their home countries but the church leaders insisted that they first gain church approval. In defiant mood AIM brought their missionaries back and placed them in the two departments still under mission direction. AIC countered by forbidding these missionaries any ministry in the churches. The mission then withdrew the promise to hand over the remaining two departments.

AIC sighed as they saw their brothers in the Anglican and Lutheran churches gliding easily into independence from their parent missions. A delegate to Synod complained, 'We have been born and established by a mother. Unfortunately we were born by the wrong mother.'[206]

Yeremiyah said (at Kola Ndoto),

Well, such matters troubled us greatly. Then we remembered that the missionaries of the AIM have those (in) authority over them; so we wrote to the CFC (Central Field Council), stating our grievances. In December 1963 the CFC came to Tanganyika and listened to both sides of the question in real Christian sympathy. They came to the conclusion that the AIC is without fault and the missionaries are at fault. The missionaries acknowledged their fault and asked our forgiveness, which of course we granted.

Fellowship was coming back again! The CFC said, 'But our brothers there is just one thing . . . the Form. Drop that altogether.'[207]

Some missionaries found the CFC capitulation tough for it reversed the guidelines that council laid down only two years previously. Although a few missionaries had disagreed with these guidelines (including their Field Director who resigned) the Field Council had followed them as best they could. Those who had thought the original guidelines correct understandably felt betrayed by the new decision.

Gladly accepting these further steps towards their goal, the Synod appointed missionaries to lead the medical and literature ministries. The bishop told them, 'You manage these departments for us until we are able to do so ourselves – when that will ever be, I don't know.' AIM's leader, Paul Beverly (his title changed from Director to Field Secretary out of deference to Tanzanian leadership) wrote, 'It is now the goal of the AIM to assist the AIC in administering these departments in such a way that the National Church will be able to handle them without the assistance of the foreign missionary.'[208]

One step only remained – mission recognition that the Church had the right to decide who they would accept to work with them. It was only a matter of time before AIM gave consent to this also.

In fact the AIC only refused the return of one missionary from leave but a number quietly asked the mission to assign them elsewhere. The missionaries felt a certain harshness from the new leadership – a legacy from the years of what the church saw as mission prevarication. If to some the bishop appeared aloof, the Field Secretaries (Paul Beverly 1964 to 1970 and Russel Baker, 1970 to 1980) formed close personal friendships with him and recognized his godliness. As dignified as an African Chief, he showed courtesy and firmness which demanded attention. 'But you could still eat with the Chief, relax and laugh together.'[209]

In twenty years from 1961, the number of AIM people serving in Tanzania fell from eighty-eight to twenty-one. At the beginning of that period evangelism and church planting marked time while the Church built an administrative machine. Then Bishop Yeremiyah asserted his old love for preaching. He travelled widely but said, 'My heart is heavy; for miles and miles we travelled – people everywhere, but no church.'

Uhuru injected vigour and confidence into evangelism. The socialist government insisted on gathering people into large communal villages. Although the experiment failed, God's Spirit turned social change to his own advantage and the Church advanced.

11

Serving the saints

When the European war broke out in 1939, the Kenya Government recruited a labour battalion from the Luo Tribe and sent them to the northern semi-desert to dig latrines and build roads. Despite good pay they soon threatened mutiny.

Mystified, the East African Command looked for an officer to resolve the problem and found a young settler who spoke the Luo language. He quickly discovered a misunderstanding: they had become soldiers expecting to wield guns, not shovels. But they could adjust to the menial tasks, as well as to the harsh environment. Their uniform upset them, especially the headgear; they hated their hats. The army issued the Luo labourer with a pill box having a flap to protect the back of his neck, and the fighting man with a wide-brimmed bush hat. The message was clear: the government valued front-line troops more than supporting soldiers.

The authorities changed the offending garments and wisely appointed the settler to command the battalion. He trained them into a crack unit of rapidly mobile engineers, and led them into battle first through the Ethiopian campaign and then in Burma.

David, soon to be King of Judah, resolved a similar issue at the Besor Ravine when he decreed, 'The share of the man who stayed with the supplies is to be the same as that of him who went down to the battle.' (1 Samuel 30:24) By insisting that all share equally in the plunder, he showed that he counted the men who cared for the base as important as those who fought.

The Luo battalion and David's small army learnt the dignity of servant ministries which support the front-line soldiers. Less obvious to them at the time, both experienced the blessing of firm, caring leaders.

Serving in leadership

The first fifteen members of AIM gladly followed their Superintendent, Peter Cameron Scott. When he died they looked to his assistant, Fredrick Krieger, to direct the infant operation, but Krieger led unwillingly and the team fell apart.

Charles Hurlburt took over and, for twenty-six years, attempted to keep the growing family of missionaries united in fellowship and in purpose. By 1920 he needed to visit teams spread over large areas, poorly connected by roads, as well as colleagues in USA, Britain and Australia. Inevitably the leader became remote. In each country missionaries elected a council and director to provide overall supervision but much of the responsibility rested on the individual in his or her location. To many, their General Director seemed out of touch and his pronouncements dictatorial.

Before Hurlburt resigned, the American Council appointed a 'Committee of Direction' but these five men in New York could never provide the vision and nurture that characterized the early days. Without international direction each council became autonomous in its own area and the missionaries, often reacting against firm leadership of the past, developed a large measure of independence. The loose organization stimulated personal initiative but stifled united action.

Twenty-nine years after the departure of Hurlburt AIM took hesitant steps again towards what he had called 'overall leadership' by establishing the International Conference to co-ordinate the work worldwide with a subordinate Central Field Council to tie the councils in Africa together. In practice the mission relished consultation but rejected control. The system faltered.

But the need for a central leadership group to serve the mission increased. In 1968 leaders stated, 'The International Conference recognizes the need for a full study of Mission Administration.'[210] They commissioned a consultancy called the Christian

Service Fellowship to perform this evaluation and then distributed their frank report (of 283 pages) throughout the mission for study.[211]

Prodded by this study, the Conference decided to change the central body to an International Council, empowered 'to provide close and effective co-operation and spiritual unity between councils and to be the final authoritative body of the Mission. It shall be charged with the formulation and co-ordination of general Mission policy and practice, at home and on the field'.[212] Heeding the consultants' advice they appointed an International General Secretary (IGS) and envisaged Associate Secretaries for specific functions. 'The International Council,' they stated, 'exercises its jurisdiction over the Mission's work through the IGS.'[213] In the flush of a new beginning the IC drew up 'Goals for the Seventies'. One of these resulted in a major outreach initiative, another in closer relationships with African churches, a third in more effective care for missionaries.[214]

Serving in support

Care for missionaries became an ongoing puzzle for the IGS and his team. Throughout the seventies work expanded while road travel became increasingly difficult and expensive. Many tried the air and found to their surprise that they could both save money and increase efficiency. A missionary, Arnold Newman, received a gift of a plane and offered to fly his colleagues at running cost only. He and his wife, Marilyn, founded AIM–AIR which multiplied to include a DC 3 and six small Cessna aircraft.

Soon we realized that missionaries would save much time if a department could purchase their supplies to put on the planes, arrange international flights, care for mission properties and provide a central banking facility. AIM–AIR grew into an organization of several departments called 'AIM International Services'.[215] It provided an umbrella to other international ministries. Jim Propst, senior doctor/engineer, and his two missionary sons established a technical consultancy to guide and help amateurs responsible for construction and engineering. Meeting a different sort of need, a psychiatrist and a psychologist together set up AIM–Care to offer therapy and to teach missionaries to counsel each other. By 1993 this bundle of services kept fifty-nine missionaries busy.

Josephine Hope Westervelt

Long before the days of the International Council, missionary families faced a most important aspect of care – the education of their children. While leaders at home recognized this priority, they did not recruit anyone specifically for it for many years. When, eventually, the mission's representatives at home publicized the need, teachers heard and responded, as convinced of God's call to Africa as any church planter.

Like many new missionaries, Josephine Hope appreciated the privilege of sailing with Charles Hurlburt. One day he drew a deckchair alongside hers and talked about Kenya. He asked, 'Would you be willing to teach the children of missionaries?' She thought for a moment about her love of teaching which she expected to use in serving Africans but why, she asked herself, should anyone be unwilling to teach the children of missionaries? 'Sure,' she replied, 'I'd be glad to.'

Everything seemed so new to her when she met the little band of missionaries in the 1906 Kijabe conference a few days after her arrival. As soon as it finished she sat her first four pupils on the dirt floor of a bare, ten-foot-square room with rough walls and a cloth ceiling, shielding them from the insects and strands of straw which occasionally fell out of the thatch. In the absence of any equipment they learnt remarkably well.

Other children arrived, both black and white, and her schoolroom quadrupled, with two rooms for the MKs (missionary kids), one for the Kikuyu and a shared chapel to emphasize Josephine's educational priority. She taught both races together in the mornings and the whites alone after lunch.

Kiambogo

Like most AIM ventures the school, with its grand title of Rift Valley Academy (RVA), began with no resources apart from an enthusiastic person who possessed boundless confidence in a God who answers. She prayed about the curriculum and received advice from the American schools in which she had taught; she asked God for teachers, books and desks and they arrived the following year; she shared with him her dream of a building to house fifty pupils and money came.

Josephine and Hurlburt selected a flat site called Kiambogo, the Place of the Buffalo, and he agreed to supervise the construction. His Indian builders were frightened when a brick kiln exploded. They searched the local ravines until they found

Kiambogo RVA, CM

semi-hard volcanic rock and chiselled it out for Kiambogo. Hurlburt surprised Josephine by inviting ex-President, Teddy Roosevelt, to lay the cornerstone.

Some missionaries walked forty miles to the ceremony on 4 August 1909. Recent settlers from Britain and South Africa, who saw RVA as the only source of quality education for their children, mingled with government officials to listen to the renowned American leader. He commended Miss Hope for 'not only . . . working for the natives but for the settlers' children and the children of your own missionaries.' With a good grasp of missionary thinking he congratulated Hurlburt on the mission policy for African education, 'I am so pleased that you . . . teach the teachers and train the trainers among their own fellow tribesmen and raise them, not to become make-believe or imitation whites . . . The men you teach can thus teach others whom you cannot reach.'[216] The missionaries rewarded him with his favourite 'real American pumpkin pie'.

Kiambogo housed only a dozen MKs and a handful of settlers' children. By this time the mission provided separate schooling for the mass of Kikuyu. Lack of furniture increased a sense of emptiness in Kiambogo. A few months after Roosevelt's visit, Josephine visited the States in search of supplies. She found more perhaps than she had anticipated. When she got back to Kijabe, a fellow missionary, Theodore Westervelt, married her and moved into RVA.

Josephine established a firm Christian foundation for RVA, stressing Bible study and prayer. To settlers and officials, who asked her to educate their children, she carefully explained that she and her staff aimed to lead each student into a Christian commitment. They rarely failed.

Just before the outbreak of war Josephine became ill. Doctors diagnosed a heart disorder and warned her that Kijabe's altitude would make it worse. Under the best conditions in USA, they reckoned, she might survive two years. Sadly the Westervelts handed the work over to others.

Many grieved over their departure. Lee Downing's eleven-year-old daughter, Lucile, had

> beautiful memories of some of my teachers who were gifted and dedicated . . . Then I have memories of others! Occasionally the Field Council had to force people to teach a term or two at RVA. Many felt that teaching white kids was not mission work — they had come to Africa to work with the Africans! Some were qualified; some were not, and most of this group were not only unhappy themselves, but made life miserable for the students.[217]

Several times lack of personnel forced the school to close for a term but by 1915 AIM policy clearly stated, 'Our missionaries' children should have the best school advantages which are possible, while their parents are taking the Gospel to the lost.'

When Erik Barnett enrolled with his twin brother in 1917, they brought the number of boys to four while the girls mustered seven. He remembered, 'We had very happy times together.' At the age of eleven he responded to a preacher by giving his life to the Lord – a commitment which still bore fruit seventy years later. When other 'European' schools opened in Kenya, the number of non-missionary children at RVA fell. The Barnett twins completed the seven years available to them at RVA and left for high school in California.

The Westervelt boys

The doctors' prognosis for Josephine Westervelt proved wrong. Although her heart condition prevented her return to Kenya she never lost her love for MKs. The Westervelts developed a ministry to MKs attending college in America, eventually moving to Columbia, South Carolina, where a University and a Bible College offered all the education the young men needed.

Josephine trained her family vigorously: the fellows cooked, cleaned, washed and ironed; they turned out their lights at ten and rose early; for breakfast they ate oatmeal porridge with lashings of milk but no sugar or salt. She forbade dating. 'You must get your education first,' she insisted, 'then you will be mature enough to know the kind of girl you need.' Although modern teachers could feel that she aimed more at control than growth, Erik Barnett says, 'We didn't chafe at the discipline. We were there to learn the best we could. As far as I know, everyone of us had an early call to missionary service.'[218] In the summer vacation they drove around the States as a family, stopping wherever a church would welcome them, to give a lively presentation on Kenya, assisted by their violins, piano, trumpets, singing and curios.

In 1932 Josephine took in girls and soon accepted families. She began offering schooling herself using some of her students to teach between their Bible College classes. One of the young women remembers

> that the first time I saw her I fell in love with her. She was very warm. There was so much love in her, she just won my heart. The men too had great confidence in her. Yes, it was maybe austere because there were no frills but MKs had no use for frills anyway. They went to her with their problems. Whatever mistakes she might be making, they accepted that she meant it for their good.[219]

Much good resulted. All but one of the eleven lads they took in returned to long ministries in Africa – three Barnetts, Linnell Davis, Propst brothers, Earl Andersen, two Stauffachers and Emil Sywulka. With the development of high school at RVA, the demand for the home in South Carolina declined.

In the mid twenties the RVA enrolment averaged eighteen and the school puzzled over staff shortages. The early thirties saw the Westervelt boys return along with other RVA graduates. Having experienced the benefits of a first-class education themselves, they wanted their own children to receive full schooling in Africa up to university entrance. Many linked this with a commitment to advance African education at least through high school. One of them, Herbert Downing, arrived at RVA to begin a ministry spread over forty-one years, during which he transformed a small and struggling school of thirty pupils into a first-class institution of more than 400 in twelve grades.

Kiambogo still sits at the heart of the RVA complex, its rugged volcanic stone testifying to the vision of the school's founder.

Roy and Judy Entwistle

Kiambogo became the ministry base for another American couple.

Roy and Judy Entwistle studied in Seattle, where they shared a home with several single students. One of these complained bitterly that throughout five high school years in America he never saw his missionary parents. As a result he neither trusted them nor their God. The Lord used his testimony to stir Roy and Judy to work with missionary children, providing education on the field so that children would not spend years apart from their parents. Hearing of AIM's commitment to care for its MKs, they applied for RVA.

Ken Downing met the boat train at Nairobi and drove them the thirty-five miles to their new home. They passed Kikuyu women bent by huge burdens on their backs, barefoot schoolchildren, and better dressed men riding bicycles or chatting outside small shops. Many peered at the newcomers and shook a forefinger to express their certainty of the approaching black rule under their hero Jomo Kenyatta, who in 1962 was still detained in northern Kenya by a colonial regime in its twilight.

Perched on the edge of Africa's huge Rift Valley at 7,200 feet, the newcomers soon understood the meaning of 'Kijabe' – 'The Place of the Winds'. Far below them the Maasai plains spread southwards towards Tanzania, pierced here and there by rugged volcanic craters, while, at their backs, forest climbed the escarpment, broken by patches of maize gardens, each embracing round thatched huts and an occasional modern, rectangular house roofed with corrugated iron.

Christians no longer questioned the validity of ministry to the children of missionaries. Thirty years earlier, when Herbert and Mildred Downing had agreed to the Field Council's request to take over RVA, friends at home could not understand why their missionaries ministered to white children rather than black and had withdrawn their promised financial support.

The Entwistles joined a staff of twenty-six missionaries looking after 150 pupils. The old Kiambogo building sat at the heart of a complex spread over twenty-five acres, seldom sufficient for the rapidly increasing educational needs of the missionary force pouring into Africa. Like the rest of the staff Roy developed a deep respect for Mr Downing (he never got round to calling him Herbert) whose pioneering background seemed equal to every building challenge. Mr Downing's quiet temperament and fluency in the Kikuyu language steered RVA through the storms of Mau Mau and now held the school on course as the surging tide of nationalism threatened to engulf it.

Dilemma of growth

In the sixties RVA faced a policy dilemma: should the school limit numbers to their existing facilities or admit all MKs and expand to cope? The Board, composed of missionaries (who are usually visionaries), opted for the latter. Enrolment exploded. Pupils crowded into dormitories built for half the number. A dorm parent found herself in the impossible situation of caring for seventy-five girls. Such rapid growth presented a daunting challenge to both Principal and Board. New buildings sprang up.

In 1976, Roy inherited Downing's mantle as Principal of a school which continued to mushroom. He reckoned never to refuse the child of missionaries. Christians who were not missionaries, coveted the RVA education for their own children, but sadly Roy had to say no to many. A trickle of African students began in 1964 and swelled modestly to forty-five Kenyans in 1993 and a dozen from Ethiopia, Tanzania and Uganda. They included two sons of Kenya's President Moi.

The Entwistles' letters to supporters share joys and sorrows. Early in 1984 they wrote, rejoicing in conversions; even children from Hindu, Muslim and Sikh homes had found Christ. But life was tough too, 'It is wonderful to have experienced the Lord's strength in seeming failure – student disciplining problems, pressures that seemed too great at times, personnel problems and misunderstandings, concerns for family members, etc.'[220]

Like the Downings before them, husband and wife teamed together in the school. Although responsible for a growing family and home, Judy taught French and mothered students.

Throughout the eighties missions across Africa continued to grow. As pressure built up on the facilities, Roy realized that only major expansion would enable the mission to maintain the generous policy of accepting every MK. In May 1987, he faced the necessity of turning down thirty applications. His board, fearing lest RVA develop 'into a large, impersonal school', advised slight enlargement to a fixed limit and thereafter to explore other possibilities. With the number of AIM children forming less than a third of the total enrolment, some Board members questioned their responsibility to provide an unlimited service to all missions. Roy, on the other hand, shuddered at the prospect of limiting missionary work in the Continent by failing to supply educational opportunities for MKs and asked, 'Has God not given AIM experience and resources in the past which qualifies them to increase this service in the future?' The more he pondered and prayed, the more he believed God wanted AIM to take a fresh, bold step. He presented the International Council with a carefully reasoned request for a second school in Kenya.

The Council met in beautiful Spring weather outside the historic city of Bath, England, and grappled with forceful arguments. On the one side Roy and many of his staff urged expansion, fortified by their call to serve missions; on the other, several board members pleaded the case for caution, afraid that AIM might divert from its prime church planting role. After many hours the Council stated its great appreciation of RVA adding, 'IC considers RVA to be primarily a ministry *to* AIM missionary children and only secondarily, if space permits, a ministry *of* AIM to other Christian agencies, African and expatriate children.'[221] While willing to assist others to set up a second school, AIM would not accept the responsibility of administering it.

Seven years later, when RVA was educating over 500 youngsters, Roy still found it painful to discuss his disappointment, unconvinced by the reasons which prevailed against it. He told the Lord, 'I don't understand; I tried to present what I thought you wanted but it is not accepted by those in authority over me. So I must humble myself to your will.'[222]

Roy and Judy built on a solid foundation of prayer, laid by Hurlburt, Holt and the Downings. Staff and students developed a daily prayer meeting and drew on the immense resource of a mass of concerned parents who interceded daily for their children and the academy. They sent out calls for special prayer at any time of crisis such as the political uncertainty which followed the death of Kenya's respected first President in 1978.

Prayer prevailed too in the daily struggle to provide a first-class education. They aimed for standards which 'will more than meet the minimum requirements of any school to which pupils may go to complete their studies.' By Roy's time university entrance was the goal for all who could make it. The staff and board invited the Middle States Association to evaluate the whole operation and treasured the official accreditation they eventually gave. They coveted spiritual results even more than secular recognition. Each precious pupil, regardless of academic gifting, must be equipped for life. The handbook stated, 'The formal objective of RVA is to bring to the attention of every boy and girl the importance of salvation of his and her soul, not only through instruction in Scripture . . . but in every phase of the school experience.'

At the same time a strange flood of new teenage mores in the homelands sent eddies into RVA, demanding careful assessment and cautious adjustment. Parents, whose picture of western behaviour patterns inevitably became outdated, puzzled over their children's behaviour and sometimes criticized the school. Even Roy's new generation of well-trained educators, coming specifically for a missionary ministry in RVA, felt the strain. Discipline suffered and students did not benefit from the spiritual training as much as the staff hoped. The effect, according to a teacher, Warren Day, was a nominal Christianity; 'The kid who really wanted to stand for Christ had a very difficult time. Everybody knew how to say what we wanted to hear but then they would be what they wanted to be.'[223]

Then three young men approached him saying, 'We want our senior year to count for Christ. We're starting an early morning Bible study and we'd like you to join us – not to lead but to be one of us.' The group expanded and then split into two. A study for girls started and soon several groups met regularly. Warren and his wife invited them all to their home once a week for fellowship and by mid year counted eighty. Next they looked for an evangelistic outreach. Shocked by a film, 'The Exorcist' showing in Nairobi, they wrote a tract and picketed the cinemas, handing it to all who came out.

A spiritual hothouse and a cultural island

Daily chapel, Sunday services, dormitory prayers and Bible classes provided a strong diet for independent-minded young people. If some put on Christianity as a cloak, which they shed as soon as they got away, a large majority followed the Lord throughout their lives; even rebels turned to the faith they had once learnt but despised. In 1993 eighty RVA graduates served in AIM, twelve of them on the staff of RVA.

Janice Dunkerton, daughter of the Field Director in Tanzania, and her husband Richard, whose father led AIM's pioneer team into Lesotho, were both RVA students. Janice kept in touch with most of the sixty-four people of her class. Ten years after leaving school, only two made no Christian profession and they did not come from Christian homes. All the rest served the Lord, over eighty-five per cent in one form or another of full-time ministry. She said, 'Even some we didn't think would last as Christians are now preachers.'[224]

Roy and Judy always regretted that RVA's demands on them prevented adequate language study. As soon as they arrived, they plunged into the school programme. They worked at Swahili in the evenings when their busy schedule permitted, but, without the opportunity for full-time study and practice, they never became fluent. Even so, they quickly befriended many Africans. Every Sunday they aimed to worship in the local church, often taking the whole school with them – an amazing mix of well-educated professional people, farmers, traders and MKs. The church expressed their appreciation by appointing Roy to the Board of Elders for over fifteen years. He knew the youngsters often found the services indigestible but persisted, recognizing their need to keep a foot in local Christian culture. The newly-awakened students found opportunities to serve the poor in many practical ways and some Kijabe folk made time to teach the Bible in Kikuyu primary schools.

Despite these links, Kijabe appeared like a western island in the midst of an African ocean. Over 100 missionaries worked in RVA, while many others served a big hospital (a centre for specialist services, training and community care), Bible School, Literature Department, African high schools, etc.

Roy wrestled with the problem. He said, 'We are always caught between the conflict of relating to an African community and preparing students to move into other cultures in the future.' Those cultures were in moral crisis and he wanted to equip men and women to live as Christians in them.

As well as entering an alien moral climate, graduates stepped off their plane at J.F. Kennedy or Heathrow Airport into a different world of malls and megamarkets, television and video, computers, calculators and fax machines. Roy and his colleagues, many of whom were MKs themselves, understood the lad who said, 'I am a combination of two cultures; I am neither and I am both.' Some felt awkward, lonely, different, rootless, insecure and misunderstood in a western world focusing on trivia in place of the trauma of poverty, war, banditry and bereavement which surrounded them in Africa. RVA staff asked, how can we prepare them for such a revolution and yet foster the rich link with Kenyan culture?

Some did not think they struck the life-style balance right. One teacher remarked, 'I find it strange to walk into a home at Kijabe and see it decorated exactly like it would be in the United States.' More harshly, two young visitors criticized Kijabe, 'It was a world apart – a world of privileged, indulged missionary children enjoying the best education that money can buy in that country; a world of happy, fulfilled, industrious, supremely secure white missionaries, spending their lives in medical, educational, and developmental programs'; but such denigration of RVA was unfair, for it suggested no answer to the educational puzzle.

As in any school, confrontation developed with the local community from time to time. Roy instinctively consulted church leaders and frequently visited a special friend, the local Bible School Principal, to seek his advice.

Roy relaxed by raising roses. First he learnt to adjust to the rich African soil and then, as the plants grew, to nurture them by weeding, pruning and watering. As with his students, planted in Africa's soil and nurtured in Christ's school, he delighted when they flowered into fragrant maturity.

Ralph and Ellen Davis

Children of missionaries, brought up in one world, eventually found themselves adjusting to another. Hurlburt also moved in two worlds; he could talk to a President in the White House or relax with a pauper in the wide African bush. Such skill, though rare, equipped a mission leader for fruitful service.

In the mid twenties, the AIM office in New York distracted perhaps by their jostling with Charles Hurlburt for control of the mission, responded slowly to the application from a Chicago couple and lost them to another mission. Despite the council's error, God prepared Ralph and Ellen Davis for future leadership by rooting them in the soils of both Africa and the West.

Moody Bible Church wanted their new missionaries to leave for Africa as soon as possible. Ralph and Ellen Davis should have waited. They endured contempt and misunderstanding throughout their first year in Northern Rhodesia (today's Zambia) because mission leaders refused to acknowledge immorality in a senior colleague. In desperation they slipped out of their mission station at night, with only what they could carry by hand, found their way to the ocean, thence to Mombasa by boat and Kijabe by train.

Fortunately they met Charles Hurlburt (the AIM Director's son, married to Ellen's sister) who invited them to join a new team for Congo. The deep wounds of rejection in Rhodesia quickly healed in the fellowship and challenge of pioneer missionary outreach. They kept moving to commence new work so that in their first five years Ellen never spent two birthdays at the same location.

Living among the Kakwa long enough to gain a handful of converts they heard John Buyse's plea for missionaries to preach to the Zandes of Equatorial Africa. Taking their most promising disciple, Yoane Akudri, they met the (young) Charles Hurlburt and three others at Bafuka to plan their long journey to the French territory. The team decided that five would travel the shortest route through sleeping sickness country, where government forbade porters, while Ralph and Ellen took all the baggage with a four-hundred-strong army of carriers through Bangassou, four hundred miles to the west, meeting up in Zemio (Map 4).

On 4 January 1926 they arrived in great style at Zemio to meet the rest of the party before the final stretch to journey's end at Djema. Hastily erecting a grass hut, they settled into the luxury of stillness after 171 days travelling 800 miles, secure in the knowledge that AIM had taken another immense step in the line of the founder's vision towards Lake Chad.[225]

Ellen survived the journey well, but she was unsure of Ralph. He lost weight over the next few months and she tried to persuade him to take a spell of assignment at home. Surprisingly he laid down two conditions, 'We'll go to the States only if you become pregnant and if God supplies the fares.' By Christmas the Lord fulfilled both. Ellen gave birth to Bob in Switzerland, where they stayed for six months before going on to America.

Thrust into leadership

After a long second tour in Congo, Ralph and Ellen were in the States again preparing to return to Africa when the General Secretary, Henry Campbell, suffered a stroke. The Chairman of the council looked for someone to help until Campbell recovered. He called Ralph. Like most missionaries he accepted a temporary administrative position reluctantly, more from loyalty to a sick colleague than any ambition. The stricken leader recovered slowly while unexpected talents surfaced in his helper. A short-term assignment solidified into an ongoing position of Assistant General Secretary in 1939 until Campbell retired two years later and the home council asked Ralph to take his place.

Without seeking it Ralph found himself thrust into a senior

position. In 1939, the American council governed the mission, held veto rights over the field councils in Africa and appointed the field directors. The General Secretary in New York served as the mission's chief executive, although the fourteen years since Hurlburt's retirement had not erased the missionaries' reluctance to submit to one overall leader.

As an experienced missionary, Ralph brought a refreshingly relevant note into the American work. Two students at the Bible Institute of Los Angeles heard him speak at an Easter sunrise service on, 'He is not here; he has risen . . . Come and see . . . Go quickly and tell.' (Matthew 28:6, 7) They said, 'On that occasion we felt the call of the Lord to come to Africa under the AIM.'[226] Young Doctor Doug Reitsma spoke for many, 'He contributed a great deal to my missionary call by his messages in Junior High days; and again in the days of application to the Mission.'[227] Ralph took a deep personal interest in everyone who crossed his path and especially any heading to Africa. With any youngster seeking guidance his fingers quickly rummaged through the pages of a Bible to find an apt verse and then his head bowed in prayer. Those who joined AIM saw him as a father.

His reputation as a speaker and administrator spread throughout the country. Many sought his counsel. On nine occasions he was elected President of the important Interdenominational Foreign Missions Association.

By 1948 AIM boasted home councils in America and Great Britain which, between them, kept parental eyes on committees in Canada, Australia and South Africa. Field councils controlled the work in Kenya, Tanzania and Belgian Congo (caring also for French Equatorial Africa and Uganda, although these soon developed their own councils). In theory the American council still led; in practice the increase of missionary numbers and ministry problems demanded decisions closer to the action. The organization seemed fragmented to three able men conferring in London – Ralph Davis, Howard Ferrin (President of American Council) and Philip Henman (Chairman of British Council). They wondered, could AIM not accomplish much more by tying these separate strands into a single structure?

They recommended an 'International Co-operating Directorate' consisting of representatives of home and field councils and led by a General Director. The mission would charge its Directorate to establish and co-ordinate mission policy 'so that there might be close and effective co-operation in all fields and countries'.[228] They envisaged a 'Field Directorate' formed by elected field directors and answerable to the international body.

Over the next seven years AIM debated these radical suggestions. In a large conference at Kijabe the members said, 'Yes, but . . .' The twin spectres of dictatorship and remote control still haunted them. Much in AIM culture fostered independence: God called each individual; he supported them through the finances and prayers of personal contacts, and developed rugged initiative by

Ralph Davis, DD

sending them into harsh conditions. Yet they saw the sense in the arguments for structural unity and direction.

The missionaries approved an International Conference instead of an International Directorate and a Central Field Council (CFC) rather than a Field Directorate. The first Conference appointed Ralph as executive officer of the larger body, calling him International General Secretary (rather than International Director – a title they feared). They asked Lee Downing's son, Ken, to serve the smaller CFC, with the title General Field Secretary.

The headless body

The new international leader of AIM expressed his enthusiasm in a letter to the missionaries, 'When Mr Hurlburt left the mission, we no longer had a liaison officer . . . to unite all the constituent parts.' He attributed the mission's success to oneness in Christ but added, 'yet there was little if anything to keep us from going apart and (to) keep us all marching in step.' He now rejoiced in 'a medium for fellowship and consideration for the work of God that we have lacked.'[229]

Although some shared Ralph's optimism, the new constitution sowed seeds of misunderstanding from the start. It gave the International Conference the responsibility 'to secure unanimity of action in all matters of major importance' but assigned it no authority. It described the lesser body, the CFC, as 'the co-ordinating authority for the work of the Mission throughout the Field'.[230] In practice the CFC made policy decisions which the Conference rubber-stamped and each field council used as guidelines for their own decision-making.

Ralph introduced a new American General Secretary, Sid Langford, to the Brooklyn office and trained him so that Ralph could focus on his own new role. But the role itself was unclear. Correspondence with his good friend, Ken Downing, indicates differences of opinion on some issues but does not acknowledge Ralph's leadership. Ralph expressed his frustration about his title in a letter to Ken two years after his appointment, 'the title of International General Secretary means nothing. I think we have misinterpreted the function of a director because we cannot get out of our minds certain individuals whom we knew as "general directors" of the past.'[231]

Later he was hurt when other leaders questioned his need for money to visit Africa, asking why he needed to go. Ken's successor as General Field Secretary, Ken Richardson, underlined the ambiguity when he wrote later that 'one of the most important advances made under the 1955 constitution was the transferring of authority to the field under CFC.'[232]

Eventually the International Conference changed Ralph's title to 'General Director' but failed to clarify his role. The change helped the American churches to understand his position, but did nothing to ease his frustration within the mission family.

Ill health forced Ralph to retire in 1962 and the mission searched for a successor. Ken Richardson wrote of 'confusion regarding the duties of a General Director' and Erik Barnett, while admiring Ralph's work, thought that a replacement 'would find himself serving under the same continual frustrations and discouragements'. As Kenya's field director, he reckoned that both CFC and International Conference were 'becoming less and less essential in our AIM organization'.[233]

Writing from the retirement home, Ralph, who had given ten years of his life trying to facilitate an unworkable structure, called AIM 'The Headless Body'. He told three leaders, 'If we do not have supreme authority in the mission, then we have minority rule, or at least its potential . . . Any body must have a head . . . The constituent parts should not be laws unto themselves . . . able to fly apart from the whole.'[234]

The mission did not replace Dr Davis for ten years. He died

on 19 August 1963. His widow received a vast array of letters from missionaries, friends and mission leaders across the world, all of whom appreciated his tremendous contribution to the cause of Christ.

Ralph's missionary service ended – as it had begun – under a cloud of misunderstanding. He felt that his difficult relationship problems as General Director contributed to his physical collapse. Five months before his death, he wrote, 'None knows the heart pangs I have had over this. I hope my successors will never have to endure the same.'[235]

George and Anne Frutchey

At the end of their careers Ralph and Ellen Davis found support in the invigorating fellowship of the AIM retirement centre. This community developed through his friendship with a successful businessman who lived close to New York, George Frutchey.

Pharmacy fascinated George. As a young man he devoted his life to serving the Lord and his fellow men through his interest in medicines. God prospered him so that his little drug store in Westfield, New Jersey, grew. He married Anne and together they were able to purchase a simple holiday home in Florida – a cottage set in twenty-eight sandy acres of fan palms, and tall trees, beside a large lake.

The Maynards, colleagues of Emil and Marie Sywulka in Tanganyika, visited Westfield. Their pioneer enthusiasm challenged the pharmacist and his wife. They heard the Westervelt boys in Westfield and determined to show their gratitude to Christ by doing more for his kingdom. They began to pray for AIM and to send gifts to the New York office. Whenever the business would allow them, they attended mission conferences, amassing an impressive knowledge of the ministry in Africa.

George and Anne, like thousands of AIM's colleagues, ministered in their own home country by prayer and practical generosity. The financial policy, emphasizing prayer rather than appeals, meant that donors were usually intercessors as well. Many became counsellors too, giving their time freely to the mission's councils. Ralph invited George to join the American Home Council.

The demands of the drug store and increasing mission and church responsibilities allowed them little opportunity to use their southern home. A tangled forest of low palms thronged their bungalow and blocked off the view of the lake; oaks and pines spread too much sombre shade, and the Frutcheys lacked both the time and the incentive needed to bring their wilderness under control.

In 1934 they invited one of the Westervelt lads, Raymond Stauffacher, to bring his bride to the cottage for their honeymoon. Around that time George discovered that another of the young men, Jim Propst, had withdrawn from the University of Pennsylvania Medical College after only one year of study because he could not pay the fees. George consulted with his own brother and together they found the $600 Jim needed to continue. Two years later the Frutcheys encouraged Jim to begin his married life with Lila at their balmy lakeside property. For many years they supported the Propsts in their fruitful ministry in Kenya.

An AIM gathering in Montrose in 1937 recognized the need for missionaries to have a home in America – an inexpensive place to stay in their nomadic lives. George and Anne wondered about their undeveloped acres in Florida.

A couple from Tanzania needed a retirement place and the Frutcheys built a second cottage on their property for them. Impressed by the number of homeless missionaries expecting to settle in America after years of service, they decided to hand the estate to AIM in January 1938. Anne called it 'Media – a place of rest after the toils of Africa before advancing into the regions beyond . . . to higher service.'[236]

Later that year another couple arrived, following thirty years among the Kikuyu, built their own house and settled down. Soon others followed suit. Bungalows sprang up; lawns replaced tanglewood; tall trees rustled above them in the warm breeze; tranquil vistas of the lake appeared for any who had time to enjoy them. In 1953 the mission built Scott Home to house people who needed extra care.

By 1993 a community of fifty-six formed a hive of spiritual activity. They lived in twelve apartments, twelve cottages, eight duplexes and Scott Home. Linnell and Martha Davis (both of them graduates from the Westervelt home long ago) arrived in 1993 to discover that,

This is no retirement place. These people are all engaged in something or other: preaching in local churches, acting as elders and deacons, correcting correspondence courses for prisoners and children. Two of our women have taught themselves Spanish so that they can minister in a Spanish church. Many visit the sick at the nursing home. We have very good prayer meetings. It's a beautiful place to live.

Another senior Westervelt boy, Erik Barnett, said, 'It's really like a family. We live in a supporting community of our own fellow missionaries. We have known the names of one another for years and we know how to pray for all our fellow workers in Africa.' Erik described the daily men's prayer meetings (which he could attend because two missionary nurses came to look after Emily at that time), cottage prayer meetings and the ongoing personal ministry of intercession in every home. Mature minds maintained an acute interest in every phase of the work overseas and a flow of younger missionaries came to enlist this vital support. Some might be frail in body, but they knew that God used them in the spiritual battle for Africa. Erik spoke for them all, 'This is a tremendous ministry to which the Lord has called us here.'

Mark and Ruth Wagnell

As Christ advanced his kingdom in Africa, Satan recognized that people who serve in leadership and in other support ministries are the Lord's front-line soldiers as much as any. He flung his arrows of misunderstanding, disappointment and frustration at them with ferocious intensity. Although he usually fought out these battles in individual lives, he always aimed at wider targets. AIM's flying programme must have upset him badly for he fought bitterly against its establishment in 1975 and has seldom relaxed his efforts since. AIM–AIR experienced few accidents but none as serious as that of 16 June 1989.

On that morning Mark Wagnell glanced out of the window of his home in a northern suburb of Nairobi and noticed the first light of dawn glistening through mist. 'A typical June morning,' he said to his wife, Ruth, 'It cleared for my last two flights to Bunia so I'll see how it looks at the airport.'

The AIM–AIR pilots always liked to get away early for the three and a half hour flight to eastern Zaire. All sorts of unexpected delays could hold them up and they had to bear in mind the possible need to fly around a storm at this time of year. He kissed Ruth goodbye and said, 'Say Hi to Jeff. Tell him I expect to be home tonight.'

The thought of their seven-year-old son, still asleep, made him feel uncomfortable as he mounted his motor bike and slipped into the early traffic. Eight weeks ago a car had knocked Jeff down in the market and broken his leg. Then a family vacation ushered in a series of problems. Changing a wheel in order to repair a flat tyre, Mark's car fell off two jacks, pinning him to the ground. He was glad to get away with just a sore rib. Paratyphoid fever kept father and son in bed for much of the holiday and frightened Ruth because they were far from medical care and had no radio with them. Jeff woke up one night screaming and hallucinating, while Mark, lying alongside him, felt an evil presence in the room. After four days they recovered sufficiently to limp back to Nairobi where they could consult a doctor.

Ruth drove Jeff the thirty miles out to Kijabe to have his plaster cast removed. Descending the steep hill in the rain, she spun on an oil slick and ended going down backwards. She stopped, unhurt but badly shaken, glad that she had not crashed into the wall on one side or plunged over a bank on the other.

Two days later a friend phoned from the States. A stroke had paralyzed Mark's father down the right side leaving him partially deaf and so confused that he could not recognize anyone.

More recently still, Jeff had woken up screaming. Terror-struck he told his mother, 'A creature is sitting on my leg.' She asked, 'What sort of a creature?' 'Black with long hairy legs,' he replied. Then he cried out again, 'It's jumped onto my arm.' Believing that a demon was troubling him, Ruth implored Christ to bind it and the boy relaxed back into sleep.

As Mark slowed down at the airport gate to make sure that the security police recognized him, he reflected that he did indeed believe in Satan's power but he also worked in a practical world of nuts and bolts, of wings and weather, and now he needed to think about the clouds. They brooded, low and dark, just 200 feet above the runway but they were not solid. He thought about the Ngong Hills twenty miles to the west.

The Ngongs, rising over 8,000 feet to five peaks, have earned the respect of all Kenya's pilots. On Monday and Tuesday Mark had slipped around the northern end of the ridge into sunshine over the Rift Valley. He decided to try it. He could always turn back if he couldn't get through.

He jumped into the Cessna parked on the apron and taxied to Immigration and Customs. Four passengers waited for him beside a trolley of carefully weighed freight. He loaded, checked seat belts, tested the ties over the baggage and locked his own belt into position. Turning to his passengers he told them, 'We usually start our trip with prayer.' Then he added, 'Lord, please care for us as we fly and bless your servants in the work they hope to accomplish in Zaire.'

A few minutes later Mark, high above cloud, searched the ground for familiar landmarks but saw only a dense grey carpet. He wondered about returning when he noticed a hill with a small valley behind and, at the far end, an opening into the Rift. Convinced that he was looking at the gap north of the Ngongs, he swung into the valley.

The green hillsides closed in on the little plane – too close to turn now if he should need to. Above, the clouds formed a dense lid. Too late he realized that bushes and rock shut the valley ahead with an impenetrable wall. He asked himself, 'Should I make a forced landing or climb?' He decided to go up.

Within three minutes of entering the valley, they struck. Mark heard the impact and raised his eyes from the instruments to see bushes flying past at 80 knots. He pulled back on the control and to his surprise saw the nose rise ahead of him. A thought struck him, 'Is this thing going to fly out of the brush?' But the next instant the machine ploughed deep into the trees and darkness closed in. Words tumbled through his mind, 'Well, this is my death in a plane crash.' The engine died.

Mark looked at his passengers, amazed that they were alive. They climbed out without a scratch. Many other planes have rammed the Ngongs but few of their passengers have escaped with their lives.

Looking round later, he found that they had flown for ninety feet through bushes on a step without touching the ground. By pulling back on the control at just the right moment, he had lifted the Cessna onto a sloping shelf covered with extremely dense brush about ten feet tall. They slid up the shelf for 130 feet before coming to rest seven paces from a big tree. Beyond that the cliff rose steeply. A fellow pilot visited the scene and commented, 'Twenty feet lower or fifty feet higher, fifty feet left or right, and no one would have survived.'

Relief gave way to remorse. He told himself that he would never act as a pilot in command of a plane again. Terror swept over him as he relived the experience. 'I had about three minutes that lasted an eternity wondering when the clouds would turn into granite and we would be splattered across the face of the Ngong Hills.' Guilt haunted him as he reminisced. 'There sat my passengers, trusting me to bring them safely through. Two seconds later they were sitting on a mountain side, alive, unhurt and wondering why I had failed them.' Shame stabbed him: already everyone at Wilson Airport was dissecting the story and soon an official enquiry would probe into every second of those fateful minutes. His conscience accused him continually, 'You wrecked one of the mission's most costly assets.'

Mark never forgot the accident that Friday. In fact, Sunday was more momentous. Ruth and Jeff went off to church but he stayed at home and cried out to God for some sort of an answer, pleading for rest from his anguish of soul.

He flipped his Bible open to Ephesians and read 'I pray that . . you may know . . . the surpassing greatness of his power toward us.' Mark asked himself, 'Why does God want me to know this?' He turned a couple of pages and was struck by an answer, 'Be strong in the Lord and in the strength of his might . . . for our struggle is not against flesh and blood but against rulers . . . powers . . . spiritual forces of wickedness.' He saw that he was in a great war and in that recognition he found peace. 'God's power is real,' he wrote next day to his friends. 'God's power is necessary; it is the only power that is sufficiently strong and it is available through prayer. Please pray for us. We feel we are under the gun, and not only us, AIM–AIR, AIM, the Church, Africa. Thanks.'[237]

Words on target

Like Mark Wagnell, African Christians often felt 'under the gun'. Their best defence lay in soaking their understanding in God's book. From the earliest days, missionaries did more than preach and serve; they prepared books – usually Scripture translations and hymns. As people across Africa learnt to read, God called some missionaries to write more for the growing hunger. In the fifties they found a new tool at hand – radio – and began to explore this way of addressing mass audiences. Even the illiterate could listen to a small transistor.

Writers and broadcasters, perhaps more than preachers, valued their tools but recognized too the importance of their targets. They asked: What is the value of great writing without reading, of good preachers without hearers, of megawatt transmitters but switched off receivers? So they studied their audiences to ensure that faithful messages matched felt needs.

At one level AIM missionaries had always understood their hearers' needs. After all, did not the inspired word diagnose the agony of human lostness and prescribe the healing balm of the gospel? Had not this message already saved millions?

But something was wrong. While people poured into the churches, they often brought baggage from the past. Like the blind man whom the Lord touched, they could 'see people; they look like trees walking around' (Mark 8:25). The Lord determined that the man should see 'everything clearly' (Mark 8:25).

In order to touch the deepest aspects of spiritual blindness, God taught others, besides the mass communicators, a radically new form of audience research. They confessed, 'It is only by active, loving engagement with the local people, thinking in their thought patterns, understanding their world view, listening to their questions and feeling their burdens, that the whole believing community (of which the missionary is a part) will be able to respond to their need.'[238]

This humble sensitivity to the hearer began to transform the approach of preachers and teachers (which, of course, included every missionary in some measure). When pioneer church planters thought along these lines, they found that the African context called them deeper into an arena of warfare with spiritual powers.

Bob and Lillian Davis

When Ralph and Ellen Davis set out for their second stint in Congo in 1928 (p. 215), their son Bob boasted a few milk teeth but could not yet walk. He spent his next eight years in Congo unconsciously learning from his small friends how to think and talk with Africans. Although his subsequent technical education at various American colleges fitted him further for a communication ministry, his childhood preparation was probably the more significant.

At Providence Bible Institute he developed his interest in radio, eventually serving on the staff of their FM station where he met and fell in love with another radio buff. Together, Bob and Lillian devoted their lives and talents to the Lord's service.

Their first enquiry about missionary service led to disappointment. Doctors discovered a faulty valve in Bob's heart which seemed to say no to any assignment overseas. They quietly pursued their interest in Christian radio wondering if God wouldn't take care of a leaking valve if he chose to send them elsewhere.

Only twenty years previously Clarence Jones had pioneered the first missionary radio station. From Ecuador the 'Voice of the Andes' resounded around South America so effectively that others followed: Far East Broadcasting Corporation in Manila and Trans World Radio in Tangier. Why not East and Central

Africa? The Davises approached AIM but received the reply, 'There is no opportunity for radio work in our fields.' They applied to another society and heard nothing in response; so they continued their studies.

Kenya's Mau Mau problem was coming to an uneasy conclusion. The colonial authorities realized that winning a war in the villages and the forests did not change minds and hearts. Successful evangelism in the large detention camps was convincing them that Christians had an answer to human need which no amount of military force or propaganda could provide. They asked the missions to broadcast their own message. The young Davises wrote, 'So, just at the time of graduation, AIM told us that there was an opportunity to use our radio abilities.'[239] They reached Kijabe in 1954, thirty-two years after Bob's parents had first set foot there.

Waveband pioneers

They timed their arrival well. Not only was Government offering free broadcasting on their transmitters, but they hit a radio boom. Kenya's 17,300 receivers in 1952 rocketed to 40,000 in three years. In remote villages ten or more crouched around each set. Without the necessity of building their own transmitter, Bob and Lillian got down immediately to the challenge of collecting and arranging material. As far as possible they wanted African voices preaching and African choirs singing.

Kenyan preachers knew nothing of time constraints. They looked at Bob in disbelief when he said, 'Please get your whole message into eight minutes' and could not understand when he simply cut them off at the end of their time. Hours of training resulted in good, crisp sermons. Wherever they found a well-trained African choir, they collected music to fill out the rest of a fifteen-minute package. If the singing was below standard they sought to improve it for they would not allow anything inferior on the air. Bob often sang in his beautiful baritone, 'I wonder have I done my best for Jesus when He has done so much for me?' What he demanded from himself, he expected from his fellow workers.

By July 1955 they were airing nine Swahili and eight Kikuyu quarter-hour programmes each month. A year later they averaged twelve in Swahili and five in Kikuyu; they had also negotiated women's slots in three languages and planned to add Kikamba and Kisukuma – their first in Tanganyika.

Listeners' letters flowed in – from educated farmers in the

cool central highlands, unchurched nomads in the northern deserts, peasant fishermen along the shores of Lake Victoria and coastal peoples wrestling with the claims of Islam.

A lonely policeman told them, 'This place is full of darkness and I have no place to go to church. I do thank the Lord for the messages on the radio. Please send me some Scripture verses to read.' A schoolgirl sent two requests: '1) I want to be saved, therefore I want you to help me by showing me how I might have peace, joy and forgiveness of my sins. 2) I want you to pray for me that I may do well in my examinations.' A young Tanganyikan chased his wife away, 'But after listening to your programmes for several months I have decided to bring her home.' An evangelist in the Mau Mau detention camps was grateful for a message one Sunday which touched the prisoners; 'Many had a change of heart and their leader stood up and said he would follow Christ from that time on.'[240]

One Sunday a Pastor Ibrahim chatted to members of his isolated church in western Kenya at the close of the service. A group of strangers approached. They told him that they had been listening to new teaching on their radio. 'We like the words we hear,' they said; 'Do you know these people?' When the pastor told them that he belonged to the same church, they replied, 'We want the Africa Inland Church to come to our people.' Two of Ibrahim's missionary friends called upon them, and found over a hundred Kisii people begging for their own resident preacher.[241] AIC sent a man into their densely populated hills to reap a bumper harvest.

The Kenya Broadcasting Service asked Bob and Lillian to provide more programmes for new transmitters in Nyeri and Kisumu. Increased broadcasting time demanded better facilities and more workers. They built a studio at Kijabe. Another MK, Ted Teasdale, joined the team and they prayed for a full-time African radio preacher.

God answered their prayers through a son of the highly respected pastor of Kijabe, Johana Nyenjeri (Virginia Blakeslee's old friend – ch. 5). Johana's wife, while struggling toward Kijabe hospital in April 1922, suddenly gave birth to her seventh child, Timothy, beside a football field. They provided him with all the opportunities that the apostle Paul gave his namesake but, at the age of seventeen, the lad 'began to be drawn by the habits of the world such as smoking and wealth.' He despised missionaries because he felt they had misled his father with the Word of God and kept him from earning a good living. 'This feeling grew,' he said, 'until I decided to leave home to get away from being deceived by my father's preaching.'[242]

Seven years later, the Lord found Timothy Kamau; 'I gave my heart to Him. He became my Father . . . I began to confess Him before men . . . Joy and peace that I had not known before filled my heart.' Graduating from Kijabe Bible School in 1955, he got his first taste of preaching to large crowds as an interpreter for the Pocket Testament League in the Kikuyu villages and detention camps. The AIC assigned him to care for three churches to the west of Kijabe. When the Navigators arrived in Kenya for a teaching ministry among the mass of new converts they sought him out to translate their materials. He saw that, 'after the Kenya Government tried to combat the Mau Mau with force, they finally realized that guns could stop the outward manifestations, but could not get at the roots that had borne such terrible fruit.' He asked God to show him how to help Africans know Christ and stand fast in him.

Early in 1959 he was chatting with Bob about Kenya, Tanganyika and Zanzibar when he suddenly realized that, through radio, 'a single message in Swahili would be understood by almost every person in these three territories'. Three months later he joined the radio department with no assurance of salary.

Timothy became known as the Radio Pastor to many East Africans. An African bishop spoke of his broadcasts reaching Muslims, 'Whenever Timothy's voice is heard on the radio, they demand absolute silence so that they might hear every word'.[243] President Kenyatta told Timothy Kamau that he listened regularly. Hearing that the Voice of Kenya ('The post Independence Kenya Broadcasting Service) had substituted an educational programme for Timothy's Friday afternoon Swahili hymn session, he insisted that V.O.K. reinstate the Christian music.

The department asked him to go to Germany in 1964 for a year of training and later to the States and Canada to represent the church's radio ministry.

Don't ask 'Why?'

When Ralph Davis died in 1963, Bob wrote to comfort his mother, 'May the Lord take the question "why?" from our hearts and replace it with an earnest and heartfelt "thank you".' In less than two years he was asking questions about his own health. Nineteen sixty-five started with forty-five minutes of air time every day, but this escalated so rapidly that eighteen months later the radio stations offered two and a half hours, stretching Bob's skills as producer and administrator to the limit. In the evenings he returned home from the studio gasping for breath, with a sense of pressure in his chest.

Back in New York the mission doctor noticed great deterioration in his cardiogram and sent him immediately to a heart surgeon. The operation seemed to go well until the surgeon tied the final stitches. Signs of heart failure unexpectedly developed. In a room close by Lillian prayed and read Psalms. God seemed to speak through Psalm 16, 'You are my Lord; apart from you I have no good thing . . . You will fill me with joy.' She said later, 'At ten minutes to three a strong conviction came over me that Bob was going Home. I told the Lord if it would glorify Him and serve His church, then I would give up my Bob.' Fifteen minutes later a doctor came to tell her that Bob had died.

To ask 'why?' seemed pointless; to say 'thank you' was very hard. The year 1965 treated Lillian harshly; she lost her mother in March, her father in October and Bob in November. In the New Year God spoke, 'As I was with Moses, so I will be with you.' (Joshua 1:5) She said later, 'I remembered that God called me to be a missionary long before I knew my husband. I asked the Lord for further direction.' A week later, African Christians and missionaries met in Kenya for their annual women's prayer conference. Moved with concern for Lillian they collected money and sent it 'for your return'.[244]

By this time AIC ran the radio department in the place of AIM. Aware of the need to maintain high technical standards, church leaders asked missionaries to manage the ministry, but both Lillian and Ted Teasdale believed Bob had been right in preparing for Kenyan leadership from the start. Teasdale declined the position of director and recommended Timothy and he, in turn, invited Ted to continue on his staff as part of an expanding team of missionaries and Africans. He asked Lillian to care for the department's money and she immediately started training Kenyan girls.

She watched the ministry spread throughout the next decade. They prepared over a hundred programmes a month in eleven languages. Hungry new transmitters of the Far East Broadcasting Association in Seychelles demanded one hour each of their English and Swahili every day. V.O.K. surveyed 4 million regular listeners and discovered that sixty-one per cent regularly listened to Kijabe and that the 'Hymns and Greetings' slots in

Swahili and Kikuyu rated second only to newscasts in popularity.[245] The Church named their radio department, 'Biblia Husema', meaning 'The Bible Speaks', carefully choosing the prefix 'Hu-' which signifies inevitability, i.e. the Bible always speaks. Biblia Husema gave birth to all sorts of communicating children: a missionary produced a monthly 'Letter From Africa' for forty American broadcasting centres; another gave his time to distributing programmes on cassette throughout Kenya; 'Afromedia' gathered a library of films and ran four cinevans every month around regular evangelistic circuits; and Ted focused on a television ministry with Voice of Kenya.

Ed Arensen, the editor of *Inland Africa*, purred (with good reason), 'the radio has brought millions to Christ. So has television. Moving pictures, once regarded as an invention of the devil, have under Christian hands drawn many to the Saviour. The tape recorder, oft regarded as a plaything, is now a preacher of gospel truth, telling the story over and over again without wearying.'

Edward and Esther Arensen

Africa opened wide to the new media. But the most powerful medium of all remained the printed page. With the explosion in education across Africa, the use of books and magazines boomed. AIM's search for writers discovered the Arensens.

They graduated from the Bible Institute of Los Angeles in 1940, married and joined AIM expecting an early departure for Africa. But war delayed them and God continued to prepare them for nineteen years before he chose to use them in mass communication to Africans. They studied linguistics at Wycliffe's Summer Institute, evangelized migrants in Arizona, acquired some building skills and then pastored a church for two and a half years before sailing for Tanganyika in 1946.

The war cut missionary numbers drastically so that, when Ed and Esther arrived, only two senior men remained. According to Ed, 'They were the Field Council and did their business out of their back pockets.' The Council assigned the new couple (with eight-month-old Jon) to the mission's first station, Nassa. Lacking missionaries for three years , Nassa's buildings had run down but the church throbbed with life under the firm care of a saintly old pastor with a scarred face. He welcomed the new helpers into his flock scattered throughout seventeen congregations.

To the west of the Sukuma tribal lands lay 'large tracts of fertile land, inhabited only by lion, leopard, various buck and tsetse fly'[246] but sleeping sickness, carried by the fly, prevented human settlement. Scientists cut down all the low brush and the flies disappeared, leaving many miles free for occupation by land-starved Sukuma. During the next decade over a quarter of a million moved.

A young teacher evangelist claimed a large area and offered to share it with any Christians who cared to join him. A strong community sprang up in the Kahunda wilderness and asked for missionary help. Ed and Esther responded to the pioneer challenge. No road led to this remote spot, 'but a small boat unloaded us bag and baggage on the shore . . . The Christians met us with songs of rejoicing and carried our things to the foot of a high palm tree.'

The settlers, some of them elders, brought their churches with them. Soon a dozen congregations sprang up within thirty miles of Kahunda. Ed and Esther ministered to the church – building, preaching, organizing schools, treating the sick and helping believers 'to reach the thousands of heathen in the surrounding countryside'.

At Kahunda Ed began to write for *Inland Africa* and to improve his photography. He built a dark-room in their grass-roofed house and supplied the home office with a stream of valuable pictures.

Ken Downing, as General Field Secretary, exercised responsibility for all AIM's ministry in Africa. In Ken's early days at Kijabe, the missionary in charge of the Bible School had installed a simple printing press operated by foot power. His students marvelled at 'a machine that could make paper talk'.[247] By the end of the fifties, the old-fashioned machine could not churn out the mass of literature needed to satisfy Kenya's voracious appetite. Two missionaries obtained a machine which, using the new offset method, could meet needs across East Africa. Downing sought a Swahili speaker, with much evangelistic and pastoral experience in Africa, who could prepare material. He asked Ed and Esther, would they consider developing a Swahili magazine at Kijabe?[248]

They knew that God had sent them to Kahunda. Both loved the work and felt strong bonds to the missionary team in Tanganyika, numbering ninety now. Their four growing lads regarded Kahunda as home; family roots reached deep into the rich soil. But they pondered Samuel Zwemmer's words, 'No other agency can penetrate so deeply, witness so daringly, abide so persistently, and influence so irresistibly as the printed page.'[249] Ed reasoned, 'The tragedy is that this influence can either be for good or for evil. It can work for God or for the Devil.' The missions had taught Africans to read, translated some Scriptures and hymns and left them with an enormous appetite for any food, good or bad, which their minds could scavenge. Ed wrote, 'The days are gone when a missionary is the African's only peephole on an outside world.' They knew their answer must be a firm yes.

Ten thousand missionaries a month

Soon after their arrival in Kijabe Ed talked about the new challenge – a magazine in Swahili, the eighth largest spoken language in the world. He wanted a vehicle for the Gospel in all its fullness, a journal which would answer questions Africans asked. Certainly it would evangelize and teach God's word – but it would also speak to other realms of everyday life. What's wrong with dancing, movies and modern jazz; how can a student decide? How can mothers improve their babies' food? 'The gospel changes lives and brings peace, mercy, love and freedom from fear. But the fact that a man has a new window in his soul seldom causes him to put one in his dark and airless hut.' For Ed and Esther, the way to achieve all this still seemed uncertain; 'We have before us a big desk, an empty file, a tremendous challenge, and God. We are glad that He is a God who specializes in impossibilities.'[250]

Africa Ya Kesho ('Tomorrow's Africa') competed with a rash of new secular magazines on the Nairobi sidewalks and in secondary schools springing up across Kenya. Ed described it as 'a man on the street type of magazine' and angled for that streetwise person with relevant articles, cover pictures of politicians, a question page with Africans supplying answers. Friends at home helped financially so that he could subsidize the price because a man earning two shillings for eight hours' work could not quickly spend them on a magazine.

In January 1961 Ed announced, 'The Africa Inland Mission has a new missionary . . . with the ability to travel from one end of East Africa to the other for the price of a postage stamp. After a year of planning and preparation *Africa Ya Kesho* is off the press and on the job.' Six months later 10,000 of these missionaries quietly penetrated book stalls on the busy streets, shops, trade schools, East African Breweries and even a school for the blind.

Ed Arensen, DD

As the first issues of the magazine rolled off the press, Esther gave birth to their fifth son and became home-bound for a while. But she could proofread and type as she cared for the family. Later she worked full-time in the office as her husband's secretary and book-keeper. He handed her another baby which needed care – the 'Kesho Tract Club'.

Ed's purpose for this new member of the Kesho family arose from his desire to involve people in distributing Christian literature. He did not believe that gospel leaflets, scattered in the wind, accomplished much but, 'the tract that counts is the one given by a Christian whose life backs up the tract's message'. Each member received up to a hundred tracts at a time with simple advice on how to use them. When his stock ran out, he could ask for another clutch, and receive more hints. Others benefited besides African readers.

A friend challenged a missionary to distribute Kesho tracts in Nairobi. 'Take these ten tracts,' he said, 'stand here on the corner and hold out a tract to the first one passing by.' The first recipient said, 'Thank you.' She took just ten minutes to hand them all out. On subsequent shopping trips, she gave out a hundred tracts before buying anything.

Ed preferred not to write himself. He maintained, 'the program needs to be from African to African. To find talented Africans is difficult. They must be trained and developed right in the job.'

He introduced a contest for African writers and followed it up with courses for new writers. They employed a translator, John Ndeti, and taught him to type. John attended Ed's courses and studied journalism for six months in the University of Nairobi. He tried his hand at the question and answer page of the magazine and then launched into full articles. In all, he served Kesho for twenty-five years. When the Kesho Advisory Board saw a gap in the market for an English magazine, they appointed

John as Editor of the Swahili publication, releasing Ed to concentrate on the new member of the family. They called it, *Today in Africa*.

On 15 October 1971, AIM turned over the Kijabe Press to the Africa Inland Church, a missionary couple remaining on the staff to train the African workers more fully. They departed in 1977 and in the next two years the press, operated entirely by Kenyans, produced a quarter of a million dollars' worth of literature in a dozen languages. The new management changed the name to 'Kesho Press'.

The 'Tomorrow's Africa' family continued to enlarge, giving birth next to a string of 'Kesho Bookshops' across Kenya, numbering six by the end of 1979. On their shelves they carried magazines and a growing army of books, all bearing the imprint of 'Kesho Publications'.

Ed once marvelled about the printed page, 'One thing about literature is that it sometimes remains many years.' Before the Arensens first left for Africa, he wrote an article for *Inland Africa* called 'The Art of Receiving' about accepting gifts from people poorer than ourselves. Soon after, *Moody Monthly* asked AIM to allow them to use it. Forty-five years later, a Baptist publishing house saw the article and wrote to Ed in retirement requesting permission to print it in their magazine.

Wasted ointment?

Shortly before Kenya's independence Ed wrote an article titled, 'To What Purpose Is This Waste?'[251] In a day of unprecedented opportunity for missionary advance some felt tempted to hold back the investment of lives and money because they faced a foggy future. He urged Christians to pour out everything for the Master just as Mary emptied her costly jar of perfume on his head. Pointing to the many AIM graves alongside African churches, he asked, 'Who would say these lives were wasted?'

Ed and Esther never withheld their precious family from the Lord. God claimed two daughters-in-law in tragic circumstances for himself during their prime (pp. 178–9). The whole family drew closer to their Lord through these tragedies. Both sons grew into positions of great influence, Jon in Wycliffe Bible Translators and Lanny as AIM's Director of Outreach. The other three sons married and joined AIM, one eventually transferring to a chaplaincy in Abu Dhabi. As Ed once wrote, 'Nothing given to God is ever lost. We only lose what we keep.'[252]

John and Dorothy Gration

Claps of thunder reverberated over Bunia, the regional centre for north-eastern Zaire. Lightning flashed around the huddled houses, shops and offices of the little town. And rain drummed on a metal roof. In the room below, seventeen church administrators and Bible school teachers had gathered to discuss a subject which sounded new to them in 1983: the relationship of the Gospel to their culture.

John Gration sat with them, straining to hear their discussion above the noise of the storm outside. Until the Simbas had forced him to leave nineteen years before, he had taught some of these men and their colleagues in the church ministries. He felt he owed them a debt. During the years of absence he had come to question his method of teaching. He wrote, 'I recognized that I had delivered many pre-packaged boxes of biblical "truth" to my Zairian students. Although the content was biblical, it did not speak to many issues, crucial to the Zairian church, of which I was only dimly aware. Furthermore, the delivery system fostered a mentality of theological dependency that matched the colonial context.'[253] In the area of Bible teaching he agreed with Ed Arensen's ideal that communication must be 'from African to African'.

Pilgrim professor

John vividly recalled the start of his theological journey, 'At the age of five I accepted the Lord Jesus Christ as my Saviour in the Sunday School of the First Baptist Church, Millburn, New Jersey.'[254]

As a young man, he planned to attend Bible school but the war intervened and he spent two years as a navy medic with 50,000 men. He said, 'I made false teeth a good part of the time (not a very heroic military career!) but God gave me the opportunity to get grounded in the Word with the Navigators and in their theme verse, "The things you have heard me say in the presence of many witnesses entrust to reliable men who will also be qualified to teach others." ' (2 Timothy 2:2) Two further years in Moody, undergraduate study at Gordon, and a year at Wheaton Graduate School prepared him for Bible school teaching in Zaire because, 'That is where the reliable men were.'[255]

A ship, misnamed *African Lightning*, crept across the Atlantic and around the Cape to arrive in Mombasa after seven weeks at sea. Disappointment awaited John and Dorothy in Zaire: the Council assigned them to supervise 125 out-schools. For three years they travelled widely and learnt. Looking back, John understands the message of the mission leaders at that time, 'John, you are not ready to teach these fellows in the Bible school. You don't know the situations they face in their little schools and churches.'

During this time God brought a new pastor to their local church at Rethy, Corneille Balongi. Often on safari together they shared insights from the Bible and common burdens for Africa and the church. At one time they literally wept in each other's arms about a situation. John found it a 'priceless experience of learning, which colored and directed my whole missionary career.' He thanked God for his studies in Greek, Hebrew and theology, 'but it's the people God brought into my life that really molded me.'

Eventually the Council sent John and Dorothy to the Linga Bible School for nine wonderful years with Eddie and Nellie Schuit. They shared the vision of pouring their lives into others and refined it into the very practical goal of developing African teachers to take their places on the staff. The Church asked John to act as Church Advisor for 8,000 believers in an area one hundred miles by eighty in addition to his Bible school work. In January 1961, he wrote under the shadow of a second evacuation prompted by death threats against westerners:

> a meeting with church leaders lasted from 8.30 a.m. to 10.15 p.m. Yes, the wooden bench became a little hard by evening, but so were some of the problems . . . No, I didn't have all the answers, but I did seek to give helpful counsel. Above all, I tried to lead my African brethren to find the answers themselves in the Word under the guidance of the Holy Spirit.[256]

Such careful preparation of leaders by the missionaries in Zaire bore fruit in the third evacuation in 1964, when all left for at least eight months and the Church found her feet. John and Dorothy settled into the Bible school in Kijabe, surprised to discover that, in Kenya, missionaries still controlled most of the work. By their third year among the Kikuyu, they were again well-settled in their own home after the loss of all their possessions to the Simbas. With RVA on their doorstep and a challenging teaching programme, they felt they had found their ministry, at least until their three youngsters should graduate from high school. But Sid Langford, the American Director, uprooted them by asking John to become his Associate Director, with responsibility for candidates.

They landed in the midst of a cultural revolution among American young people. The hippie movement, accompanied by the era of opposition to the Vietnam war, led students to question authority and tradition. They questioned what kind of a mission AIM was. How relevant to today? Had missionaries abandoned the materialism which pervaded western culture?

They forced John to think radically. In an article entitled 'Continuity and Change', he pleaded for loyalty to the purposes of the founding fathers, 'As a mission gets older, it can lose the passionate sense of mission that brought it into existence. Such a change must be resisted at every level and at every turn.' But without discriminating changes the organization could not face the new conditions and opportunities; 'Change then becomes a necessary concomitant of continuity and in reality its foundation.'

His mind ranged widely. He questioned whether AIM should remain confined to Africa. With twenty million North Americans tracing their descent back to Africa, should we not use our cross-cultural experience in seeking to win some of them for Christ? He also wondered if AIM was still too slow in fully recognizing the rising tide of African demands for equality and autonomy.

Bringing together principles of mission policy and African theology, he wrote, 'Many things we consider to be absolutes are in reality relatives. To be sure, there are some biblical absolutes that we must conserve at any cost. To relativize these is fatal. But our thinking is just as flawed when we absolutize what in reality are relatives.'

As Candidate Secretary John interacted with sharp young minds on modern university campuses. It was a new and very different generation. The 'new wine' tasted good, but John often wondered if the mission's old wineskins could contain it. In response he developed his concept of a 'plastic liner' within the old AIM wineskin, the creation of a 'special community' for this new breed of candidate. In this way they would not suddenly crack the old wineskin but could more gradually become assimilated into the larger AIM. If some of his recruits still found AIM too constricting, many survived to become key players on the African scene twenty-five years later.

To improve his ability in handling candidates, he enrolled in a doctoral programme in New York University and unwittingly laid himself open to more change. Wheaton Graduate School

called him to teach missiology. He agreed to go for an initial
one-year period. The one year stretched into many. The handful
of students multiplied; the one professor became a full
department.

Cross-cultural communication challenged Christian scholars
and missionaries in many countries. John read their work avidly
and, as he taught, grew in his own understanding. The Lausanne
Congress on World Evangelization in 1974 precipitated his
invitation to a significant consultation on the Gospel and Culture
when thirty-three theologians, anthropologists, linguists,
missionaries and pastors from all six continents met at
Willowbank in Bermuda.[257] As John taught his students in
Wheaton, he realized 'how much better I could have done in
Africa all those years before . . . Like Jonah, I prayed for another
chance.'

Breaking barriers

In 1981 John briefly visited Bunia Seminary in search of
information to help in his teaching at Wheaton. He chatted with
an African professor about strange sights and sounds that people
experience in the spirit world. His friend arrested him with the
comment, 'We don't talk to our missionary friends about this
because they just smile.' John squirmed. How much, he
wondered, has a western secular and scientific viewpoint blinded
missionaries to the Africans' understanding of ultimate reality?
He remembered how he had once taught his African students
about the Holy Spirit without ever relating to their own vivid
concepts of the spirit world.

He planned to return two years later for five-day seminars.
In preparing for them he wrote, 'I am a lecturer by nature . . .
but at all costs we must avoid the lecture method . . . it is rather
a consultation in which everyone is to make significant
contributions.'[258] He determined to arrive with sheets of blank
paper and invite the participants to set the agenda. To avoid
talking only to the well-educated French speakers, he arranged
to meet with two groups, one in French and the other in Swahili.

On the first day of each seminar John asked, 'What is the
Gospel?' After receiving a 'cascade of clichés' he enquired, 'What
is it in the Christian message which attracted you?' Exploring
together why the Christian message could be considered 'good
news', the delegates began to unearth new dimensions of the
Gospel: more than 'a forensic justification', it was also 'a release
from the bondage of sin in its various manifestations'. John

commented, 'As the excitement produced by the discovery of the richness of this simple term "gospel" became evident, I only wished that I had used this approach twenty-five years earlier.'[259]

He took up day two with a discussion of culture. Although the term sounded unfamiliar to some, the concept soon became clear as he asked how they would explain to a Senegalese, for example, the local way of life. In Bunia the thunderstorm broke just at the right moment. Speaking loudly above the roar of rain on the roof, John immediately asked if everyone in the town heard the thunder and saw the lightning. Did they mean the same to everyone? By telling him how the different tribes in Bunia interpreted thunder and lightning, they acknowledged that each cultural group explains events according to their varied views of the world around them.

With this understanding of the wealth of meaning in the terms 'gospel' and 'culture', they progressed to a discussion on the interaction between the two. John wanted to know, 'In what ways has the gospel influenced your culture?' They stressed deliverance from fear – fear of spirits, of death, of misfortune; and delight in forgiveness – rare, according to them, in pre-Christian African thinking.

By the fourth day, he found both groups ready to talk about

Rural Bible School, CM

the previously unmentionable: what areas of their context remained untouched by the Gospel? Breaking into small groups the delegates came up with an astonishing list of forty-two topics. They recognized the sensitive nature of these issues. So that, when John suggested they select three for further discussion, they insisted on a secret ballot and chose fetishism, belief in dreams and visions, and tribalism. Breaking into small groups again, they first clarified the problem and then searched the Bible for relevant data. Excited, they found a new relevance in Scripture as it not only answered questions they asked, but also raised new queries; 'The barriers between African culture and biblical truth were being gradually broken down.'[260]

Discussions continued long after John's departure and resulted in three documents; 'The Gospel and African Beliefs', 'Fetishism and Healing', and 'Tribalism'. As a result of the consultations, over half the participants found their preaching more oriented towards the real African world and several attempted similar seminars. Seminary and Bible school teachers adjusted their programmes to include this type of reflection.

Although John had deliberately avoided inviting more than one or two missionaries, his approach encouraged other like-minded educators. Gordon Molyneux, the director of a seminary in Zaire, urged his students to adopt the method. Dick Gehman and his African colleagues in Kenya, working under the direction of the Bible School Committee of the AIC, developed a system of 'Theological Advisory Groups' to stimulate the churches to recognize weaknesses and find solutions in Scripture. He challenged Africans to answer the question: 'How can Jesus Christ be made Lord of every aspect of life, during planting season, harvest, times of sickness and death?'[261]

The Director of Oicha Bible School commented on John's seminars, 'If Gration had listed in a lecture the areas of weakness which he observed in the Church and if, by coincidence, his list comprised exactly the same items that we came up with, we would not have accepted it.'[262] Instead of accepting a teacher's pre-packed truth, he wanted to pose his own questions, discover his own answers and fill his own box.

Jonathan and Margaret Dawn

The glowing embers of a dying fire warmed a partly-built house. A thread of smoke twisted around roof timbers before getting lost as it sought a way out through the thatch. A hurricane lamp, standing on a table picked out the whites of twenty pairs of attentive eyes and the pages of Bibles. The leader, a new Christian called David, began to recount some tribal history, 'The lake in the valley was not always there . . .' Two grey heads nodded for they knew the story and David warmed to his task, 'A messenger came to an upright family and warned them to leave their clan on a certain day.' 'Eeee,' assented an old man from the outer ring of darkness, 'The people had been bad. They refused to welcome strangers and were even rude to them.'

'Yes,' said David, 'The family left their ancestral home on the appointed day and five steps behind the last person, the ground split open . . .' An elderly woman eagerly took over the tale, '. . . And water rushed into the cleft and drowned all the remaining villagers.' 'And the lake has been there ever since,' concluded another.

With their attention riveted on him, David jumped into the story of Noah. An hour or two later, even the illiterate members of this Bible study group left with a message from God firmly planted in their minds.

Throughout the discussion, Jonathan Dawn crouched outside the dim circle of light quietly listening to all they said. He knew that a member of a team of five young missionaries worked almost daily with David to encourage his gift of teaching truth in a way that attracted attention. With satisfaction, tinged by a little sorrow, Jonathan looked back over ten years of leading a succession of teams to hammer out communication skills on the hard anvil of pagan village life.[263]

Who is the enemy?

Jonathan and his wife, Margaret, began the new programme called TIMO – Training in Ministry Outreach – in an unchurched Luo community close to Kenya's border with Tanzania. Over two years they sought to equip a small missionary team with skills needed to plant and nurture a church in an unevangelized community. Mission leaders hoped that more teams would follow once the programme became established, resulting in many new churches and trained, cross-cultural communicators.

Despite careful consultation with everyone concerned, misunderstandings multiplied. Fellow missionaries questioned the need for the programme: had AIM not been evangelizing for nearly ninety years? Church leaders questioned the wisdom of entering an unchurched area: was there not plenty to do at nearby Agudo mission?

AIM appointed Peter and Sally Maclure to lead the first team with Jonathan as overall coordinator. Arriving nine months before the first team, the Maclures studied Luo and helped the Dawns to plan. Taking their small son with an inherited blood disorder into a known malarial area, they knew the risk because his brother, born with the same weakness, already rested in a grave at Kijabe. He obviously needed special care. Jonathan wondered, how could he get that when his parents led a team committed to tough pioneer outreach?

Word from the sending countries made him more uneasy, 'Some potential team members have withdrawn; others lack financial support.' Would the team evaporate?

Soon after the Maclures arrived, Margaret suddenly entered hospital for an emergency operation on an ectopic pregnancy – her second major brush with the surgeons in two years. Hardly over that trauma, they heard that the AIM Council wanted Peter to leave TIMO for another leadership position. Both couples plunged into a crisis of perplexity and both found help in God.

Jonathan and Margaret realized that they were caught up in a conflict with strong forces they could neither see nor understand. Peter and Sally meanwhile fasted and prayed. After a week God answered: he wanted them to stay with the TIMO programme. Relief swept over the Dawns and Margaret commented, 'We felt like the angels were fighting for us.'

They continued to pray for the other four accepted team members, all of them very uncertain (mostly due to lack of funds). Suddenly obstacles evaporated and they arrived within a few days of each other. God's obvious answers to prayer convinced them, 'He put each of us into this team.'

That conviction soon came under fire. Highly disciplined Gloria from a Korean city found herself sharing her food, mud-walled home and daily work with relaxed Heather, reared on a farm in Oregon. Soon they hardly spoke. Separately each came to weep and pray with Margaret. Mark and Ron too discovered that their personalities clashed. All wanted to quit.

Jonathan, maybe oversensitive to criticisms from missionary colleagues, read an advertisement for a pastor to an international church in Peru and said to Margaret, 'Let's take it. No one will find us there.' Margaret's optimistic nature clouded with disappointment. A quotation from Hudson Taylor lifted them, 'It should be borne in mind that difficulties and discouragements are to be expected at the beginning of every work; and that the absence of immediate apparent results is no ground for abandoning a work begun by God.'

From the start the Dawns determined to bond the newcomers to the people they hoped to befriend. Despite some differences in lifestyle – inevitable in order to safeguard health – they expected team members to build close relationships with Africans. They spent their first days in Luo homes and came in for many surprises as their ears wrestled with new phrases and their stomachs rebelled against strange foods.

Jonathan and Margaret taught a dynamic way of language study which involved the learner choosing a few new phrases each day and practising them, over and over, with anyone willing to listen and correct. Children in particular warmed to this approach, patiently repeating the words *ad infinitum*. The experience of finding themselves counted as valued teachers intrigued the whole community. And the vulnerability of the newcomers made the Luo accept them and, later, listen to them. Some of the friendships established in those first few days still endure.

Although the people always welcomed them warmly, Jonathan and Margaret felt a sense of oppression whenever they entered the region. Margaret commented, 'Everything we attempted met closed doors.' Hepatitis knocked Mark out of the work for many weeks and Gloria suffered from an uncomfortable skin infection for most of her two years. All wrestled with recurring bouts of malaria.

Jonathan and Peter agreed that team two should move into an area an hour's walk away from Agudo and immediately set about seeking a plot. When one of the new believers offered land, they thought all was going well. Jonathan erected a small round house but wind flattened it that very night. He got it up again, only to discover that another family claimed the plot. Both families drank heavily and sought help for their claim from local witches. A curse rested on this parcel of land. One day Jonathan was caught up in an ugly brawl when men from opposing clans drew sharp knives and brandished spears. Jonathan, fearing for the life of the hothead who had started the fight, grabbed him and pulled him into the house, locking the door behind him.

Should they take the curse seriously? By now they knew that many family compounds boasted a 'spirit house' and one member who had studied witchcraft. The team asked missionaries and African pastors about handling demonic powers which so dominated the local life but few could offer guidance. Westerners thought demons sounded too odd to be true (except in remote biblical times), whereas most Luo Christians found ancestors and spirits so real that they simply feared them without challenging them.

The team called into question their own secular way of viewing life. Searching the Bible with their Luo friends, they began to see the power available to them in Christ who came to destroy the works of the devil.

When the second team arrived, fresh and full of enthusiasm, new leaders gave them a course of Bible study about spiritual warfare. They began to confront the shady spirits of evil with specific prayer and special promises from God's word. One result was a temporary lessening of the inter-family tension over land and some freedom to witness to both groups.

Three TIMO teams spanned six years in that Luo community. From the start they wanted real disciples for Christ. Each team member devoted much time to developing one or two believers, eventually sending seven off to Bible schools to prepare for church leadership. Two years after the teams left, thirty-five worshippers met week by week in the new village church with a Luo pastor cycling up the hill from Agudo to lead them. Several members of the missionary teams moved on towards long-term service elsewhere.

Warfare never let up: illness laid them low, floods forced them to evacuate, thieves visited team three twenty-one times. Howard and Phil left last. They rose on their final morning to find that most of their reasonably good clothes for Britain had disappeared overnight.

TIMO cut its teeth in the Luo region. Having watched the progress of the programme from afar, a senior church leader in another region asked for a team among the Tuken people and volunteered to help research a suitable place. He led them down the mountainous spine of the Tuken Range to the dry, barren foothills where some old men were sitting shelling groundnuts in the shade of a big tree. After listening to Jonathan and the African pastor, the men conferred together and offered ten acres for a church. Even more exciting, a woman told them, 'Five years ago I went to a big church conference far from here and was converted. Since then I've asked God every day to send people who could start a church here.'

To the visitors the population seemed at first too sparse to warrant the effort but, after much prayer, Margaret recalled that the Lord went to search for just one precious sheep. A new team leader arrived in June 1990 to learn the Tuken language and assist in preparations for team four.

Christ addresses culture

The new team in its distant valley settled into a fruitful ministry. TIMO emphasized the importance of fellowship in a team and the practice of mutual accountability. They learnt to encourage and uplift one another.

Hiking up and down the rocky foothills, they visited the round, stick-walled family compounds making friends. By asking questions of talkative Tuken people, they entered a fascinating world, rich in customs, fables and proverbs, and discovered that, rightly directed, Christians could use some of this wealth in communication. The team sought not only to teach, but to train teachers. Before long fourteen groups, totalling 200 people, met regularly to study the Bible. Not all called themselves Christians but they learnt to ask questions and to find answers in God's book. As they progressed through the Old Testament, they found cultures and practices akin to their own and then went on to see how Christ hallowed the good and transformed the bad.

At the end of the first two years there, fourteen stepped forward in baptism while others prepared for that momentous step of faith. They settled into a new congregation and a Tuken pastor, already busy with five churches, agreed to care for them with the help of lay leaders. Soon they planned two more churches and sent one of their young men to Bible college.

After ten years of solid pioneering, the Dawns passed the programme on to others. For 1994 and 1995 the mission planned six TIMO teams – in Kenya, Lesotho, Namibia and Tanzania.

Throughout their time with TIMO the Dawns had struggled against spiritual warfare. As if to warn them against complacency, Satan had one more twist for them before their departure. They set out in two vehicles to move their household goods to Nairobi for storage. Margaret, driving in front with Sarah beside her, saw a lorry approaching and decided to slow down. The brakes locked. The car skidded on the damp road, plunged into a ditch and rolled three times.

Margaret left Kenya a few days later nursing a broken shoulder and a conviction that the devil will fight to the limit to thwart any effort to communicate God's truth in a way that leads to real understanding.

13
Loving the least

A doctor in north Kenya glanced at the small boy in front of
him and noticed his skeleton, sharply outlined by clinging skin.
He sat low on a stool to greet his patient and gently drew the
lad to rest an emaciated backside against his own thigh, feeling
the boy's fever through his clothes.

The frightened eyes that looked at him bore white scars; the
mouth, pallid from anaemia, contained a few remaining teeth,
pitted and brown from fluorine deficiency. Four sockets, slightly
outside the normal tooth line, oozed pus because someone had
dug into the bone in search of ectopic teeth said to cause sickness.
He saw other marks of treatment: a rough circle of healing ulcers
on the chest where a well-meaning relative had tried to burn out
the disease; and a mass of small abdominal cuts festering beneath
a black layer of ash.

The doctor groaned as he recognized the consequences of
poverty and misguided compassion. He pondered the mass of
challenges: to provide food and medicine, to teach simple health
care to the mother and her community, to correct cruel attitudes
towards single mothers and to eradicate fear of evil supernatural
influences.

In the last quarter of AIM's first century in Africa,

247

missionaries encountered more and more poverty and children suffered most.

In many countries illiteracy and unemployment escalated while incomes (apart from those of an élite minority) fell. The lure of big cities drew people seeking work, education and pleasure; but mostly they found only poverty. Among wage earners, the new scourge of AIDS picked off many of the most able. War and drought added millions of wandering refugees and hundreds of thousands of orphans. A birth rate rising by three per cent each year further added to the strain on dwindling economies. Children under the age of sixteen formed half the population of Africa.

AIM in USA looked into its own backyard and saw poverty and injustice. Again dark-skinned mothers and children in the cities bore the brunt of the pain. The African ancestry of these Americans goaded the mission to serve them.

Katie MacKinnon

Sister MacKinnon, in charge of the labour ward of a Glasgow hospital, handed a large pair of forceps to the surgeon as he neared the end of a minor operation. She watched aghast as he drew out a minute, well-formed baby. Tearing off her gloves, she commanded the other nurses to follow her and walked out. 'It was murder,' she fumed, 'the murder of a tiny person made in God's image, and no scientific clap-trap is going to convince me differently.'[264]

Katie's strong will and quick tongue often landed her in trouble, even after she committed them to Christ as a student nurse. But she never used them more effectively than in the defence of 'the wee people'.

She applied to AIM, thinking of relieving an overworked friend at Kijabe Hospital for three months but her friend suggested that she consider a longer, more radical commitment. So, when she finally reached Kenya in 1972, she planned to serve Africa for the rest of her working life.

She arrived with lofty ideals of identifying with African culture, making friends, learning their language and sharing her faith. After only three months she saw those goals slipping. The hospital claimed her for as much as fifteen hours a day and demanded that she be on call for two nights out of three. Africans surrounded her from dawn until well after dusk, yet she hardly knew any of them. Demanding duties prevented either language study or friendship.

In the midst of a large missionary community she felt isolated. She shared a home with an American nurse, but Tara only added to her frustration. Tara wished to employ a Kikuyu girl to help in the house; Katie would have nothing to do with 'slave labour'. Tara wanted a kitten; Katie could not bear animals in the house. Tara needed privacy, but Katie loved to invite visitors to drop in at any time. They asked for different homes and received the gracious advice, 'Don't give up. Try again, and this time let God be head of your home and your relationship.'

The two young women decided to pray together every day. After persevering for a few weeks Katie began to recognize defects in her behaviour. Both slowly made concessions. Katie agreed to take on a servant who urgently needed to earn money. By Christmas Katie wrote, 'a major achievement in my first seven months has been to learn to love and respect a missionary colleague'.

Battle for the babies

The mission council unexpectedly asked Katie to move to a smaller hospital at Litein, 150 miles to the west of Kijabe. Despite her sadness at parting from Tara, excitement gripped her. She found space – not simply a three bedroomed house all to herself, but cultural space as well. With only three fellow missionaries she could concentrate much more on relating to the local Kipsigis people, learning their ways and enjoying their kindness.

Katie ran the whole programme. Although a Government hospital, 23 miles away, accepted emergencies, she treated everything else – often with a trembling hand, as when she pulled teeth for the first time.

After a honeymoon period, excitement gave way to irritability. Busy days, disturbed nights and the strains of adjusting to different values and ways of thinking undermined her peace. She could not accept the easy fatalism of her African staff when they gave up on critically ill patients, regarding death as inevitable. Part of the problem lay in her own lack of language. Frustration led her to shout too much.

The local pastor paid a painful visit. For half an hour he scolded the new missionary for her offensive behaviour and then, suddenly, he surprised her. Smiling, he reached out a hand and said, 'The Kipsigis people forgive you in spite of everything, because you love our children.'

Katie's love confronted the Kipsigis people's easy acceptance of death when she fought for the life of a two and a half pound baby. She carefully explained the treatment, even measuring out the milk for each feed, only to discover that her staff neglected the little mite. When she raged at the girls, they simply hung their heads in silence.

At last she was learning wisdom. Could it be that the girls were neither ignorant nor lax but had a reason for not feeding the premature infant. Quietly she asked her Kipsigis friends, 'How do people regard such babes?' They replied, 'These babies are not meant to live. Otherwise God would have allowed them to be born full-term.' When Katie understood them, she quietly asked them to give the treatment a chance. They fed the babe and she survived.

A woman gave birth normally at home and then died for no apparent reason. Relatives tried to rear the five and a half pound scrap but gave up and brought him to Katie. After each feed, he convulsed and vomited. Again the girls refused to care for him. 'That baby was cursed by the witchdoctors,' they explained. 'There is no point in looking after him. He is going to die.'

Katie realized that the child needed more than dedicated nursing. She explained her predicament to her three fellow missionaries and they all felt out of their depth. They opened their Bibles and read Luke's account of Jesus healing a demon-possessed man. With new clarity they realized that the Lord's power is as real today as it was 2,000 years ago. In his Name they implored God to heal the little cursed boy in the same way that he had set that man free from demons.

Back in the ward, Katie cradled the tiny emaciated frame in her arms as she dripped milk between his lips and prayed for him. He finished, shut his eyes and slept. Gently she laid him in the cot and watched. For the first time he did not vomit his feed. The Lord had touched him.

The miracle of a child set free from a demonic curse still failed to impress the staff. Katie planned a fortnight's break from the hospital – a time to relax at home, to read and to catch up on sleep – but how could she leave these two precious tots in the hands of girls who were convinced they would die, one doomed by God and the other cursed by Satan?

Suddenly the mists cleared. She decided to take them on holiday with her. All three benefited. With extra feeding, cuddling and prayer, the babies filled out and, despite rising twice each night, Katie flourished. At the end of her vacation, she decided to keep them at home. The girls, convinced at last that the children might survive, cared for them during the day and

Katie took the night calls. She felt more fulfilled than ever before; 'Surely,' she thought, 'This is God's purpose in bringing me to Africa.'

A woman arrived with her newly born premature baby. Katie asked to see her baby. 'It is not a baby. It's a monkey,' said the mother and she began to bundle it up so that she could go away. Katie pleaded, 'Please let me look after it for you.' At last she got it back to her home and unwound layers of cloth. She looked down on one of the tiniest living babies she had seen. How could she possibly care for such a vulnerable child?

A lorry drew up outside her house and doors slammed. Upset by being disturbed at this critical time she went out to demand that the driver remove a crate he had dumped on her lawn. She read her name on the label. What on earth was it? Eager fingers helped her prise boards apart and a bright child said, 'It looks like a glass box.' Inside the crate was an incubator. She wheeled it into the house, set it up and popped her precious 'monkey' inside.

God's miraculous gift of the incubator, at exactly the moment when she most needed it, spoke to her: he loved small sick babies even more than she did and he wanted her to fight for their lives. This conviction deepened a few weeks later when the mother beckoned her and said, 'I have learned something very important. There are no monkeys. There are only babies.'

Where are you Lord?

Soon Katie was a working mother with five needy babies at home and a full hospital schedule. For a time she coped, but then an outbreak of measles ran her off her feet and she found, for the first time, that the night feeds were like nightmares. Weakened by overwork, she fell prey to malaria.

Her dark enemy accused her, 'Why has God let this happen? You're a hopeless missionary. You still can't speak the language. You still lose your temper. You still haven't helped anyone to believe in Christ. And now you can't even look after the children properly.'

She opened her Bible at random hoping for words of comfort, but read of Pilate scourging Jesus. Before she could flip over the pages she felt a command to read on. Self-pity evaporated as she pondered the Lord's agony. Turning on she came to Mary, so overwhelmed by sorrow that she failed to recognize her risen Lord. She prayed, 'Please open my eyes Lord and show me where you are in this.'

Quietly God spoke, reminding her of many who came to see the children and to seek help in the hospital, creating opportunities for the Hospital Evangelist. She too was God's witness – less vocal but equally important. He told her, 'The children will take my word to their own people. Receive them, care for them and tell them of my love.'

Concerned missionaries watched Katie struggle and asked questions. Why did she keep the babies in her home? Did they satisfy a thwarted motherhood instinct? How could she continue to support a growing family on a financial allowance designed to pay the bills of a single person? Put simply (and they were too kind to be so direct): was she being selfish and presumptuous?

The first query came too close to the bone for Katie to ignore. She still sometimes longed for a husband and children of her own and she recognized that the Kipsigis babies filled a gap of loneliness in her life. But she cared for them for a more fundamental reason: she wanted to testify to her Father's love for the weakest of people. As regards money, she knew that God's tender love embraced her too, in all her own needs. She could trust him to supply whatever she required to obey his call.

When she began to care for the babies in her own home, gifts from Scotland increased without Katie making any appeal at all. Then they diminished until she was broke. One day she cooked

Waiting for water, CM

the last of her millet for the children's breakfast and asked herself, 'What's going to happen now?' Surely a cheque would arrive in the mail for God would not allow the children to be hungry. She ran out to meet the mail man to collect her letters. He responded with a smile, 'No Katie, the box was empty.'

In the afternoon five graceful Kipsigis women visited. The Lord had spoken to them during a time of prayer in their church about the importance of Katie's work, telling them to share it. Shyly one of them added, 'We bring gifts for you and the children.' Then Katie noticed the table behind them piled high with food: millet, eggs, milk, pineapples . . .

Through these Christian ladies God provided food for the children. But their visit set Katie thinking: was God planning a larger work; did he want Africans to accept more responsibility for babies in need?

The family grew from five to fourteen. The Africa Inland Church opened a second children's home and Katie offered to move there to run it. But no, they wanted an African to be in charge and Katie to supervise him from Litein. Two missionary nurses arrived to take over much of the hospital work.

A new Hospital Evangelist, Matthew, became a firm friend, calling often in the evenings to chat while he helped feed and clean the babies. One day he told her, 'This morning, when I was praying, I felt the Lord calling me to help you full time with this work.' A Dutch friend, Mrs Rookmaaker, heard about the work and offered to provide 200 Kenyan shillings a month for each baby as well as a regular salary of 600 shillings for an African manager.

Over nine months Katie, Matthew and his wife Priscilla cared for sixty-four children in their home. Fourteen premature babies thrived and returned to their families, while twenty-two recovered from severe malnutrition. Katie went to Scotland for a break, knowing that competent Kenyans would continue to care for babies in two children's homes. What should she do next?

Growth through pain

On her return to Nairobi, she visited the Church head office to discuss her assignment. If she expected recognition and even praise, she was in for a shock. She could hardly believe her ears when she heard, 'According to our information you have spent the last four years fighting with church leaders.' The leader sent her to Mulango, a drought-riven place far from her beloved, rain-drenched hills around Litein.

A warm loving welcome from the missionaries at Mulango could not eradicate the perplexity and pain. Once more the label, 'failure' hung on her. She asked herself, 'Could that unfavourable report have been accurate after all? Did I delude myself when I thought I got on well with the Kipsigis leaders?' Self-confidence plummeted to zero.

For two years the doors of the tiny hospital had been shut; now it screamed for soap and paint. From a budget of £2 the Kamba church elders expected Katie to restore and equip their clinic. Was this really God's direction for her when she was so sure of her call to serve Kenya's children?

In the midst of her trial Mrs Rookmaaker arrived for a visit and asked Katie to travel with her. When they reached Litein, Matthew and the elders turned out in force to thank the two women and to tell Katie of their sorrow when they heard she could not return to them. More satisfying still, forty-four bouncing babes welcomed them at the home. They went on to visit four other homes for children under AIC supervision. None would have commenced without the inspiration of Katie and the generosity of Mrs Rookmaaker.

Humbly Katie cleaned out the Mulango building and started to treat patients. She asked, 'If I find needy children, may I bring them to my home?' No one objected. Babies trickled in and soon the trickle became a stream. By this time Katie's little hospital thrived and she found two Kamba women to whom she could entrust most of the responsibility while she focused on the children.

Famine struck and babies flooded in. God stretched Katie's faith. Could he provide for 100 Kamba children in the same way as he had supplied the needs of the five Kipsigis long ago? She prayed and watched him answer: food arrived, buildings developed, water flowed through newly installed pipes, Christian girls applied for training. The famine began to lift but cholera broke out, and then measles. Hour after hour, day and night, Katie fought for little lives. Sometimes she lost.

Reaching home one day after her second visit to the mortuary, she lay on her bed and wept. Unexpectedly old Pastor Konzi, the local leader, looked in. He sat down on a chair beside her and asked, 'Tell me why you are crying.'

'It's so hard to understand,' she sobbed; 'the mortuary is packed with bodies . . . I don't know where God is in it all . . . I don't even have time to talk to him any more.'

The old man spoke soothingly, 'You are too tired to read and pray. I will come every day and I will pray with you and God will give us strength.'

He kept his promise, arriving often with two or three others. They read the Bible to Katie and her staff, prayed for the sick babies and breathed confidence and hope. Deaths declined; emaciated mites fattened, and the plague passed.

As the time came for Katie to visit Scotland again, she handed her Kamba babies over to trained African helpers, assured that they had both the skills and compassion they needed. By now AIC operated seventeen homes for children across the country under the overall supervision of Matthew. Katie felt her work in Kenya was complete.

At her home in Glasgow, Katie often watched the television news reports about Mozambique. Seeing the carnage of war and drought, she cried once more for the tiny people made in God's image – again men murdered them; they destroyed their homes and killed their parents; worse, they forced children to kill others.

'Lord,' she prayed; 'If I can help the children of Mozambique, I'll gladly go.' Her Lord said, 'Go.'

William and Charlene Elliott

Katie MacKinnon's move to Mozambique illustrated a new mobility in missionaries' thinking. Thom Hopler, an American missionary to Kenya, also considered redeployment, but to a radically different ministry. Kenyan friends kept asking him, 'What is the situation of the Black church in America?' . . . 'Why do no American Blacks serve as missionaries in Africa?'[265] . . . 'Why do you come to our country when so many in your own are poor?'

His friend, John Gration, was leading the mission into inner-city ministry in USA. He encouraged Thom to visit Newark City, just forty miles from the AIM office, and search for some answers. In the poverty of a disintegrating urban jungle Thom found few solutions, but many more problems – 'very complex, intensely emotional and deeply engrained.' At the heart of them all, according to the black community, lay a festering sore – white racism. In April 1971 he wrote to the American council, 'As a mission we must recognize that many of our attitudes are not acceptable to the Black church. However, our strategic position in Africa and lessons we have learned in dealing with the National Church (there) are very valuable in seeking solutions.'[266]

Thom urged the Council to 'communicate to our constituency information and attitudes that will help them close the gap between white and black' as a step towards establishing a new missionary support circle in the Black community. While recognizing that AIM should develop evangelistic and church-nurturing ministries in these deprived communities, he insisted, 'We must listen and serve for a long time before we can be "experts" . . . We should not attempt to develop our own ministry until we know more of the real need.' At the same time John Gration asked, 'Can we truly think of a more needy field than the 22 million Afro-Americans?'[267]

The Council assigned the Hoplers to Newark for a preliminary period of a year and others followed so that Thom could write, 'We may have as many as eight full-time missionaries in January.' They included three Africans, a Jamaican, and an American black girl from Harlem. Optimistically he added, 'I believe that the Africa Inland Mission is embarking on what may become one of its most important ministries in the next ten years.'[268]

By October 1980, the mission directory listed only five members serving in the Urban Ministry team, all in Newark. The American Director, Peter Stam, observed, 'We find it more difficult to recruit workers for the inner cities of USA than for the middle of Africa . . . Somehow Africa seems more glamorous and more "missionary" than the slums a few miles away.' Despite determined efforts to influence mission supporters through several articles in *Inland Africa* and an audiovisual programme, American Christians preferred to give for work in Africa. Black churches failed to respond either by sending their own messengers to Africa or by supporting black missionaries in Newark.

The council and its officers refused to lose heart. For a time they felt able to subsidize financial allowances, instead of insisting on the normal pattern of support: that a cluster of churches and individuals will commit themselves to back each worker with prayer and adequate gifts. Rather than retract they expanded, first into Patterson, New Jersey, and then into Philadelphia.

The city of brotherly love

Nearly ninety years after the birth of AIM in Philadelphia, the mission assigned its first missionary couple to minister to some of the city's immigrant communities. In 1982 Bill and Charlene Elliott, both qualified teachers, joined Timothy Academy, a school serving a mix of blacks and Puerto Ricans in a crumbling and densely populated section of North Philadelphia. They planned to stay only a year and then proceed to Rift Valley Academy but, to their own surprise, 'we started to develop a love for the ministry here' and, just three months after starting work, asked the mission to make the assignment more permanent.

Bill could remember occasions when his father, a Baptist pastor, had driven the family through inner Philadelphia to reach relatives beyond. On entering the poor areas, he would always turn to the kids and say, 'Roll up the windows and lock the doors now.' On one of these trips Bill first saw knives flash as men ran from a bar fighting. He watched in horror as red stains spread across shirts.[269]

Poverty and violence increased in the 'Puerto Rican Corridor' of the city so that by the time Bill and Char arrived at Timothy Academy, many families lived in fear of rape, robbery, shootings and stabbings. Pupils saw heroin dealers at work, each in his own patch, often protected by an armed guard on a nearby roof keeping watch for intruders.

Bill met a child's distressed mother. As he talked gently with her she explained that the previous night men broke into her sister's home, raped her in front of her family and stabbed her husband. Then the school janitor told Bill that his son had been shot by a neighbour after an argument and now lay in hospital with a serious abdominal wound. Appeal to the police in such cases might result in an arrest but the offender would probably walk the streets again next day – seeking revenge on the person who set the police onto him.

Mrs Morales, a school parent pregnant with her third child, became a widow when thieves robbed her husband's ice cream van and shot him.[270] An occasional gun fight burst out alongside the school, leaving the wounded and the dead in the street.

A missionary and another staff member worked with a converted drug dealer. Wearing bullet-proof vests and having police support, they met his bosses and safely delivered him from the business.[271]

The Elliotts arrived at Timothy Academy in 1982 as the school celebrated its twenty-sixth year with an enrolment of 283. Cartons of unsorted supplies greeted him in his office but he searched in vain for a faculty manual, a curriculum guide or even an electric typewriter. Generous schools in more affluent areas had filled boxes with their cast-off text books and sent them to their poor neighbour. Charlene's classroom for the first grade possessed neither desk nor blackboard.

At the start the school could not afford a secretary. Many days they worked from 7 a.m. often until 9 p.m. – cleaning, typing, planning, searching for furniture, equipment and books. The excitement of knowing they served God in the place of his choice buoyed them up; weariness burdened them.

Families often fled from the area. A child might attend for one or two years and then move away, only to reappear for a few months before going off once again. Many kids faced crises: a parent went to jail; a father deserted his family; or a brother joined a drug ring. Some children oscillated between three separate homes – mother's, father's, grandparent's – spending a week or two in each. In an atmosphere of violence at home and on the streets, they had little chance to learn. Their attention span in class lasted just a few minutes and many experienced difficulty in retaining knowledge from one term to the next. Sadly Bill turned away 'parent after parent whose kid was 3, 4, 5 or 6 years behind grade level.' He longed for specialists in remedial education, but such people command high salaries and Timothy Academy hardly knew where to find money to pay the regular staff.

Teachers also found the environment stressful and themselves moved on before long. If only AIM could send missionaries, committed to serving the people long term, and backed by prayer and provision from sending churches!

Faith and love on trial

Some churches, previously committed to supporting their ministry in Africa, doubted the credentials of service to an American community and ceased their help. The school board came to their aid, but every salary cut into the finances needed for running the school and for subsidizing fees for the likes of Widow Morales' three children. Through the years shortage of funds tested Bill's faith, often to the limit, but somehow God always provided both for the family and for the school.

But that provision seldom met the needs for even an average school, let alone the centre of excellence Bill felt the people deserved. He walked a tightrope, watching the budget daily, determined to avoid debt. Always he had to adjust his programme to the little money available reconciling himself to 'broken dreams for ministry'.

Facing a deficit of $81,000 one year, the Board decided to cut staff and salaries – including their own.[272] 'One person [on the staff] whose job was cut by 50% donated her lost hours to the school. Another came and asked for a $3,000 cut in pay so that someone else could remain employed.'

From their farmhouse home, just across the Delaware River, Bill drove the whole family to school every day. Christy, Nathan, Miriam and Esther, as the only white children for a time, slowly adjusted to the foreign culture around them. But eventually they made some good friends.

Soon bigger trials loomed. Charlene developed wheezing and breathlessness which the family doctor treated as asthma. In 1987 she underwent a minor surgical procedure and suddenly collapsed with a failing heart. The immediate danger passed but the doctors told her that a virus had weakened the heart muscle four years before; they thought she might live for another six months. She struggled to get out of bed although she could no longer teach. By December the Presbyterian hospital experts talked of a transplant. Four years later, although still surviving with her original heart, she suffered occasional crises now complicated by diabetes. The family mourned, 'Does God really care for us? Is he faithful? Why does he remove a valuable teacher from her class?'

The Elliotts learnt contentment in Christ from inner-city believers, who knew peace despite their lack of education, employment or money. As the bills mounted for Timothy Academy, for four Elliott youngsters away now in college, for Charlene's medical care, Bill marvelled that 'I have a roof over my head, clothes on my back, shoes on my feet, a car, receipts for paid bills and four grown children who love and serve the Lord.'

At the start of the school year in 1991, Bill calculated the budget for the year at three-quarters of a million dollars; the school bank balance stood at $4,000. Two years later he commenced the year with $100,000 in hand. He could thank God for computers, curricula, a faculty manual, policies in place, tidy financial records (audited annually) and good buildings, vastly improved from the row of houses they had inherited a decade earlier. They felt committed to an arduous process of accreditation by the Middle States Association.

For the first time in their dozen years of service to Timothy Academy, the Elliotts felt able to escape for four months. The school received more gifts than ever before during that time so a staff member said, 'Bill you need to take more time off because the more you're away, the better off we become.'

God did more than provide; he protected. Bill stands on a street corner, a violent gun-fight breaks out between police and drug dealers just fifty yards away, but no bullet comes near him. The school reports criminals for threatening children and police warn Bill that his life is in danger. Charlene meets the rascals on the street, sees their scowls and walks through them untouched. A bullet whistles past a teacher's head without striking her. Since the school first opened its doors in 1956, no child or staff member has been physically touched by violence.

Results were mixed. Of the dozen who graduated with their youngest daughter, Esther, three became single parents by the age of twenty, one was jailed for murder, police sought another for involvement in a drug-related killing and two walked with the Lord in college – one preparing for missionary service. A member of the first class of 1956 became President of the school board. Other alumni gave generously to help financially. When the school needed Christian medics to address an important meeting, they quickly found a local doctor and nurse who could testify to their early years in Timothy.

As suburban churches increasingly realized their missionary responsibility to the poor of the inner cities, financial burdens eased a little. But not sufficiently to meet the special educational needs of the city. Although enrolment once topped 320, it shrank as businesses pulled out of the inner city, federal government cut grants to such poor areas and crime escalated. By 1993, the Academy counted 220 on its books. The facilities could now accommodate 600 and Bill said, 'We could triple or quadruple the size of the school, if we could provide special education.'

The Elliotts and the AIM team in Philadelphia accomplished part of Thom Hopler's dream for an AIM ministry to America's inner-city poor. Others served women in New Jersey and Florida prisons (eighty per cent in one jail infected with HIV), young teenagers on the streets of Paterson, African students in the eastern and western seaboards and Muslims in Detroit. Their commitment helped AIM set its sights on Africa's burgeoning city poor. The vision of black and white Americans working with Africans in teams, which knew nothing of fear, arrogance or suspicion, remained mostly unfulfilled, but may have come a few notches nearer by the mid nineties. At least AIM knew by then that a major challenge existed among people of a developed but different culture, just forty miles from the American headquarters.

Caroline Gill

At the age of six Caroline developed a love for animals, especially cheetahs, and, because cheetahs lived in Africa, she wanted to work there. Her interest led her to take environmental studies at Wye College, a satellite of London University based in Kent. Early on she met some students whose intimacy with Jesus Christ challenged her formal Anglicanism. Within two months she received him as her own Saviour and he transformed her life. Deciding to serve Christ rather than seek cheetahs, she maintained her interest in Africa through the years of training college, secondary school teaching and All Nations Christian College.

Her father, listening to so much talk of Africa, said, 'Oh Caroline, you should go to Africa and see what it's like because it may not agree with you.' When he offered to pay for the trip, she decided to visit a cousin in Tanzania's principal port, Dar es Salaam. But the hot, steaming city of one and a quarter million people – many in great poverty – did not attract her. She said to herself, 'I hope I never end up here.' A country girl at heart, she loved Africa's mountains and game-studded plains. She even enjoyed sleeping in a simple village home. But when she applied to AIM, and narrowed the choice of assignment down to Tanzania, the Personnel Secretary asked, 'The Church is requesting a team for the coast which includes teachers. What about it?'

She quickly grasped Swahili and enjoyed a year of orientation in the Africa Inland Church heartland around the southern shores of Lake Victoria. Then, accompanied by our own daughter Helen, moved to sauna-like Dar es Salaam in January 1989.

A sensitive servant

Caroline and Helen Anderson set up home in a decaying estate built in the colonial era by East African Railways for their junior employees. They rented a solid little bungalow, recently squeezed onto a narrow slice of land in the midst of a jumble of African housing. By rising early, before too many of the city's taps emptied the pipes, they could take showers and fill buckets for the rest of the day's needs. Electricity fitfully powered their lights and spun their fans.

An anopheles mosquito sampled her blood and laid her low for a week with malaria. Insanitary conditions around threatened dysentery but Caroline suffered more from the effects of the pot-holed roads on a weak back and of a climate which stole her appetite. According to Helen, when Caroline returns to England, 'she has this delightful problem of needing to eat and eat as much as she can' and, when she gets back to Dar, friends rejoice to see she 'has eaten many potatoes'. But the evidence falls off in a couple of weeks.

Fortunately a neighbour sold milk from his cows, and a local market supplied them with fruit, rice, meat, fish, potatoes and beans. Although their own plot boasted no garden, coconut palms rustled overhead whenever a breeze relieved the fierce heat. Chickens and children rummaged in their garbage pit for anything interesting. If neighbours turned off their blaring radios, they could sometimes sense a rural village atmosphere in the heart of the city.

As in Philadelphia, half a world away, poverty fostered crime. Early Caroline learnt the importance of locking doors and windows when driving through crowded streets. One day a thief reached in and snatched her watch. On another, hoards of football hooligans thumped on the side of the car, then wrenched the door open, breaking her glasses as they attempted to snatch her handbag.

Helen and Caroline slept behind a steel door and barred windows. Even though they employed a night guard, armed with bow and arrows, thieves removed a succession of three windscreens until they reluctantly persuaded the landlord to build a wall around the compound and close it off with a stout gate.

They hated to erect any unnecessary barrier, either physical or cultural, because they wanted people to feel free to wander in and out at any time. Despite gates and bars, they developed many warm relationships. The Africans entertained generously (even a poor man might blow half his monthly income on a good meal for guests) and the two teachers reciprocated, believing that the grace of Jesus runs best along paths of informal friendship.

Most of their friends belonged to the five million Sukuma tribe.[273] By the time Caroline arrived, the main congregation worshipped in an airy, newly-built church in Magomeni location while three daughter churches met in school rooms and a small factory. Church leaders recognized her call to children's ministry and readily consented to her teaching in primary schools and developing children's work in the churches.

As she taught in primary schools, she realized that the schools welcomed Christians to teach Religious Education but few took up the opportunities. 'Did you know,' she enquired,

> that half the population of Tanzania is under the age of fourteen? For many years the church has ignored its younger members and concentrated on the adults. At last Christians are waking up . . . to a mammoth challenge: the street children, AIDS orphans, teenagers who face so many uncertainties and temptations as old values disappear and the extended family breaks down in the city.[274]

As part of a small team she began a programme for training lay people with a series of seminars, starting with sixty and rising to 200 by the end of 1992. Topics included 'How to Plan and Teach a Lesson', 'Visual Aids in teaching' and 'AIDS Awareness', with plenty of time allowed for discussion.

She shared her expertise in greater depth by inviting potential teachers, one by one, into her classroom to watch and learn. Each took time to develop her abilities, but eventually went off to her own school, equipped with a supply of Caroline's pictures, books and other teaching aids. Similarly, as the Magomeni Sunday School swelled quickly to over a hundred children, she worked with her best friend Martha and a band of eager instructors. They eventually took over her whole programme.

A promising midweek Bible club crowded into a church elder's flat and flourished for a while but, when Caroline went home for a few months, disappointingly collapsed.

Most of all she loved the orphans in a government home close to her own, where she held a weekly children's club and taught them about Jesus. Many became firm Christians before leaving the orphanage, some to continue into secondary education. In summer of 1993, she wrote of two who came to say goodbye. 'They asked me to make sure that their Swahili Bible correspondence courses get sent on to them. Although these boys lack earthly parents or have faced rejection, they have found a heavenly Father who accepts them unconditionally.'[275]

Early on, a young man from the Assemblies of God joined the orphanage team. Working alongside Caroline, Luoga became increasingly concerned for children and capable of ministering to them. God gave him a wife and two children of his own and his commitment increased. When Caroline suggested that they take the orphans for an occasional trip to the beach, they persuaded friends to bring five elderly cars and packed the crowd in like sardines. On Sundays he carted many off to his church. Caroline reckoned, 'He knows the children better than I do and I find it a privilege to work with him. If I left he would carry on.'

Up-front but low key

In Sukuma society an unmarried woman lacks status; they call her *mtoto* meaning 'child'. To a visitor, the title sounds demeaning and strange, particularly when applied to a highly educated and skilled woman in her thirties. But it carries hidden strengths. While an older missionary man might pose a threat to a pastor or church elder, a mtoto challenges no one. She simply influences by quiet suggestion.

But the AIC opened up to women in leadership. They agreed to women sitting on the church's governing Synod and allowed female graduates from Bible school to preach. The leaders in Dar asked Caroline to accept responsibility as an evangelist for a small church, eight miles from the city centre. She loved the challenge of preaching to a congregation of forty but carefully nurtured gifts in the congregation with an eye for future leaders.

As in many churches, growth in AIC Tanzania took place along ethnic lines. Although they used Swahili, the whole culture slanted towards the Sukuma. Of course Sukuma people felt comfortable in such a climate and responded more readily but eight per cent of Magomeni's population called themselves Muslims and belonged to other tribes. How should a Sukuma church show Christ's love to them? Among the 640,000 inhabitants of the nearby islands of Zanzibar and Pemba, the percentage was higher. Could AIC establish a church there?

To Caroline the answer seemed to be no – at least not at that time – and she tried to inculcate love for Muslims into her circle of influence. By agreeing to work under the leadership of AIC, the mission could do little more than pray for these unreached peoples and rejoice when God answered prayer by sending others.

They lived far from the rest of the mission. Apart from the annual trek to missionary conference, they might have resided in a different land. Recognizing the importance of personal fellowship and accountability, Caroline and Helen asked a Ghanaian couple and an Indian lady to meet with them every Monday evening. Without consciously aiming at a multinational group, they later added a Tanzanian and two Germans along with others. Every few months they invited Muslim friends to tea, games and testimonies. Even so they missed a leader to correct, direct and encourage them to attempt something new.

Helen described Caroline as

> a quiet person, quite happy to be at home with the things she likes – her crosswords, some good books, a few videos – and with friends dropping in for long chats. It's amazing that God has set her before congregations and classes, to sing and play the guitar, to preach and teach as an up-front person. God has used her like this but it is not her natural bent.

She never lost her love of the fastest animal on earth and one day actually saw a cheetah. Laughing, she thanked God saying, 'I fulfilled one of my life's ambitions but not in the way I expected.'

14

False paradises

In 1975 Joan and I drove south from our desert home among the Turkana to Kapsabet where she had worked as a teacher twenty years before. After leaving her with friends, I caught the plane out of Nairobi heading towards England in the full flush of spring. The Kenya committee of AIM had asked me to represent them at the International Council.

The Council sprang to life with vigorous talk about unreached people in several countries close to the mission's areas of ministry – 'the northern and coastal areas of Kenya, vast sections of Tanzania and Sudan and new fields such as the Comoro Islands and Mozambique.' Members wished to work with the rapidly growing churches in Africa to evangelize these peoples.

Sitting in the meeting, I sensed a new fire of zeal as we identified with AIM men and women in the past facing impossible-looking tasks. We decided that,

> on this, the 80th anniversary of the Mission, we commit ourselves anew to the fulfilment of our evangelistic mandate. Unreached areas, representing thousands and thousands for whom Christ died, present themselves to us as did our present fields at the beginning of the century . . . We commend to . . . our constituency, the need to pray and trust God for 100 workers in 5 years . . . together with the necessary material provision.[276]

Aware that we knew little of these tribes and nations, the council members decided to appoint a new officer (called the Associate Secretary for Outreach) to investigate, encourage and implement outreach into the new areas. To my great surprise, they asked me to undertake this task.

We soon discovered the inaccuracy of the Council's estimate: 'thousands and thousands' of unreached should have read 'millions and millions'. We also underestimated the difficulties of the enterprise. Newly independent states looked askance at preachers from the colonial west and some hid behind dense ideological barriers of Marxism and Islam.

I first tackled Mozambique, thinking (erroneously) that, a few months after winning a devastating war against Portugal, they would welcome Christian relief and development. Circling round the 1,800 miles of inland border, first in Tanzania, then Malawi, and finally South Africa, I found all entry forbidden by a regime claiming to be 'the first truly Marxist government in Africa'. In the south, pastors fleeing persecution told of others imprisoned, beaten and even killed. My mind went back many centuries to the wandering nation of Israel on the border of Canaan. Spies despatched by Moses had seen the cities with their towering walls and giant defenders and had trembled. They warned Moses and the people, 'We seemed like grasshoppers in our own eyes, and we looked the same to them' (Numbers 13:33). I looked on Mozambique and shuddered.

The next trip seemed equally unpromising. In August 1975, politicians in the Comoro Islands, off the east coast of Africa, announced their independence from France. Fighting broke out and the situation became dangerous for two AIM pioneers, Millicent Coulton and Miriam van Reenen, beginning to feel at home after only three months. The mission withdrew them. Tension eased enough for Joan and me to plan a visit. As a friend drove us from our Nairobi home to the airport, he asked, 'What do you plan to do there?' I felt like a very small grasshopper when I replied, 'We expect to meet the only believer; after that we don't know.'

The one Cormorien Christian we knew about met us at Moroni, capital for nearly half a million people in this beautiful island nation. Abdul took us to a fishing town at the north end of the island and invited us to use an unfinished building of his. The only room with a roof became our home for the next two weeks. Furniture consisted of two straw mattresses on rough, handmade beds and a tiny kerosene burner. On a rickety

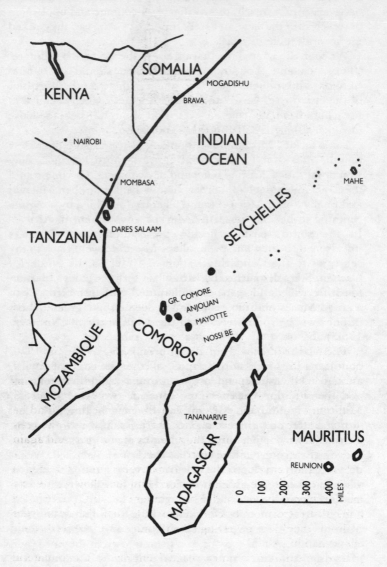

The islands off East Africa

Moroni harbour and mosque, CM

verandah, Abdul ran a small school for a dozen poor children which he called 'Give God a Chance'. With his help, Joan translated a Swahili chorus into the local language and then taught it to the youngsters. In the midst of much chat, he told us his own story.

Abdul once lived in Zanzibar where he learnt Swahili and English and dabbled in politics. Caught in the wrong political party in the Zanzibar revolution, he spent eighteen months in jail before returning home to the island of Grande Comore. A friend sent him a copy of *Good News For Modern Man*[277] and he read it. Interested, he read it once more. Excited now, he read it a third time. He devoured the amazing story again and again and, in the process, came to trust the Lord.

Persecution enveloped the new convert: his family threatened to disinherit him; neighbours derided him for following a white man's religion; the local judge brought him to court; police jailed him. Ill-treatment affected him so little that the authorities realized they were wasting their time and reduced their harassment.

During our stay, France reacted angrily to the unilateral declaration of independence by withdrawing all French personnel and cancelling an enormous grant. Doctors and nurses left the hospitals; engineers abandoned the massive generators which supplied Moroni; 130 secondary school teachers walked out of their classrooms. For all its simplicity 'Give God a Chance' did not seem a bad school at all; at least its doors remained open.

Joan and I walked around the town and some neighbouring villages, chatting with friendly people everywhere. But mostly we prayed for opportunities to serve these Muslims. We came across a handful of Roman Catholics working mainly among the French on condition that they never preached to the local people. One of them told us 'We pray to God, and they pray to God. What is the difference?' We believed that our Lord would provide us with better terms.

One day two well-dressed men tapped on our door. 'The honourable Ali Soilih wishes to meet your visitors,' they told Abdul. Abdul informed us that Ali Soilih, although the Defence Minister, ruled the state.

Abdul and I met the minister in a superbly furnished French mansion overlooking the glittering ocean. He invited us to sit in chairs covered in green and gold. I told him about the mission's practical ministries on mainland Africa and the churches which had developed. He responded, 'You've heard what the French have done? We need help and will accept it from anyone.'

The only surgeon at the main hospital gave us a more precise list of helpers he would like to see – three surgeons, three general physicians, two anaesthetists, five midwives and a hospital engineer. With the schools and other hospitals also crying out for skilled personnel, opportunities for well-qualified, compassionate followers of Jesus seemed unlimited.

We returned to Kenya in time to meet 300 colleagues at their annual conference. Several responded to this pioneer challenge, including a senior surgeon and his wife.

William and Laura Barnett

In February 1976 a small twin-engined plane climbed out of Dar es Salaam and swung east over Tanzania's sun-drenched coast. On board, Norman Thomas, AIM's International General Secretary, and a small medical team consisting of surgeon Bill Barnett, his wife Laura, and nurse Sheila Jones, headed towards Grande Comore 400 miles across the Indian Ocean.

A sparkling drop of dew

Bill, in his sixtieth year, together with his parents, spanned a large slice of AIM history since his parents' shipboard romance on their way to Africa in 1907. By the time of Bill's birth, ten years later, they already cared for Erik, Arthur, Paul and Ruth in a thatched home in Kenya's Rift Valley. Papa and Mama Barnett nurtured their children in an atmosphere of dependence on God. In the lean years after the world war, they often lacked cash but never wavered in a rock-like confidence that God would supply all they needed. Bill said, 'The life of faith in Christ was simply something we grew up with. We knew that God was right there and we could communicate with him just as well as with one another.'

Following several life-threatening episodes in his first ten years, Bill's mother said, 'God has something special in store for you. Maybe he wants you to become a doctor.'[278]

Years later, after study at RVA and the Westervelt Home, he entered Columbia Bible College, but was not so sure that Mama was right. Thanks to Papa's upbringing, he loved using his hands but he felt inadequate as a student. He wondered about going into one of the trades, perhaps as a mechanic. In the midst of this time of confusion Papa came to speak at the college.

Papa told the students that during his first seven years of walking hundreds of miles in Kenya, preaching throughout much of the Rift Valley and beyond, he saw no results. Rising before dawn one day, he went out to a damp hillside and sat down to tell God about his failure. He questioned his call and considered taking the family home to America. As darkness began to fade in the east, the land around him sparkled with a million points of light. The sun climbed above the horizon and he saw its rays glistening in the dew drops around him on the grass and leaves. He seemed to hear a voice saying, 'I don't ask you to be a Billy Sunday, a D.L. Moody or an apostle Paul. All I want is that, like one little drop of dew, you let me shine through you and reflect my light.'

Papa went on to say that the experience transformed his attitude. He continued faithfully preaching until slowly churches appeared and multiplied. Listening to his father, Bill determined to persevere with his medical studies.

He went on to premedical studies in Wheaton College, where he met a beautiful fifteen-year-old high school girl. The next year they committed themselves to wait for each other while they continued their studies. Six years later, when Bill was approaching graduation from Albany Medical School in New York, he and Laura married.

Tanzania and Kenya: restructuring and training

In 1950 they reached Kola Ndoto Hospital in Tanzania. Bill soon plunged into a heavy surgical schedule. One day he badly needed to transfuse a patient dying from a ruptured ectopic pregnancy, but no Sukuma would consent to give blood. A lady missionary offered hers. Bill called several community leaders to watch him draw out the precious fluid and then inject it into the perishing woman's veins. The visitors stood amazed as the patient opened her eyes and began talking. After a successful operation Bill never again had trouble in finding donors.

Men carried water to the hospital for half a mile on cans hanging from shoulder poles. With Papa's help, Bill dug a well, installed a pump and provided an ample supply. Spotlessly clean walls sounded hollow when tapped because, under their layers of whitewash, white ants consumed every piece of wood. Bats nested above the ceilings. Bill began to replace mud walls and thatched roofs with stone and iron.

Laura learnt to give anaesthetics between the demands of six growing youngsters. But in all the rush of life, nothing displaced the spiritual diet of Bible reading and prayer, morning and evening. The family could relax and laugh too. They loved the occasional picnic or a swim at the pool belonging to the Williamson Diamond mine down the road.

They kept a playful monkey at home. Changing a wheel on his car, Bill carefully placed the lug nuts into the hub cap behind him. As each fell into the container, the pet picked it up, sniffed it and tossed it into the long grass. Laura hung her washing on the line to dry. The monkey walked carefully hand over hand along the cord, pulling out each peg until all the damp clothes dropped into the dust.

Looking back over their eleven years in Kola Ndoto, Bill thought 'perhaps the most valuable accomplishment was the starting of a government-recognized nurses' training program which resulted in many skilled Christians serving throughout Tanzania and also some neighbouring countries.' He rejoiced greatly when Tanzanians took over the running of the hospital a short time after his departure and continued to develop it.

In 1963, returning to Africa after two years study in America, they agreed to fill a temporary need in Kijabe. The assignment stretched to seventeen years, allowing time to plan major developments in the Medical Centre and a training programme for community health nurses. He introduced a short-term training programme for young doctors from overseas and saw some dedicate their lives to Christ's service. Hearing the challenge of the Comoro Islands, Bill and Laura volunteered to go for six months and Kijabe released them.

Compassion in the Comores

High above the Indian Ocean, the travellers watched a distant shadow lengthen into a large cloud capping two volcanos. Soon a golden beach shimmered beneath them and green palms climbed the island's mountainous spine, parting every so often to make way for untidy villages. Descending over black lava scattered along the shore, the aircraft landed in Moroni.

Bill's heart sank the first time he and Laura entered the 300-bed Hôpital al Marouf. His eye took in the filthy walls, rusting beds, and refuse from bananas, mangoes, pineapples, coconuts and pawpaws which littered all the walkways between wards. Each patient arrived with relatives, who hovered over them continually with food and comfort, and camped between the beds at night.

An operating list included bone surgery, which needed a germ-free environment, and the lancing of foul abscesses – all on the same table. Every clean case became infected. Few of the staff

Kijabe hospital, CM

possessed any training and their inadequacy forced Bill and Laura to go back several times after operating to check on their patients, even calling to see them late at night. Neither staff nor patients had experienced such care before. He was never so busy that he turned away from someone who wanted to chat about his sickness or felt anxious for a relative. Long after others left for a meal or for an afternoon siesta, Bill and Laura continued quietly working in the wards.

The AIM group grew to include a dentist, an engineer, teachers, nurses, other doctors and a lab technician. Peter Brashler, the Field Secretary in Zaire, transferred in order to lead the pioneer team. Soon after their arrival they came across a church of Malagasy immigrants in Moroni and linked up. The elders asked Pete to pastor the little flock.

The team learnt to take care in evangelism, realizing that Muslim sensitivity would quickly misunderstand and take offence. Dr Bill said, 'Our service is our witness and while we can't preach, we can pray and we can answer questions.' When someone asked about his faith he testified to what God meant to him. With an anxious patient, he offered to pray. He gave Scriptures only to those who directly requested them.

One day they found an elderly patient reading the Koran. He asked them in French, 'Have you got your religious book?' Laura, fluent in French, translated the question. When Bill hesitated he continued, 'You know . . . the Injil [Good News]; do you have a Swahili version? I'd like you to give it to me. Will you?' Later, as they left the hospital, the old man called across the square, 'Don't forget that book.' A few days later they took it to him, suitably wrapped in brown paper.

Recovered and back at work, he came home a few months afterwards and told his wife, 'I want you to make me some tea. Something very important is about to happen to me.' She left him drinking and reading. Later she found him dead in his chair, with the New Testament across his face.

People noticed more than Bill's high standard of surgical care. In a community which accepted polygamy (up to a maximum of four wives at one time) and countenanced easy divorce, Bill and Laura displayed a remarkable marital stability. Bill's lack of French meant they had to go everywhere together.

An amusing comment surfaced while operating. As usual Laura administered the anaesthetic, while bearded Musa assisted Bill, and Maria looked after the instruments. Maria spoke to Musa in the local Shingazidja language and he laughed. Bill felt that the joke pointed to him and he told his wife, 'Ask him what she said.' Embarrassed and amused, Musa refused to reply. Bill persisted. Eventually Musa answered, 'She said, "You know, these old people are in love." ' In a culture where very few marriages survive, theirs was an important aspect of their quiet testimony.

President Ali Soilih cooperated with the team for two years – possibly with mixed motives. Recognizing a need for radical change, he designed a secular, Marxist state under the banner of *Mapinduzi* ('Overturning' or 'Revolution'). When he invited Pete Brashler to broadcast, he told him, 'Our Muslims teach their religion on the air, why not you?' He permitted doctors and a laboratory worker to join a hospital on the second island, Anjouan, and another medical team on the third, Moheli. But did he simply wish to use the mission group to undermine the influence of Islam?

Some ugly incidents convinced Islamic leaders that Ali Soilih opposed their religion. At the same time four people on Anjouan island became Christians. The Muslims asked him, 'Why do you allow such freedom to the Christians and oppress us?' Soilih arrested the mission's laboratory worker on Anjouan. When the mission's leader tried to intercede, he accused the team of propagating their religion and suddenly, in January 1978, he expelled them.

Even while Ali Soilih was giving the order for missionaries to leave, wealthy Comoriens in Europe were hiring an invasion force. Two months later thirty-five Belgian and French mercenaries, armed to the teeth, silently steered their dinghies onto a sandy beach north of Moroni. One group ran to the army barracks, climbed onto the flat roof and terrified the men with a hail of bullets. They surrendered at once. Another quickly overpowered the police. And the commander led a third squad up to the President's residence. In two days they subjugated the other two islands, and then released a cryptic announcement, 'The President was shot while trying to escape.'

The mission began to enquire, could the team return? Not at all sure of the answer, Bill and Laura flew to Moroni and settled into an old hotel. Many friends wanted them back in the hospital but the new leaders had invited a French team. For a time Bill worked alongside them but he faced many frustrations.

In May 1980 he wrote, 'I have a heavy surgical schedule which runs the whole gamut of all the specialities.' He averaged twenty-four operations a week, with almost no gauze for sponges; he treated three or four fractures a day with neither X-ray nor plaster of Paris; he wrestled with pain without morphine or demerol. Even aspirin was a luxury.

Three believers visited them from time to time. One told him that police had recently detained him for four days, accusing him before the religious court, 'You have betrayed your religion.' They threatened, 'Next time Islamic law will deal with you.' This meant decapitation.

The Grand Mufti, a Muslim leader, had been principally responsible for the team's expulsion in 1978. Nonetheless he consulted Bill about an unpleasant infection of his foot. For a year he had failed to get satisfaction from any doctor. Bill took him to the operating room and quietly prayed as he scrubbed his hands before making a simple incision and applying ointment. A week later the foot healed and an enemy became a friend.

The Minister of Health asked Bill to move to Mitsamiouli at the northern end of the island. He gave him considerable freedom to develop the 55-bed hospital, suggesting that he made it a model for the nation.

So the team entered another tumbledown, rusting, dirty institution with disheartened Comorien nurses who seldom received a salary. A lifetime of practical experience in Africa helped Bill build and equip a surgical unit, refurbish wards, erect a water tank with its tower, install electricity and X-ray. Soon they listed sixty operations a month.

Bill kept healthy by cycling 25 miles into Moroni. Even so his eyes troubled him increasingly. Eventually he could not see well enough to operate. Arthritis in her hips upset Laura's walking, but she still limped around the hospital with her husband. In their seventies now, their letters home breathed peace 'in knowing we are just where our Lord wants us'. But, as the decade came to an end, they realized they should leave the work in other hands. 'The Comoros,' said Bill, 'have been the most satisfying period in Laura's life and mine. We're helping people who have been neglected for years. They are very appreciative. We have touched many lives here.'

Bill and Laura knew that they could touch no life for God without his guidance and power. They passed this principle on to their six children, who all grew up to serve the Lord. The eldest, Ted, met them in Nairobi in 1987. AIM wanted him to consider becoming Director for their 728 American members and a large supporting constituency. Later Ted told the members, 'I asked my father in confidence what he thought of the idea.

He was speechless for a long time . . . he talked of always wanting God's will for me. He helped me weigh the pros and cons.' They all prayed. Ted submitted his name and the Council unanimously recommended him.

The Island's Governor expressed his appreciation in calling the nation's dignitaries to a farewell party. Bill looked into their faces, knowing that beneath their flowing Muslim robes many carried neat scars on their bodies from his knife. Towards the end, the Governor called for silence. For five minutes he spoke about Dr Bill and his wife – their care, their surprising willingness to rise during the night, their readiness to pause for a friendly chat in the midst of hectic activity. 'Above all,' he concluded, 'Dr Barnett is a man of God.'

Sad Somalia

Bill's love for Muslims stirred again two years into his Californian retirement when a friend in World Medical Missions, long-time helpers of AIM, asked if he would use his forty years' medical missionary experience in relieving the advancing disease situation in Somalia. Bill did not hesitate a moment, 'As long as I can be of help, I'm happy to go. I've had plenty of exposure to danger in the past and I'm not afraid. I know the Lord will take care of us.'[279]

The filth of the Comoro Islands failed to prepare Bill and Laura for the devastation that confronted them in Mogadishu. They came to a country looted by its own people; its public buildings, factories and many homes stripped of contents, doors, windows, and in many cases roofs, even walls; its beautiful university in a shambles. Rubble and garbage lay everywhere under an umbrella of flies.

In the midst of the mess, people grew millet and maize, tended their camels, cattle and goats, and looked for relief supplies. But fighting, disease and theft killed thousands.

Danger abounded too. Gunmen robbed a Somali doctor of his UNICEF car. As they made to drive away he hurled rocks at them in his frustration. They paused long enough to kill him. The Barnetts and their team slept and travelled with armed guards protecting them at all times. Bill kept fit by running round the flat roof of their rented house sixty times every morning.

He organized a team to visit feeding centres, where he treated up to 300 a day and held classes. Kijabe hospital sent nurses and doctors to assist on a rotating system.

Influenced by his Comorien experience, he looked for a

hospital which AIM might develop as a long-term demonstration of Christ's compassion. He wrote to his family, 'Mom and I have been asked to spearhead our thrust into Brava [125 miles south of Mogadishu] . . . establish relations with the people and town elders and then gradually begin an out patient service and a mobile community health program. We expect one other doctor, two nurses and an administrator.'

He hoped that the traditional village elder system of rule could return. But beyond that he longed to see society transformed through a true experience of God's love and forgiveness. They met some changed people like the middle-aged hunchback who told them, 'I'm a Christian; the Lord Jesus is my Saviour and I love Him.' They felt that ultimately the answer to the bitter rivalries in the Somali clans lay in the cross of Christ.

When the UN military operation turned sour, the Barnetts had to leave, their hopes unfulfilled. They returned to Nairobi to wait for an opportunity for long-term workers to heal Somalia's wounds. If younger men and women did not show up, they thought perhaps two seventy-five-year-olds might still be needed – despite failing eyes and stiffening hips.

Lilian Hurter

Joan and I remained in the Comoro Islands for eight months in 1976, based in the hospitals of Moroni and Moheli. Our team prayed for opportunities to establish work on the remaining two islands, Anjouan and Mayotte.

Mayotte's peaceful invaders

Local politicians on Mayotte wanted nothing to do with the independence movement. Rivalry between the islands dated back for nearly two centuries, when sultans vied for power. Desperate for relief from invaders, the people of Mayotte asked France to help in 1844 and paid the price by submitting to colonial rule. Although French control spread quickly over the whole archipelago, distrust between the ancient sultanates persisted.

During our first visit to Grande Comore, Ali Soilih attempted a peaceful invasion of Mayotte, commandeering the three old aircraft of Air Comores to transport himself and his supporters to the French island. One plane made it, but the French quickly scattered fuel drums across the runway to prevent the others landing. Soilih's march through the neighbouring village sparked off derisive opposition from the local people and he must have been glad when the authorities rolled back the drums and allowed him to escape.

Miriam van Reenen, one of our first pair of missionaries, wished to return accompanied by two other South Africans, Lilian Hurter and Heather Simkin. But opinion had hardened against their country since Miriam's previous visit. Soilih's government refused to give visas to South Africans.

When Joan and I visited Mayotte, puzzling graffiti greeted us, 'Indépendance = Tyran'. People said, 'You cannot distinguish between Comoriens and French; they are all French.' And France, we discovered, still remained friendly with South Africa.

In September the three ladies flew from Johannesburg to Reunion. Two days before their proposed trip to Mayotte, the army cancelled all civilian travel on the military supply plane – the only one between the two islands. The ladies set alarm bells ringing in our team with a telegram announcing their intention to travel via Moroni. To everyone's surprise no one arrested them in Moroni and, after a pleasant weekend with their colleagues there, they climbed aboard the Air Comores flight to Mayotte, where Joan and I welcomed them.

The tourist sun no longer shone on Mayotte's 'Hotel Rocher'. The taps usually remained obstinately dry. We improvised by equipping ourselves with two large cans to collect water wherever we travelled in the overcrowded Renault taxis. Food varied in quality but the cost never changed – so high that we used our own little stove to cook simple meals in our rooms.

Perched on a rock above the sea, we looked down from the hotel onto a foreshore littered with rusty cans, beer bottles, orange peel and an old sack. Close by, colourful people thronged a jetty every hour or so, waiting to surge onto the ferry which linked this tiny island with mainland Mayotte, a couple of miles away.

We boarded the ferry. Out on the water, the beauty of the place took our breath away. In one direction, God's glorious sunshine danced across the bluest ripples to a green-clad island; ahead, a mountain on the main island lifted its peak into a shroud of mist; while, encircling us to the seaward, hidden coral threw up a ribbon of white surf.

We approached the government in the person of 'Le Représentant de la France à Mayotte'. A path, guarded by an ancient cannon with two cairns of ammunition, led us in a straight line from the road to his large office building (engineered by Eiffel). We climbed a wide semicircle of stone steps with the tricolor waving above us to give a feel of faded grandeur. I made the mistake of offering the type of help for which Ali Soilih showed such hunger. With courteous dignity he suggested, 'Such help can better be used in underdeveloped countries.' France could provide all the technical assistance he needed. 'But,' he assured us, 'your religious activities present no problem.'

Housing presented a huge problem. As we followed every lead we soon found that French aid workers occupied all the western-style buildings. The five of us walked miles from village to village, day after day. Once a man we knew stopped his Peugeot 504 to offer us a welcome lift. Later we wanted to pay but he declined. 'You are my guests,' he insisted; 'and this is how we Muslims treat our visitors.'

At last we found a stone house a yard back from the only street in the village of Passamainti. Five little rooms and a piped water supply made us optimistic despite the lack of privacy and the full pit latrine. We agreed on a rent, to rise when the landlord attended to several repairs. Scouring the villages for furniture, we found a dump of rejects behind the hotel – two small double beds, two tables, a set of orphaned table legs, parts of four wooden chairs and a toilet seat. Miriam and I loaded this unusual collection onto the ferry under the gaze of a horde of interested passengers. None of them would share our embarrassment by lending a hand.

Is there an octopus?

Joan and I felt badly about leaving the ladies in such poor surroundings. As Lilian watched our DC 3 climb over the ocean, a sense of desolation swept over her. The bare, almost unfurnished house in Passamainti added to the loneliness. Opening the shuttered windows next morning, she immediately encountered enquiring faces, peering into the house to discover more of these strange newcomers. Becoming bold when they perceived the gentleness of the occupants, they bawled obscene comments.

Throughout the first year, Lilian never opened the door or front windows without seeing spectators. They showed enormous interest in every move of the ladies. Slowly it dawned on them that the young men of Passamainti believed they had come in search of husbands. With no knowledge of the language they found it difficult to correct them.[280]

They discussed how they should approach their neighbours

and decided to invite them to classes. Lilian taught English, Heather offered needlework and Miriam, knitting. Miriam asked, 'Why, in this stifling climate does anyone want to knit?' But forty came to her and the strategy succeeded in building understanding, and eventually appreciation.

Each knew that friendship was the key to mastery of the language. Lilian had known for a long time that God called her to Mayotte and she was 'one hundred per cent sure' that he wanted her to translate his Word. But as she heard everyone speaking the incomprehensible language, she asked herself, 'How will I learn it without any contacts? Will I ever be able to translate?'

Contacts came through the English class and she began to make sense of a few phrases. At the end of the first year a nurse joined them from South Africa. Being a team of four now, they could occasionally separate. Lilian and Heather visited a remote village and met a teacher whom we had befriended on a previous trip. As he was teaching in a distant school, he invited them to use his two-roomed house. A Koranic teacher, impressed by their commitment to learn his language, offered them a meal. To release them from the burden of preparing meals, he agreed to feed them regularly in return for payment. In six weeks they made immense strides in the language.

Back in Passamainti, the classes continued to break down barriers. They treasured a regular Bible study with five boys and looked forward to the day when the lads would find the Lord for themselves. A large group of young people arrived, wanting to evangelize Mayotte. They asked the ladies about local helpers and invited the five to join them. Mildly surprised that the missionaries had lived in Passamainti for over a year without leading a single Muslim to Christ, they invited the lads for daily study and, after a few days, encouraged them to decide to follow Jesus. All five agreed. Following the departure of the evangelists, the lads never returned to the ladies' Bible studies nor linked up with any group of believers.

The ladies developed several simple principles of ministry: learn Shimaore, absorb local culture, make friends, seek to serve, keep witness low key, develop Bible studies. They used a filmstrip on the life of Christ in villages with no preaching apart from a simple explanation of the pictures. Portrayals of the crucifixion, seen for the first time, always evoked complete silence. Miriam started a Bible study which eventually developed into an international church with a missionary pastor. She trained as a children's nurse and worked in the hospital for a while before moving to Anjouan Island.

A leprosy nurse joined the team and all agreed that she should work among the 20,000 people of Moheli. But she needed a companion and Lilian offered to go for a year. A step which she thought would hinder her language learning brought great dividends. On Moheli she found people from all four islands and could study the four dialects, arriving at the conclusion that the Comoriens needed two separate translations. One year stretched to five.

In 1987 Lilian returned to Mayotte. She found that her old friend, the Koranic teacher, had built a new house on the beach. She rented two rooms facing the sea and again arranged to take all her meals with the family.

Every evening she walked around the village chatting. At harvest time she helped the women in the fields. People recognized her as the adopted daughter of the elderly couple and felt comfortable. They called the couple BaLiliani and MaLiliani. BaLiliani's home lacked piped water and she took her place in the queue at the village pump. Sanitation left much to be desired, but she kept healthy and content.

Quiet by disposition, Lilian sat back in the evenings to listen to the family conversation, picking up patterns of thought and forms of speech. One evening they discussed demons. BaLiliani turned to her and asked, 'What do you think?' She talked of Jesus and his encounters, ending by saying, 'God is more powerful than Satan and his demons.' The old man responded, 'You have a powerful religion. Have you got a book that will tell me more?' Lilian told him, 'I am translating one at the moment and will give it to you when I finish.'

Although BaLiliani taught the Koran by rote, he did not understand its Arabic. As she listened to his chat she heard more and more of the Bible and observed a surprising anomaly: recognizing biblical truth but still convinced of the Koran as the fountain of orthodoxy, he attributed to the Koran what he learnt from Lilian.

Like all good Bible translators Lilian depended heavily on local people for accuracy. But where could she find them in a village without a single Christian? Several helpers came to assist in the translation but none persisted.

One day, as a cyclone poured rain upon Mzouazia, Lilian chatted to a young mother. Sitting around a fire roasting corn, she marvelled again at the intelligence of this woman despite her limited education.[281] 'Zeinab,' Lilian asked tentatively, 'Would you like to work for me?' She had in mind a dictionary she wanted to prepare. Zeinab agreed.

Zeinab soon showed interest in the Gospels and Lilian found her a valuable source of words and ideas. Lilian watched the impact of God's word on an intelligent mind studying it for the first time. Zeinab read the question which people repeatedly asked the Lord, 'Who are you? . . . Where are you from?' Throwing her hands in the air, she exclaimed in disgust, 'These people have heads like stones. He's told them!'

They read John's Gospel chapter fourteen and came to verse eight, 'Lord, show us the Father and that will be enough for us.' Lilian paused and asked Zeinab, 'What will he answer?' She replied, 'I've told you; if you have seen me you have seen the Father.'

Many months later they arrived at a difficult verse for translators, 'God made him who had no sin to be sin for us' (2 Corinthians 5:21). Lilian presented Zeinab with five possibilities and they discussed each of them. After a little thought, Zeinab suddenly said, 'So that is why he had to die!'

At times Lilian remained as the only team member on the island and found that responsibilities for Bible studies, church services and mission funds frustrated her efforts to press on with the New Testament. She wondered if she would ever complete it.

At last Lilian wrote on April 16, 1993, 'A keen sense of excitement filled me as Zeinab and I worked together. We could still run into problems. "One never knows where an octopus is lurking!" Zeinab reminded me. But there were no octopi that day, and we duly reached the final "Amen" of Revelation 22 verse 21!'[282]

David and Eleanor Duncan

One thousand miles north-east of Grande Comore, the sun-drenched beaches and forested hills of Mahe in the Seychelles drew a stream of tourists to fill 2,000 hotel beds in 1976. The government expected this figure to double in the following five years because of Britain's last gift before independence that year – a modern airport.

Few tourists would have chosen the cheap, waterside hotel. Exhausted by the long journey, Joan flopped onto a bed. Music seeped into our room from the lounge – Shirley Bassey singing,

'This is a lovely way to spend an evening'. In the face of myriad uncertainties, she thought wryly, 'I know of better ways.'

French planters from Mauritius had first found this uninhabited island in the mid eighteenth century and settled with their slaves. Britain, emboldened by victories over Napoleon, grabbed it in 1814. Later the British navy mounted a campaign against slavery along the coast of Africa. Whenever they succeeded in arresting an Arab dhow laden with this precious cargo, they dropped the liberated Africans at Mahe, where the French immediately enslaved them again.

Who ever heard of a missionary potter?

The Far East Broadcasting Association came in 1971 and recognized near ideal conditions for reaching India, the Middle East and Africa. They also discovered that almost all the 60,000 people living on the Seychelle Islands called themselves Christians but, as in some countries which had exported Christianity to them, religion was a veneer covering many evil practices. FEBA suggested that AIM assist the local people, releasing the radio missionaries for their international priorities. With the Comoro work well established, Joan and I next considered Seychelles.

An English bishop, who led the 7,000 Anglicans warned us against rocking the church boat, which sailed comfortably in a sea of sacramentalism. But in the Seychelles a partaker of communion might retain the blessed wafer under his tongue, extract it and take it to the 'Bon Homme du Bois', a sort of witch doctor, who then would add his own magic to make it a very potent charm indeed. A worshipper might buy a candle in church, give it the name of her enemy, curse it as she set it alight, watch it burn, and, when it finally spluttered out, go away convinced that her enemy would likewise perish. The bishop admitted, 'Your approach with an emphasis on personal belief is something we need here.'

The Permanent Secretary to the Ministry for Education and Social Services wondered why missionaries should come to a country which was 'ninety-eight per cent Christian'; they needed no more religion. He did nurse a concern though for 'a thousand fifteen year olds who drop out of school every year and cannot find work.' In view of the burgeoning tourist industry he asked, 'Could you not establish craft training – perhaps pottery?'

Who ever heard of missionary potters? Surprisingly we found one on the staff of RVA. Jack Wilson gladly consented to transfer and became the first of a succession of artists who shared their

experience of Christ as well as their skill. Another was David
Duncan, an English potter, and his wife Eleanor, a teacher.

Fashioning leaders

As their Jumbo settled into the approach to Seychelles Airport,
the Duncans looked down into a clear sea shimmering with the
brightest blues and greens they had ever seen. The seventeen
mile long island seemed all mountain; even the runway ran along
a strip reclaimed from the Indian Ocean. Driving away from
Immigration their driver showed them a rock face of granite and
said, 'the whole island is like that'. They zig-zagged up a track
between coconut trees and boulders until they arrived at two
bungalows overlooking the airport, giving them the impression
that they could reach out and touch the incoming jets.[283]

Other less pleasant impressions crowded in. Unexpectedly,
constant noise assailed them – crickets, bats, dogs, radios.
Steamy heat drenched them in sweat which refused to evaporate.
One evening David and Eleanor crouched behind a sofa armed
with a tennis racket and watched a rat climb up their book-
shelves. A colleague did not help by telling them about the
rat which fell onto a table in the midst of a prayer meeting. To
avoid disturbing the worship she turned a bowl upside down over
the stunned beast to imprison it until a convenient time for
execution.

David taught in the Ceramics Training Centre for eighteen
months. When Jack opened the centre six years earlier, the
mission agreed to look for capital funding and personnel for eight
years. The Seychelles Government would provide all running
costs and, after that initial period, take over the whole operation.
By David's time, the missionaries could no longer choose their
students but had to accept poorly motivated youngsters who
could think of nothing better. The hopes of the team centred
on one of their first graduates, Rodney, completing an additional
course of three years in USA.

Rodney fulfilled all their expectations. Well-trained now,
artistic and full of creative ideas, he seemed the ideal man to
take over as the missionaries withdrew. For a time the centre
boomed, but Rodney felt slighted. Surely, he reasoned, if the
government recognized his value, they would pay him better.
He departed to earn more in a tour agency. Potters' wheels
disappeared into cupboards, the kiln remained empty and new
government staff developed a woodwork programme.

When the missionaries handed the training centre to the

government, they sought to set the trained potters up in business. A cooperative society called Seypot developed slowly. Initially low standards of pottery kept sales down. Since sales dictated salaries, several disgruntled potters left. Unaccustomed to working together, members easily squabbled. Several young women became pregnant and departed to set up their homes. Only two men remained, but they became the nucleus of the society.

With missionary hands maintaining a measure of control, Seypot decided to advertise for apprentices. From over 100 applicants they chose two and left their training to the Seychellois potters. David encouraged them to develop a distinctively local form of art for themselves, as well as training them in some of the nitty-gritty of running a small business. Sales looked up. The Minister of Manpower, previously critical of the missionary team, came in his chauffeur-driven car to buy their pots. Seypot took over a small shop on the main road and invited the Minister to open it. Hearing that all the missionaries planned to pull out the next day, he arrived with TV cameras and publicly thanked them for their work for the nation.

By the end of the eighties AIM had accomplished the original pottery task but the need for 'personal belief' continued to challenge the team. They could see progress. Over those first ten years of ministry many young people passed through the missionaries' Bible studies and seminars to become active in church life. Some are now doctors and teachers; two entered the Anglican ministry, taking responsibility for major churches; another went overseas for study and joined Arab World Ministries in Marseilles. Several decided to organize their own church, called 'The Grace and Peace Fellowship', and asked AIM to help.

In contrast to the work on mainland Africa, the mission never sought to plant new churches in Seychelles but gladly assisted in the development of national churches. Twice the team provided a pastor to 'Grace and Peace', but with the proviso that the congregation seek leaders from their own ranks. David, as Team Leader, urged the elders to look for someone who could be trained. At the same time he sought a missionary to work with them, for no more than four years, in developing their own leadership talents. The elders only accepted such responsibility with reluctance. 'We prefer a missionary to organize the church,' they told David; 'If one of us initiates something, others may think him proud.'

David himself pondered the needs of the increasing number of people coming to a personal commitment to Christ. He asked the Anglican bishop French Chang Him, 'How can they grow without literature in their own language?' Bishop French offered him a room alongside the main church for a resource centre. With an office and a computer, he looked for a Seychellois counterpart and found John Jean-Louis, a recent graduate from the church's little training centre (and before that active in the team's Bible studies).

In a joint project with Lion Publishing, they translated six of the Lion Bible Story series. These sold well, encouraging them to undertake others to a total of thirteen titles by the end of 1991. Two years later David participated in the visit of Operation Mobilisation's ship, MV *Doulos*, and good literature flooded the population.

David launched a weekly Gospel music programme on national radio which he called 'Lekla Lorizon' ('Bright Horizon'). He aimed to use music to show the relevance of Christian faith to all areas of life.

In a country where over three-quarters of babies are born outside marriage, the team's 'Studies in Christian Growth' often focused on marriage, family and related ills such as abortion. David attended a Scripture Union conference on AIDS

David and Eleanor Duncan, DD

awareness in Zimbabwe. When he returned, the Ministry of Health asked him to join a task force conducting research into the sexual health of teenagers with a view to taking appropriate action.

The team based all their teaching on the Bible – but it had to be practical. With an expanding pentecostal element in the churches, they discussed healing. When they noticed threats from the Jehovah's Witnesses and Muslims, they studied the uniqueness of Christ. Aware always of the need to improve communication from the pulpits, they invited a preacher from Zimbabwe to provide an unprecedented feast of exposition spread over a week.

David welcomed Neville and Judy Marston into the team for a government assignment of training social workers. Their insistence on integrity made them unpopular with some of the students but earned the gratitude of their employer. The two-year course produced radical changes but, after they left the department, the improvement was not maintained. The Anglican bishop invited Neville to become Training Officer for the little diocese, where he hoped that a Bible-based ministry would produce more lasting fruit.

David's vision for the team focused on providing skills and resources for leaders. But more important than such technical concerns was a Christlike life. He said, 'When we depart we must ask, are people more holy? Do they represent Christ?'

Colin and Christine Molyneux

Mind-numbing fevers never took Colin Molyneux by surprise. Four years in a remote corner of Zaire, followed by seven in northern Kenya had exposed him to all manner of parasites so that, by 1979, he responded to any sore head and soaring temperature with a fistful of chloroquine tablets. On September 14th, he wondered if his mental lethargy arose from malaria, its treatment or the hectic changes of the past few months.

As he settled back into a plane seat, he could still hardly believe that he was moving his family once again. He and Christine had inherited Tom and Ruth Collins' mantle five years previously when they had arrived at Liter to find several churches full of young disciples in need of teaching. With their early training and experience in Britain's Faith Mission, Colin and Christine enjoyed both evangelism and teaching. Colin developed a

'Theological Education by Extension' programme for pastors, elders and leading women. Students studied at home, meeting regularly with their teachers to discuss the lessons. Towards the end of five strenuous years they could witness Bible-based teaching infusing the churches.

A surprising request shattered any tendency towards comfortable complacency: 'Please consider a move to Madagascar.'

Colin's reaction was negative at first: 'We've only just launched this vital ministry. Our children, Joy and John Mark, need schools and Liter is almost too remote, let alone Madagascar.'

Christine noticed that several others were moving into new outreach areas. As they prayed together she realized that 'all the reasons for not going were really quite selfish, unable to stand against Scripture and scrutiny. It just took a little while for God to enlarge our minds.'[284]

Five frail years

At the end of their first day in Madagascar, after problems with immigration, traffic jams and pickpockets, Colin and Christine could gladly have taken the first flight home. They discovered that difficulties did not ease as they persevered. They knew the language would be hard, but had not realized how hard. Eighteen months passed before Colin could put together a simple evangelistic message. He persisted and became an able preacher in Malagasy.

Even more perplexing, they developed serious misgivings about the programme. The General Secretary of the Malagasy Bible Society, Rev Jules Ramaroson, invited AIM to assist his 'League of Sowers' on a 257 hectare farm outside the city. When he first took me to the farm in 1976, he introduced eighteen poor Christians living from the rice they grew. They expected a team of their colleagues to return shortly from an evangelistic and Bible distribution trek of several hundred miles. The General Secretary believed that, with aid and expertise, he could settle four villages on the land, each housing fifteen families. Impoverished Christians would grow food, learn their faith, sell Bibles and spread the Gospel. Extra cash from the sale of farm produce might even swell Bible Society funds. Urging AIM to come he said, 'Madagascar needs the Gospel again. Our churches are cold.' The godly Pastor Jules could not visit the farm as often as he wished. He sadly dismissed the foreman when he heard that he had fathered a child with another member of the group.

Leaderless, the League of Sowers disintegrated and Jules looked to the AIM team to trigger new development.

Roland and Anne Everard sold their own farm in Kenya's highlands, joined AIM and moved out to Madagascar to take charge of the farm there, while the Molyneux family settled in Tananarive. Roly Everard, hampered by language and other limitations, struggled to reconcile the pastor's grandiose ideas with the realities of poor-quality soil and traditional farming methods. A fish farm failed and then a costly potato scheme collapsed.

Meanwhile Colin encouraged the evangelistic teams. Mostly they came from Pentecostal backgrounds whereas their hearers belonged, at least nominally, to the big Reformed denomination. Some ministers complained to the Bible Society and the treks stopped.

Five fruitful years

The Molyneux net spread wider than the farm. A large conference in the north, linked with Scripture Union, invited Colin to preach every year. The SU leader asked Colin about their plans after their five-year contract with the farm. He suggested, 'We have plenty of work you can do, so please step right over.' The new assignment took Colin to many parts of the large island, carrying SU materials, teaching and preaching.

Eventually the original farm foundered. Colin and Christine managed to relocate the few remaining settlers on a new piece of ground which the settlers chose themselves. Steadily they built up their plots and pursued their vision for evangelism.

As they traversed the country Colin and Christine realized the tremendous need for evangelism as well as for Bible teaching. Although half the population professed the Christian faith, few knew Christ. If they acknowledged him at all, many placed him alongside the spirits of their ancestors.

An elderly 'Christian', crippled in a car accident, worshipped at a royal shrine and noticed improvement in his limbs. The missionaries asked, 'Who is healing you?' Puzzled by their ignorance, he affirmed, 'By the power of the spirit of the king, God has heard my prayer . . . therefore I thank both the king and God. They are the same.'[285]

To a question about the health of his church, an Anglican minister responded, 'Our denomination is dying.' He pointed to two beautiful church buildings, which looked as though they had stepped out of the English countryside of a previous century, and said, 'One of those is my seminary where I teach only five students.' Colin and Christine joined a worship service in the other. Swinging incense censers, tinkling bells, soft candles and intoned prayers shrouded them in unreality.

In an earlier era, when Malagasy people had flooded into the congregations, missionaries built churches alongside pagan shrines. The two merged. Indicating a building on a hill-top, the priest said, 'I went up there and found sacrifices of banana, honey and salt in front of a cross . . . Visit any church and you'll find that the cross has nothing to do with Jesus Christ.'

Such a depressing diagnosis did not apply to every part of the church. Some firm believers cherished memories of revival which arose out of bitter persecution fifteen years after the first missionaries of the London Missionary Society had come in 1818. The General Secretary of the Scripture Union saw himself in the direct line of succession of those first faithful preachers. After theological training in France and Switzerland, he returned to Madagascar in 1978. With the widely respected Jules Ramaroson as sponsor and the Bible Society as umbrella he and his wife launched SU to encourage reading and understanding of the Bible. Ordination as a minister of the Reformed Church (FJKM) helped disarm opposition to his uncompromising message. SU grew so rapidly that soon it separated from its parent to stand on its own organizational feet.

A young mother of three, Miriam, attended Christine's Bible study. Throughout her life she attended church but, just after her marriage had died in traumatic divorce, she discovered a living union with the Lord Jesus. Well educated, clever and zealous, she became an effective member of a team of SU evangelists. She humbled her teachers, Colin and Christine, by her compassionate love. With great insight into Malagasy ways of covering up issues, she could penetrate to the heart of a person's problems and provide a biblical solution.

When she married a second time, Miriam walked into a mass of problems of her own. Her new husband had been a dissolute politician before he too fell in love with Christ. The law caught up with him and took him to jail for a seven year sentence. Out on parole after serving five years, he met Miriam and they felt God leading them together. Unexpectedly the prison called him back to complete his remaining two years. Miriam now had to support him in prison, care for her family and fulfil her evangelistic calling. They survived and went on to lead one of Colin's teams.

As leaders of the little AIM team, Colin and Christine looked for other openings for missionaries. They knew that the Marxist government would only allow people to enter at the invitation of leaders of Malagasy churches and organizations. This coincided perfectly both with their own desires and with mission policy. The head of the Inter Varsity organization (Union Groupe Biblique de Madagascar) invited them to find a worker at the same time as a travelling secretary of the British Universities and Colleges Christian Fellowship applied to join AIM. John and Kathy Williams found the UGBM a vigorous movement reaching from the University of Tananarive to five colleges in other major towns and many more in high schools.

A growing denomination, the Mission Evangelique au Tananarive, requested workers – some to serve in their seminary and others to pastor the ministers and evangelists in the churches. A converted English publican and a South African policeman responded.

Looking back on a decade in Madagascar Colin and Christine found reasons to praise God for the early difficult years. Without the Bible Society's invitation, AIM could not have entered Madagascar. Although the first farm failed, the second flourished. They both learnt the language, absorbed some of the culture and made friends, who provided the springboard for further fruitful service. As their time there drew to a close they said, 'Those five years with SU were the most fulfilling and profitable of any in our mission work.'

Joy and John Mark finished their studies at RVA and in Tananarive. Their parents realized that the youngsters had moved around so much that they scarcely knew where they belonged. The family made the difficult decision to return to England, at any rate for a few years, and accepted the position of mission representatives in the northern half of England, where the mission was largely unknown. They never found missionary work easy in Zaire, Kenya or Madagascar, but they learnt to develop fruitful ministries, especially at the end. Now, with missionary interest declining in the home country, they faced possibly their biggest headaches of all as they strove to reverse the trend.

15
New lessons in the south

While we developed our ministry to the islands, we continued to study the situation in southern Africa. Sister societies offered much assistance and some invited us to work closely – even in one country to the point of merging. Although we had moved far from the geographical confines of our founder's Mombasa to Lake Chad axis (p. 19) the mission held fast to its basic goal of equipping African Christians to evangelize. As horizons expanded, the need to change in order to remain true to that vision challenged us, sometimes in uncomfortable ways.

The International Council insisted that from the start 'all church-related ministry shall be organized and operated to ensure its adequate national leadership and support as soon as possible.'[286] While some ministries might require many years before achieving that goal, others could africanize much more rapidly than we previously had thought possible. African Christians had already pressed us to abandon our questioning of their ability to lead their own denominations and churches. Now we took the additional step of seeking African leadership in the earliest stages of any fresh thrust.

As new churches started, we looked for God's chosen leaders and helped train them. Of course this commitment influenced the planning of all the ministries, including the more technical, so that African Christians and churches would ultimately want to run them and find the needed resources of trained personnel and money. The IC called it 'The Repeatable Principle'. It ensured early ownership without dependence on foreign skills or funds; it also released the missionary 'to accept a fresh challenge from the Lord'.[287]

When you see fruitful opportunities all round you, it is difficult to contemplate handing over your ministry to others and moving to another situation, more strategic to the advance of God's kingdom. But many adjusted: some by modifying their programmes in the light of the IC priorities; others by painfully uprooting and moving to new areas.

Early in the eighties, the mission faced another cultural challenge – an incoming tide of workers from vigorous new churches planted in the previous century. New men and women joined from Brazil, Hong Kong, Korea, Portugal, Singapore, non-white sections of South Africa, Sudan, Uganda and Zimbabwe, and each brought their own unique interpretations of Christian life-style. They disturbed our western traditions and challenged us to learn from their insights.

Jack and Peggy Pienaar

Jack Pienaar, a native Afrikaans speaker, and Peggy, an English-speaking South African, learnt the lessons of change and became examples of cross-cultural sensitivity to many of us.

Peggy looked back over two generations of missionaries; a great uncle pioneered with George Grenfell to open the Baptist work in Congo and her father, Professor Doke, achieved renown as a linguist. Jack was descended from French Huguenots who had found shelter from persecution by emigrating to South Africa, where the family settled on a sheep farm in the dry Karoo. Immediately after their honeymoon in March 1952, the Pienaars travelled north to Kenya where they immersed themselves in the churches and in building projects. Four moves of home in as many years tried Peggy's patience, especially as she had to leave behind a flourishing garden in each. As well as setting up many new homes, they lived through the transitions in the church throughout the sixties. Jack, as a member of the Field Council, took part in the lengthy discussions which led up to the AIC assuming control over the work. More significantly, they befriended many church leaders in western Kenya and developed great respect for their maturity.

In 1972 the small AIM Committee in South Africa asked Jack to become their General Secretary. Reluctantly they pulled up their roots from Kenyan soil and headed back to Cape Town. They found comfort in living close to their family of five as they began their university careers and Peggy thought she could at last settle into her own nest.

When AIM's International General Secretary, Norman Thomas, needed an experienced missionary to investigate the Comoro Islands, he asked Jack. Fired by the needs he saw there, Jack shared his impressions with the growing AIM following in South Africa. God spoke to Miriam, Lilian and Heather at Jack's old school, the Kalk Bay Bible Institute, and they left for the islands.

What do your people need?

The pioneer witness in the Comoros encouraged mission supporters in South Africa. Interest grew, constrained only by the developing international isolation of South Africa. Jack looked for other places where his countrymen could serve in AIM and turned towards Namibia.

Nearly half of the one and a half million people in Namibia called themselves Lutherans, thanks to the efforts of German and Finnish missionaries since 1842. Liberal teaching, followed by black theology, eroded the early spiritual heritage so that, by the time of Jack's first visit in 1979, political liberation stood higher on the agenda of most Christians than biblical salvation. He found many churches but few people who spoke of a close relationship with Christ.

Politically Namibia wallowed in a bloodstained trough. From their bases in Angola, the Marxist SWAPO (South West Africa Peoples' Organization) struck into the northern half of Namibia to murder, maim and pillage. The Pienaar sons, like most South African young men, saw service in the Defence Force quartered in a string of camps along the border, from which they sallied into Angola searching for rebels.

Jack invited me to join him in an exploratory trip early in 1980. We suggested that three senior members of the Africa Evangelical Fellowship (AEF) join us and they brought a Christian Swazi (a member of the Swaziland Parliament). AEF interest in Namibia dated back to 1968 and, by the time of our safari, they counted two missionary families, both on leave.

We flew into Windhoek where we planned to meet the AEF men in their car. This modern city of 150,000 lay in a cradle of hills sparkling in sunshine. A deceptive aura of peace hung over the clean, multistorey office blocks, beautiful churches, colourful gardens with dancing fountains, well-stocked stores, tarmac roads, efficient railways and manicured white suburban homes. The once segregated African, Indian and 'Coloured' townships seemed less oppressive than their rigidly separated counterparts further south.

As we sped north, the grass at the roadside turned green, tempting a dozen families of wild pigs to scamper around searching for food. Lesser kudus fled from the road ahead of us. Don, AEF Director for Botswana, pointed to a ruined farm and said, 'Insurgents murdered a German there ten years ago.' Silently we passed the burnt-out shell of a saloon car, recently wrecked by a landmine. We arrived at a small town where well-armed guards looked us over before opening an electronically controlled gate. We bedded down in the home of an absent missionary to the light of big lamps strung along the barbed wire perimeter fence.

Early one morning, Chief Dimbare of the Hambukushu welcomed us to his home in Namibia's fertile northern belt. Standing at the entrance to his compound, we awaited his summons before advancing to shake the royal hand. Our interpreter told us with awe that one of his ancestors, a queen,

Supplies arrive at last, CM

once offered children to the crocodiles from an island in the river as a sacrifice to bring rain. By tradition rainmaking passed down the royal line, but Dimbare had either forgotten the art or lost faith in it. His interest centred more on a woman to his left who dispensed cups of beer from a large bucket to twenty mums and kids around her and a posse of men and boys sitting in front of the king. A guard with a rifle also drank as he watched us all.

Jack asked, 'What do you people need?' Royalty answered, 'Help with the gardens, mainly rain.' Jack enquired, 'What about praying?' 'Yes, we have all prayed, but no rain has come.'

Jack continued, 'Do you need Bible teaching?' 'No; we are all Roman Catholics and get plenty of that.' 'And health care?' The chief replied, 'We have clinics and an RC hospital. Yes, babies die, but that is because God has decided to take them.'

Missions and government seemed to meet their material needs but development meant handouts rather than imparting life-sustaining skills. At an agricultural centre, long pipes rotated over circular maize fields sprinkling water while a big John Dere combine harvester stood in silent testimony to generous but inappropriate technology.

Like many of the people in northern Namibia the Hambukushu came from Angola. They arrived two centuries ago. Others poured across the border throughout the Angolan civil war in the seventies, among them AEF-related Christians speaking the Luchazi language. Don recognized Israel Kanjila and extracted his story.

Israel taught school in Angola, north of the Kavango. Then he became secretary for the church hospital and leprosarium, running it himself for a long time. The MPLA (Popular Movement for the Liberation of Angola) first robbed and then destroyed the hospital. They set fire to homes and Israel watched seven of his neighbours burn to death. After capture, he managed to escape to live in the bush with his family for two years. Then he moved slowly south, losing a son to malaria, until he crossed the Kavango river and met other Angolan Christians. A refugee pastor called them into a church of two hundred.

We found Portuguese refugees too. Delayed by car trouble, Dick, our Portuguese-speaking AEF missionary, looked for a film in a small shop and met a young woman behind the counter. He talked about the Lord and found her spiritually hungry. She closed the shop and knelt on the floor to ask Christ to forgive and accept her. While we travelled on, Dick remained to share the same message with her family and friends.

By the end of ten days' road travel a picture of mixed-up religion formed in our minds. In one tribe a thin layer of Christian faith covered a tradition of immorality. In another, an elder led worship in church on Sunday and at the ancestral spirit's fire during the week. Elsewhere, Marxism and the Gospel became strange allies in the independence struggle. Individual Christians stood against the tide of compromise and occasional churches shone like beacons. Listening to a perceptive, poorly educated evangelist talking about his independent group of churches, Jack said, 'We don't want to lead these churches; they need their own leaders. We want to find out, "Can we help them?" '

Their need for trained leaders stirred Jack. As we prayed, all of us felt challenged to seek a new emphasis on Bible training, but none as much as Jack. By the end of the safari, he told us, 'I believe God wants me to offer to move up here.' Privately he confessed to me, 'Man . . . I don't know what Peggy will think!'

Peggy did not relish another move. In her mid fifties now, she needed to relearn Afrikaans, the trade language of Namibia and she knew she would find it difficult. Recalling her struggle later, she said, 'It was really quite hard as it meant leaving the family again after nine good years.' She wanted assurance of God's will, 'We prayed about it and felt convinced this was the step to take.'[288]

The two missions determined to work together and AIM suggested that the AEF administer the team. AEF then asked Jack to become the leader. When numbers built up, the missionaries elected a leader for themselves and again the choice fell on Jack. He welded them into a fellowship which seldom thought about their own organizations; some did not know to which mission a colleague belonged.

God gathered a fine group – a Portuguese Angolan with American citizenship, a Dutch evangelist with experience among Kenya's Turkana, a Korean pastor, a Zambian Bible teacher, theologians, teachers, a South African doctor, student workers, nurses – until, after ten years, Jack led a team of thirty. They emphasized churches: planting new congregations where none had existed and nurturing leaders of the established groups.

Jack and his team broke free from the old parental pattern. Instead of slowly nursing newly-born churches through childhood and adolescence until, after many years, they became mature, they expected God to establish indigenous churches from the start. In the north, they recognized that God had already launched a church among the refugees. Their role was to provide an advisor (in answer to a request from the church) and a Bible school. The school drew evangelists from war-stricken Angolan churches across the border and young Namibian congregations. With this help, both groups survived in difficult times and multiplied.

Jack attended one of the first baptismal services of the Mbukushu church. Before the presiding elder entered the Kavango, he sent a young man to chase the crocodiles away. The elder invited testimonies and then preached a long sermon before arriving at the time to immerse the new Christians. Jack reckoned the crocs could easily have returned for their meal and was glad that he had no responsibilities in the river.

Jack and Peggy ministered within the Herero independent churches, emphasizing their respected New Testament (translated by German missionaries). But converts appeared more among the young people, whom missionaries contacted outside the churches. When a number moved to Windhoek for higher education and for work, they wanted to meet together. A missionary couple opened their home and offered them encouragement.

When the couple left in October 1982, five young teachers organized their first church service and Sunday school. Four years later Joan and I joined 100 people, mostly in their late teens and twenties, as they worshipped in the lounge of one of their leaders. A tall Herero led, assisted by two men who studied theology full time with the missionary pastor. John, the missionary, told us that he acted more as counsellor than pastor and hoped soon to withdraw. He achieved his goal in 1989 when one of the two students graduated and became pastor.

These two students formed the nucleus of a Bible college. Jack and John showed us building plans for the Evangelical Bible Church complex which included rooms for the new leadership development programme. The Windhoek Evangelical Bible College, catering for tertiary level (post matric) students never grew as much as the team hoped. Soon after its launch, another denomination opened a school to develop leaders at the two lower educational strata. Jack queried, why have two Bible seminaries in one small city? After years of difficult discussion, the two merged to establish the Namibia Evangelical Theological Seminary.

Healthy faith confronts holy fire

In other areas the seeds of the gospel did not immediately grow
into churches. Missionaries needed all God's gifts of endurance.
Most of the Herero resisted.

The Herero Chief hesitated before granting permission for
Jack to build a missionary residence in his town. Finally he gave
his approval on condition that 'Mr Pienaar's church does not
interfere with Herero traditions or culture, directly or indirectly,
and that Mr Pienaar and his church do not influence the people
(youth) or dissuade them from obeying or honouring the ancestral
spirits.' The missionaries responded to this impossible demand
by ensuring that young believers drew their own conclusions from
the Word of God.

As young Herero believers multiplied friction developed.
Tribal elders told them, 'We've had the New Testament in our
language for a hundred years and you should honour it. But
remember, the ancestors have watched over us for centuries and
you must revere them.'

Herero leaders accused Jack of teaching children to disobey their
parents. They questioned him on repentance and conversion and
Jack found he could build upon their innate but unfocused respect
for God's Word. After explaining its message on these issues, he
turned the question back to them, 'If the Bible says this, what do
you want me to do?' He knew the problem centred on the
believers' refusal to venerate the spirits at the holy fire. He wrote,
'I had to explain what you do when God's Word says something
and your own traditions say something else. As an Afrikaner, with
a background of apartheid, I had to question that myself. If the
tradition clashes with God's Word then I need to obey God.'

Jack failed to satisfy the old men and they fought back. Every
important decision must come to the ancestors for their approval,
especially the matter of marriage. The bride must meet the
ancestors at the holy fire 'with her body smeared with fat of a
special sheep so that no evil will befall her.'

Missionaries refused to get involved, leaving the discussion
to a group of maturer Herero Christians. One of their number
put it this way, 'We believe that the Scriptures teach the
following:

1 The Kingship of Christ.
2 Believers should never contact the dead or seek help from them.
3 Blessing and joy are received from God alone.'[289]

They quoted the Scriptures from which they drew their conclusions, insisting that the church teach these truths and discipline believers who depart from them.

The pioneering Pienaars retired to Cape Town in January 1991. Thirty-six missionaries, two Bible schools, and many churches remained and God's kingdom continued to spread.

Donald and Sueli Potocki

Driving to work, a young pilot idly read a roadside text on a large billboard. On the return journey he glanced at it again and noticed a different verse on the reverse side. As the message changed frequently, he got into the habit of watching for it. Don Potocki found that 'after a year the words bothered me and I wanted to read the Bible.' He felt self-conscious as he walked around a big store searching for the book, but, when he found it, he read it from cover to cover, taking twelve months to complete the marathon. Well before reaching the end, he found himself speaking to the Lord Jesus as a personal friend.

The book satisfied and stimulated him so much that he gave up flying and entered Grand Rapids School of Bible and Music in Michigan, where another surprise awaited him – a missionary speaker from AIM who announced, 'We need pilots in our mission.'

Preacher pilot

Wilson Airport on the western edge of Nairobi housed AIM–AIR in a commodious building (given largely by the Christoffel Blindenmission in Germany because of AIM's airborne assistance to sufferers from eye disease). For over a year and a half Don flew out of Nairobi to facilitate the pastoral, health care and evangelistic efforts of the churches' servants, secure and satisfied in his missionary calling.

Typical of his concept of mission, he wrote from Kagando hospital in Uganda in July 1985, after bringing an eye doctor for a round of clinics and operating sessions. A coup closed the airports and people asked him what he planned to do while waiting. 'I told them I would write letters and sermons. "Do you preach?" they said. "Yes I do," I replied. They had me preach in their local church . . . fourteen sermons in twenty days . . . plus house to house evangelism and teaching in the hospital wards.'[290]

Back in Nairobi he was working on his plane in the hangar,

when the AIM–AIR manager leant over the balcony and called, 'Hey Don, how would you like to go to Mozambique?' Don replied, 'Where's Mozambique?' The manager could not tell him much more, except that I had enquired about Don's availability. He told Don, 'You'd better go and talk to Dick.' The story I recounted unsettled him.

Ten years before, my attempts to enter Mozambique thwarted (p. 267), I reported the information I had gleaned to mission supporters, stimulating much prayer. A friend in Harare, Zimbabwe, put me in touch with a Mozambiquan evangelist who invited us to visit and, surprisingly, obtained visas. In August 1983, my friend drove me to Beira through a dozen army check points, past a bridge damaged by rebels and another completely destroyed. At one point, where the road and railway converged, we saw two railway carriages recently blown up with great loss of life.

As we approached the city a banner across the entrance to a big cement factory proudly called, 'Workers of the world unite'. But no one worked in this factory. A huge mill sat idle; cranes along the wharves of a once busy port stood stark and still; Beira railway station silently collected rubbish and rodents. The Indian Ocean pounded miles of empty beach, once thronged with holiday-makers. Most restaurants and shops kept their doors closed for they had nothing to sell.

Every night our evangelist host took us to a different church and we discovered remarkable life in the midst of economic collapse and Marxist oppression. Throughout seven years of war against the Portuguese colonial regime and eight more of communism the Gospel quietly spread through Mozambiquan evangelists. The resulting new churches shone with devotion and zeal but stumbled for lack of teaching. Our evangelist host told me, 'God gave me the gifts of an evangelist, not of a teacher. He has established many churches through my preaching and now I have to serve these people and I am not able. Why don't you send us teachers and set me free for the people who have never heard the Gospel?'

When Joan and I returned the next year for two weeks of teaching in the churches, we heard the same call for teachers as well as the cry, 'Please tell people to pray for poor Mozambique.'

'AIM has three goals for Mozambique,' I told Don; 'to preach in the churches, to develop pastors, to train Mozambiquan missionaries for the unreached.' Several mission leaders respected

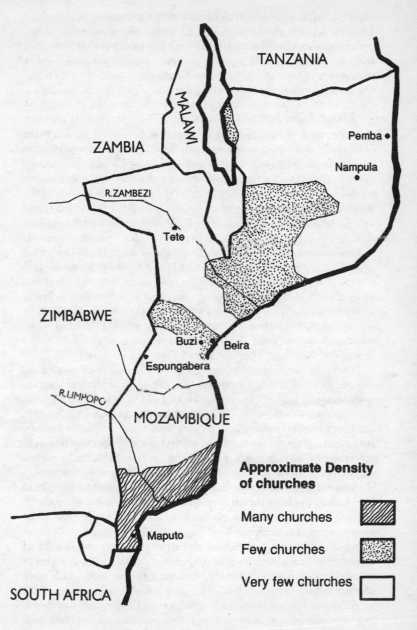

Mozambique: density of churches 1983

Don's preaching gifts. Would he consider leaving flying, for a while at least, so that he could concentrate on this ministry?

Although he loved flying, Don was not wedded to it. Leaving Kenyan friends posed a more difficult challenge, particularly Douglas and Jane in whose home he taught a weekly Bible class. They wept together, prayed and reluctantly decided he should go.

'We've got the power'

Emotion choked Don at Nairobi airport as he waited for our flight to Harare. I arrived late with little luggage and we checked in together so that he could share my baggage allowance. We prayed briefly with Don's friends and dashed through immigration to be the last two for security check in the departure lounge. Don suddenly told me that he had Kenyan cash in his pocket and ran back to offload it on his friends but they had left. The metal detector squealed over keys in his trouser pocket and the policeman asked, 'What's this?' 'It's money,' cried Don in his guilt and pulled two thousand shillings out. We tried to explain that he had come prepared to pay for excess baggage. Naively Don said, 'Let's pray.' 'What,' answered a uniformed woman, 'You break the law and want to pray!' Don looked dazed; in his mind he could sense prison doors closing behind him. Suddenly the woman said, 'Go!' Don seemed not to hear. I closed his briefcase, grabbed his hand and we ran.

It was his Rubicon. As he relaxed in his aircraft seat, Don remembered that 'they that wait upon the Lord shall mount up with wings as eagles' (Isaiah 40:31 AV). He said later, 'The Lord put that verse in my soul; I can't forget it. Leaving Nairobi Airport after calling to the Lord in a very tense situation I finally mounted up on wings.' His gratitude for deliverance wrought an iron-like determination to press on into Mozambique no matter how hard the way.

A harsh test of that determination awaited him in Harare. In the midst of dilemmas about visas and vehicles, he phoned his mother in America to say farewell. She stunned him with news that liver cancer was threatening his father's life. He told me, 'Dad is sinking towards a lost eternity. I wonder if I should go to him.' He wrestled with God's call, so powerfully confirmed by the experience in Nairobi Airport, and his duty to his dad. World Vision helped get his visa and asked him to drive a VW Golf of theirs into Mozambique and he decided to drive to Beira, still tormented by doubts. On 7 December 1985, AIM's first missionary entered Mozambique in a little yellow Volkswagen, wondering if he should be heading westwards rather than to the east.

The fog of uncertainty lifted as soon as he tasted the welcome of Mozambiquan Christians. Whenever he walked into a church, they asked him to preach, prepared or not. He called sinners to repent and many responded; he fed believers and they said, 'We want more please.'

His mother called to say his father had died. He shared the shock with his new brothers and sisters. 'You must go to your family,' they insisted and, in their poverty, collected money for an air ticket out of Harare. Unconvinced he left for the border, asking God to guide him. At the border, Mozambiquan immigration officials refused to let him cross without an exit visa. He returned to Beira with the words singing in his head, 'What he opens, no-one can shut; what he shuts, no-one can open.' (Revelation 3:7) Living conditions did not improve much at first. Money transferred to his Beira account from New York in January 1986 had not arrived by July. Appropriately he saw a sign on the bank manager's door, 'Director of the Invisible'. He shared an apartment in a high-rise block 'where the cockroach is king of the beasts'.[291]

A church 150 yards from his home expected the congregation to attend meetings every day, twice on Tuesday, Friday and Sunday. They wanted Don to preach at every one. His team leader said, 'That's not good enough. Limit preaching to Sunday so that you can spend your week in learning Portuguese.' But his Portuguese did not improve and the leader enquired about his study habits. He replied (with a hint of criticism in his tone), 'How can I not preach God's word when they ask me?' The answer came when he left for his first leave at home and the leader said, 'Yes Don, we want you back; but first you need to spend a year in Portugal.'

After a year of full-time language study, he still felt far from fluent. Back in Beira again, he found conditions worse than before. Rebels often destroyed the electricity supply into the city and water flowed uncertainly through the pipes. Anyone venturing outside city boundaries must be sure his vehicle would not break down for he never knew when bullets would whistle around it or a mine explode beneath. Incidents were rare but frightening.

A pastor asked Don to preach in his church at Dondo, twenty miles from the city. Don told him that he could not go without a car and, in those days cars in Beira were as scarce as gold.

On a Sunday he preached in his own church on a favourite text, 'All power is given unto me in heaven and in earth. Go therefore and teach all nations . . .' (Matthew 28:18, 19) He waxed eloquent, 'ALL power. Don't worry about the power; we've got the power. GO and preach the Gospel.' Afterwards the Dondo pastor approached him and said, 'I've got a car for next week – George's.' Don knew that baling wire and scotch tape scarcely kept George's car together. He would not go round the block in it. He politely declined, 'I don't know that it would be good to go in *that* car.' 'Don't you remember what you just preached?' asked the pastor, 'We've got the power, we've got the power; all we need to do is go.' Don felt as small as Tom Thumb.

George's car made it to Dondo and back. After dropping passengers at the Beira church, an explosion echoed off the surrounding buildings. George stuck his head out of the window and called, 'Hey brother Donald, we just blew a tyre.'[292]

A live-in linguist

Joan and I visited Don after his fortieth birthday. Joan always felt a motherly responsibility for the mission's bachelors. 'You know Don,' she gently chided, 'You need someone to look after you.' Don grinned and shrugged his shoulders. He mumbled something about his age and added, 'There's not much chance of finding a wife here.' Joan replied, 'I'm asking the Lord to send one.'

The suffering all around him pushed such thoughts to the back of Don's mind. The pastor who headed his group of churches invited speakers from Zimbabwe for a conference at Chimoyo, close to the border. Police expelled the guests and arrested all the leaders. The prison governor told the pastor 'You believe in God. Let God provide your food.' God did. Christian friends nearby heard of his plight and helped. He planted all the seeds he saved and eventually supplied other prisoners as well as his own family. When fighting engulfed the prison the pastor jumped into a pit latrine. Afterwards, friends took a long time to locate the source of his subterranean cries.

In 1989 the Marxist regime softened. Don's pastor friend invited him to another conference in the Chimoyo church with the same Zimbabwean speakers. The pastor pointed to some government officials and said, 'Those are the men who arrested us.' This time they came to praise not to persecute.

Preparing preachers meant more to the team than simply

preaching. They consulted twenty-four pastors representing fourteen church organizations before establishing the Sofala Bible Institute in a suburb of Beira. The churches repeated the request for pastors' training which must be in-service as the pastors could not leave their congregations. Soon forty students met four times a week for two hours in the evening. They crowded into two containers for their classes but slowly, as money came in, they bought land, laid foundations and gathered materials. They dreamt of a higher educational level of intake, leading to higher standards in graduates.

In December 1992 leaders of government signed a peace accord with the resistance. Soon roads, closed for over a decade, opened. Missionary Aviation Fellowship expanded the opportunities for travel and the team (numbering twenty-four workers in 1993) fanned out – to Espungabera close to Zimbabwe and Buzi among the Ndau, to Muslims in the northern centres of Pemba and Nampula and to masses of people, displaced by civil war in the north-west.

Don still stuttered whenever he conversed in Portuguese although surprisingly he preached fluently. God planned language help beyond all his imaginings – a native Portuguese speaker living permanently in his own home.

The first Brazilian joined AIM's Mozambique team in 1987 and others followed including Sueli de Freitas. Fluent in Portuguese, they could start teaching as soon as they arrived and also commence work on an African language. Sueli plunged into a group of seven churches, determined to develop evangelists who could win and then teach the children. One church asked her to teach right through the Bible which she gladly attempted but, at the same time, trained a young man who could continue the classes after her departure. For Sueli expected God to move her northwards to the Lomwe people and, to this end was already studying their language.

But Don changed all that. Moving fast (or so it seemed to onlookers) he proposed to Sueli and soon married her. Wisely they went home immediately so that their families could adjust to the cross-cultural union. Don found that 'my mother, brothers and church received Sueli very well and, in Brazil, I had the same welcome.' Joan commented, 'You can never tell the power of prayer!'

Don and Sueli taught for a while in the Bible school. Their letters told us of a visit to the remote Tete Province with the Missionary Aviation Fellowship. Next they moved there to commence again the cycle of evangelism, teaching believers, and training leaders.

Richard and Barbara Dunkerton

Ntate Mosoang sat up and pulled a thick blanket around him to protect himself from the freezing night air, so different from the atmosphere of his dream. As his mind cleared of sleep, he recalled the vision of painful thirst, a strange white man who slaked his agony with cool water and the vivid conviction that God was revealing his plan to send a missionary to his remote village in the mountains of Lesotho.

While awaiting the fulfilment of the dream, he worked. First he burnt bricks and built three rooms for the expected guest. Then he called his family and friends every evening to read the Bible and pray. The word spread across the hills and valleys that anyone in serious trouble could go to Mosoang's home for prayer and help. They came, on foot and on horseback, from miles away – the sick, the sinner, the demon-oppressed and the deranged. Some, relieved by this ministry of intercession, used their own homes for the same purpose until fourteen such centres functioned. Still Mosoang waited.

One day a light aircraft swept low over the village. Had he known, this was a step towards the fulfilment of his dream. The Missionary Aviation Fellowship (MAF) surveyed the whole high mountain area (two-thirds of Lesotho) to discover the unmet medical and spiritual needs.

MAF found much untreated sickness and many people superficially christianized but still untouched by the gospel. Large sections, poorly served by roads, could be cut off completely in the harsh winters. They offered to fly government health care personnel into the high villages and asked AIM to cooperate in the evangelistic task.

Hawtrey Judd, our South African leader, and Jonathan Dawn, just sharpening his teeth on TIMO, conducted a preliminary survey for AIM, and the International Council expressed interest. In September 1984 Hawtrey drove me from Johannesburg to the capital, Maseru, where we stayed with the Bittenbenders. They had flown us in Kenya but were now working with MAF.

Don Bittenbender took us to the MAF centre at Maseru airport and showed us the hangar next to theirs, blown up the previous year by the Lesotho Liberation Army in one of the violent political struggles which characterized this little land. We boarded his Cessna and climbed above the so-called 'lowlands' (the height averages 1,500 metres) and headed east. Soon the land rose beneath us: a jumble of jagged peaks, deep gulleys and tumbling cascades. Ahead the snow-covered Drakensburg range reared its head to 3,480 metres.

We bumped to a stop on a strip perched on a ridge and climbed out. In contrast to the brightly coloured blankets worn by all the adults, the country struck me as universally brown – brown grass, brown houses, brown cattle and brown oxen pulling ploughs which turned up brown furrows. The forewoman of a 'food for work' programme claimed responsibility for building the airstrip and the local headmaster galloped up on his horse to underline the importance of this medical scheme. I asked, 'Why can I see no trees?' They replied, 'The people needed the wood to protect them from the severe winter frosts.' Someone added a sinister note, 'Spirits live in trees.'

We flew on to another strip, Tebellong, where Swiss missionaries ran a hospital with a vigorous community health project. Although the homes seemed scattered, they told us that many people lived in the vicinity. Three parishes of the Lesotho Evangelical Church (LEC), each comprising several congregations, attempted to meet their spiritual needs. But the doctor and his wife confessed that they themselves had arrived twenty years previously as missionaries with little idea of the good news of Christ. They encountered him only recently while on leave in Europe. They asked, 'If a missionary couple can be so ignorant of the gospel, how can we expect the churches to flourish?'

Back in Maseru we called on people in the denominational offices and parachurch organizations. Several confirmed the need to evangelize the inaccessible valleys but also opened up another concern. A pentecostal pastor told us; 'Our people need training; this is my greatest burden. The Lord sent you for this is the time he plans to turn Lesotho upside down.' Leaders of the big Lesotho Evangelical Church (LEC) talked about training evangelists and lay leaders out in their places of ministry. One elder told us, 'For ten years we've been praying about an extension ministry but have been unable to start,' and the seminary Principal added, 'Maybe the Lord has heard our prayers for a person to head it up.'

Veterans become novices

Dick and Barbara Dunkerton provided the immediate answer. These two teachers first arrived in Kenya in 1954 during the tense days of Mau Mau and later served in various church planting ministries in Tanzania where, 'After twelve years, we felt it was time to move on to avoid the church building up a dependency on us.' Back in a Kenya Bible school, they taught for three years until 'we were able to persuade the church leaders to appoint a Mkamba principal.'[293] They took another post – national coordinator of Theological Education by Extension (TEE) – and sought to train lay leaders for the rapidly multiplying churches across Kenya. Eight years later, AIC responded to Dick's repeated suggestions by appointing a Kenyan coordinator. Once again they could say, 'We were ready for a new assignment and were open to going to another country.'

On the day they left their assignment with AIC Kenya, the International Council, unknown to the Dunkertons, approved the mission's entrance into Lesotho, initially with a team of Bible teachers, one at least with experience of TEE in Africa. After much prayer, Dick and Barbara believed God wanted them to go.

They arrived in Lesotho in June 1986 ready to apply one of Dick's axioms, 'Before you become a teacher, you must be a learner.' At the age of fifty-eight they considered themselves new missionaries again, facing a different culture and a difficult language. In arranging their work, we approached the LEC first, bearing in mind the advice of a South African missionary, 'Humbly take what you're offered and get stuck in.'

Not all LEC missionaries regarded them as kindly as that South African. Some hesitated because the Dunkertons did not seem to have the reformed denominational background they favoured and others disliked their strong view of the importance and infallibility of the Bible. But the eleven men who constituted the ruling Executive Committee welcomed them gladly, particularly the Principal of the Seminary who would be their immediate supervisor. They agreed to Dick's request for a year to learn the language before starting on TEE.

Walking along the pathway to their classes, children greeted them respectfully, 'Good morning grandfather, good morning grandmother.' Some dropped into their home in the afternoons to correct pronunciation and on Sundays to assist Barbara in Sunday school.[294]

The LEC covered the lowlands and lapped into the mountains

with a network of 100 parishes served by seventy-one ministers. A minister might have as many as nine or ten churches and depended on evangelists to run these. Of 300 evangelists, only a third had qualified through a three year Bible school course. Dick offered to help others by taking the training to them rather than insisting that they come to study in a central institution. In fact they trained themselves by following a series of workbooks in the Sesotho language. Each day required them to cover a few pages and each month their teacher discussed their work – collecting written tests, talking over problems and setting more material for study. Dick spent much of his time in preparing the books, correcting papers and travelling to each of seven centres for the monthly classes.

Ninety-six commenced the programme, each recommended and encouraged by his or her own church. Even though Dick went out to their areas, many needed to travel one or two days to attend the monthly review and fellowship time. One month Egbert apologized for his absence during the previous session. He had set out but came to a river in spate. His determination to cross could not prevail over his reluctant horse. An evangelist spoke for most when he thanked Dick, 'I have waited many years for an opportunity to study the Bible.'[295]

Josephine told her class that members of her church asked, 'What has happened to you: your messages and ministry are so much better?' Leaders of LEC decided that six years in extension classes would qualify an evangelist as if he had spent three in residential Bible school. The first group of forty-five graduated in November 1993. Meanwhile LEC sent a minister to Daystar University in Nairobi to prepare to continue the programme when the Dunkertons retired.

Barbara carried on a ministry to the children, as well as teaching English and counselling students in the Bible school and seminary.

As Dick and Barbara read the history of the early missionaries to Lesotho, they prayed for the church to recapture the zeal and holiness of the early days. Convinced that God only renews his church through the preaching of his Word, they gave themselves to preaching and to preparing preachers. As they got to know the high mountains better, they realized the force of the MAF assertions that many of the people there – perhaps half a million – lacked any opportunity to hear the good news of the Lord Jesus. They asked AIM to recruit a team for this urgent task.

As the team grew to thirteen by early 1994, Dick, anxious to avoid duplication, placed missionaries with existing organizations – a church in Maseru, Mosoang's home, Tebellong hospital, a LEC parish, a Youth With A Mission team. Keen to prevent dependence, he urged them to train Basotho replacements.

Ntate Mosoang opened his home to the newcomers and several lived with his family while they learnt Sesotho and took their first stumbling steps in preaching. Latest to settle in his frosty climate and warm fellowship, Gary and Linda Casady transferred from Kenya. They trotted out to visit surrounding villages on their own horses and looked to MAF for more distant travel. As he watched the water of God's life satisfying many thirsty people, Mosoang thanked God for the fulfilment of his dream.

Sonya Kim

Sun Ok Kim was born in the city of Jin Ju, close to the southern end of the Korean peninsula, in June 1948. After her second birthday war shattered the nation as North Koreans, supported by hordes of Chinese, flooded through the country and captured Jin Ju on July 24th. They set up the headquarters of their ninth infantry division in the city and immediately closed all the churches. Sun Ok's father joined other men of fighting age in a grim game of hide-and-seek to keep out of the clutches of communist press-gangs.

One of these young men, standing outside the local Presbyterian church, heard a solitary aircraft. Looking up he recognized the American star on the side of a B 29 bomber. An incendiary fell onto the church steeple, setting the whole building ablaze. A few days later, a massive air raid destroyed the city centre.[296] Within six weeks General MacArthur chased the communists out of Jin Ju and finally pushed them north of the 38th parallel.

Christians quickly rebuilt their church. An aunt took Sun Ok Kim to worship there from the age of six and she became a regular member. Her father, a nominal Buddhist, objected to her faith and twice locked her up to prevent her going to church.[297] But the little disciple grew in the midst of a fellowship refined by trial from its earliest days.

Before the communists, colonialists had oppressed the people of God. In 1907, when Japan was tightening its grasp on defenceless Korea, the Lord strengthened his young churches. A pastor, teaching a group in Pyongyang, the capital, had to give way as one after another cried out to God confessing sin. People continued in prayer for hours. A wave of conviction swept across the country, leading thousands to forgiveness and peace. God was preparing his children for a tide of persecution which flowed for thirty-five years under a cruel Japanese occupation.

In Jin Ju Japanese soldiers arrogantly attached their flag, with its rising sun, to the pulpit. When Christians refused to bow their heads before it, they nailed the church doors shut. Christians met in secret, often well before dawn; many went to prison and some died rather than compromise. Under the communists, they experienced a second era of opposition, more severe than the first. They learnt to depend upon God alone, drawing on his resources by a disciplined delight in prayer.

Sun Ok remembered little of the war years but knew that her parents struggled to provide for the growing family. At the age of fifteen she regularly came home from school to find her mother away at her trading and her father busy tailoring. Responsibility for feeding and caring for five younger brothers rested largely with her.

'Elder Sister' kept a tight rein on the boys. She immediately punished any dishonesty. If they refused to accompany her to church she sent them to bed without supper. They learnt respect; one said later that he 'always thought of her as next to God'.

She completed teacher training by the age of twenty and took her first job. She worked hard for the church as well. Soon she was sent to a distant school. On Saturdays she called the children to Bible study and worship, much to the disgust of the vice-principal and some parents who complained. Suddenly she was moved again, to a school with only three classrooms and even further from her home. Although it had the feel of a punishment posting, she threw herself again into the work of the Lord and eventually planted a little church.

By January 1980, after eleven years of teaching, she felt God wanted her to move on. Uncertain of the way ahead she set aside three days for fasting and prayer. Then she applied for a three-year course at her denomination's leading seminary, Chong Shin in Seoul city.

While Sun Ok Kim studied in Seoul, she witnessed two Korean miracles, one economic and the other, spiritual. Despite the continuous threat of invasion from the north, Korea surged forwards. Education and hard work thrust the country into the modern age of technology and the economy boomed. At the same time, evangelists planted new churches at the rate of six each day and seminaries multiplied to prepare pastors.

After three years Sun Ok won her diploma with honours (the only woman in a large class to gain that distinction) and decided to stay two more years to gain a B.A. in education.

A mission to missionaries

The seminary offered an optional 'Training in Mission' class, taught by a Professor Son Young-jun. He lectured in English and she went along mainly to improve her knowledge of that language. But the subject fascinated Sun Ok. Around this time she took the name of Sonya. In the cold winter of 1983 the professor planned a month-long Missionary Training Institute (MTI) for thirty-six of his students and she offered to assist him with administration. Six months later, he organized his second MTI and told her, 'Sonya, now you are the captain.'

While Professor Son continued as Director of MTI, he left much of the control in Sonya's hands. As well as lecturing herself, she kept hearing challenges to missionary involvement and began to feel that God wanted her to become a missionary herself. After the fourth MTI Professor Son invited her to join a small party on a visit to Kenya.

A generous cash prize from the seminary provided her fare. Travelling in the great Rift Valley, mingling with churches and missionaries, she became certain of God's call to Africa but wondered where. The party returned to Korea leaving Sonya in Nairobi to assist a Korean minister in planting two churches in a shanty suburb. But she felt restless, as though God was preparing her for something else. The professor wrote from Seoul, suggesting that she return home and apply to AIM.

While she waited in Seoul for the mission's response, the seminary President asked her to be his personal assistant and Professor Son requested her help every six months for MTI. In his absence she could now run MTI herself.

By this time over a hundred pastors, students and their wives attended each course. The natural Korean drive, prayerfulness and dedication to hard work had resulted in enormous church growth. This was now breaking out into vigorous missionary commitment. But most of these students knew only the Korean culture: MTI sought to prepare them for work with missionaries from many nations, for mastering new languages and serving different peoples. Without these skills, their great vigour could founder in frustration.

Meanwhile Sonya's application met inexplicable delays. AIM wanted to accept her and to assign her back to the country she knew – Kenya. But for AIC in Kenya, assignment could only come through the Africa Inland Church and the leaders seemed reluctant. Some independent Korean missionaries had agreed to work with AIC and then did their own thing without submitting to local pastors and elders. The resulting misunderstanding made the bishop hesitate before accepting a Korean from AIM. But the delay multiplied Sonya's perplexities: Jin Ju church leaders asked, 'Why is our missionary stuck in Seoul when we sent her to Africa?' A graduate of MTI enquired, 'Is AIM prejudiced against Koreans?'

Eventually, AIM decided on a different assignment – five months in England to improve her English and then a teaching post in Lesotho.

Approaching the Lesotho Evangelical Church's main centre, Morija, for the first time, she read huge figures painted high on the cliff face above the settlement, '1833–1983'. It commemorated 150 years of missionary ministry to the Basotho people. The work of the Paris Evangelical Missionary Society had borne fruit through much of the country. Sonya found that the church remained committed to many good enterprises – social justice, education, health care and literature production. But the evangelistic fervour of the early pioneers had largely evaporated. The team leaders, Dick and Barbara Dunkerton, helped her settle in and adjust to the new surroundings.

The Lesotho Evangelical Church asked Sonya to teach in their English Medium School, originally set up for the children of missionaries, but now, in 1988, catering for Basotho children. The Headmaster told her, 'Sonya, it's good that English is not your first language. You can better appreciate the problems others experience in learning it.' She enjoyed the children and they responded to her happy temperament. Bible classes for adults and fellowship with the Dunkertons and an elderly teacher from the American Peace Corps kept her busy. She expected to spend the rest of her working life there.

A summons from Seoul suddenly changed her plans. Professor Son's training programme was becoming too big for him to handle. In addition to the two courses of a month each in summer and winter, he now led longer sessions in spring and autumn for a smaller number. Extension travel to encourage the many graduates in their scattered ministries took him away frequently and he needed efficient help. Three years after Sonya's arrival in Morija he asked AIM to send her back to MTI to assist temporarily.

With a dozen Koreans in the mission, AIM saw the importance of adequate preparation before they left their own country and recognized that Sonya possessed both the gifts and experience they needed. She stepped off the plane straight into the rush of a new course – arranging teachers, sifting through applications, fixing accommodation, advising everyone and marking exam papers. Although many respected pastors now attended MTI, they submitted to 'Elder Sister's' friendly firmness.

Sonya kept her gaze on Africa. Realizing the fundamental importance of training leaders for the churches, she determined to upgrade her theological qualifications by studying for a year at Columbia Bible College in South Carolina and then offered to serve the AIC in Tanzania.

Towards Koreans in AIM she felt a special responsibility. Most missionaries find their greatest challenge in adjusting to African culture, but Koreans in an international society experienced a more painful adjustment to westerners. They thought that colleagues regarded them as 'too Korean' and resented their lack of fluency in English. Back at home, churches urged them to join the increasing number of Korean missions and criticized them for joining AIM. Sonya told me, 'Feeling like everyone's target, they easily lose heart and slip into anger, self-will and further errors.' One told her that she felt 'like a fish on a slab waiting to be sliced up.' Yet both Sonya and her mentor, Professor Son, believed that Korean missionaries become most effective in an international fellowship.

She pleaded with AIM leaders. 'Please be patient and try to understand.' Asian courtesy prevented her saying that AIM could learn much about prayer, zeal and hard work from our Korean members – if only all could persevere in God's school.

16

Grapes instead of giants

A Kenyan Christian, asked to address a missionary prayer conference, chatted about Paul's relationship to his young disciple, Timothy. She looked out on a sea of white faces and asked, 'Where are your Timothys?'

Peter Scott planned that AIM should spread the gospel through African evangelists. Since his time, council minutes, magazine articles and conference messages repeatedly dwelt on the theme of 'working ourselves out of a job'. Increasingly the mission focused on developing Africans who would lead the work of the kingdom. But how could leaders of church and mission know when missionaries should hand over their tools and move on? If they left too soon, the church would suffer; if they stayed too long, Timothy might never appear.

The puzzle presented itself in both the old countries of service and the new. Why should we continue working in Zaire when we could see churches multiplying, maturing and producing godly leaders? How long should we plan to stay in Mozambique and Lesotho? The answer seemed to lie in prayerful appraisal of the churches in an area and especially of their ability to accomplish God's purposes without help from outside. Such delicate judgments required not only the partnership of the churches but, wherever possible, their leadership.

The Kenyan AIC leaders, prodded by Peter and Roda Mualuko, started training African missionaries. They welcomed students from other countries as well as their own. One came from Chad – Peter Scott's ultimate objective.

While moving far from Scott's projected line of advance, AIM never abandoned his original goal. On at least three occasions mission leaders seriously considered entering Chad, only to hear that other societies could evangelize its peoples. When, however, the Evangelical Missionary Alliance called a conference in London in 1983 to consider Africa's hunger belt, delegates quickly realized that double famine afflicted the people: they lacked both bread and the Bible. Challenged to survey Chad, AIM discovered that it scored higher in unreached people-groups than any other country in the part of Africa we served.

Certainly developed churches existed in Chad, but mostly in one corner of the land. Mature enough to accept their responsibility to plant churches across their own country and humble enough to acknowledge that they would never do it without outside help, they invited AIM to share the task. So ninety years after Scott's vision in Westminster Abbey, his successors stood on the shore of Lake Chad as guests of an African denomination planted by a sister mission.

William and Ruth Stough

Bill Stough's parents, Paul and Rachel, arrived in Zaire in 1929. His father supervised a network of schools and churches while his mother cared for the Rethy Academy for missionaries' children and their own three children. Sadly Rachel died after fourteen happy years of marriage and subsequently Paul Stough married a teacher at the academy, Betty Quackenbush.[298]

Father and son

The Gospel spread widely at that time. Paul knew of country, far to the west, which no missionary had visited. Even the Africans he asked knew nothing of the people down there on the grassy plains. Exploring it himself, he came across the Babendi people and returned to tell the Christians.

A young man, blind in one eye, asked if he could go to teach the Babendi. Paul warned Tomasi that they might beat him, starve him, perhaps kill him. 'But Bwana', he replied, 'The Lord Jesus suffered for me; certainly I can suffer a little for him.'

The Bendi Chief arrested Tomasi, put a rope around his neck and commanded soldiers to force him to run to the government centre. Wherever they rested, villagers enquired why he was detained. He replied, 'For preaching the gospel of Jesus who died for your sins' and went on to tell them the way of salvation. Imprisoned at the government post, he passed on the same message to his guards. Next morning the judge ordered him to be laid on the ground and lashed with a hippo-hide whip. He thanked God for the soldier assigned to flay him, 'My preaching the previous night made him friendly and he did not hit me as hard as he should.'[299] Released, he continued to preach and God established churches among the Babendi.

Persecution matched church growth across north-east Zaire. Bill and his wife, Ruth, arrived in Aba as missionaries just two years before the storms of the sixties broke upon the church. Concerned to help people make a living as well as to find the secret of living in Christ, Bill taught boys woodwork in a vocational school at Aba. But after six years, the Simba rebellion forced them out. They worked for eighteen months in a Kenyan secondary school and then returned to find a purer and wiser church emerging from the ruins of Zaire.

The total evacuation of the AIM encouraged the remaining Zairois church leaders to take charge of the whole programme of the mission and church and bind it into one. When the missionaries went back, they determined to affirm the new spirit of African leadership. For Bill, this meant a further eight years of training boys before handing the Aba trade school over to Zairois teachers. He and Ruth then felt free to minister more widely in the churches. Working under the District Church Council, Bill and four other pastors developed an extension programme. Using carefully prepared teaching books, they imparted a vision to pastors and elders for helping young disciples grow in their faith. As they grew, they learnt how to share Christ with others and then help new believers in their first steps of faith.

Despite the training emphasis by the Stoughs and many others, evangelism outstripped development. In the churches, as persecution abated, zeal diminished. Numbers of members multiplied but lives limped along at a low level of holiness.

By 1978 eleven ordained pastors cared for sixty-four churches in the Aba Section, helped by just four evangelists. The Section President, Rev Kanda Olego, complained to a visitor that the Christians failed to give enough to support their pastors and evangelists. So the leaders spent time in their gardens rather than in teaching God's word. Christians then questioned, 'If they don't teach us, why should we support them?' Olego went on to show how this lack of teaching ruined families. He said, 'Over the last year we celebrated only one wedding in all of our sixty-four churches. Fathers – many of them church elders – demand such a high bride price for their daughters that the young people cannot afford to marry. They simply live together.'[300]

Kanda Olego worked closely with Bill and welcomed the new emphasis on extension training. Although hundreds benefited, they both knew that they were tackling only the edge of a vast need.

Bill and Ruth watched with alarm as tribal divisions caused a rift in the denomination. One group felt neglected in elections; they also disagreed about leadership patterns. Years of patient negotiation swallowed time which should have been used in teaching.

Throughout the eighties poverty increased. In 1974 the local currency, a 'zaire', was worth half an American dollar. By May of 1993, one dollar exchanged for two and a half million zaires and five months later the figure had reached twenty-five million. Such economic collapse reverberated throughout the whole of CECA. Giving, however generous, failed to support the church leaders and their offices; congregations could not pay Bible school fees for their students; the sick had no money for medicines; teachers went many months without salaries.

Most peasant Christians relied on their gardens and survived. But if a child became sick, parents with no cash for medicine faced the stark choice: depend on prayer alone or consult the witch doctor. In such a crisis the temptation to revert to ancient superstition became almost overwhelming.

In 1992 Bill approached the end of his period as 'Branch Executive Officer', the leader of the AIM members in Zaire. He could look at great results from the mission's eighty years of ministry – 2,000 congregations, 400 pastors, 2,000 evangelists, and some great Christian leaders able to take their places alongside any in the world.[301] Despite this great work of God, Bill felt uneasy. His own son increased his unease.

Research and renewed commitment

The Stoughs' eldest, also Bill, commenced missionary service in Zaire in 1991. During his second year, he joined another missionary, Steve Wolcott, in an extensive survey of the northern part of CECA's work. Influenced by the mission's experiment with TIMO, they set out on a 3,000 mile safari to identify the needs of the people and think how the church should tackle them. In particular, they wondered about a ministry by a team of five, including themselves.

Bill and Steve found themselves in a vast decaying land of collapsed buildings. They reported that 'skeletons of stripped mill buildings, warehouses, and residences of the once booming cotton company dot the Zande area.' Likewise, 'the church in many places is stagnant and dying . . . witchcraft and traditional standards of morality hold sway.' As in Rev Kanda Olego's area fourteen years before, pastors and evangelists supported themselves from their gardens and could give little time to teaching and sermon preparation.

The leaders expressed their own desolation saying, 'We are at the end of the world and nobody cares.' The mission had certainly succeeded in establishing a church and moving on, but 'this "phase out" was forced and not planned and has left an immature church.' The needs for Bible training, youth work, health care, education, literature, literacy, economic and agricultural development seemed almost overwhelming. In their view, workers must 'encourage the existing initiative of the church in such a way that it will stand and continue to grow after the missionaries leave.'[302]

In another section, called Faradje, they found the church situation similar but with the additional problem that many locations lacked any Protestant church at all. Bordering Faradje, large sections of four other tribes remained unreached. The denominational leaders decided that a team of long-term missionaries should settle in the Faradje Section. Later, as they gained experience, they could separate to provide 'seed members' of new teams for the Zande and other areas.

In April 1993, Bill senior called sixty-three missionaries to meet in Rethy to seek God's plan for the future and invited Alan Arensen, the mission's Director for Outreach, to lead a discussion spread over a week. The elected members of the Branch Committee had prepared the ground by drafting mission objectives, which they circulated to all the members before the forum for study. By the start of the meetings, they listed four: to plant new churches, especially among unreached peoples; to assist churches to develop a spiritual vitality which would enable them to reproduce themselves; to enhance the ministries

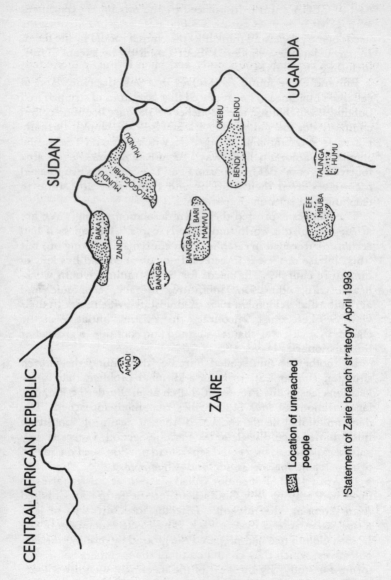

Unreached peoples in Zaire 1993

of church leaders; and encourage the church in her ministry to all the needs of people – spiritual, mental, social, physical, moral, etc.

They gave a day to the study of each objective. Arensen first invited everyone to write two subsidiary goals for an objective. Through group study and open forum, punctuated by much prayer, they refined these to four or five goals for each objective.

With this method, each member of the forum felt they owned the statement. They planned to survey the whole of the vast area of Zaire in which their Church operated, searching for unreached people, deciding ways of evangelizing them, recruiting new workers, fostering prayer, spreading information to other segments of the mission. They thought about a more effective use of music in the worship of the church, and the demands of a rapidly increasing number of young people, slow to respond to traditional approaches. With church leaders helping them, they decided to offer seminars on such matters as financial management, spiritual warfare, family life, leadership characteristics and Christian life-style. They pondered the community development programme, education, technical needs of church and mission, and health care – all in the overarching concern to glorify Christ and advance his kingdom.[303]

The President of CECA, who joined them, commented, 'The missionaries are now thinking in the way of the early missionaries – to get the gospel out.' Perhaps he took the view that missionaries, in the complexities of life and ministry had lost some of the fire of pioneer commitment. Certainly they left the forum inspired with renewed vision to proclaim a full Gospel and to prepare faithful Timothys.

Jonathan and Dorothy Hildebrandt

Jonathan could not hide his surprise when an African student told him, 'We think you are the man God sent us,' for he had already written to ask for a transfer from Mangu High School. Embarrassed, he asked the boy, 'What do you mean by that?'

'Last September we started meeting secretly for Bible study in our dorm,' the lad explained. 'The Father Headmaster accused us of organizing an illegal club because school rules insist that any group must have a staff member to vouch for it. He disbanded our little Christian Union and expelled our leader. In November we began asking God to send us a Christian teacher to sponsor us; so you must be the one.'

Jonathan thought a while. Coming to Kenya as one of 100 graduates sent from Columbia University in New York City, he had been surprised when the Kenyan education authorities sent him to a strongly Roman Catholic school. He had told the American Brothers in charge about his own beliefs and they also had questioned if he would fit. So he had decided to move. But now these boys asked him to fulfil the purpose for which he believed God had sent him to Kenya – to foster the faith of high school students.

'I tell you what,' he said; 'You get the boys together to pray while I talk to the headmaster. I will offer to withdraw my letter if he will allow you to meet for Bible study.'[304]

The bargain did not please the headmaster for he had to choose between allowing the Protestants to meet and losing a teacher he needed. In the end he agreed and Jonathan spent two years developing a fellowship in which several teenagers found Christ and many got to know him better.

Facilitating the faithful

By the time Jonathan completed his contract with the government, he knew God wished to use his teaching talent in equipping African Christians to serve their Lord. He returned to the States to work for a Master's degree in African history from Northwestern University in Illinois, followed by a year of biblical studies in Trinity, Deerfield. On 3 January 1969, he arrived in Nairobi at 10 p.m. as a new member of AIM. Next morning, still reeling from jet lag, he travelled twenty miles north to Kagwe high school. His predecessor thrust handing-over papers in front of him saying, 'You are the new headmaster. Sign here!'

After eighteen months Jonathan, up to his eyes in lessons, could rejoice that several lads returned from a Bible camp in April 'with a real desire to communicate the gospel to their classmates'. Partly as a result, 'twenty persons received Christ as their personal Saviour this past term.'[305] One of these boys went on to study at Scott Theological College and in USA before returning to teach at Moffat Bible College at Kijabe. Years later, he met another witnessing faithfully as a laboratory technician.

He wrote in his letters home to ask prayer that a Christian

Kenyan take his place, 'This has been my goal from the start at the high school. So over the last three years I have been erecting buildings, organizing the office, building a professional staff and giving a Christian direction to the school.'[306] He decided to move on. Hearing an appeal from the AIC for Bible school instructors, he accepted a post at Ukamba Bible Institute, Machakos. While here he married Dorothy Downing (daughter of Ken and granddaughter of Lee).

Teaching African church history, Jonathan could find no suitable text book. So he produced his own material, managing always to have a new chapter ready for each lecture. After completing the course, he mimeographed the material and offered it to other Bible schools. Because of their enthusiastic acceptance, he revised it into thirty-three chapters and sent the book to African Christian Press in Ghana for publication. He showed that 'Christianity is not a recent arrival in Africa, nor some sort of imported religion from Europe. Rather, it is a dynamic worldwide faith that has been part of Africa for nineteen long centuries.'[307] The book met a need much wider than Jonathan had anticipated and became required reading for many theological schools across the continent.

The AIC wanted a new Bible school at the coast. Jonathan initially reacted to the idea in the same way as many, 'We don't need another because those we have are not yet filled.' When Frank Frew, the mission's leader in Kenya, asked him to move to Mombasa to launch the school, he forced Jonathan to face the question of its importance. He came to see it 'as unique in two ways. Firstly, I felt that the future of the church in Africa was going to be urban and here was a city Bible school. Then too I was struck by its Islamic setting and I thought that our pastors needed to learn sensitivity in their approach to Muslims.'[308]

Any doubts about God's planning evaporated as he heard Frank's story about the site. By the early seventies, all suitable properties in Mombasa carried a price far above mission or church resources. Looking at a map in the Land Office, Frank asked the cost of one vacant lot and received a very low quote. He enquired, 'Why is it so cheap?' and his heart sank when he heard it was a swamp. Talking to local people at the site, he found that a rim of higher ground always escaped flooding and he decided that, because of the shortage of money, he would advise the church to take it. Soon after, the Municipal Council, alerted to the health hazard, drained the swamp and the property's value shot up. The Council asked the church to return it but Frank refused to part with the title deeds. Then, after the Bible school's start, the government erected a new bridge to connect Mombasa Island with the mainland, placing its northern end right at the entrance to Pwani Bible Institute.

With financial help from America (through the Christian Nationals Evangelism Commission), the AIC sent ten Kamba missionaries to the largely unreached Giriama tribe. As people responded to their preaching, Jonathan realized that the Giriama churches could become strong only if pastored by Giriama. So he welcomed several Giriama men into his first class in January 1975. After four years of training they left to minister to their own people. As AIM had done in the early sixties, the older Wakamba missionaries questioned the maturity of these Giriama graduates and wondered, 'could they trust these converts with leadership?' Like AIC leaders of a previous decade, the Giriama asked, 'Why can't the original Wakamba missionaries trust local men to lead?'

Jonathan always insisted that training be practical. He rejoiced, just nine months after Pwani opened its doors, that students had started their second church.[309] On Tuesday afternoons he took them out to evangelize. Usually they stood at the end of the bridge to greet pedestrians pouring home from work. If a person responded, they chatted about the Lord. Jonathan soon noticed that his students avoided anyone wearing a white, pillbox hat. 'Why do you not talk to Muslims?' he asked. 'What's the use?' they replied: 'They are hard and won't listen.' In order to convince them that Christ loves Muslims and can draw them into his kingdom, Jonathan encouraged Christians with an Islamic background (like Abdul from the Comores) to join the school.

At Pwani he laid the foundations for others, although he regretted not staying long enough to install an African principal. Frank Frew again asked him to move – this time into Frank's own office in Nairobi – in order to care for the 300 AIM folk serving in Kenya.

Despite the demands of two lively sons, Dorothy managed to help with secretarial work. Since missionaries now came directly under the supervision of AIC, they related to the bishop, Wellington Mulwa. He welcomed the assistance of overseas personnel as the 2,200 churches of his denomination now catered for a million people (out of the total population of Kenya numbering 14 million).

Sometimes they wondered about the importance of mission administration but after four years they wrote, 'We have found our time in Nairobi rewarding just by knowing that we have helped scores of people to get to their places of ministry and assisted them to do a more effective work in the place where God wants them.'[310]

Before they left for further study in USA, the new bishop (Ezekiel Birech) asked them to prepare for another venture – perhaps one of the most important ever undertaken by the AIC.

Preparing African missionaries

Bishop Ezekiel wondered why his Kenyan missionaries ran into so many problems. He questioned, could AIC prepare missionaries better for the stresses of their new ministries?

A friend of his called Edward Limo owned a farm near the growing town of Eldoret in Kenya's high western plateau. In gratitude to God for prospering him and his family, he gave thirty valuable acres to the church. Ezekiel asked that they use the land for a missionary college.

Jonathan inherited a project possessing two vital resources – land and enthusiasm – but little else. Daunting deficiencies stared him in the face; he needed a fence, a site plan, an architect, electricity, water, curriculum, funds, and the goodwill of AIC nationwide. The vision had started in Kenyan hearts and he determined to build on this asset from the start. He shared his sense of an awesome challenge with a committee appointed by the church. Limo and Birech told them that the answer lay in God's hands; 'This college will become a reality only by prayer.' They decided to begin prayer meetings on the site and called Christians across Kenya to join them on 5 February 1984.

Jonathan spoke with great feeling from the text, 'Call to me, and I will answer you, and I will show you great and mighty things, which you do not know' (Jeremiah 33:3). Afterwards he counted some of the great things God did that day: 1,500 Christians met on the site to worship for four hours; they prayed for the unreached tribes and nations; leaders from all the AIC regions publicly accepted Edward's gift of the land for a missionary college; the church officially approved an architect's site plan, and the people gave $6,700.

But they needed much more. AIM and British TEAR Fund (The Evangelical Alliance Relief) added to locally-given money. Jonathan built the first house and classroom. An overseas donor offered two-thirds of the remaining $65,000 needed for phase

Missionary Training College, Eldoret, CM

one as long as the AIC could provide a third themselves. But a severe drought curtailed Kenyan harvests and the Christians had little to give. As the deadline approached, AIC still lacked over $5,000. Ezekiel asked Jonathan to request the American donor to allow a two-week extension of the time. He told Jonathan, 'I have a friend who once said he wished to give toward the college.' Jonathan asked, 'But can he provide $5,000?' 'I don't know but I think so,' Bishop Ezekiel replied; 'So let's just be patient.'

Jonathan felt far from patient as he saw the distant donor's offer slipping away. The bishop phoned Jonathan, 'I have a cheque for you.' Jonathan gasped when he saw the amount — $10,000. He was even more amazed to read the signature — 'Daniel T. Arap Moi' — Kenya's President.

Before banking the money, he visited the local manager of the Kenya Power company, who had delayed in bringing his lines to the site. Jonathan told him, 'We have a benefactor who'd be very happy to know that you kept to your agreement to install our electricity. Maybe you'd like to see his cheque.' Within weeks the cables reached the college.

Jonathan only considered applicants if they had completed a standard Bible school course and two years of pastoral experience. Students spent several weeks living among unreached people in order to root study into practical mission. With that introduction, a year poring over anthropology, cross-cultural communication and the biblical foundations of mission made sense. They could also understand the need to spend time in learning to repair a motor cycle, to build and to cook strange foods.

During the first seven years, the college drew over 100 students from Chad, Ethiopia, Kenya, Madagascar, Sudan, Tanzania, Uganda and Zaire. Most graduated into strategic outreach ministries. Alfred and Ruth Chepkwony were typical of many. After completing the course, AIC sent them to the Sabaot people in western Kenya. Along with two AIM couples, they planted four new congregations, trained local leaders and established a nursery school. When tribal unrest made the area unsafe for foreigners, they judged that the time had arrived for local Christians to support their own churches and they headed north to Kalokol among the Turkana.

In April 1993 Bishop Ezekiel invited Jonathan to address several hundred AIC leaders. He reminded them that, from 1971, when AIC accepted responsibility for the work in Kenya, the church grew from approximately half a million adherents to two million. AIM membership worldwide also increased during that period from 789 missionaries in five countries to 1,212 in fifteen. But, since 1984, the number of AIM missionaries in Kenya fell. The figures demonstrated 'our confidence in AIC to bear the major responsibility for continuing ministry in Kenya'. While AIM was willing to respond to their requests for personnel, 'we need to be able to push ahead in other areas too'.[311]

Even while he spoke, Jonathan thought of a team in far-off Chad. An AIM group, in partnership with a Chadian couple he had trained in Eldoret, was planning to forge the final link in Scott's vision.

Ben and Winsome Webster

Ben and Winsome Webster emigrated to New Zealand with their young family in 1959. Ben's agricultural expertise and Presbyterian conscience led them to assignments with the Food and Agricultural Organisation of the United Nations in Cyprus, Turkey and Sudan. Following postings in Cambodia and India, World Vision contacted them in their New Zealand home to ask if they would consider Ethiopia. Ben preceded Winsome to Addis

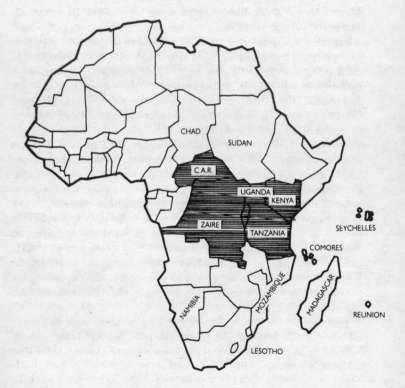

AIM in Africa 1993

Ababa. By the time she was ready to follow, he was in Nairobi to meet her with the news, 'The World Vision director doesn't want me. He says I'm not a Christian.'

Winsome was less surprised than Ben because she had recently met the Lord Jesus in person and understood what the director was talking about. Back at home she had encouraged their son to attend the Capernwray Bible School. 'We've time on our hands,' she exclaimed to Ben, 'Let's go ourselves.' In two breathtaking weeks in Lancashire, Ben also entered a saving relationship with Christ.

Everything changed. A voracious appetite for God's word sent them onto a longer Capernwray course. A new urge to serve the Lord pushed them into AIM. They established an irrigated agricultural scheme for the Turkana in North Kenya. From the start they consulted the local Turkana about the details. Wherever possible they left decisions to them. Tribal leaders criticised them for not employing earth moving equipment and diesel pumps but they were determined to keep the technology simple enough for the people to maintain without depending on outside resources. Ten years after their departure, the gardens were still producing.

They moved north into Sudan, answering a request from ACROSS (the African Committee for the Rehabilitation of South Sudan) that they head up a settlement programme for 23,000 refugees, who had fled from drought and war in Chad. After a year the Islamic Government requested ACROSS to withdraw, but not before Ben and his team had the scheme running well.

They were out of a job when AIM was listening to the challenge of unreached tribes in Chad and looking for someone to lead a new thrust. They possessed the qualifications, two questions troubled us in the mission's International Office. Was it fair to ask a couple now in their early sixties to undertake such a rugged pioneer ministry? And was it wise? Chad had experienced twenty-five years of turmoil since independence and, at that very time, war was escalating. Ben and Winsome quietly responded, 'We believe God wants us in Chad. We are not getting any younger. Please may we go.'

Hand in hand

For two months, early in 1987, they crisscrossed a five-hundred-mile strip centred on the River Chari. Many friends cried daily to God for their protection. No army met them. No bandits shot at them. No mine exploded beneath their vehicle. In fact a peace, unknown for years, settled across Chad. Everywhere friendly villagers welcomed them. Despite great poverty, pastors, church elders and chiefs entertained them with simple generosity.

Settling in their low camp beds in a village, they were disturbed by the throb of a big drum. A few weeks later a chief, fifty miles away, told them that the drummer had pounded out a message, which was picked up by others and passed on, to inform a group of rebels that visitors had arrived by car, but they appeared harmless. Even so, armed men came in the night to check their vehicle while they slept inside.

Sixty tribal groups had settled along the river, some long ago and others recently. About half of these came from the well churched areas of south-western Chad, bringing their faith with them. But they had little impact on the recently Islamized tribes native to the river area. Other societies – like the Worldwide Evangelization Crusade, Action Partners, The Evangelical Alliance Mission – encouraged AIM to work alongside them. Most of the missions had formed a cooperative fellowship linked with the Eglise Evangelique au Tchad (EET).

The President of the EET, Rev Thomas Kayé, once a missionary himself to the tribes around Lake Chad, told the Websters, 'We used to have missionaries in the north but war destroyed our plans. The church is not asleep. We are now turning eastwards. We are praying that God will send five new Chadian missionaries out each year.' Poor government policies, drought and fighting impoverished the church in material terms but suffering enriched her immeasurably. Fine men and women graduated each year from her training colleges. 'But we cannot do it alone yet,' cautioned Kayé, 'We need to work hand in hand with you.'

The EET sent an experienced pastor, Philémon, and his wife to join the new missionary team. His easy outgoing personality and knowledge of six languages multiplied the team's effective-

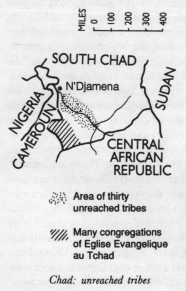

Area of thirty unreached tribes

Many congregations of Eglise Evangelique au Tchad

Chad: unreached tribes

ness in further surveys. They preached everywhere they went and treated the sick. When they were not travelling, the team lived in the little town of Ba Illi, consisting of a jumble of rectangular, mud-walled houses, the same light brown colour as the surrounding sunbaked plains. The Websters' four small rooms squatted around a sandy courtyard. A corrugated iron roof forced up the daytime temperatures and drove anyone, who had the time to relax, out to a palm leaf shelter in the yard. A woman brought their water by hand and bundled their laundry to the river. The bath was a bucket on a bench under the open sky. All the neighbours knew them. Well dressed Muslims, walking home from the mosque at dusk, paused for a chat. Lively children danced up for a quick handshake. What the missionaries lacked in home comforts, they made up in cordial relationships.

After four and a half years of intense research, Ben reported to the EET, 'In order to get some idea of the task before us, I have tried to make a list of all the 181 peoples in Chad . . . as well as the 135 languages that they speak.'[312] An astonishing 115 lacked any church and could count on no more than a dozen missionaries. He urged more detailed research for many of them with a view to drawing up an overall strategy.

As well as surveys, the church needed servants. Ben talked it over with Pastor Kayé and shared a dream of a missionary training centre at Ba Illi for Bible college graduates with pastoral experience. Kayé lived in Chad's second largest town, Moundou, and worshipped with a thousand others in a church pastored by forty-year-old Moise Baou. When Moise heard the decision to establish a missionary training centre, he discussed it with his wife and both concluded, 'God wants us to train missionaries.' The EET sent them first to the Eldoret Missionary College in Kenya and later invited Jonathan Hildebrandt to come and advise them on their programme.

In the prevailing spirit of cooperation, Action Partners assigned a Dutch builder and his British wife to build the missionary centre. Meanwhile a member of The Evangelical Alliance Mission commenced a study of the Kwong language with a view to encouraging literacy and preparing Scriptures in their tongue. A Chadian joined him and wrote about his work in a new village, 'In January I started the work from nothing. I began by asking the village chief to beat the drum to call the people together. Praise God, on the 30th May he established the missionary church . . . Sometimes we have fifteen, twenty or thirty at our service. The chief has given his heart for conversion, but some village elders are pulling him back . . . I thank the powerful God because it is by his hand that things are going well. As for me, while I am a missionary in this place there is thirst famine and fatigue.'[313]

Maurice Wheatley, once the British Director of AIM and his wife Joan asked to be relieved from their position in the International Office so that they could take over as Team Leaders when Ben and Winsome retired. The Director of the Church's Health Care in Zaire, a citizen of Luxembourg, and his wife requested a transfer in order to assist the EET to design a health care programme for the unreached tribes. An American nurse from the Rift Valley Academy in Kenya offered to assist. Others arrived from America, France, Holland and New Zealand.

Ben and Winsome handed over to the Wheatleys in 1992. Soon after their departure news of a Chadian missionary colleague reminded them that they would never retire from the battle of prayer. Gabriel was beginning to see some fruit among the Ndam. Riding home on his bicycle, he met a bandit who shot him, robbed him, and left him to bleed to death on the sandy track.

AIM began with a dream and a death. As that dream neared fulfilment a century later, blood again sealed it. God has given other visions; some were dangerous, all were demanding. Confronting them missionaries usually felt their own weaknesses. Charles Hurlburt set a trend during his first visit to Africa in 1899: 'Like Joshua and Caleb who returned from the promised land looking at gigantic grapes instead of enormous giants, so Hurlburt returned from his inspection of Africa.'[314] With God's help the grasshoppers vanquished these giants and the grapes multiplied.

At the start of a second century of ministry, AIM confronts a new breed of giants. They stalk Africa spreading war, famine and AIDS. They force impoverished millions into rural refugee camps and huge urban slums. Strengthening old faiths with new ferocity, they jealously guard most of the northern half of the continent and seek captives elsewhere. Into multiplying churches, they take advantage of the gross shortage of Bible teachers by injecting error. Modern giants may be cleverer than those who confronted Scott and Hurlburt, but they are no less awesome.

A new breed of grasshoppers has arisen too, more black than white and numbering millions. While most of AIM's 1,150 missionaries still come from western lands, mature Africans in their partner churches far outnumber them and usually lead the new assaults. Facing difficulties, disease and danger, they need Hurlburt's spirit if, like Caleb, they will scoff at the giants, 'Do not be afraid because we will swallow them up. Their protection is gone, but the Lord is with us.' (Numbers 14:9).

References

Chapter 1   A dream dies
1   John 10:16 (AV).
2   *Vision and 50 Years After* (Africa Inland Mission, 1945).
3   J. C. Pollock, *Moody Without Sankey* (Hodder and Stoughton, 1963), p. 114.
4   J. Stauffacher, 'History of the Africa Inland Mission' (undated typescript), p. 8.
5. Ibid., p. 2.
6   Johann Ludwig Krapf, *Travels, Researches and Missionary Labours During 18 Years Residence in East Africa* (Trubner, 1860), p. 133.
7   Willis Hotchkiss, *Then and Now in Kenya Colony* (Fleming H. Revell, 1937), pp. 14 and 15.
8   Peter C. Scott, *Hearing and Doing* (March 1896) (magazine produced by AIM).
9   Margaret Scott, *Hearing and Doing* (March 1896).
10 Hotchkiss, *Then and Now*, p. 31.
11 Ibid., p. 45.
12 Peter Scott, *Hearing and Doing* (May 1896).
13 Margaret Scott, *Hearing and Doing* (March 1897).
14 *Hearing and Doing* (January 1896).
15 Hotchkiss, *Then and Now*, pp. 57 and 58.
16 L. Severn, letter in *Hearing and Doing*, dated 7 September 1897.
17 *Hearing and Doing* (January 1896).
18 Hotchkiss, letter in *Hearing and Doing* dated 18 December 1898.
19 Hotchkiss, letter in *Hearing and Doing* dated 6 May 1899.
20 Hotchkiss, *Then and Now*, p. 149.

Chapter 2   A seed germinates
21 K. Richardson, *Garden of Miracles* (AIM and Victory Press, 1968), p. 43.
22 C. Hurlburt, 'Address at the House of Rest in London

on 6 May 1921', quoted in T. Cope, 'The Africa Inland Mission in Kenya – Aspects of its History (1895–1945)' (unpublished M.Phil thesis, London Bible College, 1979).

23 *Hearing and Doing* (August/September 1897).

24 C. S. Miller, *The Life of Peter Cameron Scott* (Parry Jackman, 1955), p. 51.

25 *Hearing and Doing* (January 1896).

26 J. Stauffacher, 'History of the Africa Inland Mission', p. 3.

27 C. Hurlburt, Letter to 'Fellow Members' dated 1 July 1914 (AIM).

28 Hurlburt, Letter to AIM workers in German East Africa dated 3 July 1913.

29 Cope, 'AIM in Kenya', p. 38.

30 Ibid., p. 29.

31 E. C. Miller, 'Venture of Faith' (private publication 1969).

32 Cope, 'AIM in Kenya', p. 103.

33 Hurlburt, quoted in Cope, 'AIM in Kenya'.

34 Constitution of the AIM, Article VI, Section 1 (AIM, 1912).

35 Hurlburt, Letter to British Home Council, 30 November 1921, quoted in Cope, 'AIM in Kenya'.

36 R. A. Smith, Letter to Hurlburt dated 9 April 1926, quoted in Cope, 'AIM in Kenya'.

37 Carl Becker, *God's Faithfulness* (Evangelical School of Theology, Pennsylvania, 1981), p. 33.

38 H. D. Campbell, Letter to T. Marsh dated 10 August 1925, quoted in Cope, 'AIM in Kenya'.

39 Hurlburt, Letter to E. E. Grimwood dated 10 November 1926.

40 C. S. Miller, *Life of Peter Cameron Scott*, p. 43.

41 W. Hotchkiss, *Then and Now in Kenya Colony*, pp. 71 and 72.

42 Ibid., p. 89.

43 Stauffacher, 'History of AIM', p. 14.

44 Ibid., pp. 17 and 18.

45 *Hearing and Doing* (July 1903).

46 Cope discusses this fascinating issue in 'AIM in Kenya', pp. 25–6.

47 Dr Philip Muindi, personal comment.

48 Cope, 'AIM in Kenya', p. 40.

49 R. Macpherson, *The Presbyterian Church in East Africa* (Presbyterian Church of East Africa, Nairobi, 1970), p. 88.

50 *Hearing and Doing* (April–June 1915).

51 Macpherson, *Presbyterian Church*, p. 131.

Chapter 3   Under British, German and Belgian rule

52   C. P. Groves, *The Planting of Christianity in East Africa*, Vol. III (Lutterworth Press, 1955), p. 74.

53   G. Stauffacher, *Faster Beats the Drum* (AIM, 1978), p. 29.

54   *Hearing and Doing* (October – December 1909 and January 1910).

55   G. Stauffacher, *Faster Beats the Drum*, p. 83.

56   J. Stauffacher, 'Side-tracked for 2000 Years' (AIM pamphlet, 1912), p. 11.

57   G. Stauffacher, *Faster Beats the Drum*, p. 103.

58   Josephine Westervelt, 'On Safari For God' (AIM book, undated), p. 144.

59   Ibid., p. 147.

60   G. Stauffacher, *Faster Beats the Drum*, p. 141.

61   Ibid., p. 164.

62   Raymond Stauffacher (unpublished notes, undated)

63   Westervelt, 'On Safari', p. 39.

64   G. Stauffacher, *Faster Beats the Drum*, p. 79.

65   Ibid., p. 139.

66   Ruth Shaffer, *Road to Kilimanjaro* (Four Corners Press, 1985), p. 47.

67   J. Gration, 'The Relationship of AIM and its National Church in Kenya between 1895 and 1971' (unpublished Ph.D thesis, University of New York, 1974), p. 151.

68   Ibid., p. 152.

69   Quotation taken from *Beyond the Kikuyu Curtain* by H. V. Blakeslee. Copyright 1956, Moody Bible Institute of Chicago. Moody Press. Used by permission.

70   Taken from the book *From Jerusalem to Irian Jaya* by Ruth Tucker (p. 15). Copyright © 1983 by The Zondervan Corporation. Used by permission of Zondervan Publishing House.

71   Marie Sywulka, 'Workers Together With Him' (AIM, undated pamphlet), p. 5.

72   K. Richardson, *Garden of Miracles*, p. 70.

73   M. Sywulka, 'Workers Together', p. 8.

74   Richardson, *Garden of Miracles*, p. 124.

75   *Inland Africa* (September to October, 1961) (magazine of AIM).

Chapter 4   Straining the Nets

76   Eileen Vincent, *No Sacrifice Too Great* (SWEC 2nd ed. 1988), p. 93.

77 British Home Council Minutes (AIM, London, 3 March 1913).
78 Letter entitled 'The Belgian Congo Party' signed by J. S. Holden (chairman), D. P. Robinson (Hon. Home Director), C. E. Hurlburt (AIM, London 1913).
79 Vincent, *No Sacrifice Too Great*, p. 166.
80 K. Richardson, *Garden of Miracles*, p. 142.
81 T. Cope, 'AIM in Kenya', p. 72.
82 British Home Council Minutes (19 September 1919).
83 A. Buxton, Foreword to N. Grubb, *C. T. Studd, Cricketer and Pioneer* (The Religious Tract Society, 1933), p. 5.
84 The following quotations are from Edith Gardner, 'African Travels' (unpublished and undated manuscript in the possession of Dr Rex Gardner, Sunderland).
85 The following quotations are from C. S. Miller, *Obedience of Faith* (AIM, 1935).
86 The following quotations are taken from Beatrice T. King, *Moro Sheeba* (Moody Press, 1957).

Chapter 5 Cultures clash
87 J. Glenden Rae, 'A Historical Study of the Educational Work of the Africa Inland Mission in Kenya' (unpublished M.Ed. thesis, University of New Brunswick, 1969), p. 11.
88 T. Cope, 'AIM in Kenya', p. 27.
89 *Hearing and Doing* (July 1897).
90 *Hearing and Doing* (August/September 1897).
91 J. Gration, 'Relationship of AIM', p. 350.
92 R. Gehman, *Doing African Christian Theology, An Evangelical Perspective* (Evangel Press, 1987), p. 11.
93 Ibid., p. 10.
94 A. Shorter quoted in D. Bosch, *Transforming Mission* (Orbis, 1991), p. 343.
95 The following quotations are from Lucile Downing Sawhill, 'My Childhood in Africa' (unpublished and undated manuscript), p. 4.
96 *Inland Africa* (December 1927).
97 Minutes of Philadelphia Missionary Council (6 May 1895).
98 C. S. Miller, *The Life of Peter Cameron Scott*, p. 46.
99 A. J. Temu, quoted in Cope, 'AIM in Kenya', p. 37.
100 Gration, 'Relationship of AIM', p. 52.
101 Cope, 'AIM in Kenya', p. 49.
102 Gration, 'Relationship of AIM', p. 158.

103   *Inland Africa* (February 1928).
104   Gration, 'Relationship of AIM', p. 168.
105   Cope, 'AIM in Kenya', p. 43.
106   Gration, 'Relationship of AIM', p. 163.
107   Minutes of Kijabe Conference 1916 quoted in Cope, 'AIM in Kenya'.
108   Letter from L. Downing to Hurlburt dated 16 May 1924, quoted in Cope, 'AIM in Kenya'.
109   Rae, 'Historical Study', p. 38
110   Gration, 'Relationship of AIM', p. 163.
111   Ibid., p. 179.
112   Letter from L. Downing to H. Campbell dated 19 January 1938 in Ibid.
113   Letter from H. Nixon to R. Davis dated 10 May 1939 in Ibid.
114   Gration, 'Relationship of AIM', p. 176.
115   The following quotations are from Blakeslee, *Beyond the Kikuyu Curtain* (see end note 69).
116   R. Macpherson, *The Presbyterian Church in Kenya*, p. 74.
117   Jomo Kenyatta, *Facing Mount Kenya* (Secker & Warburg, 1938), p. 133.
118   Minutes of Kijabe Conference (29 May 1921).
119   Gration, 'Relationship of AIM', p. 140.
120   Ibid., p. 147.
121   The following account is from Blakeslee, *Beyond the Kikuyu Curtain*.
122   T. F. C. Bewes, *Kikuyu Conflict* (Highway Press, 1953), p. 42.
123   Ibid., p. 45.
124   The following quotations are from K. N. Phillips, 'From Mau Mau to Christ' (Stirling Tract Enterprise, 1958), p. 14.

Chapter 6   Progress and Peril in Uganda
125   Most of the following quotations are from the letters of Albert Vollor to family members (unpublished letters from 1923 to 15 September 1928 in the possession of R. Vollor).
126   K. Richardson, *Garden of Miracles*, p. 190.
127   Margaret Lloyd, *Wedge of Light* (unpublished, undated), p. 80.
128   Ted Williams, *It Came to Pass* (personal publication, undated, in possession of Mrs Muriel Williams), p. 98.
129   Most of the following quotations are from an interview with

Seton and Peggy Maclure, Wadhurst, Kent in November 1991.

130 Lloyd, *Wedge of Light*, pp. 8–10.

131 Ibid., p. 76.

132 Laura Belle Barr, Letter to 'Friends' (AIM, 2 January 1981).

133 Ibid.

134 C. Kinzer, 'Report on West Nile District, Uganda' (AIM, 1981).

135 The following account is from Ted Williams, *It Came to Pass*.

136 Ted Williams, *Probably Not, The Story of Kuluva Hospital* (AIM, London, undated booklet).

Chapter 7   Growth and crisis in Congo

137 The following account is from Earl Dix with B. P. Young, *Earl Dix, Adventurer for God* (Buena Book Services, 1987).

138 The following account is mostly from W. J. Peterson, *Another Hand on Mine* (Keats Publishing, 1967).

139 Carl K. Becker, *God's Faithfulness* (Evangelical School of Theology, Myerstown, 1981), p. 87.

140 Peterson, *Another Hand*, p. 119.

141 Becker, *God's Faithfulness*, p. 100.

142 Ibid., p. 110.

143 Ibid., p. 132.

144 Most of the following quotations are from an interview with Joyce and David Richardson, Enfield, 3 June 1992.

145 Ken Richardson, *He Giveth the Increase* (AIM, 1955), p. 29.

146 Communauté Evangélique Au Centre De L'Afrique (CECA) which paralleled the Africa Inland Mission in Anglophone countries.

147 The following account is from Peter Brashler, *Akudri* (Cascade, 1990), p. 224.

148 K. Richardson, *He Giveth the Increase*, p. 56.

149 Brashler, *Akudri*, p. 192.

150 David Richardson, Letter to author dated 31 January, 1994.

151 Brashler, *Akudri*, p. 16.

152 David Richardson, Letter to author.

153 Homer Dowdy, *Out of the Jaws of the Lion* (Harper and Row, 1965), p. 24.

154 Ibid., p. 50.

155 Joseph Bayley, *Congo Crisis* (Victory Press, 1966), p. 132.

156 Ibid., p. 178.
157 Dowdy, *Out of the Jaws of the Lion*, p. 169 and Bayley, *Congo Crisis*, p. 184.
158 Interview with Charles Davis at Pearl River, New York, 25 March, 1993.

Chapter 8   Spread across Kenya
159 The following account is from Stuart M. Bryson, *Light in Darkness* (Parry Jackman, 1959).
160 The following account is from K. N. Phillips, *Tom Collins of Kenya* (AIM, 1965).
161 Tom Collins, personal account to the author in 1957. The *East African Standard* (September 1950) reports the official enquiry.
162 This account draws on Peter Mualuko Kisulu, *A Missionary Called Peter* (Kesho, Kijabe, 1983).
163 Alan Checkley, interview, East Calder, 13 May 1992.

Chapter 9   Towards Africa's heart
164 John Buyse, *Inland Africa* (January/March 1935).
165 Peter Brashler, *Change: My Thirty Five Years in Africa* (Tyndale House, 1979), p. 192.
166 John Buyse, Letter to friends, from Ara, Congo, 17 January 1918.
167 K. Richardson, *Garden of Miracles*, p. 158.
168 *Inland Africa* (March 1927).
169 *Inland Africa* (February 1927).
170 *Inland Africa* (June 1931).
171 *Inland Africa* (June 1935).
172 *Inland Africa* (January 1939).
173 Seton Maclure quoting Psalm 81:10 in interview with author.
174 Interview with Martha Hughell and Barbara Battye at Media, USA, 12 May 1993.
175 *Inland Africa* (September 1953).
176 *Inland Africa* (July 1954).
177 *Inland Africa* (March 1963).
178 Interview with Doug and Gill Reitsma, East Calder, 4 August 1991.
179 Interview with Pastor Singa Alfonse, Rejaf, Sudan, 13 March 1977.
180 *Times* (London, 1 March 1989).
181 *Independent* (London, 15 November 1988).

182 *Sudan Times* (10 July 1988).
183 The Reitsmas' letter to 'Dear Friends', 5 December 1989.
184 *AIM International* (British edition, Winter 1993) (Magazine of AIM).
185 Reitsmas' letter, September 1992.
186 Prayer requests, *AIM International* Office (5/6 February 1994).
187 D. and G. Reitsma, 'AIM Sudan Report' (February 1994).

Chapter 10 The wind of change
188 American Home Council Minutes (14 December 1960).
189 *Inland Africa* (November 1962).
190 K. Richardson, *Inland Africa* (March 1964).
191 *Inland Africa* (September 1965).
192 Aim Constitution, Articles VII and IX (1955).
193 Central Field Council Minute No. 4/59 (24 June 1959).
194 CFC, 'The Relationships of the Mission and the Church' (AIM memo, April 1960).
195 J. Gration, 'The Relationship of AIM and Its National Church', p. 288.
196 Minutes of the Joint Meeting of AIC Executive and AIM FC (AIM, 1 December 1964).
197 Minutes of Kenya FC (AIM, May 1969).
198 Gration, 'Relationship of AIM', p. 320.
199 *Inland Africa* (January 1972).
200 Kisula, 'Maisha Yangu Tangu Kuzaliwa' [My Life Since Birth] (unpublished and undated autobiography in Swahili).
201 Ibid.
202 Minutes of AIC Synod (February 1961).
203 Kisula, address to the AIC, Kola Ndoto, early 1964.
204 Kisula, address.
205 Central Field Council Memo, 1961.
206 Interview with R. Baker, Laurel Springs, 29 March 1993.
207 Kisula, address.
208 P. Beverly, letter dated 2 December 1970, quoted in Gration, 'Relationship of AIM', p. 279.
209 Interview with P. Baker, Laurel Springs, 29 March 1993.

Chapter 11 Serving the saints
210 International Conference minute 42 (1968).
211 Christian Service Fellowship, 'Report of Evaluation Study of the Africa Inland Mission' (24 July 1970).

212 Constitution of the AIM, Article VII (1972).
213 Job description of IGS, appended to Minutes of International Council (May 1972).
214 IC Minute 17/72.
215 IC Minute 25/75.
216 'Address of Colonel Roosevelt made at the laying of corner stone of school building, Kijabe, B.E. Africa, 4 August 1909', by kind permission of the archivist of the Billy Graham Centre, Wheaton, Illinois.
217 Lucile Downing Sawhill, 'My Childhood in Africa', p. 41.
218 Interview with Erik and Emily Barnet, Media, 12 April 1993.
219 Interview with Linnel and Martha Davis, Media, 11 April 1993.
220 Roy and Judy Entwhistle, Letter to Friends, January 1984.
221 International Council Minute 45/87.
222 Interview with Roy Entwhistle, Bawtry, 8 May 1993.
223 Interview with Warren Day, Pearl River, 1 April 1993.
224 Interview with Richard and Janice Dunkerton, Laurel Springs, 28 March 1993.
225 K. Richardson, *Garden of Miracles*, p. 209.
226 P. Brashler, Letter to Mrs Davis, Bob and Lillian, 9 September 1963.
227 D. Reitsma, Letter to Mrs Davis, 23 August 1963.
228 R. Davis, Aide memoire, 5/6 June 1948.
229 R. Davis, 18 June 1955.
230 AIM Constitution 1955, Articles VII and IX.
231 R. Davis, 24 May 1957.
232 K. Richardson, Letter to R. Seume, 19 March 1963.
233 E. Barnett, Letter to R. Seume, 5 June 1963.
234 R. Davis, Letter to R. Seume, 2 January 1963.
235 R. Davis, Letter to S. Boehme, 29 March 1963.
236 Obituary for George Frutchey, *Inland Africa*, January 1959.
237 P. Wagnell, Letter to W. and S. Ewing, 19 June 1989.

Chapter 12 Words on target
238 Lausanne, Willowbank Report, in *Explaining the Gospel in Today's World* (Scripture Union, 1978), p. 25. © Scripture Union, used by permission.
239 The following quotations are taken from R. and L. Davis, Letters to Friends (July 1955–June 1962).
240 *Inland Africa* (July 1962).

241 *Inland Africa* (November 1962); Davis, Letter to friends, late 1961.

242 T. Kamau in *Inland Africa* (November 1962).

243 Davis, November 1963.

244 Interview with Lillian Davis, Pearl River, 15 April 1993.

245 Davis, Autumn 1968.

246 *Inland Africa* (May 1958).

247 *Inland Africa* (October 1979).

248 E. Arensen, Letter to author, December 1993.

249 *Inland Africa* (March 1960).

250 Ibid.

251 *Inland Africa* (January 1961).

252 E. Arensen, Letter to author, December 1993.

253 J. Gration, 'Willowbank to Zaire', *Missiology* (July 1984).

254 J. Gration, AIM application form.

255 Interview with J. Gration, Wheaton, 9 April 1993.

256 Gration, Letter to Friends, January 1961.

257 Lausanne, Willowbank Report.

258 G. Molyneux, *African Christian Theology* (Mellen, 1993), p. 275.

259 Ibid., p. 277.

260 Ibid., p. 283.

261 R. Gehman, *Doing African Christian Theology*, p. 110.

262 Kile Kpala, quoted in Molyneux, *African Christian Theology*, p. 300.

263 Interview with Jonathan and Margaret Dawn, London, 18 January 1993.

Chapter 13 Loving the least

264 The following quotations are from Katie Mackinnon with Lynda Neilands, *Love Breaks Through* (HarperCollins Publishers Ltd, 1988).

265 Thom Hopler, *A World of Difference* (IVP, USA, 1981).

266 Thom Hopler, 'Report to American Home Council', 15 April 1971.

267 J. Gration, *Inland Africa* (October 1971).

268 Thom Hopler, 'Report on Urban Ministry' to American Home Council, 1971.

269 William Elliot, Audio-tape, September 1993.

270 *Inland Africa* (Spring 1987).

271 *Inland Africa* (May 1986).

272 William Elliot, Letter to Friends, 10 September 1991.

273 Patrick Johnstone, *Operation World* (Operation Mobilisation, 1993), p. 527.

274 Caroline Gill, Letter entitled 'The Dar Daily', 1 December 1992.

275 Gill, Letter to A. Dix, 20 July 1993.

Chapter 14 False paradises

276 International Council Minute 11/75.

277 *Good News for Modern Man* (American Bible Society, New York, 1966).

278 W. Barnett, taped biographical notes, September 1993.

279 *Oregon County Register*, 7 January 1993.

280 Interview with L. Hurter, East Calder, 21 January 1994.

281 L. Hurter, 'South Up North', September 1993 (news sheet by South African AIM).

282 Ibid.

283 Interview with David and Eleanor Duncan, Birmingham, 4 May 1992.

284 Interview with C. and C. Molyneux, Sutton Bonington, 10 September 1993.

285 Lanny Arensen, *AIM International*, Winter 1989.

Chapter 15 New lessons in the south

286 AIM 'Policies and Procedures', 01.

287 International Council, Minute 13/87.

288 Interview with J. and P. Pienaar, East Calder, 4 August 1993.

289 Godwin Murangi, *The Holy Fire And Christian Marriage* (1989) (Pamphlet).

290 D. Potocki, Letters to friends, 27 July and 16 August 1985.

291 D. Potocki, Letter to friends, 29 March 1986.

292 D. Potocki, tape, September 1993.

293 D. and B. Dunkerton, tape, September 1993.

294 Dunkerton, Letter to friends, May/June 1987.

295 Dunkerton, Letter to friends, June 1988.

296 Elders of Jin Ju Presbyterian Church, Interview, 29 July 1992.

297 Interview with Sonya Kim, Seoul, 28 July 1992.

Chapter 16 Grapes instead of giants

298 Interview with William Stough, Bawtry, 8 May 1993.

299 Paul Stough, 'Biographical Notes' (unpublished, early 1990).

300 R. Anderson, Diary (unpublished, 14 November 1978).
301 Statistics from William Stough, May 1993.
302 S. Wolcott and W. Stough (Jnr.), 'Report of Zanderland and Faradje Section' (29 May 1992).
303 'Statement of Zaire Branch Strategy' (AIM, April 1993).
304 Interview with J. and D. Hildebrandt, Bawtry, 8 May 1993.
305 J. and D. Hildebrandt, Letter to friends, 22 August 1970.
306 Ibid., 3 January 1972.
307 J. Hildebrandt, *History of the Church in Africa* (Africa Christian Press, 1981), p. xi.
308 Interview with Hildebrandts, 8 May 1993.
309 Hildebrandt, Letter to friends, September 1975.
310 Hildebrandt, Hildebrandt Habari, September 1982.
311 J. Hildebrandt, 'Working to Reach Kenya for Christ Since 1985' (lecture to Africa Inland Church, Kenya, Leaders' conference, April 1993).
312 B. Webster, 'The Work Still To Be Done in Chad' (Report to Leaders of Eglise Evangélique au Tchad, November 1991).
313 M. Wheatley, Letter to friends, October 1993.
314 W. Peterson (Ed. *Eternity* Magazine) typed article (untitled, unpublished, undated: AIM, Pearl River, New York, USA).